The Nature of Politics

Ohio University Research in International Studies

This series of publications on Africa, Latin America, Southeast Asia, and Global and Comparative Studies is designed to present significant research, translation, and opinion to area specialists and to a wide community of persons interested in world affairs. The series is distributed worldwide. For more information, consult the Ohio University Press website, ohioswallow.com.

Books in the Ohio University Research in International Studies series are published by Ohio University Press in association with the Center for International Studies. The views expressed in individual volumes are those of the authors and should not be considered to represent the policies or beliefs of the Center for International Studies, Ohio University Press, or Ohio University.

The Nature of Politics

STATE BUILDING AND THE CONSERVATION ESTATE IN POSTCOLONIAL BOTSWANA

Annette A. LaRocco

Ohio University Research in International Studies
AFRICA SERIES NO. 98

Ohio University Press
Athens

Ohio University Press, Athens, Ohio 45701
ohioswallow.com
© 2024 by Ohio University Press
All rights reserved

To obtain permission to quote, reprint, or otherwise reproduce or distribute material from Ohio University Press publications, please contact our rights and permissions department at (740) 593-1154 or (740) 593-4536 (fax).

Figure 4.1 on page 155 © 2021 from *Tribal Innovators: Tswana Chiefs and Social Change 1795–1940* by Isaac Schapera. Reproduced by permission of Taylor and Francis Group, LLC, a division of Informa plc. This permission does not cover any third party copyrighted work which may appear in the material requested. User is responsible for obtaining permission for such material separately from this grant.

Printed in the United States of America
Ohio University Press books are printed on acid-free paper ∞ ™

31 30 29 28 27 26 25 24 23 22 21 5 4 3 2 1

Library of Congress Cataloging-in-Publication Data

Names: LaRocco, A. A. (Annette Alfina), 1988– author.
Title: The nature of politics : state building and the conservation estate in postcolonial Botswana / Annette A. LaRocco.
Other titles: Research in international studies. Africa series ; no. 98.
Description: Athens : Ohio University Press, 2024. | Series: Ohio University research in international studies. Africa series ; no. 98 | Includes bibliographical references and index.
Identifiers: LCCN 2023042512 (print) | LCCN 2023042513 (ebook) | ISBN 9780896803336 (hardback) | ISBN 9780896803343 (paperback) | ISBN 9780896803350 (pdf)
Subjects: LCSH: Environmental protection—Political aspects—Botswana. | Nation-building—Botswana. | Postcolonialism—Botswana. Classification: LCC TD171.5.B55 (print) | LCC TD171.5.B55 (ebook) | DDC 363.70096883—dc23/eng/20230913
LC record available at https://lccn.loc.gov/2023042512
LC ebook record available at https://lccn.loc.gov/2023042513

For DOR and MB

Contents

List of Illustrations
ix

Acknowledgments
xi

List of Abbreviations
xiii

Introduction
1

1
Lay of the Land
Conservation and the State in Botswana
51

PART I AUTHORITY

2
Coercion on Botswana's Conservation Estate
73

3
Democracy, the *Kgotla*, and Promises of Consent amid Conservation
114

PART II TERRITORY

4
Land and Ownership on the Conservation Estate
151

5
Infrastructure and the Contours of Settlement, Tourism, and Conservation
191

PART III IDENTITY

6
Conservation Restrictions and the Construction of Criminalized Identities
229

7
Promises of Modernity and Failures of Development on the Conservation Estate
261

Conclusion
305

Appendix
Primary Source Interviews
321

Glossary of Setswana Terms
329

Notes
331

References
353

Index
381

Illustrations

Figures

I.1. Map of Botswana	40
I.2. Botswana land-use map	40
I.3. Botswana district map	41
2.1. Antipoaching sign in Sankuyo	109
3.1. *Kgotla* in Khwai	125
4.1. Map of the Bechuanaland Protectorate in 1940	155
4.2. Map of the Central Kalahari Game Reserve	163
5.1. *Mokoro* station, Ditshiping	212
5.2. Traveling to Ditshiping by *mokoro*	212
5.3. Unfinished community-built bridge, Ditshiping	214
5.4. Community-constructed bridge, Xuoxao	218
6.1. Collected thatching grass in Boro	238
6.2. Ostrich eggshell beads in West Hanahai	249
7.1. Map of veterinary fences across southern Africa	293
7.2. Elephant-control sign in Sankuyo	298

Tables

I.1. Community organizations by research site	39
I.2. Interviewee characteristics	44
I.3. Interview respondents by research site	45
4.1. Land characteristics in Ghanzi and Northwest Districts	174

Acknowledgments

While I cannot list them all individually, this project owes everything to the scores of people on Botswana's conservation estate who welcomed me into their communities, their homes, and their lives. They shared their experiences with me generously, and they have my utmost respect and gratitude. I am grateful for the research permission I received from the Ministry of Environment, Wildlife and Tourism and thank the many members of the Department of Wildlife and National Parks who spoke with me during my fieldwork. My institutional homes during my fieldwork, the Department of Political and Administrative Studies at the University of Botswana and the Okavango Research Institute, provided invaluable support and assistance. I am especially appreciative to Zibani Maundeni, Joseph E. Mbaiwa, Dorothy Mpabanga, and David Sebudubudu.

Thanks to colleagues, mentors, and coauthors who assisted this project in its various stages over many years—Jocelyn Alexander, Maha Rafi Atal, Ronald Seabo Badubi, William Beinart, Louisa Cantwell, Simukai Chigudu, Christopher Clapham, Stephanie Diepeveen, Toyin Kolawole, Kentse Madise, Emmanuel Mogende, Rufusiah Molefe, Kabo Motswagole, Eva Namusoke, Alexander Noyes, Glen Rangwala, Ludo Sabone, Jamie Shinn, Sharath Srinivasan, and Elizabeth Watson. I am grateful for the support of Florida Atlantic University and my colleagues in its Department of Political Science, especially Rebecca LeMoine,

Jeffrey Morton, and Angela Nichols. I also must thank my graduate school compatriots of Portugal Street, who have been eagerly anticipating this book's publication. My thanks go to the editorial team at Ohio University Press, who patiently assisted me and answered my many questions as I navigated my first experience writing a solo monograph.

This research was generously funded by a variety of sources over many years, including the Cambridge International Trust and Trinity College, the Cambridge Political Economy Society, the Smuts Memorial Fund, the University of Cambridge Conservation Research Initiative, the Department of Politics and International Studies, the UAC of Nigeria Travel Grant, the Rouse Ball Research Fund, the Walter D. Head Graduate Fellowship, the Alumnae Association of Barnard College Graduate Fellowship, the Bob Male Research Fellowship, the Center for Peace, Justice, and Human Rights, and the Dorothy F. Schmidt College of Arts and Letters at Florida Atlantic University. This support has facilitated the data collection and completion of this book.

Though not complete reproductions, some material here has been published elsewhere. I appreciate the permission from the relevant publishers to include it. A condensed version of chapter 5 was published as "Infrastructure, Wildlife Tourism, (Il)legible Populations: A Comparative Study of Two Districts in Contemporary Botswana," *Environment and Planning E: Nature and Space* 3 (4): 1074–95. A similarly abbreviated version of the first half of chapter 7 appeared as "Botswana's Hunting Ban and the Transformation of Game-Meat Cultures, Economies and Ecologies," *Journal of Southern African Studies* 46 (4): 723–41. A small portion of chapter 3 describing the historical context of the *kgotla* was published in "Fall from Grace or Back Down to Earth? Conservation and Political Conflict in Africa's 'Miracle' State," *Environment and Planning E: Nature and Space*.

Finally, I send gratitude and love to Mom, Dad, Cathy, Lucia, Michelle, Leo, Dominic, Olivia, Christopher Mark, and the rest of my friends and family for their patience and support.

Abbreviations

BDF	Botswana Defence Force
BDP	Botswana Democratic Party
BTO	Botswana Tourism Organisation
CBNRM	Community-Based Natural Resource Management
CHA	Controlled Hunting Area
CITES	Convention on International Trade in Endangered Species of Wild Fauna and Flora
CKGR	Central Kalahari Game Reserve
DWNP	Department of Wildlife and National Parks
IUCN	International Union for Conservation of Nature
MGR	Moremi Game Reserve
RAD	Remote Area Dweller
SI	Survival International
SGL	Special Game Licence
WMA	Wildlife Management Area

Introduction

The early days of the fieldwork that informs this book were a blur. In a very short period of time, I needed to hire my assistants, find a vehicle and housing, and develop research relationships, in addition to the numerous bureaucratic hurdles to be surmounted, not the least of which was receiving my research permit. I spent the first two weeks shuttling between various offices in Botswana's capital, Gaborone, to secure the appropriate interviews, paperwork, and signatures. Once I was finally issued my permit, I spent a few days settling in at the University of Botswana's Department of Political and Administrative Studies, which would be my institutional home for the duration of my fieldwork.

I was sitting at my desk in the department's offices when a senior faculty member came to welcome me. We chatted amiably about my background and my project. I spoke about the logistical tasks I needed to complete in the capital before traveling to the rural areas in the country's north and west, and I mentioned how my government research permit had just been approved by the Ministry of Environment, Wildlife and Tourism (MEWT).[1] I walked her through the questions I wanted to ask in my research as well as the empirical phenomena I thought would be interesting to explore: antipoaching strategies, the newly announced hunting ban, land disputes and histories of evictions, human-wildlife conflict, and resource-use restrictions, among others. After all of this, she looked at me somewhat incredulously and then turned toward the doorway to make sure no one was in the hallway. She closed the door behind her, and with just the two of us in the office she asked, "How did you ever manage to get a research permit? The conservation issue is very hot right now, and the government is very sensitive about this kind of research."[2] For me, this one interaction early in my fieldwork became emblematic of some of the core issues at the center of my research: the political nature of the environment and the central role of the struggle over environmental concerns in the state-building process—that is, the nature of politics.

Ten months later, this interaction was in stark contrast to a conversation I had at my home institution, a long-standing and in many ways traditional politics department at an elite university in the United Kingdom. Upon returning from my fieldwork, I presented some of my preliminary analysis at a conference for doctoral students hosted by the department. After my talk, the head of the department, a distinguished and well-known scholar of international relations, noted that he found my research fascinating but so very different from what he thought of as "politics" and quite unusual compared with the doctoral projects presented by my various colleagues. This echoed the sentiments I frequently heard from others in the department: Really didn't my work belong in a geography department or perhaps in development studies? How "political" was *biodiversity conservation*—to the head of the department a seemingly benign, if not uniformly positive, concept—when juxtaposed to the big questions probed in the offices, libraries, and seminar rooms of venerable departments of politics: questions about democracy and political behavior and sovereign statehood and citizenship. The obviously political nature of my work in Botswana—and how it was received by scholars, interview participants, and government officials there as plainly and clearly being in the realm of what political scientists analyze and indeed the self-evidently controversial and sensitive nature of these questions—contrasted with the ways in which my work was often viewed as an interesting curiosity in a traditional politics department in the United Kingdom.

These contradictory bookends at the beginning and end of my fieldwork confirmed what had become clear to me throughout my months in Botswana's rural areas—that the *nature* of politics has an understudied explanatory power and this is more readily apparent in certain venues than in others. This is especially true in the postcolonies of the Global South, where control of land, resources, and territory were a central crucible forging authority during the colonial project and beyond. That environmental policies were constitutive to, and illuminating of, the state-building process was almost obvious to individuals living on Botswana's conservation estate, though they would be unlikely to frame it in such terms. What was self-evident among my informants was that contestations over land, environment, and natural resources were one of the most important venues, if not the primary one, through which they interacted with state authority and situated themselves within the wider polity. Questions of the environment are core questions about the politics of a society: they speak to the way power is enacted, how citizens imagine themselves, and how a country prosecutes its international relations and tends to its global reputation.

The environment and politics are mutually constituted; this book probes the co-productive relationships between conservation policies, citizen subjectivities, political authority, and political economy in places deemed important for the project of global biodiversity conservation. The decisions made relating to land and environment are politically salient features of the state-building process. Human-environment relations highlight questions central to political inquiry and necessitate analysis of global processes, social institutions, cultural subjectivities, and manifestations of power. Human interactions of, in, and with the environment reveal new dimensions of political authority. While the role of private corporations, NGOs, and international institutions have expanded greatly in the arena of biodiversity conservation, the use or non-use of natural resources remains, in large part, directly controlled by the state or controlled with the state's consent. In addition to being a physical space on which people live, land and environment play a role in how the state and territory are defined and are relevant to how resources are made productive. More specifically, biodiversity conservation operates as an important political lens because it illuminates the relationship between the state and territory, tensions around a state's drive to make territory and populations productive, and the manner in which territorial control is linked to citizenship and belonging. Elements of state authority, territory, and identity formation intersect in conservation policy.

This book is concerned with the nature of the state and citizen-state relations in contemporary Botswana. The aim of this book is to examine the state from the vantage point of the *conservation estate*, a key theoretical innovation that encapsulates the wide swath of land devoted to biodiversity conservation, a concept that is further articulated below. I argue that the rural space of the state in postcolonial Africa is more heterogeneous than often accounted for in the broader scholarship on rural politics. The deployment of the analytical conception of the conservation estate brings this to the fore and helps to address this gap. By examining this particular kind of territory—at once both liminal and pivotal to the state—I uncover the paradoxes that lie at the heart of the state-building project and the powerful mythologies and imaginaries that allow for the (re)production of the social order. The nature of politics is complex, contingent, dynamic, and highly variegated across space. In addressing this complexity, this book examines a series of conservation policies, strategies, and logics of state action as well as their reception by people living in conservation areas in contemporary Botswana. Key empirical phenomena addressed in later chapters include the enforcement-first approach to antipoaching, a nationwide ban on hunting enacted from 2014 to 2019, limitations and restriction on the use of wildlife products, relocation of residents from conservation areas, and the conservation of globally important charismatic species, such as the African bush elephant (*Loxodonta africana*).

Introduction

The Politics of Protected Areas

Protected areas have always served purposes beyond the imperatives of biodiversity conservation and are typically embedded in and central to a wide array of political and ideological projects (Corson 2010; Corson et al. 2014; Dongol and Neumann 2021; Hodgetts et al. 2019; Vandergeest and Peluso 1995). In a global context, the setting aside of land for conservation can be politically instrumental: it signals an apparent commitment to green values at relatively low stakes for the broader populace of a country. It does not require a national reckoning with fossil fuel emissions, consumption levels, or economic development. Moreover, the conservation estate can be harnessed for explicitly political purposes—such as the push to transform the post-Soviet states into a "European Green Belt" or the initiative to bring regional stability and prosperity to formerly white-ruled southern Africa via transfrontier conservation areas, also known as "peace parks." These political objectives may or may not align with ecological ones but nonetheless should be interrogated in their own right (Carruthers 2012).

It is necessary, especially in the postcolonial Global South where there is a large conservation footprint, to engage with histories of the environment, which have ably probed the origins of protected areas (Beinart 2003; Beinart and Hughes 2007; Carruthers 1995; Gissibl, Hohler, and Kupper 2012; Grove 1995). Historians have documented the origins of parks as political projects in the "civilizing" mission (Gissibl, Hohler, and Kupper 2012), in nation building (Meskell 2011), in identity formation (Alexander 2006; Ranger 1999), and as part of transnational political movements and epistemic communities (De Bont 2017). This historical literature is insightful and valuable context that guides this project as it reckons with this social and political category of land in its contemporary manifestation, the conservation estate. I am looking at how the conservation estate is rendered as part of the iterative, evolving process of state building and how it mediates the fundamental relationship between the state and its citizens. The conservation estate makes up a substantial percentage of land in many African countries, such as Botswana, Tanzania, South Africa, Kenya, and Gabon. The status of these lands are live political issues, with many NGOs, corporations, and governments advocating for their further expansion. For example, the Half-Earth coalition of scholars and practitioners argues for the setting aside of half the world's land for the purposes of biodiversity conservation (Wilson 2016). Critics say that much of this territory would presumably be located in the Global South, and Africa in particular, and that such a measure would come at the expense of citizens of postcolonial countries (Büscher et al. 2017). Brockington, Duffy, and Igoe (2008) note that the number of protected areas has increased since the 1980s as a part of the ongoing process of neoliberalization of the environment rather than being just a relic of colonial land control across the Global South. While there are protected areas on every inhabited continent, Africa, Latin America, the Caribbean, and Asia constitute the bulk of the world's conservation estate. In fact, the regions identified as global conservation priority areas are almost entirely in the Global South (Mascia et al. 2014). For instance, officially gazetted protected areas account for 16 percent of the land area in eastern and southern Africa (Death 2016b). It is this context that makes the lens of environmental politics particularly relevant to debates regarding postcolonial statehood, especially on the African continent.

The study of politics is often used to shed light on environmental policy processes, and the policy outcomes that result from political jockeying are used to frame issues, theorize problems, and promote interests (Keeley and Scoones 2003). This orientation is a mainstay of political ecology, which is a literature focused on the political and economic conditions and constraints that dictate the access and control over land, the use or non-use of resources, and the sociological dimensions of ecology and natural resource management. The typical structure of this analytical frame has been that for scholars to understand conservation, they must examine the state. As Brockington notes, "If we are to understand conservation policies in Africa we need to look at the behaviour of African states within globalised conservation discourses and with respect to large-scale movements of capital and ideas" (2005, 103). While agreeing with Brockington's supposition, I suggest that the converse is also true. If we want to understand African states in the postcolonial era, we can and should examine their conservation policies. Death's work resonates with this analytical inversion.[3] He does important work in retheorizing the environmental, or "green," state in order to argue that there is a "longstanding centrality of environmental and ecological imperatives to the production of states in Africa" (2016a, 120). He suggests that "the African state is actually a product of particular attempts to govern land, species, human populations, water resources, and so on" (Death 2016a, 123; see also Ramutsindela and Büscher 2019). Relevant to this book is Death's assertion that the "greenness" of the so-called green state can be evaluated by the way in which environmental imperatives are linked to core state functions—like stability, order, legitimacy, territorial control, and political economy—rather than the state's environmental "performance" along ecological metrics (Death 2016b). This provides a helpful point of departure for my project, which confirms and extends Death's proposition that the environment is central to African state building and provides space for the examination of the state from the empirical position of the conservation estate.

This project engages with bodies of academic literature from African politics and political ecology. This introduction begins by further articulating the key arguments of the book and then continues with an examination of biodiversity conservation and introduces my deeper theorization of the concept of the conservation estate. Next, it critically engages with three significant bodies of literature that guide the inquiry. First, I discuss constructivist theories of the state in relation to Africanist political science; second, I examine the literature related to the politics of land and authority; and, third, I situate this work within scholarship concerning the rural-urban divide and the manner in which it interpenetrates with the phenomenon of conservation. Following that, it discusses the methodological approach undertaken for the research presented here. Finally, I close with an overview of this book's structure and chapter outline.

Analytical Aims

Drawing from the insights in Death's 2016 monograph *The Green State in Africa*, this book examines how the logics and strategies of conservation function as part of the postcolonial state building in Botswana and how contestations over this process shape the relationships between the state and its citizens. Before delving into the analytical framework, the terminology around "citizen" and "citizenship" in this context warrants further attention. I am using the word "citizen" in this context in its most theoretically neutral sense. I recognize that it is a highly fraught term—especially within Africanist literature where the distinction between citizen and subject in the postcolonial state has been richly theorized by Mamdani (1996). In my book a "citizen" refers to a Botswana national, a member of the postcolonial political unit of the Republic of Botswana. This is a Motswana in the non-ethnic sense, someone who is eligible to hold a Botswana Omang (national identity card) and passport, whether or not they are in possession of one. I use the demonym "Batswana" to describe all citizens of the country regardless of race, ethnicity, or linguistic background, while also recognizing the ethnic register with which the term "Batswana" may also be used. In fact, the question of ethnicity and its import on the conservation estate and in citizen's subjectivities is a major focus of this book's section on identity and will be thoroughly examined in later chapters.

Key Arguments

This book, which is a close empirical study of a specific case—contemporary Botswana—seeks to elucidate claims and broader understanding with respect to the common characteristics of social and political lives lived on the conservation estate. By examining the complex and multivalent project of state building from the vantage point of conservation estate, I make three key interventions.

The first argument relates to the conservation estate itself. This book puts forward a definition of biodiversity conservation that is tied to its political elements, distinct from ecological or biological conceptualizations. The component parts of conservation as currently operationalized—control over land, policing of human behavior, the structuring of the authority that allows or disallows certain subjectivities—render the conservation estate a political phenomenon that may be analyzed separately from considerations about "nature," "wilderness," or ecology. (This does not diminish these concerns but rather shifts attention to other important outputs.)

The "conservation estate" is a useful heuristic for the understanding of politics. Through the lens of the conservation estate, one can observe processes and technologies of state building and the way they are experienced by a very particular type of political subject—typically rural and often marginalized, living on the conservation estate. The conservation estate also gives credence to existing analytical narratives focused on the uneven, contingent, and multivalent aspects of the state. It provides a new, productive way to observe this phenomenon. The conceptualization of the conservation estate helps to explicate two subsequent arguments, which are nested within this concept, about rural differentiation and obstacles to rural resistance on the conservation estate.

The first of these, and the book's second key argument, is related to the nature of citizenship across the conservation estate. There is a differentiation of citizenship across territory, beyond the rural/urban divide that has been the focus of much of the literature relating to the spatial contingencies of citizenship in postcolonial Africa. Taking a view from the conservation estate, there is a clear and apparent variation of experience *within* rural spaces. The particularities that are characteristic of the conservation estate alone alter the relationship between the state, its citizens living on this category of space, and their compatriots living elsewhere across the breadth of Botswana's territory, including other rural dwellers not subject to the technologies of conservation. The logics and practices of conservation inevitably overlap with human residency, and the resultant social aspects of the conservation estate—seen through the variable nature of the citizen-state relations—are worthy of analysis. This book examines the features of human life on the conservation estate and analyzes flora and fauna in relation to human populations, insofar as how this category of land, and the resources found therein, mediates citizen-state relations. The commonplace distinction between "citizen" and "subject" in African politics does not adequately capture the unique identities and subjectivities generated by the conservation estate. There is an additional category of "political" being created at the nexus of human-wildlife interactions, a political subjectivity created by the proximity of wildlife and conservation. This kind of rural subject cannot be understood without considering the unique imperatives created by the copresence of wildlife, especially charismatic species that activate global interest.

Wildlife plays a role in the state-building process in often unaccounted for ways, though some scholars like Youatt (2020) meaningfully engage in political analysis that is interspecies and planetary. Such insights allow for the observation of how nonhuman animals impact the social and political worlds of humans. Co-residency with wildlife is not simply an ecological reality but also produces the unique conditions and subjectivities on the conservation estate, which work to construct conservation-adjacent people as marginal to or deviant from the larger state-building project. In this case, the spatial differentiation of citizenship happens despite Botswana's adamant insistence on an equal and nondiscriminatory state in the postcolonial era. Indeed, state building in postcolonial Botswana is premised upon the notion of a unitary state and a unified populace. State claims of undifferentiated rights (explored at length in the next chapter) are used as the logic to centralize conservation policymaking and the economic benefits of tourism and to discredit specific identity and location-based claims. However, this posture ignores the very contours of conservation that create differentiated citizenship in practice for those populations already marginal to the state project. The ostensible "equality" of all citizens promoted in national discourse impacts whether people on the conservation estate imagine themselves as insiders or outsiders in relation to the state project. Their perceived alienation from the overtly articulated notions of statehood and citizenship makes real their question as to whether they are disenfranchised tenants or legitimate citizens. The state-building project produces an outcome where conservation-adjacent people experience a vastly different set of lived circumstances from other Batswana, including those living in rural areas that are not dominated by the logic of conservation. These differences include not only the presence of wildlife as an intermediary in citizen-state relations but are also constituted in varying ability to move freely, the spatial organization of their communities, livelihood opportunities, and the role of state surveillance and scrutiny. While differentiation is not an inherently new proposition, as scholars have long elucidated key distinctions between urban and rural experiences in Africa, it is important to recognize the degree to which this diversity exists within rural contexts, as well.

The third argument of this book is that the unique characteristics of the conservation estate impact the ability of local people to negotiate or contest state-building processes. Contestation of and resistance to conservation policies are not simply about grievances related to the impacts of the policies alone but also serve as points of negotiation with a state perceived on the conservation estate as paradoxically distant yet coercive, unfamiliar yet omnipresent. The conservation estate is a particularly apt empirical venue to explore the dynamics of the multifaceted state and the way in which resistance may be constrained. The case of Botswana provides further evidence of the inability of the projects and logics of the state to be entirely coherent, which results in two key features. On one hand, the apparent inconsistency of state action, which results from the multivalent nature of the state-building process, leaves it open for critique by the people of the conservation estate. Yet, on the other, this muddled condition also works to confound resistance as the would-be subjects of state projects have difficulty in determining where to focus their opposition. While contradictions present opportunities for robust critique, they also work to vex resistance.

The flexibility or indeterminacy of the state as seen from the conservation estate does not necessarily render it more equitable. Room for negotiation does not mean resistance always works, and agency and maneuvering alone cannot preclude an inequitable outcome in the distribution of power or resources (Peters 2004). The paradoxes of state building make resistance and countervailing political organization difficult. The overt and explicit logics of the Botswana state, like democracy, consultation, equality, and participation, do not line up to the policies experienced on the conservation estate in practice. Thus, the script of resistance is limited because of the gulf between the state's clearly expressed mythology and its muddled and contradictory actuality. There is no guarantee of a relationship between the articulated logics and the actual policies on the ground, as such local resistance strategies are often aimed at co-opting and redeploying a state logic that is mythical or imaginary and not actually manifest in the quotidian processes of the state.

These three interconnected theoretical arguments will be further elucidated and evidenced in subsequent empirical chapters. The next section of this chapter provides deeper theorization of the concept of the conservation estate before critically engaging with three significant bodies of literature framing this book's arguments.

Theorizing the Conservation Estate

According to the United Nations Environment World Conservation Monitoring Centre, nearly 15 percent of the world's land area falls within one of the 238,563 protected areas recognized internationally (UNEP-WCMC, IUCN, and NGS 2018; Adams 2020). Clearly there is a large spatial footprint of the world's protected area endowment, with a substantial proportion of this land area found in postcolonial spaces of the Global South. Sub-Saharan Africa is home to over one thousand protected areas, of which thirty-six are additionally inscribed as UNESCO World Heritage Sites (Death 2016b). More broadly, the expansion of the conservation estate is a common goal in international environmental institutions, in epistemic communities of conservation biologists, and in the global conservation movement. They are broadly understood to be the way you "do conservation." Protected areas are widely seen as necessary, good, and the de facto standard bearers of conservation policies (see Corson et al. 2014; Garland 2008; Murdock 2021). This book does not investigate the ecological efficacy or performance of conservation; rather, the analysis of the conservation estate is an assessment of these spaces that goes beyond the ecological rationales articulated in their provenance. There is much existing scholarship in both the social and natural sciences that interrogates these debates (e.g., Oldekop et al. 2016). Those questions, while important, are secondary to this endeavor, which examines what the conservation estate does politically. The central focus of this book is not a question as to whether these spaces are "working" in an ecological or biological sense (worthy as that inquiry may be) but rather what they are *doing* politically, socially, economically, and culturally. It takes seriously "the ways that environmental and ecological imperatives have often functioned to extend the power of state institutions and political elites" (Death 2016b, 68).

Conservation and statehood became deeply intertwined in the twentieth century, first as a justification for colonial rule in Africa and later as a means to declare the state's right to determine the shape and nature of human-wildlife-environment relationships (Beinart and Hughes 2007; Dunn 2009; Neumann 1998). In Africa specifically, protected areas sit at the heart of conservation policy (Brockington, Duffy, and Igoe 2008; Duffy 2010; Ramutsindela 2007) while also serving as one of the most visible legacies of colonialism. Furthermore, international governance around biodiversity conservation continues to be a pervasive point of contact between postcolonial Africa and the Global

North (Adams and Mulligan 2003; Garland 2008; LaRocco 2019). Two points are worth considering. The first is that while colonial in origin, the largest expansion of protected areas globally occurred from 1985 to 1995, a process clearly taking place in the postcolonial period and tied to the growing neoliberalization of conservation (Apostolopoulou et al. 2021; Brockington, Duffy, and Igoe 2008; Brockington and Duffy 2011; Büscher, Dressler, and Fletcher 2019; Castree 2008; Holmes and Cavanagh 2016). Second, biodiversity conservation is about the control of land, resources, and people. In short, it is about power (Ellis 1994). It is a primary venue through which the relationship between many rural people and the postcolonial state is mediated. Conservation, a multiscalar yet ultimately hyperlocal issue, dictates access to the very basic building blocks of life: water, food, and shelter. These issues are critically important not just to local politics but also to the scope and stretch of political authority throughout a state.

In describing the "peculiar territorial regimes" of protected areas, Gissibl, Hohler, and Kupper (2012, 7) begin to capture the scope of my focus on the conservation estate. The conservation estate is a key analytic and a category of space worthy of political consideration and deeper theorization. Heretofore, the conservation estate has been a descriptive term most frequently used in the natural sciences to describe the totality of land set aside for conservation. It is often used unproblematically, as a value-neutral metric used to account for the collection of different arrangements such as protected areas, buffer zones, forest reserves, and private wildlife ranches. Thus far, it allows for quantification—how much "conservation" is going on—as opposed to a more qualitative focus on what this means in situ. In much of the natural sciences, the term is left undefined, and its meaning is implicit (Brownlie and Botha 2009; Kliskey 1998; Norton-Griffiths and Southey 1995; Clark et al. 2009). It is most prevalent in scholarship in the fields of environmental management, conservation biology, and tourism studies as well as literature about conservation in New Zealand and Australia (Matunga 1995; Norton 2000; Taiepa et al. 1997).

The conservation estate has also been used in the social sciences (Büscher and Fletcher 2015; Homewood and Sullivan 2004), but the definition is again most typically left implied. However, there are a few instances of definition within the literature. Writing in *Conservation Biology*, Dietz and Czech say, "The conservation estate is generally defined as the collection of areas reserved for conservation purposes" (2005, 1482–83). Elsewhere Hulme and Murphree note that a nation's conservation estate may include "species, habitats or biodiversity" (1999, 278).

This book seeks to analytically sharpen the conservation estate as a concept. The conservation estate does not simply encompass areas officially gazetted in the name of conservation (parks, reserves, management areas) but also envelopes the interstitial and liminal zones that are not formal "conservation spaces" barring human residency but nonetheless are dominated by the imperatives, logics, and practices of conservation as a suite of policies. Moreover, the conservation estate is a conceptual space for examining the lived politics of the state, wherein conservation policies become both (and simultaneously) limiting factors on the available political opportunity structures and subjectivities of its inhabitants and also a creative force in the processes of state building writ large. Therefore, a key innovation is the theorization of the conservation estate as a social category of land that can be used in the analysis of politics. My inquiry focuses on how the peculiarities of social, political, and economic life on the conservation estate create different lived experiences and shape the contours of citizenship of those residents of the conservation estate. Ong's concept of graduated sovereignty, which she draws out from her research in Southeast Asia, is instructive here as it encapsulates the differential experiences of citizen-state relations as they manifest on the conservation estate. She argues that "different sectors of the population are subjected to different technologies of regulation and nurturance, and in the progress assigned to different social fates" (Ong 2000, 58). This results in the intensification of social differences, which in turn fragments citizenship in a country. Moreover, in analyzing the concept of state sovereignty, particularly in the Global South, it "must be rethought as a set of coexisting strategies of government within a single national space" (Ong 2000, 72). From Ong's insights, I argue that by observing the state and the state-building process on the conservation estate, the multifaceted, variegated nature of politics comes into focus. The conservation estate creates a place-specific and differentiated political opportunity structure. Behavioral and institutional policy choice options open and available elsewhere across the country, including in rural areas whose purpose is deemed to be primarily not related to conservation, are non-operable in conservation estate contexts. The conservation estate creates a set of structural impediments that limit the menu of livelihood choices and therefore economic opportunity.

Vandergeest and Peluso's "political forest" is a useful comparative model of how a similar and related concept has been operationalized in the social sciences (1995, 2015). Their pathbreaking scholarship on the political forest allows analysts to see beyond conventional understandings of environments as having particular ecological characteristics in order to assess and analyze their social, political, and historical features—as political entities in their own right. They argue, succinctly, that forests are "produced through politics" (2015, 173), a finding that is directly relevant to my theorization around the conservation estate. The political forest does not map precisely onto formalized ecological definitions of forests created by international institutions, nor is it only defined by the broadly recognizable image of a forest consisting of tree cover and associated wildlife. Rather, the political forest, like the conservation estate, is a site of embedded and imbricated political logics taking place on particular type of environmental terrain and ultimately constituted by its political histories and the lived experiences of state territorialization. Over the years, their insights have informed a variety of scholars tracing the state-making and subjectivity-constructing dynamics of the political forest in numerous global contexts beyond Vandergeest and Peluso's original empirical venue in Southeast Asia (Devine and Baca 2020). This provides an example of how a theoretical framework developed in a specific socio-ecological context can have wide purchase beyond the immediate empirical venue where the concept was originally formulated and bears relevance to the potential concept portability and generalizability of the "conservation estate" as elaborated in this book.

Why the Conservation Estate Matters

By insisting on the conservation estate as an analytical category of land, a focus of analysis separate from ecological "outcomes," this book does three important things. First, it engages with the reality that many countries in sub-Saharan Africa have significant percentages of land set aside for conservation, and this fact must be accounted for in the mainstream scholarship of land politics in Africa. For example, the two most conserved countries in the world are Tanzania (with over 50 percent) and Botswana (39 percent). South Africa, Namibia, Gabon, Kenya, and Zimbabwe also have large conservation estates. The significance of these spaces has received greater attention in political ecology and critical conservation studies but less so in the discipline of political science, which tends to focus on other categories of land. Second, it recognizes that while there is a rich literature engaging with the alienation of land to white settler communities, the historical division of land ownership in Africa is not simply about Black and white but also Black, white, and green (MacKenzie 1988; Murombedzi 2003, 2010). This dispossession can, and does, occur in states without a history of settler colonialism and direct expropriation, thus the conservation estate can have utility for understanding processes of land alienation outside of the "usual suspects" of former minority-ruled states. In fact, biodiversity conservation is a contemporary manifestation of broader process of land alienation and dispossession in Africa. This has been recognized by a robust scholarship on contemporary "green grabbing" across the continent and beyond. Fairhead, Leach, and Scoones define green grabbing as "the appropriation of land and resources for environmental ends" (2012, 238), which can be situated within the broader phenomenon of land grabbing, largely in the Global South (Borras et al. 2011; Dzingirai 2003; Hall 2011). Therefore, the conservation estate must be seen as part of a larger landholding system that is unequal, often connected to identity—whether racial, ethnic, or geographic—or related to particular livelihoods and lifestyles (Magome and Murombedzi 2003; Murombedzi 2003, 2010). Finally, the concept of the conservation estate fills an empirical gap in the scholarship of rural African politics, which is overwhelmingly focused on agrarian and agricultural dynamics, an orientation that fails to capture that land *non-use* can be as politically significant and wide-reaching as land use.

The use of the conservation estate as an analytical framing device is helpful because it crosscuts through various tenure regimes and encompasses all kinds of land devoted to conservation. For example, in Botswana the conservation estate covers parcels of state land (Chobe National Park and Central Kalahari Game Reserve), communal/tribal land (Moremi Game Reserve), and private freehold land (Ghanzi and Tuli Block wildlife ranches). The conservation estate allows researchers to speak to issues and phenomena that transcend conventional divisions in land tenure and envelops the heterogeneous tenure arrangements that fall under the umbrella of conservation. This is all the more important because of the way in which a significant proportion of African wildlife and conservation policies fall outside of conventional protected areas and persist in buffer zones, management areas, and private ranches, calling for a broader scope of where the logics of conservation predominate (Awiti 2012; Dongol and Neumann 2021; Gadd 2005; Neumann 2000; Palfrey, Oldekop, and Holmes 2021; Sinthumule 2017). Furthermore, new innovations taking place on the conservation estate—be they neoliberal payment-for-ecosystem-services models or transfrontier conservation areas—all need to be reckoned with in this category of land and political space.

Development of analytical language to deal with these politically unique spaces is paramount because this type of land-use arrangement is pervasive, dynamic, and growing in scope. Designating land as protected areas is one of the most commonplace understandings of conservation on a global scale. Parks are seen as synonymous with conservation, and the inscription and protection of large tracts of land is articulated as a key policy tool for how to "do conservation." The role of the international conservation regime in pushing states to incorporate more land into their conservation estates is substantial, particularly with respect to countries in the postcolonial Global South. The Convention on Biological Diversity (CBD) aims to inscribe 10 percent of each ecological region as a protected area. Furthermore, its 2020 target, agreed to in 2010 in Aichi, Japan, as a Strategic Plan for Biodiversity, urges the inscription of 17 percent of terrestrial areas and 10 percent of coastal and marine areas under legal conservation regimes (Adams 2020). Similarly, many development aid packages include contingencies for the expansion of new or existing protected areas, often, though not always, under the guise of REDD+ or other carbon-offset-based policy initiatives (Cavanagh and Benjaminsen 2014). There is a broad consensus that land-based systems of protected areas are the cornerstones of conservation. The "discursive and geographic expansion" (Corson et al. 2014, 191) of this kind of territory is viewed as a metric of success in international conservation circles. This enthusiasm at the level of international governance persists despite concerns about the ecological effectiveness of this mode of conservation and questions of social justice surrounding the distribution and impact of these regimes around the world. Nonetheless, the hegemony of protected areas is manifest as they "have come to represent assumptions of mutual understanding of what conservation has been, how it should be pursued, and to what ends" (Corson et al. 2014, 192).

However, their success is predicated upon appealing to broad and disparate audiences who can imbue their own particular political project on these spaces. These might include goals in pursuit of carbon sequestration through forest sinks along a payment-for-ecosystems model, sustainable development, and poverty alleviation or investments in financial or reputational portfolios. The creation of conservation spaces is politically malleable. It can be many things to many different actors, some of whom are more equipped to operationalize their vision for protected areas. In the "hotspot" focus of the global conservation movement, particular spaces around the world become imbued with a kind of global valence, and these select regions become the objects of increased international attention as part of a "global" natural heritage and capital exploitation, most often through wildlife tourism (Brockington and Scholfield 2010; Holmes 2011; Igoe, Neves, and Brockington 2010; Murdock 2021). Landscapes that can be claimed as part of a global commons or resources that can be claimed as part of a global environmental heritage (such as iconic species or charismatic megafauna) become the focus of international attention, and international actors stake a claim in the decision-making process and management. Global claims are legitimized over particular spaces in specific ways (Corson et al. 2014, 193). The intensity of international focus on the conservation estate differentiates these territories from other parts of the rural landscapes, to the benefit or detriment of non-conservation rural spaces, communities, and people.

Influential transnational NGOs such as Conservation International argue that protected areas of the conservation estate are the most important tool of conservation. These more traditional actors have been joined by newer, more radical organizations such as Nature Needs Half, which advocates for the expansion of the conservation estate, arguing that, as the name suggests, half of the world's land area should be put aside for conservation purposes.[4] Groups such as these push beyond the CBD's Aichi goals, which they regard as insufficient. These efforts are supported by a constellation of natural scientists and activists (Cafaro et al. 2017; Noss et al. 2012; Watson et al. 2018; Wilson 2016; Wuerthner, Crist, and Butler 2015) in advocating for 50 percent of terrestrial surface area to come under a protective conservation regime. Social scientists have been most critical of this position. For example, Büscher et al. (2017) have pushed back on these calls, noting that while popular and becoming increasingly more so, the project is neither socially just nor politically feasible. Such an endeavor would inevitably have to be subsidized on the backs of poor, rural dwellers in the Global South and would involve radical physical and economic displacement among a subset of the global population that is already marginalized and least culpable for the problems of global environmental degradation and emissions-fueled climate change. In the midst of these global discussions, it is all the more essential to evaluate how the conservation estate inheres in state building and how it impacts the daily lives of those living in these spaces.

Moreover, there is a disconnect between the consensus position regarding the importance of conservation spaces and pushes to expand protected areas for biodiversity conservation and their debatable return on ecological goals. Protected area downgrading, downsizing, and degazettement (PADDD) has become a point of contention. Downgrading a protected area consists of increasing the scope and intensity of allowed human activity within the space, changing the daily technologies of conservation that impact local residency, livelihood, and resource-use patterns. Downsizing is decreasing the size of the protected area itself, and degazettement is the promulgation of legal changes that do away with an area's protection status altogether. However, conservation scientists note that PADDD is not inherently negative and could have positive conservation outcomes, depending on context (Mascia et al. 2014). Fuller et al. (2010) argue that while the thoughtful degazettement of some conservation spaces might have salutary effects on ecological outcomes, degazettement retains a negative connotation and the process is controversial. As members of the conservation movement tend to focus on extending existing areas and expanding to new sites, they recognize that repealing the protected status of conservation spaces may be politically difficult to untenable. Nonetheless, they argue that the expansion logic may not be the best for ecological goals; considered contraction and reallocation of conservation may be necessary in order to prioritize the most impactful use of protected areas. Therefore, political characteristics might explain why degazettement of areas of the conservation estate is unlikely, even if there may be sound ecological reasons for such a rollback. The factors mitigating against such policy choices cannot be explained by conservation biology alone. For example, competition for land in Africa makes many rural people view the conservation estate as ripe for degazettement. So why, then, have few states taken the popular (and perhaps populist) stance of downgrading the conservation estate and opening that land for agrarian production? This book considers the varied interests and incentives that align in favor of keeping them. It argues we must understand the political role they play in state building, including its international dimensions, in order to analyze their perseverance and longevity across the rural landscape.

Theorizing the State

As this inquiry is concerned with the role and scope of conservation in the process of state building, it is necessary to situate my argument within the scholarship of the state. Three characteristics of this book's theoretical framing of the state are elucidated below: the state is socially constructed; it is not reified or uniform, though still vitally important for social organization; and though the state is multifaceted and rife with inconsistencies, this is not an indicator of weakness per se. Finally, from this more global theoretical perspective, I then engage with Death's specific analysis of the environmental state building in Africa.

First to consider is the constructed nature of the state. In contrast to commonly held Western norms of statehood and sovereignty—which define the state by a set of territorial and behavioral criteria rooted in a particular European historical experience (Clapham 1996; Jackson 1990; Jackson and Rosberg 1982; Migdal 1988; Samatar and Samatar 2002)—various authors approach the state from the assumption that statehood and sovereignty are socially constructed ideas (Biersteker and Weber 1996;

Dunn 2009; Hansen and Stepputat 2001; Hagmann and Péclard 2011; Risse 2011; Weber 1998). Many scholars have challenged the central assumption that fully consolidated statehood, as seen in the Western model, is the appropriate yardstick with which to measure states and governance processes around the world, noting that this rigid conceptualization creates a global bias that delegitimizes non-Western political arrangements (Agbese and Kieh 2007; Doty 1996; Dunn 2001; Gabay and Death 2014; Grovogui 2001; Helle-Valle 2002; Risse 2011; Strang 1996).

When Western notions of sovereignty defined in terms of Weberian criteria for statehood are used as a universal measure, African states are often characterized as "weak" (Clapham 1996; Griffiths 1995; Herbst 2000; Jackson 1990; Samatar and Samatar 2002). This notion of weakness is echoed by scholars suggesting that state building in Africa should be viewed through structural and materialist lenses, focusing on the role of geography, territory, and demography (Griffiths 1995; Herbst 2000). Yet many scholars are dissatisfied with this and present a socially constructed state, an approach that is more revealing. Biersteker and Weber (1996) provide a useful definition of "social construction" as it relates to state building. They characterize "social construction" as consisting of the interactions between identities and practices. The state, as both a theoretical phenomenon and an empirical reality, is not static but rather contested, defined and redefined, and made real through lived experience. Pillay suggests eschewing the conceptualization of a fixed, ideal type in favor of understanding the state as "from its concrete manifestations in specific temporal and geographical junctures. The injunction here is to think about the political sphere as a constitutive domain, rather than constituted one" (Pillay 2018, 8). Rather than this notion of the territorial state being a given, it is crafted, constructed, and maintained through a series of social processes. This is the premise from which I approach state building. I understand the state as created through "the production of a normative conception that links authority, territory, population (society, nation), and recognition in a unique way and in a particular place" (Biersteker and Weber 1996, 3). Moreover, in Death's assessment, the "state can be treated as the effect of governing rationalities, an assemblage brought into being by reiterated practices, rationalities, and technologies and held together via discourses of sovereignty and the myth of the state" (2016b, 12). This social construction requires maintenance through discourses, practices, and technologies. For example, throughout this book I use "discourses" to mean narratives, rhetorics, and imaginaries linked to the conservation estate. I use "practices" to describe the behaviors, policies, and legal decisions related to the maintenance and expansion of the conservation estate. I use "technologies" to describe the tangible manifestations used to operationalize discourse and practice into material reality, such as fences, maps and delineations, antipoaching patrols, and public education efforts. They may be interactive, mutually enforcing, or contradictory.

Next, the socially constructed state is not uniform, reified, or entirely cohesive; it is instead an indeterminate yet powerful concept. Abrams (1988) warns against the pitfalls of studying the state as if it is a concrete and fixed entity and urges scholars to approach the state both as a system and as an idea, encompassing tangible and material institutions as well as the notional, normative dimensions of the state. Instead of being driven by a definitive programmatic logic akin to the type of coherent "authoritarian high modernism" described in Scott's *Seeing Like a State* (1998), this work envisions a more multifaceted and less ordered approach to the state, such as the one laid out by Hansen and Stepputat (2001). The theoretical reification of the state constructs the "state as a thing: a more or less unified entity that can be the subject of actions such as deciding, ruling, punishing, regulating, intervening and waging war," whereas an approach that acknowledges the quotidian and "prosaic" qualities of the state accounts for its "heterogeneous, constructed, porous, uneven, processual and relational character" (Painter 2006, 754). This attends to both the state's geographical unevenness, as well as the contestation over the normative imaginings of the state. As a result, states have a tendency to put forth contradictory and ambivalent practices. Nonetheless, the state remains a primary lens of analysis in the study of politics; whole discourses relating to identity, citizenship, territory, recognition, and authority are embedded in the imaginaries of the state. The state is an organizing concept for modern society, even if it is constructed and imagined in ways that may be fluid and shifting. Following from this, state building is an iterative act of maintenance, one that is always a site of contestation.

Third, the state's multifaceted nature is not a sign of weakness. The contested nature of the state is not a function of it being "weak" or "failing" or "quasi"—terms often applied to states in Africa—but rather characteristic of all state-building processes: a series of continually contested, reimagined, and renegotiated relationships between rulers, those they seek to rule, and the territory on which they attempt to articulate authority. Biersteker and Weber note, "The identity of the territorial state is not given, but is constituted through complex, overlapping, and often contradictory processes" (1996, 278). States are historical processes that are embedded in social forces and function as the products of institutions, policies, and the practices of bureaucratic state agents as well as discourses and imaginaries. This line of analysis shies away from discussions of "weak" versus "strong" states, instead favoring a rich empirical accounting of the state from a particular ethnographic vantage point, which in this book is the conservation estate.

Tying together these various strands in the introduction to their edited volume *States of Imagination*, Hansen and Stepputat argue that the state remains central to how we imagine social organization, *even if* it is vexed, confused, and contradictory. They suggest that the state is both inadequate and indispensable—home to various contested hegemonies but also a fundamental concept used in the ordering of social and political life in postcolonies (2001, 2). Hansen and Stepputat maintain that the state is a powerful lens for the empirical study of social and political relations, suggesting that the "imagination of the state [is] the great enframer of our lives" (37). The contemporary state is constructed and maintained through mythological dimensions: imaginaries of what the state is and does. This scholarship is often used to critique and retheorize the literature around postcolonial statehood. This book is embedded in this empirical turn, wherein analysts urge studies of the state to focus not on juridical understandings of state and stateness but rather on the phenomenon on the ground, the experiential and lived politics of the state. This body of literature challenges the notion of a top-down, scientifically driven "logical" state, as Hansen and Stepputat note, "Maybe it is the very idea of state actions as guided by an abstract, omniscient, and rational intelligence ... that constitutes the very core of the myth of the modern state" (15). Following from this, I resist analyzing the state as a monolith; there are limits to state power, and indeed power is grounded in various actors and institutions. State building is an ambiguous project even if it appears coherent. Contradictory impulses and implications are not pathological but rather intrinsic to the nature of the state itself, resultant from the myriad actors, logics, and interests that overlap in this contested process. Varied and imperfectly aligned agendas create a constellation of different interests all operating under the banner of state building. This processual contingency is not limited to states in postcolonial Africa or the Global South but manifests even in those "Weberian" archetypes.

Finally, Death's monograph *The Green State in Africa* (2016b) centers environmental governance at the heart of his analytical narrative of African states in the postcolonial era. His work articulates the empirically identifiable connections between state building and various processes of environmental governance. He argues that political contestations around the environment are so vital to African politics and have such explanatory power that our understanding of states on the continent is lacking without them. Moreover, this process is constitutive and iterative, wherein contestations over environmental issues produce the African state (2016b). While noting that existing scholarship aimed at theorizing "green states" has tended to eschew analysis of cases in the Global South in favor of wealthier countries conceived of as environmental vanguards like the Nordics, Death highlights that "the politics of land and conservation are of more central importance to contemporary African green state effects than many states elsewhere in the world" (2016b, 3). Indeed, in arguing this, he notes that in countries like Tanzania, Botswana, and South Africa "conservation is more deeply embedded in state policies and national identity" (2016b, 76). Why is this the case? Death explains: "Conservation has played a very different role in African state formation than in Europe or North America. In Africa . . . vast conservation parks preceded independent statehood, and protected areas became closely bound up with practices of state building, border enforcement, and the penetration of the state into rural areas" (2016b, 76). By examining state building from the empirical site of the conservation estate in Botswana, the local and spatially contingent aspects of the process are made apparent, and the misalignment between the mythic imaginary of state and the lived experiences of the state is brought to the fore. Furthermore, despite its constitutive importance, I suggest that the conservation estate is one empirical arena where these mythologies begin to become unstuck. In Botswana, state imaginaries about consultation, belonging, participation, and development are untethered from the realities produced by the particular conditions of biodiversity conservation. Importantly, the ubiquity of paradox does not negate the significance of the state in the lives of those subject to its authority, as being "fraught with internal inconsistencies and contradictions . . . has not necessarily weakened the state in terms of the capacity of policies and designs to create social effects" (Hansen and Stepputat 2001, 15–16). Apparent inconsistencies, hypocrisies, and contradictions from within the state-building project result from the fact that there is no overarching grand design but rather that the endeavor consists of a variety of parochial state buildings informed by particular normative, economic, and political interests.

Land and the African State

The aim of this book is to probe the state-building process from the empirical milieu of the conservation estate. This necessitates a reckoning with politics of land, most particularly in rural settings. However, as will be discussed below, while conservation is primarily a rural endeavor, it does implicate urban spaces too. As a decidedly spatial form of governance, conservation occurs in a particular place and landscape (Neumann 2005). This puts the territorial nation-state in a unique position to claim control over land and resources and to invoke authority over their regulation. The act of exerting control over a common space, superseding any existing local claim to the land, is part of the performance that can bring a state into being.

Examination of the conservation estate in relation to the politics of land is not simply revelatory with regard to who dictates and influences the practices and policies of conservation. It also provides insight about the nature of postcolonial state building. Both conservation and state building are fundamentally concerned with what people can or cannot do in their environments and what institutions and structures are empowered to set the limits on human behavior. Conservation, being embedded in land, is also inherently about spatial control, determining where people can (and should) live across a territory and the subsequent strategies that maintain this sociospatial order. Considering all of this, conservation policy in fact serves multiple purposes to postcolonial states. These objectives often transcend ecological impulses and are political in their own right.

Conservation is place-based, tied to land, and can problematize competing systems and cosmologies of ownership. Much scholarly attention has been paid to the centrality of land tenure in African politics (Alden Wily 2001, 2008; Alden and Anseeuw 2009; Amanor and Moyo 2008; Berry 1993, 2009; Boone 2013, 2014; Lund 2008; Ntsebeza and Hall 2007; Peters 1994; Ramutsindela and Sinthumule 2017; Toulmin and Quan 2000). Importantly, land can be conceptualized as territory (which has a political connotation and is governed but not owned) or as property (which has both spiritual and legal connotations and can be owned but not governed) (Lund 2013; Peluso and Lund

2011). The process of defining land as a territory allows or disallows for certain kinds of use (or non-use, as it were), imbues the state with a custodial role, and mandates appropriate types of mobility and economy for residents. The definition of land as territory, territorialization, is a strategy for controlling resources and their users (Vandergeest and Peluso 1995). The construction of land as territory makes it the realm of the state. Territoriality relates directly to authority—because as territory (rather than as property), space is governed or managed, whereas property confers specific and bounded rights to the owner(s).

State interventions with regard to land, settlement, and resource use are rooted in the need to assert state authority and shape political identity (and presumably allegiance) as well as play a role in local social relations (Alexander 2006; see also Radcliffe 2001; Saugestad 2001). Land plays a unique role in the manifestation of "legitimate" authority as well as in the contestations that may limit it (Alexander 2006; Badiey 2013; Lund 2008). Contestation, negotiation, and center-local debates about authority—who has it, and who is subject to it—are commonplace in the politics of the environment and the state (Anderson 2002; Gibson 1999; Peters 1994). In state building, a variety of actors attempt to assert rights to land and articulate their visions of the state using the medium of land and land tenure. These processes are not exclusively top-down but rather can also be sites of "the social process of contestation, negotiation and conflict that are at the heart of the state-building enterprise" (Badiey 2013, 58). Boone and Lund (2013) suggest that land plays a critical role in how various actors use these repertoires to make claims, which, in turn, construct the state and conceptualize authority, citizenship, and jurisdiction.

Biodiversity conservation, as it is currently operationalized, is dependent on attention to, regulation of, and control over land. The section below situates the unique features of the conservation estate within the broader literature of land politics and the state, notably the work of Boone and others. However, in the analysis of land and state building, areas devoted to conservation are often characterized as exceptional or left out of analysis entirely (Boone 2003; Maclean 2010), despite the fact this type of land is a significant and growing category of space in Africa and elsewhere in the Global South. Going back to the colonial era, land control served as a means to enforce state authority over people and, in many cases, limit mobility (Boone 2014). The creation of the conservation estate was a key mechanism in actualizing these processes, thus a more fulsome discussion of conservation's role is necessary. The ability of the colonial, and indeed postcolonial, state to allocate "unused" or "unoccupied" land—land deemed to not have been made "productive," often misread as terra nullius (Dominguez and Luoma 2020; Hendlin 2014; Sapignoli 2018)—is tied to the birth of the conservation estate. This book seeks to meaningfully distinguish the conservation estate as a category of socially relevant space while not needlessly separating conservation areas from the broader literature of rural social relations and land politics that are central to the study of the state in Africa. In pursuit of this, this book widens the scope of land politics to explicitly include the conservation estate as a distinct concept predominately (though not exclusively) found within rural space but one characterized by different logics and imperatives from rural, agrarian land deemed "productive." Of particular importance is the way in which state building on the conservation estate complicates the "rural" experience. State policies on the conservation estate make life qualitatively different for those who live there, manifesting in a separation from both more "conventional" rural experiences and the experiences of those living in urban spaces.

Rurality and the Conservation Estate

The preponderance of conservation in remote and peripheral areas requires attention to analyses of *rural* land politics specifically. This does not imply that the conservation estate cannot be relevant to urban or peri-urban localities but rather that engagement with the existing literature of the rural is paramount. Rural Africa, home to the vast expanses of land that produce tropes about wilderness and primitivity, can appear opaque to the political scientist. This seeming opacity is particularly relevant for political scientists who rely on survey data that, while improving, is still less reliable in more remote areas. As Boone notes, "Most political analysts have not looked for or seen structural differentiation and institutionalized political forms in rural Africa; many seem to have simply assumed the absence thereof" (2014, 19–20). Throughout her oeuvre, her focus on rural contexts is clear and well articulated. Boone has been one of the foremost proponents of recognizing the goings-on in rural spaces as key for political understanding and analysis. Across her body of work, she has emphatically given attention to rural places and people as valid loci of political study. She challenges political science research that has seen rural Africa as "invariant across space" (2014, 12) and enriches understandings of statehood in African countries by taking seriously the national implications of subnational distinctions. It is not just that the micropolitics of these localities matter but that what happens politically in these spaces is often of national importance. Despite rapid urbanization in Africa's growing megacities across the continent, approximately 60 to 70 percent of the population lives in rural areas. These spaces are home to substantial voting blocs and ruling parties often derive crucial support from their rural "heartlands."

Boone is certainly not alone in her attention to rural Africa. Numerous scholars who have engaged with rural spaces and populations have argued there is a qualitative difference—regarding both the nature of citizenship and the policy environment—in how the postcolonial state treats inhabitants of rural territory, as opposed to urban dwellers. Rural territory constitutes an integral, yet ambiguous, role in the postcolonial state (Bates 1981; Boone 2003, 2007; Hoon and Maclean 2014; Maclean 2010; Mamdani 1996). While some scholars such as Bates (1981) characterize the central state as overbearing, perhaps even all-powerful in rural areas, others including Boone (2003, 2007) argue that rural territory, remote from central power, is a site of negotiation and bargaining between rural power brokers and the central state, deeply impacting the way marginal spaces are incorporated into the postcolonial state. A middle ground suggests that variations in state formation at the central level shape rural areas in vastly different ways (Maclean 2010). This approach provides scope to consider how even states that fall short of overbearing dominance in rural areas still retain a significant potential to transform institutions, spaces, and communities found therein. Common throughout these differing analyses is the idea that there are dynamic and important linkages between the center and rural territory as well as potential transformative effects on state building at both national and local levels.

Perhaps the most influential study of the wider ramifications of rural politics is Mamdani's *Citizen and Subject: Contemporary Africa and the Legacy of Late Colonialism*, which suggests that the rural/urban divide of the bifurcated state crafted by colonial rule continues to play a substantial role in the nature of politics in the postcolonial state in Africa. He argues colonial divisions that created variegated lived experiences of authority on the part of the rural "subject" and urban "citizen" have yet to be fully remade or reimagined in the postcolonial era, with implications for postcolonial citizens and polities. Mamdani's work is primarily focused on analyzing the impactful differences between the rural and the urban in postcolonial Africa. However, the rural/urban binarism may mask the deeper complexities and variations across rural spaces. Indeed, this line of analysis does not fully account for the internal differentiation of rural territory with respect to the conservation estate, which is a central concern of this book. That is not to say that rural Africa—home to Mamdani's "subject"—has been theorized as uniform or monolithic. Elsewhere scholars helpfully attend to the variations of the rural state over space and time in a manner that enriches work of earlier scholars like Mamdani, while expanding the breadth of our understanding regarding the diversity of rural sociopolitical arrangements (Boone 2014; Maclean 2010; Rabinowitz 2018; Turner 2009).

As noted above, Boone's work—both her 2003 *Political Topographies of the African State: Territorial Authority and Institutional*

Choice and her 2014 *Property and Political Order: Land Rights and the Structure of Politics in Africa*—are important pieces of scholarship on the politics of land, rural politics, and the interactions between local elites and the central state. Her work focuses predominantly on the rural agrarian state and argues for the heterogeneity of subnational configurations across the rural space of a state. She recognizes variation within rural society to a greater extent than other scholars focused primarily on the urban/rural divide. Boone captures these rural variations by looking at regional differences in political institutional design, wherein she argues that the local context of state institution-building matters a great deal to the outcome of political authority and expression of state power. This analysis is emphatically focused on the political character of rural property regimes and takes seriously the structures of land and property that make rural African spaces and populations governable. Boone is attuned to the multiplicitous nature of these structures across space and time and argues that these institutional variations have explanatory power for how and why rural populations are linked to the state. She argues that "Africa's land regimes turn out to be far more varied and politicized than existing analysis has recognized" (2014, 3). Similarly, another comparativist, Rabinowitz (2018) characterizes the ability to generate goodwill in the countryside as an existential need for leaders to stay in power, in what she calls "a rural political strategy." With this heuristic, she recalibrates the central questions in the analysis of rural-urban dynamics in Africanist political science by suggesting that rural spaces are not neglected or merely sources of resource extraction to serve urban populations but rather constitutive of state power and leader longevity. Her empirical analysis, like Boone's, is trained upon an assessment of agricultural policies. Across these works is a tendency to equate "rural Africa" with agrarian societies dependent upon on agricultural production. A key locus of analysis in this work is on agrarian cash cropping, which does not adequately deal with other rural land-use strategies, such as conservation or transhumant pastoralism. In Boone's 2003 typology of local political systems, she notes that areas of land used by "nomadic" groups for subsistence activity would not be regarded as worth intensely incorporating into the state and thus would be left to their own devices: "It is really a catch-all for rural societies that are not engaged in commercial agriculture. Labour-exporting zones, nomadic societies, and zones of pure self-provisioning fit into this category. They are regions that are weakly incorporated into the modern state: builders of the French colonial empire referred to them dismissively as '*l'Afrique inutile*'" (2003, 323–24). I suggest that Boone is correct to center her analysis on the political variations that occur across the breadth and scope of rural Africa but that she does not sufficiently deal with a critically important category of land. Boone's geographical and empirical focus tends to leave out exactly the kinds of zones that became the backbone of the conservation estate across Africa—the places deemed wild, remote, and unproductive in a commercial sense. The spaces deemed weakly incorporated and left to their own devices by her framework are, in fact, sites of intense processes of negotiation, contestation, capital production, and state building. By moving the empirical attention to the conservation estate, in contrast to Boone's analysis of strictly commercial agrarian spaces, this book works to enrich the scholarship on land and rural politics by examining an understudied category of land—the conservation estate—as a vantage point for understanding the nature of the state in postcolonial Africa. Many typologies of land do not account for spaces of conservation, which are predicated not on material production associated with agrarian economies but rather on the purposeful absenting of these livelihood behaviors in pursuit of a wildlife tourism strategy and the restrictions around production superimposed on land deemed as part of the conservation estate. The spaces of tourism-driven *aproduction* (in the agrarian sense) may constitute a quarter of a country's land area and are becoming, for a whole host of reasons discussed later, increasingly commonplace in the twenty-first century. Hendlin notes that conservation "values—highly—precisely those lands that are fallow, unused, and wild" (2014, 157). Boone mentions, somewhat in passing, that parks tend to exist under statist land tenure and that they are off-limits to producers (2014, 38). While broadly true, this fails to capture the more expansive ways in which the logics of conservation have become dominant across a variety of tenure regimes—statist, communal (or, in her gloss, "neocustomary"), and private freehold land. Similarly, this omits the ways in which the logics of conservation extend well beyond the specifically demarcated confines of a protected areas and into buffer zones and Wildlife Management Areas where residency is permitted but various forms of production typically undertaken by resident would-be "producers" are limited, curtailed, discouraged, or outright banned. Assessing the conservation estate is an important added nuance here. Furthermore, we cannot simply think of the conservation estate as just another type of "state land" because it is far more diverse than that, occurring across state, communal, and private freehold land regime types.

Finally, by accounting for the particularities generated above and beyond distinctions in land tenure, the conservation estate captures the way in which the bifurcation laid out by Mamdani is more plural, incorporating urban, rural, and "wilderness" spaces. A greater distinction is needed between the rural, with its connotations of agrarian production, and the often-forced aproduction of so-called wilderness spaces of the conservation estate. An expanded analytical nuance of urban/rural/wilderness works to confirm and extend Mamdani's influential and far-reaching conceptualization of power and citizen-state relations in Africa and adds depth of understanding to the various sociopolitical arrangements found in the rural space through the examination of the conservation estate. Earlier scholarship has shown there are differences to the way citizens interact with structures of power in an urban setting compared with a rural setting. What sets this third category of space—the conservation estate—apart is the way in which social and political configurations are often masked as purely environmental conditions necessitated by biology or ecology. In rural areas outside of the conservation estate, people and communities are less subject to the hegemonic invocation of global conservation science as the rationale for reordering their lifeworlds, though this is certainly not absent, recalling, for example, the imposition of colonial-era rangeland science and other interventions in agronomy (Leach and Mearns 1996). Nonetheless, in many cases, though certainly not all, there is greater room for negotiation and maneuver for rural dwellers living far from a global biodiversity "hotspot" or lucrative tourism installation than is available to those citizens residing on the conservation estate. Examined throughout this book is the reality that on the conservation estate the basic functions of life are circumscribed in ways uncommon outside this zone. Yet the limits to certain kinds of land-use practices, settlement patterns, and livelihood approaches on the conservation estate are not strictly ecological but rather human-made, and thus political, restrictions. This book develops a richer model accounting for the political variance of rural space and its impact on postcolonial state building. It captures the diversity of rural spaces in Africa by theorizing more concretely around the conservation estate, which is a cross-cutting institutional form. It may span (and in the case of Botswana does span) numerous land tenure regimes—state, communal, freehold—and produces material, discursive, and subjective commonalities in these varied institutional contexts. Like in Vandergeest and Peluso's political forest, it is the unique politics that makes the conservation estate what it is, not the ecology.

The theoretical framework I have outlined above recognizes the importance of rural geographies of the conservation estate generally and with respect to the specific empirical case study of Botswana. However, conservation, and therefore the lens of the conservation estate, is certainly not limited to the rural. It is growing and dynamic land use that is being expanded in novel and creative ways, enveloping nontraditional spaces outside of the rural periphery—ranging from the suburban-type gated "eco-communities" in Hoedspruit, South Africa (Koot, Büscher, and Thakholi 2022) to urban conservation spaces in Cape Town (Ferketic, Latimer, and Silander 2010; Swanepoel 2013) and prominent cases like Nairobi National Park. The latter is a longstanding gazetted protected area within the Nairobi metropolitan area, ten miles from the city's central business district and adjacent to the country's major transit hub, Jomo Kenyatta International Airport (Mwangi, Zhang, and Wang 2022; Okello, Kenana, and Kieti 2012). While the book's empirical arguments are decidedly oriented toward the rural, I endeavor to avoid a rural spatial bias in considering how this concept may be broadly applied in other contexts. In the conclusion, I will come back to the question of the role of the conservation estate in non-rural spaces and suggest how the conservation estate may operate beyond the empirical case at hand.

Research Methods

This book argues for a resituating of conservation within the framework of state building in postcolonial Africa. It does so by introducing the heuristic of the conservation estate and through case study analysis of Botswana. Botswana as a case study has several characteristics relevant to this research. It has set aside nearly two-fifths of its land for conservation, only behind Tanzania as the most conserved country in the world, and despite rapid urbanization many Batswana live in these rural areas. Botswana is home to large populations of wildlife, particularly charismatic megafauna, including the most elephants of any nation on the continent.[5] Throughout its postcolonial history, Botswana's government has included conservation as a major domestic policy focus and foreground it in its interactions with the international system (Mogende and Ramutsindela 2020). While Botswana's already large conservation estate, wildlife endowment, and parochial environmental histories make it, to some extent, idiosyncratic, the global push to expand the size of protected areas in other "less conserved" countries of the Global South implicate the empirical findings of this book in a variety of contexts where there may be global pressure to grow the conservation estate.

Broadly speaking, Botswana's conservation estate features two distinct areas: the riverine and wetland system of the Okavango Delta and Chobe River in the north and the desert ecosystem of the western Kalahari—colloquially referred to as "the desert" and "the delta." There are both ecological and touristic differences between these regions (Barnes 1991). The northern areas of the country have larger wildlife populations and riverine ecologies, while the western Kalahari is more arid and features desert ecosystems. The research for this book spans conservation-adjacent communities in both Botswana's northern wetlands ecosystem and the western Kalahari, creating a more holistic methodological approach through which to develop insightful countrywide findings.

Data collection in both the desert and the delta allows for the development of the argument that the conservation estate has evident political and economic commonalities, even if it is diverse in ecology (e.g., arid versus wetland) and land tenure (e.g., state versus communal land). This book widens the analytical aperture by connecting both spaces. They are analyzed by their shared features despite distinct ecological contexts, ethnolinguistic diversity, and different land tenure and economic systems. Their shared characteristics warrant comprehensive analysis. Therefore, despite protected areas and Wildlife Management Areas existing at diverse geographic locations across Botswana's north and west, this book considers these spaces as a single social category—the conservation estate—sharing commonalities in their social and political features rather than strictly ecological ones alone. Important sociopolitical characteristics that unite geographically distinct, and at times ecologically dissimilar, areas of the conservation estate include limits on residency, restrictions on livelihood opportunities, the failure of national rural development strategies, heightened physical and psychological dangers related to wildlife, low or attenuated

Introduction

infrastructure penetration, the manner of their historical incorporation into the colonial state, increased securitization and deployment of military personnel, and specific land tenure configurations unique to locations zoned for conservation.

I conducted fieldwork in one district in Botswana's delta, Northwest District, and one in the desert, Ghanzi District. Within each I conducted interviews in the district capitals, Maun and Ghanzi Town, and in a series of village research field sites. Villages were selected based on two criteria to ensure that they could be classified as being "on the conservation estate," both in terms of location and institutional and socio-ecological arrangements: they would either be within a conservation area (such as a Wildlife Management Area) or adjacent to a protected area (or inscribed natural UNESCO World Heritage Site) and home to a community-based organization (either active or defunct) with connections to Botswana's Community-Based Natural Resource Management (CBNRM) program (see table I.1).

Table I.1. Community organizations by research site

Northwest District
Shakawe: Trust for Okavango Cultural and Development Initiatives
Sankuyo: Sankuyo Tshwaragano Management Trust
Boro, Ditshiping, Xuoxao: Okavango Kopano Mokoro Community Trust*
Mababe: Mababe Zokotsama Community Development Trust
Khwai: Khwai Development Trust
Ghanzi District
D'Kar: Kuru Development Trust
East Hanahai, West Hanahai, Kacgae: Xwiskurusa Community Trust
Groot Laagte and Qabo: Huiku Community Trust
New Xade: New Xade Management Trust (defunct at the time of fieldwork)
Bere: Bere Community Trust (defunct at the time of fieldwork)

Note: OKMCT is a multivillage trust that also includes the delta communities of Xharaxao, Xaxaba, and Daunara, not visited during fieldwork. Trust details provided by Department of Wildlife and National Parks CBNRM liaison officers in Maun and Ghanzi Town.

FIGURE I.1. Map of Botswana. *Source:* CIA World Factbook.

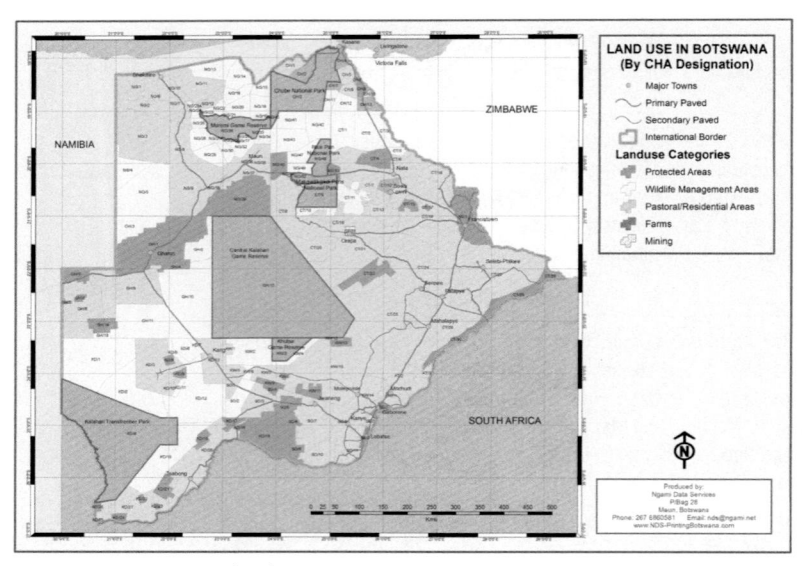

FIGURE I.2. Botswana land-use map. *Source:* Ngami Data Services.

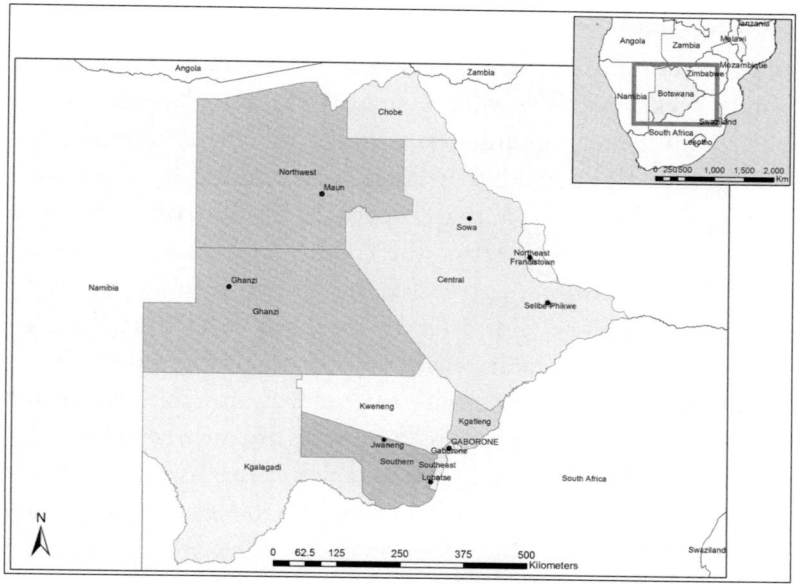

FIGURE I.3. Botswana district map. Map by Michelle LaRocco.

Data collection for this project spanned from August 2013 to April 2014 and then again from July 2014 to September 2014, with a follow-up trip in June and July of 2017. It focused on qualitative data because the perceptions, narratives, and imaginaries that constitute citizen-state relations on the conservation estate were paramount. At the core of my data collection were numerous conversations with individuals living on the conservation estate. My dataset consists of 284 semi-structured interviews with 385 individuals in Northwest District and Ghanzi District as well as with government officials in Gaborone, in addition to participant observation and document analysis. Interviewees included local residents living on the conservation estate, civil servants, elected officials, conservation practitioners, and tourism operators, among others. Interviews were secured for this project through a combination of targeted and snowball sampling. In communities where I conducted research, I would begin my interviews by having conversations with the village *kgosi* (chief) or *kgosana* (headman), both to secure research permission in the village and to initiate the data-collection process in the community. Similarly, I would seek interviews with members of the village development committee, community trust board members, community escort guides (local wildlife scouts), and any locally deployed government officials. From there, I engaged in snowball sampling, interviewing local members of the community. Interviews were semi-structured; they were flexible but in-depth in character. I began each interview with a list of topics to cover but allowed for the possibility of interviewees introducing other issues into the discussion. Typically interviews lasted forty-five minutes to an hour, with some as short as fifteen minutes and others as long as two and a half hours. To supplement this approach and to gain a broader perspective on the publicly consumable state-sponsored narratives, I relied on document analysis of secondary sources from government sources and state media.[6]

A note on chronology. The fieldwork for this book was conducted from 2013 to 2017, during the presidential tenure of Ian Khama. President Khama has been an important and influential figure in the politics of the environment in Botswana, dating back to before his term as the executive. However, his successor in the presidency, Mokgweetsi Masisi, despite being Khama's vice president and a member of the same ruling party, notably clashed with the former president with regard to several conservation endeavors. Their relationship eventually deteriorated, became acrimonious, and saw the reversal of several environmental policies championed during the Khama era, including a nationwide hunting ban and the arming of civilian wildlife officers (LaRocco and Mogende 2022). Where relevant, I address the changes in policies that have occurred since the research for this book was conducted. Nonetheless, despite the overturning of some specific policy initiatives and the dramatic confrontation between Khama and Masisi in the lead-up to the 2019 national election, the *longue durée* trends regarding the relationships between land, wildlife, the state, and citizens in postcolonial Botswana remain analytically apt. Moreover, this book avoids framing its analysis around a single individual or policymaker. Environmental policymaking and a focus on biodiversity conservation has long been a salient feature of postcolonial Botswana, appearing consistently throughout the varied presidential administrations since independence (Mogende and Ramutsindela 2020).

Throughout my fieldwork, all recorded interview data were transcribed, and written notes from unrecorded interviews were annotated. Once this process was completed, the finalized notes, translations, and transcripts were transferred into MAXQDA software for qualitative data analysis, which allowed for the grouping of information and categorization of interview responses in a holistic and systematic way. The reliance on direct quotes from my interviewees, especially those from the rural conservation estate, is a deliberate decision made throughout this book to emphasize and privilege local voices and perspectives. This approach had both ethical and analytical rationales. From an ethical perspective, I am committed to conveying local perspectives in order to address interview respondents' concerns that they are "not heard" in issues concerning conservation, a sentiment that came up consistently in geographically distant communities and across all periods of my fieldwork. Analytically, I am interested, in part, in the perceptions and subjectivities on the conservation estate, which are elucidated from local voices. The quotes chosen are highly representative and very frequently were echoed by multiple other respondents. For the sake of coherence and brevity, when multiple interviewees expressed the same idea, I present one fairly typical utterance.

In addition to interviews with people living on the conservation estate, this book is informed by numerous interviews with government officials, who were, almost to a person, incredibly generous with their time and insights. They often offered complex and nuanced perspectives about their roles in enacting state policy on the conservation estate. Where informative to do so, I use their position or title at the time of our conversation, though some individuals may of course be in different roles by the time of publication. However, I am mindful of the small and intimate bureaucratic community in Botswana where individuals may be readily identified by their names or initials within relatively small departments. As such, all government informants have been anonymized. Similarly, all respondents residing on the conservation estate have been anonymized or given pseudonyms. Where appropriate they are also categorized by a descriptor of their position (e.g., *kgosi*, tourism operator, member of a village development committee, member of parliament; see table I.2). Time has elapsed since my data collection, and I have endeavored to note if I am aware of a change in position on the part of civil servants or elected officials.

Table I.2. Interviewee characteristics

	Interviewees
Government	
Elected officials (e.g., MPs and councillors)	7
Civil servants	51
Parastatal employees (e.g., Botswana Tourism Organization)	5
Tourism	
Photographic tourism	7
Commercial safari hunting	5
NGOs	
Conservation and development	24
Multilateral donor practitioners (e.g., USAID, UN)	6
Private landowners	10
Northwest District dwellers	
Traditional leaders	6
Local residents	134
Ghanzi District dwellers	
Traditional leaders	8
Local residents	122
Total	385

Note: Some interviewees overlap in two categories (e.g., a private landowner who is also involved in the tourism industry). In this case the interviewee is listed only once, based on their primary characteristic, as judged by the author.

Table I.3. Interview respondents by research site

	Interviews	Interviewees
Gaborone	27	28
Northwest District		
Maun	36	40
Shakawe	14	21
Sankuyo	20	31
Boro	9	10
Ditshiping	9	13
Xuoxao	7	11
Mababe	18	29
Khwai	16	21
Ghanzi District		
Ghanzi Town*	29	38
D'Kar	11	12
West Hanahai	14	23
East Hanahai	7	10
Kacgae	13	18
Groot Laagte	12	22
Qabo	6	13
New Xade	19	23
Bere	17	22
Total	284	385

Note: The figures for Ghanzi Town include interviews conducted on nearby freehold farms.

My research assistants were vital to the data-collection process because almost all of the interviews that took place in conservation-adjacent communities were conducted in Setswana, with my assistants acting as translators.[7] Recognizing the limitations of translation and interpretation, in addition to my on-the-ground translators I employed two other Gaborone-based assistants to act as secondary transcribers of my recorded data.[8] This was an attempt to mitigate some of the risks of translation by allowing me to get a second opinion about interview responses from first-language Setswana speakers, who could highlight instances where they felt the initial translation was slightly amiss. In addition to my long-term research assistants, in each community I employed a local resident as a guide and community liaison, accompanying my research assistant and me around the village. These people were not only interlocutors vital to securing interviews, but they also helped me navigate sensitivities in often-researched communities, providing contextual background and insights my research assistant and I would have otherwise missed.

Book Structure and Chapter Overview

This book is divided into three parts, each focusing on a facet of state building: authority, territory, and identity. The parts illuminate how the dynamics of the conservation estate figure greatly in where, how, and in what manner citizens may live across the state's territory and inform their subsequent interactions with both co-local wildlife and the state. They work in concert to develop the three core arguments of this book: the overarching one about the conservation estate as a sociopolitical category and the two nested arguments about rural differentiation and local resistance.

Three thematic subquestions guide this book's inquiry into the state-building functions of biodiversity conservation. The first area of this research focuses on the nature of authority, coercion, and consent in state building. Here I concentrate on the way in which logics of conservation sit at the interface between the state and its citizens in terms of how people are permitted to live and act in areas dominated by the imperatives of conservation and how such terms are enforced or accepted. The second line of inquiry is concerned with the control of land across territory. It is focused on where and how citizens may occupy space and the manner in which spatial organization in conservation coincides with and complicates social organization. The third thematic area of this research is related to questions of identity, development, and livelihoods. In short, it is concerned with the ways in which conservation intersects with who citizens are and how the logics and imperatives of conservation may shape, construct, or distort these subjectivities and identities. Throughout these three sections, this book is attentive to the role of the international system in the state-building process and the relationship between the state and its citizens in the globalized context of the conservation estate.

Taken together, these three areas of focus inform the arguments presented here and constitute the basic terrain through which the book is organized. From an empirical perspective, these lines of inquiry are explored across the two research regions in Botswana described in the previous section. While some scholars emphasize the local as primary setting for the state-building process, others suggest that the loci of state building occur at local, national, and transnational levels (see Hagmann and Péclard 2011). I argue that from certain analytical vantage points both conditions may occur simultaneously; in this case, various levels overlap on the conservation estate. Local people view the conservation estate as "home"—a source of everyday livelihoods as well as a marker of identity and difference within the larger Botswana polity. National-level actors view the conservation estate as a vital state-level resource, both economically and as a symbolic representation of Botswana's peace, tranquility, and stability. Global actors conceptualize Botswana's conservation estate as part of the world's natural heritage and a vital component of the conservation strategy aimed at Africa's charismatic wildlife on behalf of the global community.

Before progressing to the book's empirical analysis, chapter 1 contextualizes the case study and situates the reader in the specificities of Botswana's postcolonial state-building ethos as well as considers the fundamental contours of biodiversity conservation and wildlife tourism in the country. This provides a baseline for the subsequent empirical chapters in which the arguments unfold.

Part I, "Authority," comprises two chapters. Chapter 2, "Coercion on Botswana's Securitized Conservation Estate," focuses on the nature of authority and coercion, examining the use of the military in conservation enforcement and antipoaching projects on the conservation estate. Using the scholarship on securitization as a lens, it examines how state authority is created, maintained, and performed in unique and exceptional ways on the conservation estate. It also examines how the people of the conservation estate may inhabit and behave in areas dominated by the imperatives of conservation and how such terms are enforced or accepted, arguing that the resultant discourses, practices, and policies of conservation create a securitized state of exception. Chapter 3, "Democracy, the *Kgotla*, and Promises of Consent amid Conservation," delves into the tension between the securitized logic that has been deployed in the name of conservation and Botswana's ostensible commitment to democratic norms of consent and consultation, substantiating core arguments about the limitations of local resistance and the mediation of wildlife in citizen-state relations. It problematizes the role of the "expertise," the impacts of co-local charismatic species, and the outsized influence of the Western gaze on the conservation estate and examines how these factors influence citizen-state relations. This chapter probes the perennial questions of accountable authority in nominally democratic states: Who counts, and who is counted?

Part II, "Territory," comprises two chapters. Chapter 4, "Land and Ownership on the Conservation Estate," is concerned with the control of land across territory. It is focused on where citizens may occupy space and the manner in which spatial organization in conservation coincides with and complicates social organization. It examines the tension between the state's promotion of complete non-use of natural resources (i.e., preservation) and its preoccupation with private property rights, which creates exceptional zones in Botswana's freehold land on the conservation estate and bolsters the arguments about the sociopolitical ramifications of conservation and differentiated rural space. This chapter examines how various land tenure regimes on the conservation estate impact the relatively muted but still influential racial politics of the state-building project. Chapter 5, "Infrastructure and the Contours of Settlement and Tourism," focuses on the material and instrumental technologies that shape the contours of territorial control on the conservation estate, examining the dispensation or denial of infrastructure and the perceptions, subjectivities, and relationships produced therein. Using the dialectic of legibility/illegibility, this chapter argues that distinct logics of tourism and the desires of tourists to view a "peopleless" wilderness substantially alter the relationship between the state and its citizens on the conservation estate and creates a deeper differentiation in the state-building project that cannot be accounted for by only thinking about divisions between "rural" and "urban."

Part III, "Identity," comprises two chapters. Chapter 6, "Conservation Restrictions and the Construction of Criminalized Identities," investigates questions of development and identity and the subjectivities produced by their interaction. It is concerned with the ways in which conservation intersects with who citizens are and how the logics and imperatives of conservation may shape, construct, or distort these subjectivities, often creating categories of criminalized citizenship for local residents. In chapter 7, "Promises of Modernity and Failures of Development on the Conservation Estate," I delve into the contradictions between conservation and the logics of rural development in Botswana. The unique and spatially contingent restrictions experienced on the conservation estate result in citizens who cannot take advantage of top-down state development programs that are central to state narratives, thus further alienating and marginalizing these populations from the political center and their co-nationals.

Finally, the conclusion explains how the chapters described above bolster the claims of this book: that the conservation estate is not only a relevant empirical venue through which to study state building and citizen-state relations and the varied experience of rural citizenship in particular but also that through this investigation it becomes apparent that the state's multifaceted, contradictory logics guiding state building complicate attempts at negotiation and resistance on the part of local residents. The rest of the book explores in detail the manner in which central imaginaries of the state-building project in Botswana begin to fragment on the conservation estate and interrogate the subsequent responses on the part of residents and state authorities. Here I explore the portability of the concept to different empirical venues and consider future trajectories of the core arguments in light of climate change, biodiversity loss, and debates about the necessity of growing the conservation estate.

1

Lay of the Land
Conservation and the State in Botswana

The broader arguments of this book are drawn from close analysis of the conservation estate in Botswana. While it does present in its conclusion generalizable claims about the conservation estate as an analytical category to be explored, the specific context of Botswana is relevant as the book's primary case. The following chapter interrogates the country's historical trajectory and considers the relevant analytical literature regarding the state, economy, and conservation that establishes the baseline upon which the book's subsequent empirical chapters are built.

The State and Economy in Botswana: An African Miracle?

National imaginaries are central to the way the state articulates itself (on the conservation estate and beyond) and the manner in which local people envision themselves as part of, or separate from, the collective mythos. In Botswana one of the preeminent discourses relies on the country's identification as an "African miracle" both in academic and journalistic circles. Botswana has long been lauded as one of the "strongest" states in the developing world, with some scholars suggesting it is the "most successful state on the African continent" (Eriksen 2011, 265). Much of the theorization of Botswana's statehood is comparative in nature, often done with an explicit eye to the rest of the continent. In their 2002 volume *The African State: Reconsiderations*, Samatar and Samatar go as far as to create a continuum of African states with the spectrum running from Somalia to Botswana—Botswana as the exemplary standout and Somalia the abject failure, with other states found in between. They lay out an evolutionary typology of African states: the integral state, the developmental state, the prebendalist state, predatory state, and the cadaverous state. They argue that Africa has no "integral state" but that Botswana is the premier example of the next best thing—the developmental state. Notably, even the organization of their book echoes the concept of a linear progression through state "types" and begins with the "best" and continues on to the "worst."

While Botswana is often touted as an African miracle in terms of economic performance and political governance (Samatar 1999), there is a lively literature debating Botswana's "exceptionality" on several fronts (Good 1992), including the nature and quality of Botswana's democratic bona fides (Botlhomilwe and Sebudubudu 2011; Cook and Sarkin 2010; Danevad 1995; de Jager and Sebudubudu 2017; Good 1996, 1999, 2008, 2009; Good and Taylor 2007; Maundeni 2002, 2005; Mogalakwe and Nyamnjoh 2017; Molomo 2000; Molutsi and Holm 1989; Poteete 2012; Selolwane 2007; Taylor 2006; Wiseman 1998), the role and place of identity and ethnicity in the state (Gulbrandsen 2012; Hitchcock 2002; Mazonde 2002a; Nyamnjoh 2004; Nyati-Ramahobo 2002a; Sapignoli 2018; Solway 2002; Solway and Nyati-Ramahobo 2004; Werbner 2002, 2004; Wilmsen 2002), and the categorization of Botswana as a "developmental state" (Acemoglu, Johnson, and Robinson 2002; Hillbom 2008, 2011, 2012; Hwedi 2001; Jerven 2010; Leftwich 2000; Leith 2005; Maundeni 2002; Mbabazi and Taylor 2005; Molomo 2001; Picard 1987; Poteete 2009b; Taylor 2012; Tsie 1996).

Certainly some of the praise for Botswana's postcolonial success at state-building appears justly warranted. At independence

Botswana only had six or seven kilometers of paved roads, an 80 percent illiteracy rate, and approximately thirty university graduates (Good 2008; Fawcus and Tilbury 2000; Livingston 2019). Its inauspicious start notwithstanding, Botswana is now considered a middle-income country with some of the highest growth rates of the twentieth century. Yet, despite many positive macroeconomic indicators, inequality and poverty are high, especially among ethnolinguistic minorities (Hillbom 2011; Sapignoli 2018; Zips-Mairitsch 2013). These economic inequalities reflect social and political inequalities in a country where "poverty is an historically structured and highly pervasive element in the political economy of Botswana" (Good 2002, 65; see also Iliffe 1987; Gulbrandsen 2012; Mogalakwe and Nyamnjoh 2017; Mbaiwa 2017; Nteta, Hermans, and Jezkova 1997).

One school of thought that is generally quite celebratory of Botswana's postcolonial political and economic trajectory praises government planners, bureaucrats, and politicians as orderly, efficient, and committed to "sound policy" (Acemoglu, Johnson, and Robinson 2002). Implicit in these arguments is the assumption that state actors are operating from and in response to a coherent, articulated vision of stateness dedicated to "modernization," growth, and efficiency. Botswana's bureaucracy is frequently described as generally free from "politics" and demonstrating good governance. Nonetheless, characterizations of Botswana as an African miracle and an African success story are not without their critics. Good (1992) highlights some of the pitfalls of the "exceptionality" narrative, including the pervasive problems of inequality, high unemployment, Tswana ethnic chauvinism, and the shallowness of democratic practices. In later work, he further theorizes that Botswana's electoral democracy is skewed toward the elite and wealthy, characterized by a highly empowered executive, centralized policymaking radiating out from the capital, and limited protection of democratic rights such as free speech and assembly. This has been echoed by scholars like Mogalakwe (2003), who argues that the miracle moniker is, in fact, a case of "mistaken identity" and that more sustained engagement with the historical and contemporary context reveals substantial shortcomings in the country's governance and economy.

There is a wealth of scholarship examining Botswana's political and electoral system (e.g., Bauer and Taylor 2005; Brown 2020; Good 2008; Poteete 2009a, 2012; Taylor 2003; Maundeni 2005; Molutsi and Holm 1989; Picard 1985; Seabo and Nyenhuis 2021), much of which is critical of the limits of Botswana's democracy (e.g., de Jager and Sebudubudu 2017; Good 2008; Molomo 2008; Poteete 2012; Taylor 2003). Despite multiparty elections every five years since independence, there has never been a changeover of power from the ruling Botswana Democratic Party (BDP). The first-past-the-post electoral system has favored the BDP in terms of vote share to seat share in the legislature. It has also faced a highly fragmented opposition, ensuring continued control even when losing the popular vote, as happened in the 2014 elections (Poteete 2015). Moreover, there are four specially elected MPs who are, in effect, appointed by the ruling party, further bolstering the government's numerical advantage in the parliament (Bauer and Taylor 2005; Taylor 2003; Poteete 2012). It is clearly a dominant-party system, not dissimilar from regional neighbors Namibia and South Africa, with their own dominant parties, the South West Africa People's Organisation and the African National Congress, respectively (Sebudubudu and Botlhomilwe 2012; de Jager and du Toit 2012).

In light of the confluence between electoral democracy, elite capitalism, and limited democratic rights, Good terms Botswana's governance system as "authoritarian liberalism" (1996, 1999). De Jager and Sebudubudu (2017) argue that Botswana is not a full-fledged liberal democracy, and indeed some traditional institutions have authoritarian tendencies (see chapter 4), and political norms of deference to the executive are commonplace, along with a "growing intolerance of opposite views by the political leadership" (Botlhomilwe and Sebudubudu 2011, 332). Others have contributed to this analysis by suggesting the institutional weakness of the parliament vis-à-vis the executive has led to an overly empowered presidency with few checks (Bodilenyane 2012).

Influential scholarship emphasizes the importance of institutions of private property for Botswana's economic success (Acemoglu, Johnson, and Robinson 2002; Robinson and Parsons 2006). This literature identifies the key role of Botswana's independence-era elites in protecting and promoting a relatively conservation economic orientation toward private property and redistribution and argues this is an essential feature of Botswana's macro-level prosperity (Mogalakwe 2003; Samatar 1999). Scholars tend to agree that a united and dominant elite class at independence sought economic growth and political stability, both from points of critique (Good 1993, 2008; Kgomotso 2011) and praise (Leith 2005; Picard 1987; Samatar 1999; Stedman 1993). A common rejoinder from skeptical scholars is that this orientation has led to growth without development, making inequality of economic and social relations systemic rather than aberrant (Hillbom 2011; Nteta, Hermans, and Jezkova 1997). Jerven (2010) is particularly critical of the "African miracle" from an economic perspective. He suggests that the celebration of Botswana's macroeconomic performance mischaracterizes the absence of bad policies as indicative of the adoption of proactively "good" policies, thus overdetermining the supposed miracle. Despite the lively debate in the academy, scholarly literature regarding the state and economy is used to bolster the state's position, and government authorities aggressively police this image, so much so that academics and journalists challenging the African miracle narrative (such as political scientist Kenneth Good) have been deported. Taylor (2006) provides a full account of Good's deportation and the manner in which it was directly related to his scholarly activities contesting the African miracle claim, ironically for highlighting the unchecked power of the executive in Botswana's political system, the very institution able to effectuate his own deportation without meaningful oversight or judicial review. Despite pushback in the scholarly literature of the last decade, the discourse promoting Botswana's exceptionality in economic and political characteristics remains prevalent in the media and among policymakers, think tanks, and governments as well as among some academics. It has relevance for this inquiry as a primary imaginary of the state in the postcolonial era and will be explored in later chapters. As much of the academic literature has been celebratory, national elites have seized on this scholarship to shape their own narrative (Good and Taylor 2008). The exceptionality discourse is consistently emphasized by state authorities; senior leaders often make speeches in foreign capitals, touting Botswana as a democratic and economic success and recently as an internationally recognized environmental success (Mogende and Ramutsindela 2020). In the first decades of the twenty-first century, the African miracle narrative has been closely associated with conservation and tourism, both of which have been construed as proxies for the country's stability, apparent lack of corruption, and focus on "good" policy. The next section examines the context of conservation and wildlife tourism in Botswana.

Tourism and Spectacle on Botswana's Conservation Estate

The Department of Wildlife and National Parks (DWNP) is the government agency tasked with the maintenance, monitoring, and upkeep of the conservation estate in Botswana. It is a constituent department of the Ministry of Environment, Natural Resources Conservation and Tourism (MENT). The history of the department illustrates some of the key themes to be examined in this book's empirical chapters. The DWNP was established in 1957 during the colonial era, nine years prior to independence, as the Elephant Control Unit of the Bechuanaland Protectorate. It was primarily concerned with the management of wildlife populations in order to prevent losses in arable and livestock agriculture (Campbell 2004). Its founding operating principle was that wild animals were pests from which "productive" pursuits such as farming and husbandry needed protecting. This mentality has shifted dramatically over the past seventy years, and this book is focused, in part, upon the ways in which contemporary policies are perceived by residents of the conservation estate to be more attentive to the needs of wildlife and serving the interest of the nature tourism sector than to managing the complex interactions between people and wildlife. Before further examining this dynamic, a point of terminological clarification is needed. This project avoids the use of "ecotourism." As Butcher (2007) notes, the term is laden with assumptions and perceptions of the industry—it is good for the environment and local community—that may not be borne out by the facts. To avoid potential greenwashing of the ecological credentials of this practice, I use "nature tourism" or "wildlife tourism" instead.

Throughout much of Africa, the interrelated phenomena of conservation and tourism are ascendant claims on land. In certain regions they are often prioritized above long-established forms of land use associated with agriculture and pastoralism. In the era of neoliberal conservation, it is through an income-generating tourism industry that conservation is most frequently justified. However, while usually described as a win-win endeavor, it is an economic choice marked by trade-offs, as noted in the rich literature of critical conservation studies. Neoliberal conservation is a complex, multiscalar phenomenon that entails dimensions beyond economics alone. It is productive of new forms of governance in the places where these logics become pervasive. The social impacts of neoliberal conservation include the reshaping of political subjectivities, the commodification of spectacle, the widening of inequalities, and the unequal distribution of impacts (Holmes and Cavanagh 2016; see also Apostolopoulou et al. 2021; Brockington, Duffy, and Igoe 2008; Brockington and Duffy 2011; Büscher, Dressler, and Fletcher 2019; Castree 2008).

The neoliberalization of conservation can be seen in the ways in which the marketing of the conservation estate through tourism is a central part of Botswana's national economic strategy and indeed an additional manifestation of the miracle state narrative. The importance of this sector to the country's economy has increased over the past several decades, and as early as the 1990s it was identified as a key growth sector for the economy (Pfotenhauer 1991). In recent National Development Plans, as well as the public discourse around developmentalism, public-private partnerships in tourism are emphasized as an essential avenue toward economic growth and diversification of the economy, in line with the neoliberal model of conservation (Atlhopheng and Mulale 2009).

Botswana's postcolonial national economy has, for the most part, been driven by natural resources across various sectors. Historically, much of the focus has been on Botswana's diamond economy (Good 2008; Hillbom 2011; Leith 2005), but, as noted above, the wildlife-based tourism industry has rapidly become an important sector. By 2007 tourism was the second-largest industry in Botswana (Mbaiwa and Darkoh 2009). According to the World Travel and Tourism Council, in 2019 the tourism industry accounted for 9.6 percent of the country's GDP.[1] The relative importance of the industry was starkly highlighted in 2020–21 with the global coronavirus pandemic shutting down international guest arrivals and negatively impacting Botswana's economy in a profound way.

While both of Botswana's key industries—diamonds and wildlife tourism—are resource-driven, not all resources can be extracted and made productive in the same manner. Mineral deposits such as Botswana's diamond reserves are stationary—their exploitation requires control of territory as the primary requirement for extraction and resource use. Floral and faunal resources—the landscapes and experiences that create wildlife tourism as an experiential commodity—are quite different. Because of the diffuse nature of wild animals and wild products (compared with Botswana's endowment of kimberlite diamonds, which require intensive infrastructure for extraction), in theory any citizen could capture the benefits from wildlife resources. Existing over vast and remote spaces, animal and plants may be used and exploited by a variety of actors at many scales—including both subsistence and commercial use. Thus, state-led exploitation of conservation-related resources requires control over both land and people to a greater extent than Botswana's other natural resources. The mobile quality of wildlife resources further complicates the role of resource use, non-use, and its subsequent political effects. Human and wildlife populations must coexist to some extent. Animals move and share land and other vital resources like water with human populations and often come into conflict with people. Therefore, the management of wildlife requires the regulation of human behavior, creating a direct policy trade-off between the state's preference for wildlife conservation—and the potential wealth created on the conservation estate—and its obligations to its human citizens. The exploitation of wildlife resources for national gain is not a question simply of economy but also creates a situation wherein citizen-state relations are shaped and structured in relation to the inherent trade-offs that result from large wildlife populations, producing a critical fault line between those citizens living with wildlife (and associated industries) and those who do not.

In the late 1990s, in recognition of the unique impacts of biodiversity conservation and in line with regional trends, Botswana began its community-based conservation program, known as Community-Based Natural Resource Management (CBNRM), with the aim to decentralize management and benefits to local conservation-adjacent communities (see Nelson 2010). However, CBNRM has had mixed results and has not lived up to the lofty claims of local, community-sensitive conservation and development (Blaikie 2006; Swatuk 2005). Since the program was officially enacted in the government's 2007 CBNRM Policy, it has become increasingly more centralized and implemented from the political center, limiting local input and autonomy. Scholars have noted that this process of centralization is tied to the logic of the unitary developmental state—that natural resources are considered national resources and no subset of citizens should have greater claim to the benefits and advantages from these endowments (DeMotts and Hoon 2012; Poteete 2009b; Poteete and Ribot 2011; Rihoy and Maguranyanga 2010). This remains pervasive, despite the fact that there are specific and place-based costs to living on the conservation estate and sharing space with wildlife and other impacts of biodiversity conservation.

Unlike other types of raw materials that are famously extracted from the African continent and used to power Western industrialization, conservation and associated wildlife tourism industries are focused on "commodifying *in situ* natural resources" (Fletcher 2010, 172), clearly implicating the conservation estate as the mechanism that makes this exploitation possible. Non-consumptive use (like photographic tourism), while seemingly an oxymoron, has been conceptualized alongside a suite of neoliberal conservation projects as "Accumulation by Conservation," or AbC (Büscher and Fletcher 2015). While the diamond industry is perhaps one of the archetypal extractive industries on the continent, the elevation of Botswana's wildlife tourism in importance has supplemented the extractive model of capital exploitation with a primarily *attractive* model, akin to Büscher and Fletcher's AbC, wherein the state leverages the attractive natural capital of the land, resources, and wildlife of the conservation estate in order to bring tourists to Botswana for the in situ use of their resources. Thus, along the logics of AbC, the wildlife tourism industry creates wealth—often at the national level or for domestic or international elites (LaRocco 2016; Mbaiwa 2005, 2017; Mbaiwa and Hambira 2020)—but also dispossession on the conservation estate. The commercial use and commodification of the flora, fauna, and landscapes within these localities substantially differentiate these spaces from other rural areas lacking the kind of attractive natural capital that appeals to foreign tourists. Safari-goers, after all, do not fly halfway around the world to gawk at cows and other livestock, notwithstanding the value and importance of domesticated animals in Batswana society. This, in turn, impacts the lived experiences of citizens who find themselves born in a unique territory that is lucrative, highly sought after, and known to the world.

Tourism, like diamonds, is a luxury good with a highly elastic demand, a characteristic that emphasizes the reliance of the industry on international tourists.[2] It is an experiential rather than a material commodity, and because of this the perceptions and preferences of foreigners often drive demand and shape local realities. In this way, it is both subjective on the part of the tourist and wrapped up in discursive ideologies that are significant far beyond any given tourism interaction. Importantly, in the tourism and conservation industries across the continent, the tourist experience is curated and translated most often by white interlocutors—professional tourism guides, celebrity conservationists, and wildlife documentarians and photographers (Brockington 2009; Fox 2018; Garland 2008; Kepe 2009; Mbaria and Ogada 2016). These individuals typically hold outsized importance in the tourism industry and significantly impact how the conservation estate is perceived and consumed by foreign visitors, most often coming from the Global North.

Igoe's work examining the role of spectacle and capital probes the way in which imagery and imagined spaces have become central components of contemporary processes of conservation and tourism (2010, 2016). Wilderness spaces, and specifically the conservation estate, on the African continent are uniquely important in this visual discourse, as Adams describes the essentializing impact of globally circulating images of "'Africa' as a generic wilderness whole, epitomized by *The Lion King* and wilderness tourist brochures" (Adams 2020, 8). Botswana's biodiversity conservation has a performative element. It tends to focus on and highlight visually appealing capstone species such as elephants or large predators, which capture the attention of safari clients and funding of the international conservation movement. These are often known as "charismatic megafauna." Cloete provides a good working definition: "those animals, in particular elephants, which have achieved international star status and have been accorded moral significance" (Cloete 2008, 257). The special status afforded to African wildlife by non-African observers is conveyed through literature, film, and television documentaries. An exemplar of this genre is the 2020 Disney nature documentary *Elephant*.[3] Shot on the striking landscapes of Botswana's conservation estate, it follows the story of an anthropomorphized elephant herd whose travails and triumphs are narrated by Meghan Markle, a member of the British royal family and a stereotypical celebrity conservationist. This kind of visual spectacle constructs the charismatic megafauna as the key subject of the landscape and trains the Western gaze to Botswana's conservation estate and the megafauna found therein. Moreover, through the assignment of moral subjectivities, these animals become embedded in debates about animal rights, conservation, and the dynamics of human-wildlife interaction (Martin 2012). The focus on specific animals is the result of a significant shift within the conservation movement toward an approach encompassing animal rights. This approach interprets animal rights as a culmination in the evolution of ethical thinking characterized by the expansion of "the circle of ethics" to include animals and against speciesism (Singer 1985, 9). This position is bolstered by mounting scientific evidence of the cognitive abilities of animals, their social relations, their capacity for communication, and, to a certain extent, their ability to reason. This perspective pushes for the consideration of the intrinsic value, rather than resource value, of nonhuman animals (Regan 1985).

However, Gibson (1999) identifies the copresence of wildlife as a key heuristic in the analysis of politics in southern Africa. He argues that conflict over wildlife is fundamentally about public authority: who inhabits powerful institutions, who sets the rules, who benefits or loses from particular policy choices, who can take part in the remunerative spectacle tied to charismatic animals and iconic landscapes, and which constituencies have the ability to impact these decisions. Copresence of especially charismatic creatures is relevant to the political identities and subjectivities of the humans of the conservation estate, who often find themselves vying with nonhuman animals for prioritization in the state-building project as well as in the wider political economy of conservation.

Identity on the Conservation Estate

In addition to being tied up in the politics of land, the maintenance of the spectacle of charismatic megafauna, and the global political economy of neoliberal conservation, the conservation estate is embedded in Botswana's unique history of identity, ethnicity, and contested notions of indigeneity. The conservation estate is home to a significant percentage of non-Tswana Batswana as well as many of Botswana's white citizens. This makes relevant the ways in which relationships among Botswana's heterogeneous people are an important part of analysis of the state-building project and the mythologies found within, especially in the context of the conservation estate. Throughout Botswana's history, political organization has been used to empower Tswana-speaking groups at the expense of others. In 1966 newly independent Botswana set about constructing a unitary nation-state across the entirety of the politically and ethnically heterogeneous territory that once was the Bechuanaland Protectorate. Sapignoli describes this process:

> Like other newly independent states, it presented itself as ethnically neutral in order to claim its legitimacy in postcolonial Africa. In this case, however, ethnic neutrality was ultimately pursued not through the suppression of all tribal markers, but through promoting the supremacy of a dominant identity. The status of minorities was articulated in a project that can be best described as the creation of a "melting pot" under Tswana domination. Marginalized groups were called upon, in the interest of national unity and prosperity, to subsume their languages, politics, and practices within the dominant, national model of Tswanadom. (2018, 91)

This process elevated the culture, language, and status of the largest and most politically powerful group, the Tswana. Botswana, literally meaning "Nation of the Tswana," operates from the assumption that "all citizens must assimilate to a certain national language (Setswana),[4] culture (dominant Tswana culture), and ideology ('typical' Motswana)" (Zips-Mairitsch 2013, 380–81; see also Anderson 1982; Nyamnjoh 2004; Sapignoli 2018).[5]

Botswana's emphasis on national unity as well as nonracial and non-ethnic politics was a courageous departure during the era of minority rule in southern Africa. For the first fourteen years of its postcolonial history, Botswana was nearly entirely surrounded by hostile, white-ruled states, and its economy was precariously tied to apartheid South Africa. In light of this, the strong stance toward non-ethnic nation building taken at independence, especially by Botswana's first president, Sir Seretse Khama, was both risky and laudable (Armstrong and Bennett 2002; Parsons, Henderson, and Tlou 1995; Saugestad 2001). President Khama's rejection of ethnic politics was a reaction against apartheid South Africa's system of tribal homeland Bantustans. Yet, in rejecting Bantustans and their shallow promise of "separate development," Botswana was not constructing the postcolonial state as non-ethnic but rather as a mono-ethnic polity with a predominance of Tswana cultural, political, social, and linguistic modes.

Botswana is only a mono-ethnic polity to the extent that "Tswanadom" has been successfully imposed on other groups (Datta and Murray 1989; Nyati-Ramahobo 2002b; Parson 1984; Solway 2002). The last census to record any statistics related to ethnicity occurred in 1946 under the colonial government. The postcolonial state has made it an intentional policy that no ethnic figures are gathered when conducting census enumeration, allowing for actual diversity to be downplayed in pursuit of a vision of national unity. But the monoculture image masks the multicultural reality of Botswana (Mazonde 2002a; Nyati-Ramahobo 2002b; Saugestad 2001). Solway, recalling Gladney (1998), argues that majorities are made, not born, suggesting that the process of Tswana majoritarianism is all the more noteworthy because "'minorities' may, if taken together, constitute a majority of the country" (2004, 130). Therefore, "minority" in this context cannot be understood in a numerical sense alone but as a sociopolitical, economic, and legal status of disadvantage (Solway and Nyati-Ramahobo 2004).

In its contemporary political project of state and nation building, even after the fall of apartheid Botswana equates homogeneity with unity and stability and emphasizes the negative connotations associated with "tribalism" as a caution against ethnic identification (Saugestad 2001). Historical evocations of South African apartheid and genocidal Rwanda are used as rhetorical foils to Botswana—what could be if the Pandora's box of ethnicity is allowed to open. There is a particular disinclination toward ethnic claims around indigeneity. Sapignoli describes the state's orientation thus: "There can be no distinct rights for those claiming indigenous status, since the state is premised on the same undifferentiated rights for all citizens. Indigenous rights introduce a dangerous form of tribalism to African politics, the argument goes, which can only be overcome by emphasizing constitutional uniformity and equality" (2018, 168).

Nonetheless, ethnic politics are not stagnant. The 1990s saw an increased awareness, dynamism, and political agitation within and among minority ethnic groups, and the early 2000s saw the state respond with some efforts to account for diversity (Molomo 2008; Werbner 2002, 2004). The Balopi Commission explored the status of the Constitution of Botswana, which listed the eight Tswana tribes as "major," compared with the other "minor" tribes, as well as the composition of the House of Chiefs. However, the changes to the constitution prompted by the Balopi Commission are viewed by many scholars and activists to be more cosmetic than substantive (Nyamnjoh 2002, 2004, 2007; for further discussion, see Good 2008; Molomo 2008; Nyati-Ramahobo 2009; Sapignoli 2018; Solway 2004).

Gulbrandsen's 2012 monograph *The State and the Social: State Formation in Botswana and Its Precolonial and Colonial Genealogies* argues that the modern postcolonial state in Botswana grew from and is embedded in symbols and institutions of precolonial Tswana authority, which is informed by a cosmology emphasizing hierarchy as essential for peace, stability, order, and prosperity. He notes that historical continuities in the exercise of power and legitimate authority on the part of the ruling elite as well as mainstream society remain important for the imagining of the state as it is currently constituted. This apparent consensus has been key to the creation of subjectivities within the state framework without the necessity of violence. Gulbrandsen argues that the peaceful nature of authority in Botswana is a noteworthy characteristic: "Botswana prevails to a great extent because the ruling group's domination is achieved and reproduced in relation to the population with a *minimal exercise of perceived violent, coercive power*" (2012, 13, emphasis in original). Despite, in his view, the limited use of violence, the state's reliance on "repressive practices and structures of domination" is apparent (2012, 317). He suggests discursive domination is manifest through the interchangeability of the words "Tswana" and "developed" in state discourse, an issue I unpack at length in part III. This was facilitated by the use of the *kgotla*, a traditional Tswana institution that functions as a sort of town hall meeting, where the state has been able to inculcate a discursive emphasis on consultation and dialogue.[6] However, the kgotla is not simply consultative or democratic in the contemporary sense but rather embedded in Tswana hierarchies of power—it a difficult venue to access by women, ethnic minorities, and youth—and works to normalize Tswana modes of authority and governance, even if they mask inequality (see chapter 4).

Despite Tswana dominance, Solway (2002) argues that the effectiveness of Botswana's postcolonial state institutions has led to and facilitated minority ethnolinguistic activism. She argues that the durability of the judiciary and the sustained presence of opposition political parties have allowed for the incremental expansion of ethnic recognition to the point where minority political agitation can flourish (Solway and Nyati-Ramahobo 2004; Werbner 2002, 2004). Yet among the political elite, grievances from minority organizations are often seen as threatening territorial integrity, especially by San cultural and political groups, whose calls for recognition are deeply tied to land ownership, residency patterns, and the governance of natural resources (Kiema 2010; Ngo'ong'ola 1997; Sapignoli 2018; Saugestad 2011; Zips-Mairitsch 2013). Some minority groups, such as the Kalanga,[7] European-descended Batswana, and Indian-descended Batswana, are quite well positioned in government, business, and education and have been able to situate their politics from an orientation of relative parity. These important exceptions notwithstanding, non-Tswana groups are severely disadvantaged (Molosi-France 2018; Nyamnjoh 2007). In particular, the San remain on the fringes of society, with little political representation and comparatively fewer educated elites. San people continue to have the most unequal access to state institutions and the weakest ability to articulate grievances, and they demand low accountability from those in power. As indigenous peoples, the San "face a basic dilemma in which people on the margins of states are required to develop high levels of expertise and administrative capacity, which they are often prevented from achieving by their conditions of marginalization" (Sapignoli 2018, 165). At the extreme end of this line of thinking, Nthomang (2004) argues that the San, especially through the Remote Area Dwellers Programme, live under continued colonization by the current government, with San people being the most marginalized group of citizens. He goes on to suggest that the primary objective of government interventions among the country's San population is assimilation by "becoming Tswana."

This lengthy examination of the ethnolinguistic context of Botswana is important to the subsequent arguments of this book because of the ways in which the prevalence of minority ethnolinguistic communities overlaps with spaces of conservation and implicates the disparate and varied ways in which the state intervenes into the population across urban, rural, and the conservation estate. Moreover, the location of the conservation estate in predominantly non-Tswana areas is not coincidental. Areas of lesser Tswana dominance were often deemed as marginal "wilderness" and incorporated as protected areas or given over to freehold tenure.

The two districts where I conducted data collection for this research, Ghanzi and Northwest, are demonstrative of this phenomenon. Sixty-seven percent of Ghanzi's land is zoned for wildlife, including the single largest reserve in the country, Central Kalahari Game Reserve (CKGR) (Twyman 1998). The CKGR, at 52,347 square kilometers, is Africa's second-largest protected area after Selous Game Reserve in Tanzania, constituting 9 percent of Botswana's land area (Hitchcock and Holm 1993; Hitchcock 2002). Ghanzi District is home to a large population of San, many of whom have been removed from the CKGR over the past two decades (Kiema 2010; Sapignoli 2018). Ghanzi is often informally referred to as a "bushman district" because of the demographic size of the group (an estimated 40 to 50 percent of the population) rather than as a reflection of the San's economic, political, or social dominance (Hitchcock and Holm 1993; Solway 2009). Ghanzi is also home to a significant and long-standing population of white Batswana. Permanent settlement of Afrikaner families in Ghanzi began in 1898, and by the early twentieth century English-speaking settlers became more common, though they still tend to be outnumbered by Afrikaans speakers. This group is important in the political and economic milieu of Ghanzi District due to its ownership of the bulk of the freehold land in the Ghanzi Farm Block (Gillett 1970; Barnard 1980).[8]

The Northwest District is home to the Okavango Delta, the world's largest inland delta and a Ramsar protected wetland (Mbaiwa, Stronza, and Kreuter 2011) and UNESCO World Heritage Site since 2014.[9] The district includes Moremi Game Reserve as well as the Tsodilo Hills historical site. It is contiguous to Chobe National Park in neighboring Chobe District. This area is also one of the most ethnolinguistically diverse regions of the country. San people such as the Bugakhwe, Ts'exa, and Anikhwe have the longest histories of residency in the region,[10] followed by the Bayei, who migrated south from Central Africa in the early eighteenth century. In the postcolonial era, the district is home to Bayei, San, Batawana (a Tswana subgroup), Hambukushu, Herero, Basubiya, and Ovambo people. In Northwest District there is also a smaller community of white Batswana as well as a larger number of European-descended foreign workers employed in the tourism industry or as conservation practitioners (Gressier 2015). The Batawana, who identify as ethnically Tswana, are the most dominant group politically and economically, though they were the last major group to arrive in the area. The Batawana primarily reside in the environs of the district capital, Maun, while other groups inhabit the outlying rural areas (Bolaane 2013; DeMotts et al. 2009; Tlou 1985).

The distribution of non-Tswana ethnic minorities tracks quite closely to the conservation estate across Botswana, a condition that will be analytically important to the development of this book's arguments. This is not coincidental but relevant to the foundation of the conservation estate in parts of the country peripheral to the Tswana core of state. Botswana's conservation estate is inhabited overwhelmingly by those citizens outside of the mainstream ethnolinguistic majority. It is not that minorities are limited to the conservation estate (there are non-Tswana people throughout the country) or that ethnic Batswana are absent from the conservation estate but that ethnolinguistic minorities disproportionately reside on the conservation estate. As such, the conservation estate is home to residents who encompass a series of imbricated marginalities: they are geographically, economically, and ethnolinguistically peripheral to the state and the state-building project.

Taken together, the contextual material of this chapter has established the ground upon which the empirical arguments of this book are built. The theoretical and empirical debates about the nature of Botswana's political and economic systems, its links to the global wildlife tourism industry, and the country's unique demographic history will figure in the analysis of this case study. The role of the conservation estate in state building and the structuring of authority, territory, and identity will be examined in detail in the subsequent sections.

Part I

Authority

2

Coercion on Botswana's Conservation Estate

The 2013 television documentary *Poaching Wars* aired on the British television channel ITV while I was conducting the initial fieldwork in Botswana for this project.[1] Not long after its first broadcast, I received messages from friends and colleagues back in the UK asking if my research was anywhere near as exhilarating and dangerous as the content of the short series. In it, Tom Hardy, an action film star, dons rugged safari gear while shadowing the antipoaching operations of the Botswana Defence Force (BDF) as they traverse the country's remote northern wilderness by plane, in boats, and on foot. Not only does he spend time with rank-and-file BDF soldiers and their officers, but he was able to secure an interview with the country's minister of environment, who spoke proudly about Botswana's militarized approach to biodiversity conservation, and the shoot-to-kill policy, in particular. While the film was largely made for international audiences, the implicit claims about the nature of coercive authority on the conservation estate are felt by everyday citizens, whose perspectives do not figure prominently in the film's narrative. The evocative imagery in the series is not unique to Botswana; drones, airplanes, and helicopters—aerial military assets as conservation tools—are a growing feature of conservation practice across the region (Bugday 2016; Massé 2018). However, in this case, the specific image of military aircraft used in service of conservation amplifies the extent to which the logics of conservation are imbued with the capacity to create and manifest state authority in ways that are ancillary to the ecological concerns conventionally associated with conservation policy. Not only are there deep interconnections between the conservation estate and Botswana's military establishment—this martial footprint in the service of conservation is also a key vector of differentiation of the conservation estate from other spatial and political categories in the Botswana state. Coercion, both potential and realized, in the service of conservation and the securitization of the conservation estate indicate how control over and dispensation of rights to resources and land are central to political power in Botswana. The performance of force on the conservation estate is integral to the structuring of authority in contemporary Botswana.

In examining the myriad ways that power and authority are manifest in the state-building project, this chapter explores the lifeworlds of Batswana living in areas dominated by the imperatives of conservation and how this construction of citizen-state relations is unique and contingent upon the conservation estate. It is concerned with the tension between the securitized logic deployed in the name of conservation and antipoaching and contrasts with Botswana's ostensible commitment to democratic norms of consent and consultation, examined in the subsequent chapter. In Lukes's (1974) view, one "face" of the exercise of power is the ability of the certain actors to set the terms of the political agenda in such a way as to foreclose avenues for bringing demands into the contestable realm of politics. I suggest that this is at work in the securitization of Botswana's conservation estate. This chapter grapples with the way controversial conservation policies such as the securitization of antipoaching, a focus on charismatic species conservation, and the national hunting ban implemented from 2014 to 2019 work to fragment relationships of consent between the ruled and the rulers, creating a situation wherein the state's authority, while potent and often highly visible, is considered illegitimate by a significant swath of the rural population living on the conservation estate. This occurs alongside the majority of the country's citizens consenting to the securitization discourse. It is on the conservation estate that consensual mechanisms of authority (which may have been more rhetorical than actual to begin with) break down and are unable to mask the coercive structures of force accompanied by the securitization of the environment. These contradictions work to create spaces of exception on the conservation estate, wherein Batswana living on this specific type of territory face a qualitatively different kind of citizenship and experience different interactions between themselves, the state, and co-local wildlife compared with their fellow citizens not residing on the conservation estate.

This chapter is divided into three sections. The first provides an overview of literature investigating the violence of conservation and engages with the Copenhagen School's conceptualization of "securitization" as an analytical lens for understanding coercive conservation's role in building state authority. The next section contextualizes this analysis in Botswana, probing the logics of coercion and force that dominate when the conservation estate is securitized in response to a perceived (or actual) crisis of poaching. The securitized approach to antipoaching is connected to global ideas instrumentally linking poaching with transnational scourges like crime and terrorism as well as domestic concerns about state authority, force, and performance of sovereign authority. The section examines how conservation institutions, practices, and local interactions become securitized. This has far-reaching implications for citizen-state relations, as is demonstrated by this chapter's third and final section, which evaluates the power of the state in creating and shaping subjectivities of residents on the conservation estate through the constructed discourse of "poaching" and "poachers" and the mediating role played by co-local wildlife in citizen-state relations.

Violent Environments of Conservation

Historically conservation has been shot through with violence (Neumann 2001, 2004a; Peluso and Watts 2001). Scholars, particularly in environmental history, have noted the ways in which environmental management and biodiversity conservation have been intertwined with violent projects of empire and colonization (Beinart and Hughes 2007; Dowie 2009; Gissibl, Hohler, and Kupper 2012). However, the coercive tendencies of conservation enactment, especially in the Global South, are not simply relics of an imperial past but also present in the contemporary practice of environmental policies (Duffy 2014; Dunlap and Fairhead 2014; Lunstrum 2014; Marijnen, De Vries, and Duffy 2021; Verhoeven 2014). In the 1980s a heightened concern about poaching, notably the so-called ivory wars in East Africa, resulted in militarized enforcement of biodiversity protection and widespread use of exclusionary "fortress conservation" models, which separated people from protected areas, often by coercive means (Brockington 2002). The very name of fortress conservation evokes the martial valence that is pervasive in much conservation practice. Despite an interlude in late 1990s and early 2000s where there was emphasis on participatory, community-based conservation endeavors that sought to incorporate rather than exclude, the contemporary discourse, in large part, reaches back to the framing of the ivory wars and is dominated by tropes of war, battles, and the "fight" to save biodiversity in not only policy framings but also in popular culture and increasingly in social media discourses around conservation practice (Büscher 2016; Duffy 2014, 2016; Lunstrum 2014, 2017). These violent environmental policies shape the state-building process. In fact, Ramutsindela and Büscher argue that "the acceptance of violence as the 'new normal' in protected areas in Africa also reconstitutes state-civil society relations" (2019, 11).

Across a variety of regions, threats to wildlife and biodiversity conservation are described using martial language and are wrapped up in anxieties surrounding migration, rebellion, crime, and terrorism. Concern about wildlife crime has become part of government security strategies, both the developed countries of the Global North, which most often shape global security postures, discourses, and institutions, and among countries in the Global South that are home to most of the world's remaining charismatic megafauna. In honor of World Wildlife Day in 2015, the then secretary-general of the UN, Ban Kimoon, released the following statement:

> Illegal trade in wildlife has become a sophisticated transnational form of crime, comparable to other pernicious examples, such as trafficking of drugs, humans, counterfeit items and oil. It is driven by rising demand, and is often facilitated by corruption and weak governance. There is strong evidence of the increased involvement of organized crime networks and non-State armed groups. . . . Illegal wildlife trade undermines the rule of law and threatens national security. . . . Combatting this crime is not only essential for conservation efforts and sustainable development, it will contribute to achieving peace and security in troubled regions where conflicts are fuelled by these illegal activities.[2]

Global discourses concerning poaching and wildlife crime frequently invoke the specter of organized crime, guerrilla warfare, and even terrorism. Media reports and international policy proclamations have laid Africa's poaching problem at the feet of notorious groups such as the Lord's Resistance Army, Al-Shabaab, and Boko Haram, regardless of the flimsy empirical evidence for such claims (Duffy 2014; Pennaz et al. 2018).[3] Duffy's 2016 article "War, by Conservation" elegantly presents the manner in which conservation has been integrated into larger global structures of security. Protected areas are increasingly seen as spaces of security risk on a national and global scale. Scholars have identified this phenomenon around the world (Büscher and Fletcher 2018; Kelly and Ybarra 2016), including in Latin America (Bocarejo and Ojeda 2016; Devine 2014; Ojeda 2012; Ybarra 2017), South Asia (Dongol and Neumann 2021; Dutta 2020; Peluso and Vandergeest 2011), and Africa (Kelly and Gupta 2016; Lunstrum 2014; Marijnen 2018; Massé and Lunstrum 2016; Neumann 2004a; Trogisch and Fletcher 2022). However, the connections between conservation and security have their own particular history in southern Africa, where the poacher-as-terrorist trope that has been reanimated in the past decade has its roots in the Cold War–era rhetoric of white minority–ruled governments (Ramutsindela 2016).

Green Militarization

There is a large and growing literature critically assessing the embedded violence in global conservation practice. Variously described as "green militarization" or "armed conservation," the militarization of conservation has been analyzed by a variety of scholars (Duffy 2014, 2016; Lunstrum 2014; Büscher and Ramutsindela 2016), with empirical examples of violent conservation enforcement in Tanzania (Mabele 2017; Weldemichel 2020), South Africa (Büscher and Ramutsindela 2016), and Mozambique (Massé and Lunstrum 2016). Lunstrum (2014) suggests that the spatial dynamics of protected areas, along with the prevalence of particular "political-ecological values" related to territory and stateness, allow for the coming together of conservation and militarization. Moreover, critical conservation scholars have noted the overlap between tourism and militarism on the conservation estate (Massé and Lunstrum 2016; Dunn 2009; Ojeda 2012; Marijnen and Verweijen 2016; Trogisch and Fletcher 2022) and how these practices produce what Ojeda (2012) characterizes as "green pretexts" for violence. While the focus is primarily on state practice, the violence of conservation is not limited to state actors alone. Large international NGOs such as the World Wildlife Fund have provided financial support for conservation-focused private security and paramilitary operations across the continent (Ramutsindela 2016; Neumann 2004a; Büscher and Fletcher 2018).

Securitization and States of Exception

Many of the scholars cited above opt for the term "militarization" in their analysis of coercive conservation environments (Duffy 2014; Dunlap and Fairhead 2014; Lunstrum 2014). Though insightful and useful to the endeavors of this book, in my analysis I have chosen to use the term "securitization," more in line with the Copenhagen School's conceptualization of state authority. This is because I suggest it is not only the tactics and techniques of military institutions leveraged in the service of conservation that require scrutiny but also that the logics, discourses, and exercises of authority to which these institutions are tied and by which they are informed warrant further inquiry. While the discursive work certainly informs the material presence of "militarized" conservation, the term "securitization" more accurately captures the way in which the language of security and authority percolates through social communities and gains purchase among most in Botswana society, even if it remains highly contested by those living on the conservation estate. It is not simply that the government of Botswana deploys its military in service of conservation but rather that most political subjects not resident on the conservation estate have accepted the government's supposition that this is necessary and legitimate for their safety and for the nation's prosperity. This invokes the "securitizing speech act," articulated by scholars of the Copenhagen School, and also draws in the work of philosopher Giorgio Agamben, whose theorization around states of exception (2005) is analytically important for the conservation estate. Agamben's language of exception has been utilized elsewhere in analysis of environments. Dwyer, Ingalls, and Baird note in their study of forestry policy in Laos that a security exception produces "a suspension of everyday governing to defend the state against a putatively grave threat" (2016, 208). Therefore, the broader political work of conservation is done through the series of securitizing moves, discussed below, that situate these spaces as outside the realm of "normal" politics.

For the Copenhagen School, "security" is defined as "the sovereign authority's ability to legitimate the use of emergency measures in the face of exceptional threats" (Hansen 2012, 529). The process of securitization moves any issue that has been "securitized" into an "emergency" setting. Once there is an "emergency," the regularized contestation and negotiative structures of "normal" politics do not apply. The question of who or what is in need of "security" and from whom or what security working against is therefore not a given reality to be objectively perceived but rather created and constructed through the process of invoking security through a securitizing speech act and legitimated by the populace at large (Buzan, Wæver, and de Wilde 1998). As Wæver suggests, "By uttering 'security' a state-representative moves a particular development into a specific area, and thereby claims a special right to use whatever means are necessary to block it" (1995, 55). In "normal" politics, issues are up for debate. The merits of each side are equally worthy of consideration and must be weighed with respect to a variety of stakeholders in society. Disagreement and dissent are manifest in this process. Framing an issue as an existential threat insulates it from the typical regime of adversarial politics. Securitization firmly places an issue outside, and even above, the rules that would dictate the conventional processes of governance. It gives state actors the freedom to take any action that is deemed vital and necessary to rectify the current "emergency."

Actors are differentially capable of invoking "security." Certain actors such as national elites and those in positions of power in the existing political system are better placed to utilize a securitizing speech act, depending on their ability to be identified as legitimate and recognizable by appropriate constituencies. This may be done by controlling the spaces of political debate or promoting the securitized orientation from an already privileged institutional position (Abrahamsen 2005; Verhoeven 2014; Wæver 1995). Securitization helps to explain the ways in which power is manifest in the exercise of authority by the state. The process of invoking "security" in biodiversity conservation makes state priorities and state solutions preeminent by enveloping the environment in a realm of politics above debate. The means by which the environment is "protected" becomes embedded in a state's control over the use of force to produce particular outcomes on the conservation estate.

While the original proponents of securitization theory highlight the discursive securitizing speech act as essential, further scholarship has argued that securitization is increasingly tied to images as a communicative and performative medium. Williams highlights the importance of "televisual communications—often broadcast and received well beyond the political borders and cultural boundaries of their production—[which have an] impact on different audiences, and the securitizing consequences that may follow from this fact" (2003, 527). This helps to inform and unpack the international dimensions at work in the justifications of securitization, particularly around charismatic megafauna species. Many of these animals, such as elephants and rhinos, are claimed by the world as part of a global environmental patrimony but become referents of security in specific and particular contexts—primarily on the conservation estates of the Global South. The securitization that takes place at various scales mandates the inevitability of violence in these unique spatial contexts. It legitimizes state coercive behaviors that might otherwise be seen as extreme. The use of force to defend co-local wildlife from the threat (or perceived threat) of humans becomes normalized and sanitized and is constructed as necessary and legitimate (Duffy 2014; Neumann 2004a; Verhoeven 2014).

Securitization can produce material outcomes and have beneficiaries (Floyd 2010). In their analysis of the overlap between securitization and neoliberal conservation, Massé and Lunstrum (2016) identify a mode of accumulation by securitization wherein armed antipoaching operations produce dispossession not only in pursuit of a set of ecological values but for capital extraction too. They argue this securitization is "not just about conservation, but about producing a secure space—for wildlife and capital—that will enable profits via tourism" (234). Securitized conservation has a political logic beyond ecological imperatives. Constructing whole communities living in conservation areas and with co-local wildlife as "threats" produces the conditions that facilitate their easier policing and clears the way for the development of exclusionary enclave safari tourism (Mbaiwa 2005).

Following from this overview of securitization, the next section explores its dynamics on Botswana's conservation estate and examines how these considerations play out in the empirical context of Botswana's antipoaching policy and with other conservation policies like the hunting ban. In its current form, the anxiety around poaching—the unauthorized use of state wildlife resources—as linked to crime, violence, and even terrorism places biodiversity conservation in the register of national security interest, territorial integrity, and state stability. As will be expanded at length in later sections of this chapter, Batswana officials make arguments about the supposed link between poaching and groups wishing to "undermine democratic rule in African states and to fund terrorism, armed militias and rebel groups engaged in internal and cross border conflicts."[4] This echoes a growing "securitization" of global environments both by international actors and domestic leaders in their respective countries.

Securitization and Antipoaching

> Botswana is a country renowned for its wildlife where the full might of the military is pledged to protect it and their closely related tourism industry.
>
> —*Poaching Wars*, ITV wildlife documentary[5]

Many of the innovations in the so-called war for biodiversity have been made through the use of private military contractors or the arming of conservation rangers supported by NGOs or international donors. Duffy (2014) suggests that the prevalence of these nonstate coercive entities like private military firms in conservation highlights deeper questions about the nature of state power in Africa. She argues that the linkages between authority, the ability to use force, and sovereignty are disrupted by the insertion of private actors into this realm. The case of Botswana offers an alternative empirical venue to assess the intersecting logics of state power and securitized conservation. Botswana has largely eschewed the privatized model of coercive conservation enforcement by empowering its own military—the BDF—in the task of antipoaching and biodiversity control. The long-standing posture, dating back to the 1980s, to utilize the state's own military institutions in order to secure wildlife is illuminating. Rather than employ and deploy private means (such as military contractors or armed rangers who operate under the auspices of NGOs) in the coercive enforcement of conservation goals, as is increasingly common in Africa, the BDF is the main, though not exclusive, agent. With this policy choice, conservation becomes a piece of statecraft. The Botswana state is both utilizing a securitization discourse quite common to international conservation and at the same time buttressing its internal ability to project force over its own territory. While the securitization move may be echoing similar trends on the continent and beyond, it is localized in a very particular way in Botswana and is used to empower the state's own authority structures. Indeed, Dan Henk, a former US military attaché in Botswana who has written extensively about the use of the BDF in conservation policy, credits the use of military force in conservation for the country's reputation as an "African success story" (Ramutsindela 2016; Henk 2007).

The state has long securitized its discourse about the environment, particularly around biodiversity conservation. Government statements often refer to the need to "secure" Botswana's wildlife.[6] In doing so, Botswana creates an expansive notion of security. Poaching is broadly understood within the key government agency tasked with the upkeep of the conservation estate, the Department of Wildlife and National Parks (DWNP), as "a national security issue. That's how it is perceived."[7] In this context, protection of wildlife can be read as the preeminent environmental concern of the nation. While encapsulating a wide range of practices, "poaching" has been cast as an issue of national security, seen to threaten both the state's territorial integrity and its claim to a monopoly of the use of force within its borders. The head of the DWNP Anti-Poaching Unit at the time of my fieldwork told me that "poaching is a national security threat. We have a lot of open country, and on the Namibian border people can come and go. Of course, there is collusion between local people and poachers who are from outside."[8] His statement illustrates the anxiety related to the vastness of territory and perceived porousness of borders, factors that embed concerns around poaching into a larger disquiet about the cohesion and durability of the state and its authority and produces an insider/outsider dichotomy by associating suspect foreign nationals with local residents of the conservation estate, thus implying increased state surveillance of the latter may be necessary.

The concern around the "illegal wildlife trade," an oft-used stand-in for "poaching" or "illegal hunting activities," is a stated central policy focus of the DWNP and other environmental agencies. However, the number of poaching incidents within Botswana is opaque, and independently evaluating claims by either the government or conservation-focused NGOs is difficult, and often these various sources are not in agreement. Not only are incidents of animal mortality not disclosed regularly, but the number of people killed or arrested in wildlife law enforcement operations are also not made publicly accessible in a comprehensive manner.[9] Nonetheless, the pervasive tenor of "threat" is hegemonic, even without independently available information.[10] Throughout my fieldwork, respondents working in the government or in the tourism industry regularly emphasized their concerns about poaching, while also touting that despite this threat to wildlife, Botswana was far safer than other countries on the continent. This was framed around the government's decade-long commitment to using the military for conservation enforcement, with other countries cast as a harbinger of what is to come if the military option is not adequately exercised. A commercial tourism operator, who was also previously involved in the government's rhino conservation program, noted, "It [poaching] is well below that in Tanzania, Zambia, Gabon, those places. It's well below that, but we'd be naive to not believe it's coming here. I believe we have the greatest wild herd of elephants, African elephants, left in the world. They [poachers] will come.... Our leadership understands this, and they've put in place protection. [The] Botswana Defence Force is ... mobilized."[11] He articulated a position of constant vigilance, which is common in securitizing discourses ranging from terrorism and drug trafficking to, in this case, wildlife crime. Those who either do not see a threat or actively contest the nature of the security threat are deemed "naive" and not fit to guide policy so vital to the survival of the state. A record of success, in this construction, is not viewed as an argument for revisiting the exceptional nature of securitized politics but rather a vindication. The deputy director of the DWNP echoed a similar line of argument: "We have been able by and large to keep out the poachers. But we are not sitting on our laurels. We are very aware that what is happening around us will most likely find its way here if we are complacent."[12] The centrality of the border and the inside/outside dichotomies are apparent in his statement. This line of thinking is one of "Fortress Botswana," wherein the seeming onslaught from abroad necessitates the decisive and overwhelming show of force to act as a deterrent to poaching and as retribution for any poaching that does occur within Botswana's borders. This discursive positioning of securitization justifies the deployment of troops on the conservation estate, as opposed to other law enforcement mechanisms more readily associated with civilian life such as the police, heightening the state of exception. A senior DWNP official argued, "You have guys who are basically coming in at ungazetted points [along the border] heavily armed, so it's war. So, you need your defense force to come in and play a significant role."[13] This situates the military as the appropriate actor and renders the conservation estate as a unique place for securitizing moves on the part of the state. Many interviewees from the wildlife establishment (particularly the DWNP) explicitly described poaching as being committed by ex-combatants from neighboring countries,[14] who used "weapons of war."[15] This evokes the connective tissue between the anxieties of statehood and wildlife protection. The historical context here provides insights into why this reasoning is not only rational to some extent but also commonplace among many government officials. The cross-border raids and incursions from the minority-ruled states during the apartheid era become the substrate upon which cross-border poaching raids are understood in the twenty-first century. Moreover, just as Botswana was constructed as a bastion of democratic, majority rule during the era of apartheid and racist minority governments across southern Africa, contemporarily, amid high levels of poaching, Botswana proactively imagines itself as an island of safety and tranquility, and its officials fiercely dispute reports of poaching that may shatter this imaginary.[16]

While the intellectual roots of the Copenhagen School focus on the discursive dimensions of securitization, Floyd (2010) argues that securitization is not simply about the securitizing speech act but also about the subsequent *securitizing moves* that follow on in policy. Her work is meaningfully attentive to the ways in which securitization is not simply discursive but often also necessitates changes in institutional behavior. She further refines this concept by describing what she calls "agent benefitting securitization," wherein institutional rewards in the form of budgeting, attention, and bureaucratic support redound to the actor invoking securitization, thus providing a justification and raison d'être. Following from Floyd's insights, the next sections examine securitization from three perspectives: institutional securitization, practical securitization, and the securitization of interactions between citizens and the state on the conservation estate. This analysis begins below with consideration of securitized institutions of state authority on the conservation estate.

The BDF, the DWNP, and the Securitized Institutions of Conservation

> The country is so vast and so much open country, animals roam so freely we need ten thousand pairs of eyes in every corner.
>
> —Head of DWNP Anti-Poaching Unit[17]

The institutional transformation of the bodies tasked with conservation policy in Botswana reveals the pervasiveness of securitization throughout the postcolonial period, providing insight into the nature of authority on and across the conservation estate. First, there is the BDF. Its primary objective in the early days of the independent republic was to act as bulwark against incursions by the militaries of its white-led neighbors amid the violence of southern Africa's liberation struggles. Historically, its internal deployments in the border areas hinted at the national anxiety about the unstable regional system and the threats it posed to Botswana's sovereign territory. Contemporarily, even with the fall of neighboring minority governments, the domestic use of the BDF echoes this outward-looking unease, this time with poachers being perceived as the key external threat, despite this posture often being a point of contention in regional international relations. Though beyond the scope of this chapter, it is worth considering the manner in which securitization embeds conservation policy into international relations. Because Botswana is landlocked and centrally located in southern Africa, its conservation estate sits at a regional environmental nexus and is party to several transfrontier conservation areas (Ramutsindela 2007). These potential ecological and political interconnections heighten state anxiety around the national border, which is often shorthanded as a concern about the intrusion and trespass of poachers from neighboring countries. As a result, scores of Namibian and Zimbabwean nationals have been killed under the shoot-to-kill policy, assumed to be poachers. This has created diplomatic tensions with neighboring states arguing these actions amount to extrajudicial killing and many family members arguing their deceased relative were engaged in legal activities like fishing on shared waterways between the two countries.[18]

Antipoaching is promoted as one of the flagship duties of the BDF, with the need to protect wildlife species as one of the major tasks of the country's national military. Deployments to the conservation estate for the purpose of protecting wildlife are routine parts of soldiering in Botswana. This role has been explicitly assigned to the BDF for over thirty years and constitutes a principal mission. The BDF first became involved in antipoaching in 1987 when former president Khama was the BDF's commanding officer.[19] (He was a military officer before entering the realm of electoral politics.) It began as a specialized effort, but by 1989 the mission of antipoaching was expanded beyond the elite Commando Squadron special forces unit to include the BDF's regular personnel. A large and visible military presence has been maintained ever since, primarily in the country's north. Beginning in 2004, a minimum of four companies at a time patrol the conservation areas, and all BDF soldiers, not just special forces, can expect to spend approximately three months of the year on antipoaching operations.[20]

Despite the high praise given to Botswana for the use of the BDF in conservation (see Henk 2007; Bugday 2016; Mogomotsi and Madigele 2017), there is debate about the effectiveness of military deployments in obtaining specific ecological outcomes. A group of scholars concerned about the broader implications of the trend toward using militaries in conservation enforcement note that the black rhinos endemic to Botswana became extinct in the country *after* the BDF took control of antipoaching in the late 1980s (Duffy et al. 2019). Therefore, the presence of the BDF may not be able to demonstrate much about effective conservation policy per se, but it can illustrate how the nature of state authority and state building play out on the conservation estate. BDF personnel do not have any particular conservation expertise. In fact, animals are brought to military training sessions in order to acclimate new recruits to their presence and give them a rudimentary sense of their behavior (Bugday 2016). This may be attributed, in part, to the fact that most recruits do not hail from the conservation estate and are thus unfamiliar with certain aspects of the environment that might be more common knowledge in conservation-adjacent communities. One potential rationale given for this differentiation in recruitment was highly unequal educational attainment among the population in Botswana, with rural communities on the conservation estate having fewer high school graduates than other regions. Nonetheless, it is notable that despite conservation policy being a central task of the armed forces' current mandate, the emphasis is not on the ecological criteria of natural resources management but on the enactment of state authority and coercion across the conservation estate.

The institutional securitization described above creates a coercive, enforcement-first paradigm of conservation practice in Botswana that has become hegemonic. Poaching, or the threat of poaching, is conceived of as a low-intensity conflict brewing in Botswana's remote areas and therefore a feature of conservation estate. The BDF's primary mandate is antipoaching, whereas the DWNP is responsible for conducting a wide range of functions related to the conservation estate. While wildlife officers from the DWNP are tasked with all aspects of conservation management—issuing permits, dealing with tourists, environmental research, operating their own antipoaching unit, community outreach, and problem animal control and compensation[21]—BDF units are tasked with antipoaching enforcement alone.[22] Despite the myriad institutional tasks assigned to the DWNP, it remains relatively underresourced compared with the BDF in conservation areas. In line with a securitized approach empowering institutions of state violence, the BDF is better equipped in terms of manpower and matériel resources. Because the environment of the conservation estate is problematized primarily as a security issue, the military is viewed as the appropriate responding institution. Other parts of the institutional complex nominally tasked with conservation become sublimated to and often dependent on the BDF. DWNP officials complain of a lack of resources and personnel, especially compared with the BDF. The regional wildlife officer in Maun recounted that the oversight and control of the conservation estate is dependent upon the presence of the BDF: "With Botswana Defence Force, they have a lot of soldiers in the area, manning the gates, doing the patrols. So, because of their numbers, they can cover a wide range of area. And they also have equipment—better equipment than us and the police.... Whenever there is any report of poaching, when we call on them they come and assist us real quick."[23] Not only is the practice of enforcement on the ground a core mandate of active-duty military personnel in the conservation estate, but the institutional structures of the DWNP are also slowly becoming more militarized and recreated in the image of a security-oriented organization. DWNP officials describe the inertia of the department moving in favor of a more robust antipoaching agenda. In addition to its reliance on the BDF, the antipoaching unit within the DWNP has been made its own division and strengthened institutionally, compared with other DWNP units focused on nonenforcement aspects of wildlife management and conservation.[24] The antipoaching unit grew by one hundred officers in 2014 and by another seventy-five in 2015.[25] With the preeminence of antipoaching in environmental management, other aspects of conservation policymaking get lost: the mundane, quotidian stuff of human-wildlife conflict and compensation, problem animal control, environmental education, and so on. All of these presumably require other skill sets and responsibilities than those prioritized in military training. This tilt in favor of enforcement is felt throughout the department and represents a myopic view of what conservation is—the process of securing the environment from human interference and trespass. The alternative departmental nodes, many of which operate along a more consultative framework and require community interactions, have been disempowered relative to the financial, institutional, and discursive support given to security-focused endeavors.[26] Officials working in various departments, including Problem Animal Control (the unit tasked with dealing with human-wildlife conflict),[27] CBNRM,[28] Park Maintenance,[29] Research,[30] and Community Education,[31] all felt inadequately staffed and underresourced. Consequently, the upper echelon of the DWNP often features retired BDF officers in leadership positions, including a former major, a former colonel, and a former major general at key posts throughout the decade of the 2010s.[32] This results in a kind of inertia of securitization. As the old adage goes, when one's only tool is a hammer, every problem looks like a nail. As the power of the securitized actors within and outside of the department became amplified, it created a securitized feedback loop of sorts. The most capacitated institutional bodies, be they the BDF or internal DWNP antipoaching units, have the most resources and get the most responsibility. Therefore, policy implementation is iteratively constructed in their image and according to their strengths and expertise. This results in an enforcement-first paradigm of authority building that predominates above other considerations on the conservation estate.

I do not intend to suggest that these institutions are monolithic or that there is no dissensus with regard to enforcement-first, coercive modes of conservation policy implementation. There is a noticeable divergence from this approach among district-based wildlife officers and junior staff at headquarters. Several of these interview participants questioned the efficacy of a securitized "enforcement first" approach to biodiversity conservation and the manner in which the department engaged with communities in the conservation estate. They often highlighted the contradictory nature of a security-focused presence contrasted with the tenets of participation and local buy-in frequently emphasized in government outreach and environmental education programs coming out of less institutionally powerful divisions of their department. Despite the apparent institutional strength of the antipoaching wildlife posture, a junior-level DWNP staffer suggested securitizing conservation cannot lead to improved ecological outcomes. He instead argued that the enforcement paradigm was merely a stopgap rather than a sustainable solution to the tensions created by wildlife policies and resource-use restrictions commonplace on the conservation estate: "I personally don't think that enforcement and more enforcement and more enforcement will bring that much change. . . . People should know why it's so important to conserve, how they're going to benefit in the long run. Because if they don't know that, we'll have jails full, no matter what you do."[33] The securitized enforcement-first orientation, which short-circuits the ability of those living on the conservation estate to view themselves as part of the wildlife system, produces social trespass. It creates outsiders of the most "inside" population of Batswana imaginable, the people in communities with long and well-documented histories of living on the land now categorized as the conservation estate, whose lives and livelihoods today depend on the health and longevity of their immediate ecosystem. This very dynamic was described by many residents of the conservation estate. A middle-aged San man living in the village of Mababe asserted that members of his community would work alongside the government in conservation enforcement if it had a role for them and if they were given a reason to do so: "I would make the community more responsible [for conservation], which would also make them more active in protecting our natural resources because it is their business. They would not allow criminals [poachers] to kill the animals because they would be the main source of income and living for the members of the community."[34] Recognizing the saliency of statements like the one above, many of the people tasked with implementing conservation policies are deeply skeptical of the efficacy of securitized approaches, but nonetheless this policy paradigm remains dominant in state practice on the conservation estate. A senior official at the DWNP headquarters in Gaborone described this incongruity: "On the one hand, communities will see us coming in force, but at the same time we'll be preaching that we are still with you, we still want you to really have ownership of these things."[35] The multifaceted nature of the state-building project on the conservation estate is formed by a broad constellation of interests and logics, which may in fact operate at cross-purposes. Not only do local people find the exercise of state power contradictory or conflicted, but also those public servants tasked with implementation find these policy positions fragmented and incoherent. The privileging of enforcement approaches occurs because enforcement is a blunt instrument, wrapped up in a legitimizing discourse of national security—a securitizing act. It is easier from an implementation perspective to put more antipoaching personnel and matériel out in the field than to win over populations that have long been at odds with government priorities on the conservation estate.

This does not suggest that the enforcement-first paradigm is more sustainable, effective, or has more longevity. In fact, many critical conservation scholars have argued the ecological impacts of securitized conservation may be a net negative (Duffy et al. 2015, 2019; Witter 2021). However, the institutional dominance of securitized conservation in Botswana helps illustrate a central argument: conservation is not an ecological endeavor only. The act of securing the environment is not done based on the effectiveness of this approach from a conservation or ecological perspective alone but rather because securitization is informed by other logics, such as the need to structure authority, forcefully maintain the integrity of the state's borders, justify deployment of the armed forces, and police the behavior of conservation-dwelling citizens in addition to foreigners (be they the much sought-after international tourists or the much feared, transgressive Namibian, Zambian, or Zimbabwean "poachers").

The conservation estate in Botswana is vast and remote, adjacent to the state's territorial boundaries and marginal to the population centers that are home to political power. The militarized interventions of conservation are "spatially amorphous," sometimes resulting in spillover beyond the confines of protected areas that envelops nearby people and communities (Duffy 2016,

238). This territorial extensity causes great anxiety on the part of those tasked with managing it. The head of the DWNP's antipoaching unit expressed this, saying, "It's a vast area for our troops to control, and that's what keeps me up at night."[36] The spatial and geographic scope of the conservation estate presents challenges to its management and provides insights into why the securitized paradigm is prevalent. The size and expansiveness of the conservation estate is often invoked as a reason for increased surveillance and manpower deployment to the remote areas of the country. Conservation enforcement, therefore, becomes a means of folding in these spaces under state structures and making them subject to state authority. One of the deputy directors of the DWNP cited the potential for the conservation estate to act as safe haven for undesirable people and behaviors as a justification for the presence of law enforcement agents in these regions, creating states of exception where traditional modes of law enforcement can be replaced by military deployment: "These are very huge protected areas, and of course . . . it's a plus to have them because the bigger your protected areas, the better in terms of conservation. But, of course, the bigger they are also the more it means that people take advantage of their isolation to engage in illegal activities. And, therefore, we are then required to have men on the ground to look after and monitor what is going on in those protected areas, apart from management of wildlife that are found within those areas."[37] In the last sentence of this quote, the interviewee appealed to a logic above and beyond conservation alone by noting that monitoring and surveillance "apart from the management of wildlife" was an essential part of the mission of conservation enforcement, a unique set of circumstances that allow for this kind of state of exception of the conservation estate not easily replicable or justifiable on other spaces of state territory. Following from this position, it is unsurprising that in addition to the BDF, the Directorate of Intelligence and Security has become fully enmeshed in the antipoaching mechanisms, now considered a constituent institutional part of conservation implementation in

Botswana.[38] As such, conservation enforcement is not only about bodily force used in the exercise of authority but also about surveillance and monitoring as a means of social control and coercion. The quote from the head of the antipoaching unit that began this section indicates as much. In order to control the perceived threat of poaching, "ten thousand pairs of eyes" are specifically enumerated (for surveillance) as critically important. The deployment of military force and allied security and intelligence institutions into these areas on the conservation estate operates not only in the service of protecting natural habitats but also as a means of controlling, regulating, and sanctioning the people and behavior of those inhabiting this vast section of Botswana's national territory in accordance with assumptions and priorities determined by the state.

The Shoot-to-Kill Policy and the Securitization of Conservation Practice

> If a person has a weapon and they challenge our security forces, at that standoff distance you don't know, you are not interrogating what country they come from. The response is the same.
>
> —Tshekedi Khama (minister of environment, conservation, natural resources, and tourism, 2012–18)[39]

The securitization of conservation institutions is paralleled by the securitization in the practical implementation of conservation policy itself. The enforcement-first paradigm is underpinned by assumptions that construct conservation-adjacent people, who are very often indigenous to the land of the conservation estate, as criminals, trespassers, or proto-poachers. This is highly relevant because of the rules of engagement that predominate on the securitized conservation estate empower the use of force upon the presumption of illegal behavior or trespass with little oversight. This is frequently described as "shoot-to-kill," wherein armed agents of the state are able to use lethal force to protect environmental resources, typically wildlife. Shoot-to-kill policies are not unique to Botswana but have been employed at various times in conservation areas in countries like Malawi, Tanzania, Kenya, and Zimbabwe (Duffy 2014). While ostensibly for poachers—who are often described as quasi-military combatants—this application of state coercive force inevitably envelops ordinary citizens. Botswana has a long history of employing a shoot-to-kill policy on the conservation estate, linked to the BDF's deployment described in the previous section (Henk 2007). During the period of my fieldwork, the Khama government was very vocal in asserting this as a legitimate method of antipoaching enforcement in the face of a world where armed poachers penetrated the country's borders. While there have been some shifts of conservation policy under President Mokgweetsi Masisi, like the removal of automatic weapons from wildlife officers (LaRocco and Mogende 2022), incidents of BDF use of force against poachers, or suspected poachers, remain commonplace across the conservation estate. This pervasive threat of state violence is unique and specific to this area of the country and is another axis along which the conservation estate is exceptionalized.

As noted earlier, Botswana's shoot-to-kill policy has resulted in diplomatic tensions with neighboring countries, notably Namibia and Zimbabwe, whose citizens have been killed by antipoaching operators.[40] While the "foreignness" of typical victims allows for the policy to be slotted into a national security and sovereign protection valence and implicates regional dynamics of Botswana's international relations, the policy impacts are not limited to noncitizens. Shoot-to-kill makes no distinction between suspected foreign poachers and suspected poachers from Botswana.[41] While the extrajudicial killing of foreign poachers is potentially transgressive of human rights norms, the manner in which a certain subsection of Batswana citizens—those on the conservation estate—are subject to this singular mode of state violence complicates the imaginary of a peaceful, rule-bound Botswana. Of course, the country still utilizes capital punishment, and the judicial system has applied the death penalty to individuals convicted of murder.[42] However, poaching is not a capital crime, nor are those *suspected* of poaching even given the presumption of innocence.[43] The nonchalance with which officials speak of the shoot-to-kill policy reflects how embedded and normalized it has become, part of the securitizing discourse that makes poachers, would-be poachers, and suspected poachers akin to enemy combatants, placing poaching in the realm of war rather than that of law. Moreover, despite its legality, the judicial death penalty is highly contested in Botswana, in both the political and legal realm.[44] If there were an execution of an accused criminal without trial, it would be viewed by nearly all citizens, and especially by the urban elite, as entirely unacceptable and against the democratic norms of the nation's self-image.[45] In fact, high-profile cases of police killings in Gaborone have attracted much attention over the years (Good 2009), whereas the victims of shoot-to-kill on the conservation estate remain mostly anonymous and unremarked upon. The contrast is telling. The shoot-to-kill policy has been carefully lifted out of the realm of normal legal procedure and exceptionalized. It is placed within the discourse of security, a move that manufactures consent on the part of the broader populace. The securitization of conservation practice in the form of shoot-to-kill removes it from the rigors of political and legal scrutiny, and it becomes taken for granted by most citizens not living on the conservation estate.

Bugday (2016) details the way in which securitized conservation does receive plaudits from within Botswana society. However, her analysis relies primarily on informants from the military and on media reports from national papers, which in Botswana are overwhelmingly based in Gaborone. Little analysis engages with people living on the conservation estate, a vantage point that produces a very different perspective. When analysts laud the rule-bound, civilian-controlled military in Botswana, they fail to capture the perspective of those on the conservation estate, where the relationship looks very different. As noted earlier, there is little transparency of statistics of deaths of suspected poachers or of arrests and incarcerations.[46] In fact, the most consistent public reporting appears in media outlets of neighboring countries—Namibia, Zambia, and Zimbabwe—whose citizens are routinely impacted by this policy. However, the general opacity makes efforts to shift the debate around the shoot-to-kill policy highly problematic. The government's unwillingness to disclose these figures shrouds this issue in the cloak of "national security," restricting any contestation and employing the state exercise of authority as predominant and paramount, in line with the securitized closure of debate described by scholars of the Copenhagen School.

As further evidence of the ways in which the shoot-to-kill policy has been moved from the realm of normal debate into emergency politics, supporters of Botswana's antipoaching approach—including nonstate actors like conservation activists and tourism operators—regard it as an example for the rest of Africa to follow,[47] and they have lambasted the government even when incremental changes have been made to the military posture of antipoaching, including relatively minor changes initiated by President Masisi to remove certain weapons from the DWNP, while maintaining the full array of the BDF's matériel.[48] Alongside proponents in the policy space, some scholars have endorsed the shoot-to-kill policy, arguing that it is a justified conservation strategy and that concerns about human rights and the rule of law are specious because "parks are war zones and that rules and principles of war ought to be implemented" (Mogomotsi and Madigele 2017, 54), further invoking an Agamben-like state of exception, using some of the very language he highlights in his critique of state power. They cite support from NGOs, the private sector, and "international tourist clientele" and note that shoot-to-kill has "been used in various countries without significant outcry from the international community" (Mogomotsi and Madigele 2017, 54). Far from that, they argue, there is evidence of public support for these policies, and they urge other countries, including South Africa, to follow Botswana's lead.

The broad consensus regarding shoot-to-kill is a result of shifting norms and a solidifying of the securitization discourse, part of a transformation not only of institutions but of the practice of policy implementation. In his 2007 monograph, Henk notes how in the early days of antipoaching operations the Botswana Police Service attempted to investigate the killings of poachers as homicides and insisted on conducting interviews with members of the military as murder suspects, seizing the weapons involved as evidence, and scrutinizing the facts of each case. The BDF strongly rejected this process, claiming "their honor [was] now somehow tarnished with *unwarranted implications* of illegality" (Henk 2007, 66, emphasis mine). Analysts have further suggested that it would be inappropriate for the police to scrutinize military behavior because it "would have bogged down the BDF operations" (Bugday 2016, 203). It is only through the political work of "securitization" that this type of force is insulated from the usual criminal justice procedures that predominate in Botswana's adjudication of capital crimes. (It should be noted again, of course, that poaching is not a capital crime and that if adjudicated according to established norms would result in imprisonment, not execution.) What Henk's anecdote illustrates is that the Botswana Police Service was attempting to approach the death of individuals within Botswana, their perceived and actual jurisdiction, with attention to the legal statutes that bound their work. The BDF was not willing to oblige. The securitized operation of the army exists in a separate sphere when it comes to the rules of engagement in the conservation estate, differentiating the modes of state authority on this category of political space. The unique construction of poaching as superseding the normal order of the legal system is pervasive and creates a state of exception (Agamben 2005) wherein the rights to legal procedures no longer hold and the imperatives of safety and security preempt both normal politics of negotiation and the rule of law that affords individual rights and protections. The declaration of poachers as a security threat abrogates their rights to due process, and the majority of people in Botswana, but not those on the conservation estate, take the government at its word regarding the validity of the security threat of poaching. Subsequently, this shifts the dynamics of citizen-state relations on the conservation estate and introduces other entities as key subjects of state security.

Securitization, Wildlife, and the People of the Conservation Estate

> Poaching is utilizing for your own good at the expense of the nation. It is stealing from the nation.
>
> —DWNP regional wildlife officer, Ghanzi and Kgalagadi Districts[49]

A central argument of this book is that those individuals living on the conservation estate experience citizenship within the state in highly differentiated ways compared with their counterparts living elsewhere across Botswana's territory, as a feature of the unique state-building characteristics at play in these areas. The securitization of conservation institutions and practices result in securitizing the basic interactions between this specific class of citizens and the state. This is further complicated by the way in which securitization of conservation envelopes another category of being, whose regular presence is unique to the conservation estate: wildlife. When the moral community of who belongs under the umbrella of state protection is expanded to include wildlife, when national security is extended into the realm of wildlife protection, as it is in Botswana, an inadvertent impact is that some citizens perceive themselves as pushed out from under this guarantee of protection and subjects of state coercive scrutiny rather than subjects warranting security themselves. While the securitization discourse may be remote and esoteric for other Batswana, it deeply impacts the political subjectivities of people on the conservation estate.

Securitization can work to dehumanize or depoliticize the people of the conservation estate and simultaneously humanize and politicize the charismatic animals that become the primary referents of security in these contexts—the species thought to be protected by securitized antipoaching—and that are often elevated above the humans with whom they share the ecosystem of the conservation estate. Henk (2007) argues that the relatively low population density of the conservation estate facilitates securitized approaches to wildlife protection due to the fact that most citizens live far from the impacted areas. He writes, "The military was not obliged to contend with an angry peasantry whose land use rights had been arbitrarily abrogated in the recent past. The country's relative prosperity and ready availability of domestic livestock products also significantly reduced the local incentive for poaching" (2007, 173). While he is accurately portraying a broad swath of Batswana society, his analysis erases the very concerns of those living on the conservation estate in favor of the majority of Batswana who reside far from these contexts. Their numbers are smaller, but their lived experiences are markedly different and in fact exhibit many of the characteristics dismissed by Henk: they have relatively recent histories of dispossession through conservation (especially those from indigenous communities); they deal with restrictions of livestock production, short-circuiting those livelihood opportunities; and they generally have not shared in the country's macro-level prosperity, despite sharing their lives and communities with the charismatic wildlife and landscapes central to the tourism industry. These animals, especially elephants, are frequently rendered using politically terminology that evokes human qualities and political subjectivities on the part of wildlife. Mike Chase, a prominent Motswana ecologist said this of Botswana's elephant population: "The elephants that we've collared in the Okavango have trekked nearly five hundred kilometers across three international boundaries. . . . A lot of our elephants were essentially *political refugees*. They fled to the safety and security of Botswana, moving away from poaching [emphasis mine]."[50] This is a kind of anthropomorphization that works to cast Botswana—specifically the securitized conservation estate—as a sanctuary, a place of peace and tranquility where charismatic megafauna can roam once they have escaped the political turmoil beyond the borders. It puts the plight of elephants on par with humans in a region with a recent history of violent minority rule, refugee flows, and liberation struggles. In doing so, this rhetoric also serves to highlight Botswana's unique history in southern Africa as a haven during the era of minority rule, often now construed as a haven in light of poaching and the violence of wildlife crime. Not only does this do the work of imbuing Botswana's nonhuman inhabitants with human qualities—and indeed human rights as "refugees," a category that evokes clearly defined obligations to states in the international system—but it also reinforces the strength and stability of Botswana's international borders and internal authority. According to the 1951 Convention Relating to the Status of Refugees, a refugee is "someone who is unable or unwilling to return to their country of origin owing to a well-founded fear of being persecuted."[51] Affixing this appellation to wildlife like elephants would confer in them the agentic ability to flee "persecution" and mandates the ability of co-local wildlife to have subjective anxiety about their safety. This rhetorical maneuver of putting the potential suffering of elephants on par with human suffering by turning them into "refugees" has the effect of expanding the referents of state security in a way that not only humanizes elephants but also depoliticizes the grievances humans have with how the state chooses to protect wildlife populations. The global and continental anxiety around the survival of elephants as a species has created a moral positioning in Botswana where animals become the focus of political attention, often to a greater extent than co-local human populations. This situation is unique to the conservation estate. The presence of certain kinds of globally important wildlife trains the gaze of international observers on the people and places that share their existence with charismatic megafauna. The conventional understanding of a citizen-state relationship then becomes expanded into a *citizen–state–charismatic megafauna relationship,* often with influential international actors claiming to speak on behalf of the nonhuman animals of the conservation estate.

The concept of the conservation estate as encompassing all types of land that are subject to the logic of conservation, not just those delineated as national parks, helps in the explanation of securitization's impact on political subjectivities. The securitization of conservation occurs not only in officially gazetted protected areas but also in Wildlife Management Areas, where human residency is permitted. In these spaces, the securitization discourse renders animals the subjects of defense and protection, and local people who live alongside this wildlife become potential threats. This results in a group of citizens whose ability to freely move across territory is circumscribed in ways not seen elsewhere in the country. By casting resource use (potential or actual) as a national security threat, the first assumption if a local resident is found outside the spatial confines of their village on the conservation estate is that they are participating in illicit behavior. Interview respondents who live in villages located on the conservation estate suggest that it is the threat of state violence, embodied by the presence of the BDF and other enforcement-first conservation actors, that keeps people within the confines of their communities, not necessarily their satisfaction with the life and livelihoods they find therein. This is all the more important when considering these populations have cultural histories of foraging and lifestyle patterns premised upon mobility. A resident conveyed the kind of enforced sedentarism that exists due to the security atmosphere: "They [the soldiers] are not just protecting the park nowadays; they are all over the place.... The soldiers are here to stop people from stealing wild animals inside the park."[52] Several interviewees describe the situation they experienced as a transfer of land to the armed forces—that these areas have become the prerogative of the state military, and to be found beyond the village boundaries was understood locally to be a crime. The interviewee characterized this as a full transfer of the authority of the land over to the military, forcing local people to question their legitimate occupation of the land: "It [land] belongs to the soldier because we used to roam this land freely, we could easily walk from Sankuyo to

Khwai [villages in Botswana's northern conservation estate] without having to account to anyone as to where we are going alone on foot. Nowadays the soldiers think that if you are traveling on foot you are a criminal."[53] The reordering of spatial politics and the perceived imposition of fixed and hardening boundaries for human presence was reiterated during my fieldwork in community after community on the conservation estate. This contrasts with other non-conservation rural areas where village limits are less strictly perceived and are more akin to a series of concentric circles emanating outward, rather than a stark dichotomy between village and the space deemed the purview of conservation and thus subject to becoming a securitized state of exception. Moreover, in areas of the conservation estate where people are limited in their mobility due to enforcement-first approaches to wildlife management, elephants are given the freedom to move throughout human communities, frequently eating or damaging crops unmolested. They are perceived locally to obtain rights and freedoms that co-local humans are often denied, without the concomitant obligations required of other moral agents.

Perhaps unsurprisingly, community relations with conservation enforcement officers are generally not good. Community escort guides are individuals employed by village conservation trusts in order to monitor the flora and fauna present on the community's allocated piece of land.[54] In theory, these are the local people tasked with monitoring local use of natural resources as well as patrolling and reporting any suspicious behavior possibly related to poaching. These individuals have bought into state-sanctioned ideas about conservation, tourism, and development and are invested in seeing themselves as part of a conservation "solution" that takes into account both local people and the needs of the larger state. Many of them explicitly think of themselves as bridging interlocutors between the state and their communities.[55] In any form of participatory conservation, these are the members of the population viewed as the vanguard of local environmental protection, but the coercive use of force that characterizes a securitized environment leaves little space for them. The exercise of authority through modes of consent would ostensibly privilege these actors, yet in a lengthy conversation with a community escort guide in the village of Sankuyo, the frustration of community escort guides became apparent: "We will not do regular patrols because it will be done mostly by the government, especially the police officers and the army officers. And maybe the police and the army officer . . . are not much experienced on the wildlife, so maybe it could be a negative impact to the community."[56] These mediating figures are pushed out, and they perceive that their communities have no say, or stake, in nearby land and resources made alien to them by the securitized practice of conservation. Moreover, this interviewee highlighted a major concern about the occupation of the conservation estate by the armed services—that military personnel are not geared toward environmental management or community outreach but rather see most situations through a security lens. This is perhaps not surprising, considering this sentiment echoes similar concerns expressed by institutional actors not convinced of the merits of the enforcement-first paradigm. The military actors who become tasked with "doing conservation" in the form of antipoaching patrols are embedded in sets of norms, procedures, and regulations that create a martial orientation to the world wherein every interaction is potentially with a deadly foe. This leaves no room for the other important functions of the wildlife authorities, including the community outreach and education needed to inculcate an air of legitimacy around the exercise of authority. Engagements with the local communities living on the conservation estate are informed from a position that favors the logics of coercion rather than the development of a relationship of consent. The above interviewee continued: "They can shoot to kill. They don't negotiate. It is the rule that if you are found out in the bush doing poaching, then you have to be shot to death."[57] This is demonstrative of the manner in which the legitimacy of authority for those on the conservation estate differs from the wider polity. In this location, legitimacy is predicated not on the cooperation of the citizenry in agreement with state actors but rather upon the threat of force. It is all the more telling that this assessment comes from one of the community members, a community escort guide, mostly likely to be predisposed to the government's stated conservation goals, and yet even he views the operations of conservation authorities as bounded and directed by coercion. For those on the conservation estate, the BDF and other conservation enforcement authorities do not operate as a symbol of government-provided security but rather as state expressions of force.

The pressure of surveillance in pursuit of (potential) illegal activities characterizes the relationship between the state and the local people found on the conservation estate. A man in the Ghanzi village Groot Laagte expressed his frustration: "We only see Wildlife [DWNP] in the village when they are patrolling or looking after some trouble. They are viewed badly. When you see them, they are hunting for people who are eating wildlife."[58] This statement was a powerful discursive inversion of who and what is being hunted and speaks to a commonplace register through which people perceive conservation policies enacted and enforced in their daily lives. For this man, the DWNP is "hunting" the people of Groot Laagte for the crime of "eating wildlife," which he clearly does not view as a crime at all. Moreover, there is an implicit desire for the DWNP to fulfill other functions of a conservation agency, including focusing on problem animal control. Managing human-wildlife interactions and conflicts is fully within the agency's remit. However, locally the department is not viewed as balancing the equities of its mandate—protecting the environment while *also* recognizing and ameliorating grievances of the citizenry. In a community that is harried by frequent instances of human-wildlife conflict, the residents believe themselves to be the ones in the state's crosshairs, so to speak. For this respondent, because of the failures of collaborative approaches to these problems ("We only see Wildlife [DWNP] in the village when they are patrolling"), the ability of the state to exercise legitimate authority through consent is lost. Thus, force is the primary mechanism through which the state is able to bend communities to their conservation agendas.

This discussion of the securitized environment of Botswana's conservation estate has used the term "poacher" freely and often. However, to fully grasp the empirical situation of state authority, force, and power on the conservation estate, the very idea signified by the word must be interrogated. The notion of a poacher is important to examine in this context; despite the commonplace state rhetoric aligning "poacher" and "foreigner" presented in the previous section, there are myriad ways in which local people become or, more important, begin to see themselves as poachers. The term is fraught with assumptions about legality, illegality, trespass, and criminality. Poaching can encompass a wide variety of activities, ranging from killing an animal that is not specifically enumerated in a hunting quota or game license in order to consume its meat or the killing of an animal in order to sell its wildlife products—skins, tusks, horns, bones—on a lucrative market. The process of securitization of the environment creates poachers as omnipotent and omnipresent; they become an enemy that warrants the use of military force as the only viable option for its defeat.

Seen in this process is what Bourdieu observes in the power of naming. The act of naming an actor—say, a "hunter" versus a "poacher"—is an exercise and demonstration of the power to categorize the world and to shape social understanding through discursive contexts. Classifying certain behaviors as part of particular subjectivities operates to construct, maintain, and control social and political meanings, influencing institutions and the relationships between political subjects. It is the actors with the power to name—to subsume sets of behaviors under particular monikers—who establish the contours of the system or, as Bourdieu suggests, to "create the world through naming" (1991, 105). Names are neither arbitrary nor insignificant; it is language that creates and consolidates social categorization (Bourdieu 1977). The designation of people as "poachers" or set of behaviors as "poaching" is not just semantic but rather part of the political projection of power and authority, in this case on the part of the state vis-à-vis a subset of its citizens. With the act of poaching constructed as a violation of national treasure, any citizen who does this is rejecting their allegiance to the state project.

Following from Bourdieu's focus on language and the power of naming, the discursive positions of securitization work to dehumanize local people living on the conservation estate, who are often viewed with suspicion and wariness. Duffy (2014) notes that "poachers" are constructed as dangerous, which is done by demonizing them as outsiders who are threatening the integrity of the state with violence. Since the late 1980s, the rhetorical register used in Botswana to describe poachers has been one of foreignness. This certainly originates from the palpable anxiety about foreign trespass during the volatile era of minority rule in the region. Scholarship indicates that combatants on various sides of the liberation wars were, in fact, engaged in illegal offtake of wildlife (Ellis 1994; Ramutsindela 2016). However, the pervasiveness of the characterization of poachers as foreigners has present-day consequences on the conservation estate. While at first glance it appears that Botswana adheres to this same insider/outsider dynamic in its public pronouncements around poaching, further examination demonstrates the ways in which certain citizens—specifically those living on the conservation estate—are constructed as outside the mainstream, potentially dangerous, untrustworthy, and requiring surveillance. In Botswana this has the effect, perhaps unintentional, of capturing citizens in this discourse. This is amplified by the ways in which protected areas and the conservation estate geographically overlap with areas inhabited by indigenous populations and contribute to the essentializing representation of these people (Bocarejo and Ojeda 2016) and further construct these populations as aberrant to the mainstream. This coincides with other contexts where scholars have observed that the definition of a "security threat" in conservation violence is often done along axes of difference wherein "the state participates in interpellating non-dominant populations

FIGURE 2.1. Antipoaching sign in the village of Sankuyo: "Be responsible. Wild animals belong to us. No poaching. Do not kill wild animals without a permit. Preserve nature." Author's photograph.

with cultural, linguistic, class, and national markers of difference as territorial trespassers—as invaders or interlopers" (Lunstrum and Ybarra 2018, 116). As the line is blurred between "poacher," "outsider," and "enemy," local citizens become caught up in this discursive dragnet. The power of securitization limits the ability of already marginal citizens to contest the rhetorical configurations of "good" and "bad" that have purchase among the majority of the populace and state authorities. Some people living on the conservation estate begin to self-adopt the category of poacher as they see their intersubjective understanding of themselves becoming associated with the identity of a poacher or a potential poacher. The production of the identity of poacher as pervasive creates a guilt-by-association mentality on the conservation estate, part of what Witter and Satterfield describe as the slow violence wrought upon the "chronically liminal" (2019, 275).

Many respondents from the DWNP argue that if only local people appreciated the value of biodiversity, they would not need to be subject to the oversight of state authorities. The regional wildlife officer in Maun noted, "If people eventually will appreciate the existence of wildlife, then we won't have to be sending our officers to go and patrol to see if people are poaching or not because communities will then be the law enforcement officers."[59] This places the onus on the local residents to ensure their freedom from surveillance through compliance with the state-dictated orientation toward wildlife. This highlights a contradiction in the way that state-directed policies have played out. By making certain behaviors (including something as innocuous as being out in the bush near their communities) "deviant," the ability for communities to self-monitor is diminished. This necessitates that securitized conservation becomes the solution to a problem—clandestine extralegal hunting and resource use—made in part by state policies to begin with. What is lost in much of the securitization discourse is the social and political context for poaching. Hübschle (2017) investigates the motivations of poachers and argues that their continued marginalization in terms of loss of land and resources access rights associated with conservation has explanatory power. During the 2014–19 moratorium on hunting, respondents described a breakdown of the local social norms that dictated how resources were to be used. An older woman in Kacgae in Ghanzi District remarked, "Before people were very careful about what they hunted. But now because they are very afraid of Wildlife [DWNP], they will go out to poach quickly and just kill whatever they can see."[60] Here she draws an interesting distinction between the practice of hunting, which was done locally under a set of disciplining social taboos, and that of poaching, which is done quickly, carelessly, and in pursuit of whatever protein is readily available. This situation was presaged by a conservation practitioner who worked with conservation-adjacent populations for decades. This interviewee suggested that the blanket hunting ban implemented over a five-year period would not be the end of hunting but rather make it clandestine and unregulated: "You know the thing with hunting is that they [the government] can try and ban it . . . but they'll just drive it underground. They'll [local people] just carry on poaching. So, I'd rather have them on board a properly controlled and managed system and see it as their resource that they [local people] are looking after and get them involved in antipoaching rather than just outright trying to police everyone."[61] The reordering of citizen-state relations on the conservation estate during the period of the hunting moratorium provides an illustrative example of the state-building capacities of conservation practice in the sociopolitical space. When hunting was driven underground, local residents were discouraged from engaging in the protection of wildlife in a collaborative manner. This then necessitated that the state use surveillance and policing as a means to monitor and uphold its policy on the conservation estate, transforming the relationship between state authority and residents. The hunting ban, therefore, created the kinds of subjects—poachers—that it sought to prevent.

This chapter has argued that state use of an environmental securitization discourse has constructed the monitoring of conservation policies as integral to the state's ability to exercise its sovereignty and concurrently constricted the space for debating such a claim. Conservation is largely about power, which is often unequally distributed between citizens and the state. The process whereby securitization predominates on the conservation estate functions as a modality of "state and subject formation" (Kelly and Ybarra 2016, 173). This chapter has examined how the precipitating "securitizing speech act" of securitization theory—rendering wildlife protection as central to state security, sovereignty, and territorial integrity—is followed up by a series of securitizing acts. These include the transformation of institutions and practices of conservation along a securitized paradigm of enforcement first and also the subtler reconfiguration of citizen-state relations on the conservation estate.

The military in Botswana is a key institutional and practical actor in conservation enforcement. The expansive use of a security orientation in conservation betrays an anxiety about the nature of state control and the penetration of borders and removes resource-use issues from the realm of political contestation. The citizenry of the conservation estate becomes constructed as an "enemy within" that is possibly dangerous but also perhaps redeemable through education and outreach, though the previous section detailed how these kinds of endeavors are institutionally marginalized with the DWNP. The dehumanization of individuals seen to be poachers is coupled with the humanization of charismatic wildlife, in such a manner that makes it permissible and justified for state shoot-to-kill policies (Büscher 2016). This is particularly prevalent in many online forums, where Botswana is often held up as a model (Lunstrum 2017). Moreover, the glossy imagery presented on the social media accounts of many antipoaching actors can create a type of antipolitics whereby the violence and trauma of antipoaching is masked for broad audiences in favor of consumable and marketable hero narratives (Massé 2019). Conservation-adjacent citizens are not expected to consent to these environmental decisions but rather to obey them. This facilitates a particular construction of a "poacher" as foreign, criminal, and dangerous to the integrity and stability of the state, a construction that precariously differentiates conservation-adjacent people from other rural dwellers. This discursive orientation captures within it citizens of Botswana, complicating and confusing the ways in which operations to end poaching are understood to be externally focused endeavors of statecraft but simultaneously structuring domestic relations of authority between ruler and ruled.

3

Democracy, the *Kgotla*, and Promises of Consent amid Conservation

In February 2014, a month after the official start of a hunting ban that would ultimately remain in effect for five more years, I had a striking conversation with a man in the village of Kacgae in the western Kalahari.[1] The man, in his midthirties, wanted to know when I had heard about the hunting ban. During this period of my fieldwork, and in this region of Botswana's conservation estate, it was an ever-present topic of conversation and came up without prompting in nearly every conversation I had, both in and outside of formal interview settings. Replying truthfully, I told him I first became aware of the impending hunting ban in late November 2012, a full fourteen months before its implementation, from a BBC news report.[2] I told him that the structure of my research project was built around the knowledge of the impending ban and that I had planned to be in Botswana when it first took effect.

My response saddened this man. He said that he had spent his whole life on the conservation estate and that, as a San man, he felt a cultural affinity toward the practice of hunting. And yet he had only heard about the ban several weeks before its implementation, through a Radio Botswana broadcast he happened to catch.[3] For him, the difference of when I heard about the hunting ban encapsulated his frustrations. "The *makgoa* always are more important," he said. "You knew before we did."[4] This confirmed all of his suspicions: a foreigner, a *lekgoa*, knew a year before he did that his lifestyle and livelihood would be fundamentally altered by his own government. This interaction was representative of sentiments I frequently encountered during fieldwork. I often came back to this conversation over the next months and years as I tried to rectify this interaction, and so many others, with consistent, emphatic state discourses about Botswana's local modes of participation and democracy.

This chapter examines Botswana's discursive attention to consent and democracy and the limitations faced in pursuit of this particular state imaginary by people on the conservation estate. It considers local repertoires of resistance to the securitized paradigm described in the previous chapter. Local people—inculcated with mythologies of democracy, consultation, and participation—attempt to utilize these state-promoted discourses to illustrate their apparent incongruity in the way the conservation estate shapes their lives. Local resistance to lack of consultation in conservation policy and the pervasive use of force in a securitization paradigm adopts the form of the state's outwardly projected imaginary—Botswana as a democratic country that values and seeks the input of its citizens—to contest the contradiction as it occurs on the conservation estate. In particular, the countervailing authority logics of securitization and democracy embedded in the same state-building project produce a world in which typical modes of resistance seemingly available to all Batswana—such as the deployment of voting in order to activate a relationship of democratic accountability or the voicing of grievances at the *kgotla* (Tswana town hall)—become short-circuited for those citizens living on the conservation estate. The limits of this strategy to overcome the securitized paradigm of conservation is central to a key argument of this book—that local resistance on the conservation estate is vexed by the presence of countervailing state logics and differentiated citizen-state relations.

The core imaginaries of the state—in this case around democracy, consultation, and participation—become tested, fraught, and begin to collapse on the conservation estate due to a host of conflicting and contradictory logics apparent in the state-building process. From within this constellation, local people are left with a handful of strategies for negotiation, contestation, and resistance. This array of potential points of contestation does not necessarily provide a clear path for resistance, and local responses decrying failures of democratic norms on the conservation estate miss the ways in which the process of securitization of this conservation space has largely removed these policies from a fully participatory realm, rendering them exceptional in relation to the rest of the body politic. This chapter deals with this central dilemma: local peoples' persistent focus on the failures of the state to live up to its own participatory rhetoric is a rational response but one that is frequently stymied. When the logic of securitization predominates on the conservation estate, the invocation of democratic norms, those proudly espoused by the state itself, results in frustration, blockage, and resignation. To illustrate this, this chapter introduces the democratic imaginary that pervades the state and the way in which it directs local resistance toward mechanisms like the kgotla and voting that are problematized by the trends of securitization and top-down authority described previously. This further highlights the exceptionality of the conservation estate as a category of sociopolitical space in Botswana—caught between the imaginaries of democracy and the discourses of security. Conservation-adjacent citizens attempt to assert their apparent right to participate as Batswana but find that conventional, even traditional, modes of consultation are complicated due to the unique situation created by conservation. Finally, the elevation of the needs of co-local wildlife, as well as the preferences of international observers, raises key questions on the conservation estate: Who counts, and who is counted?

The Kgotla, Tradition, and the Democratic Imaginary in Botswana

> The tradition of the Kgotla provides a strong base on which to build a decentralised democracy. Democracy must be extended down to the level of community in a way that allows ordinary people to see that their views have been freely sought and seriously received.
>
> —*Vision 2016—a Long Term Vision for Botswana*[5]

A valuable source outlining Botswana's officially constructed and publicly consumed image of statehood is the document *Vision 2016—a Long Term Vision for Botswana*. Commonly referred to as Vision 2016, it is a government manifesto produced in the late 1990s by the Presidential Task Group on a Long Term Vision for Botswana, which encapsulates the aspirations for Botswana over the two decades leading up to the fiftieth anniversary of the country's independence in September 2016. The document's purpose is to shape the contours of postcolonial Botswana, and it is more aspirational than a fine-grained policy pronouncement. Demonstrating the self-imagination of the Botswana state and expressing the country's avowed priorities, Vision 2016 is useful in understanding state discourses that inundate the daily life of most Batswana—in schools, on the radio, and in interactions with government officials. The document encompasses a broad range of ideas and aspirations, but of particular note is the way in which it promotes the idea of national stability, the unity of all Batswana, the norms of consultation and democracy, and the notion that "the management of the environment and the control of natural resources must be shifted to the level of the community."[6]

A central pillar of Botswana's idealized future described in Vision 2016 is the country being "An Open, Democratic and Accountable Nation."[7] "Democracy" as an idea and as a mode of legitimate authority is important to Botswana's self-conceptualization, with leaders articulating the history of the kgotla as evidence for the country's indigenous traditions of participatory governance. The kgotla is a complex and nuanced institution that sits at the nexus of Tswana traditional authority, the government civil service, and postcolonial electoral politics (Gulbrandsen 1995, 1996, 2012; Kuper 1970; Maundeni 2002; Mogalakwe 2006; Molutsi and Holm 1989; Mompati and Prinsen 2000; Odell 1985; Roberts 1985; Schapera 1984; Vaughan 2003; Wylie 1990). With the kgotla system held up as an exemplar, leaders throughout the postcolonial era have emphatically localized the concepts of democracy and democratic decision-making, rejecting the notion of their importation from the West and evoking their roots in precolonial Botswana history and culture. Former vice president Peter Mmusi emphasized this mythos, noting, "We haven't learned democracy from America or England. It is inborn.... [It] grew from a system developed by our forefathers" (quoted in Wylie 1990, 211). Evocations of precolonial, consensus-based political cultures can be found articulated by many early independence leaders across the continent, including Botswana's founding father, Seretse Khama (Fawcus and Tilbury 2000). This is in keeping with much Africanist political theory that argues these elements of precolonial political traditions can render greater legitimacy to citizen-state practice in the postcolonial era (Maundeni 2004).

Embedded in this discourse is Vision 2016's call for extensive exercise of *therisanyo*, or consultation, across all levels of society in line with the apparently indigenous practice of democracy. Consultation is, in the Tswana system, about the consent of those who are ruled. Botswana's postcolonial state motto, *Puso ya botho ka botho* (Government of the People for the People) (Gulbrandsen 2012, 196), bears a strong resemblance to a traditional Tswana proverb, *Kgosi ke kgosi ka botho/merafe* (The chief is chief by virtue of the people/tribe) (Wylie 1990, 210). Both convey a sense of a check on the power of the rulers by the people being ruled and imply a spirit of consensus and consent. It is worth noting, and will be discussed at greater length in this chapter, that most Batswana living on the conservation estate are not ethnically Tswana, the group from which these traditions originate. However, this has not prevented these populations from deploying these sentiments in their contestations with state authority.

The rhetorical emphasis on therisanyo is echoed by subsequent state self-narrations. Throughout the postcolonial period, the widely articulated imaginary with regard to the conditions of political authority in Botswana was that major decisions would require extensive consultation across the breadth of the country. While this proposition was at times more theoretical than real in a straightforward sense, this mythology promotes the idea that popular, even "traditional," democracy exists above and beyond the act of participation in procedural elections. With the emphasis on therisanyo, legitimate authority in a democratic polity is constructed not only as procedural or representative democracy commonplace in Western democratic theory but also as a mode of quotidian democratic praxis. However, the gulf between the theory and practice will be explored below. Botswana has largely hewed closer to a procedural model of democracy, with the regularity of its free and fair elections (notable on the continent) and its emphasis on civil and political rights, rather than social and cultural rights. Nonetheless, state discourse tends to orient toward the imaginary—how the state describes and presents itself—around precolonial norms of consent and consultation.

The primary site of consultation is the kgotla, regardless of whether or not it meets the lofty ideals espoused in Vision 2016. The kgotla, which encapsulates a rich history of precolonial origins as well as colonial and postcolonial adaptations, is both a physical place (usually situated at the center of any village or settlement) and an institution imbued with particular norms and social rules. It is perceived as the main venue through which leaders and officials address citizens. As such, the interactions at the kgotla have been constructed as integral to the formation of state imaginaries on the part of both ruler and ruled. In the government's 10th National Development Plan, language first introduced in the Vision 2016 document is used to describe the importance of the kgotla in the state's self-narration: "Vision 2016 sees the tradition of the Kgotla to be providing a strong base on which to build democracy; that through the use of the Kgotla, democracy must be extended down to the level of community in a way that allows ordinary people to feel that their views have been freely sought and taken seriously received."[8]

This excerpt exemplifies the elevation of the kgotla in state discourses as a locally cognizable metric for assessing the practice of legitimate authority. It suggests that the state sees itself, or at least presents itself, as wielding authority through the people based not only on a representative basis but on a participatory one as well. Beyond holding free and fair elections every five years (often a primary, though certainly not only, external metric for democracy) Botswana crafts a local legitimation of authority distinct from common external metrics. Outside of the academy, the kgotla itself is little recognized by foreign audiences (such as international rankers of democracies) but acts as an internal legitimizer for local society. For example, the democracy ranking produced by Freedom House, which is often cited in media and incorporated into datasets and quantitative analysis in political science, makes no mention of the institution of the kgotla.[9] Botswana's external plaudits for its democratic norms focus on the frequency and consistency of elections, perception of low corruption, rule of law, and the independence of the judiciary, among others. It is noteworthy to contrast how the domestic focus imbues greater significance to consultative forums of consensus. The kgotla is held up as the gold standard—the means through which to contest policies, announce support, or articulate grievances. While the *dikgotla* (the plural of *kgotla*) exist alongside "freedom squares" (which were established in the 1960s as a means for communication outside of traditional structures), they are still the main forum for communication with government officials and elected representatives (Lekorwe 1989). Integral to Botswana's socially constructed vision of its own stateness is the notion that the kgotla exists to connect local people to their government. The kgotla is described as more permanent, deep, and meaningful than electoral contests held every five years. The proposition of citizen involvement in policies and governance often reiterated by government officials and in state media with high-ranking cabinet ministers articulates the position that "people's right for governance does not end with ballot paper."[10]

Importantly, the aim of Vision 2016 is not only to ostensibly guide government policy—it is explicit about its role in state building and the creation of citizen subjectivities. It frames its purpose beyond a dry policy document to promote the ambitious goal to "change the mindset of every Motswana."[11] Indeed, the document calls for a "concerted campaign" to instill its stated values in the populace, noting that "the ideas behind the Vision must be communicated and explained as widely as possible, using every medium available, including the press, radio and television, the schools and university."[12] This becomes integral both to the creation of citizenship in the postcolonial era and to the construction of the relationship between citizen and state. How this plays out—or is confounded—on the conservation estate is central to understanding the unique sociopolitical contexts on this category of land.

The Kgotla and Its Discontents

Despite the stated enthusiasm for the kgotla in Botswana self-narrations, a critical eye is required. Not all observers of, or indeed participants in, the kgotla system are as sanguine about its role in postcolonial Botswana society. Some argue it represents not localized democracy but rather a form of imposed traditional authority (de Jager and Sebudubudu 2017). Its provenance as an institution from the precolonial Tswana *merafe*, or proto-states, has been highlighted as key feature of the creation of a postcolonial society around Tswana norms, culture, language, and traditions, at times to the detriment of non-Tswana Batswana (Gulbrandsen 2012). Scholars have argued that the kgotla, as an institution, is a central feature of the process of mono-ethnic state building around "Tswanadom" in the postcolonial era, with its preeminence in the national imagery highlighting the extent of so-called Tswanafication of non-Tswana ethnolinguistic minorities (Gulbrandsen 2012; Nthomang 2004; Sapignoli 2018). Others have argued that the assimilationist logic of rendering the kgotla a national institution reflects the skewed power dynamics of their operations, which tend to reinscribe marginalities upon participants who are non-Tswana, women, or youth. They have noted that dikgotla remain spaces of inequality for women, minorities (especially the San), and young people (Lekorwe 1989; Mompati and Prinsen 2000). Quite often the main performative aspect of the kgotla—the dialogue between the ruler and the ruled—is the most highly choreographed moment. Those local residents able to ask questions of visiting officials are restricted to three or four individuals, usually with the people and questions determined beforehand by a screening process (Sapignoli 2018). Nonetheless, over several decades of consistent state promotion of these ideals in the public sphere, conservation-adjacent Batswana appear to take promises of consultation and participation as credible parts of the state's mythology and express dismay when they appear to fall short, as the empirical data presented below describe. The next section will engage with the question of what happens when local people attempt to operationalize the seemingly open, participatory forums of consultation on the conservation estate.

Consultation and the Kgotla on the Conservation Estate

> There was no official communication with us. I thought we were supposed to be informed officially by way of a kgotla meeting.
>
> —Resident of Boro[13]

The role of the kgotla is more than just rhetoric for many of the state's frontline workers. Government bureaucrats and conservation practitioners emphasize the need to use the traditional function of the kgotla as a consultative forum when making decisions, especially those related to the environment and resources.[14] A senior official in the Department of Wildlife and National Parks described the way in which many public servants consider kgotla consultation as central to state practice and integral to their imagining of their own role as agents of the state. He said, "First and foremost you have to consult. In our case consulting means going to the grassroots—going to the kgotla meetings."[15] This reflects a genuine buy-in from many frontline government workers tasked with the practical responsibility of engaging with the people of the conservation estate. As described below in further detail, throughout the data collection for this project there was some disquiet within this segment of state actors when they felt this consultative process was overlooked, compromised, or merely performative. Yet on the conservation estate the ideal of consultation has not always aligned with the actual rollout of policy, and there are numerous examples of the gulf between the theory of community consultation and the effectuation of policy. This can include lack of consultation around long-standing practices going back decades, like the use and presence of the Botswana Defence Force in conservation communities, but also discrete, impactful changes like the 2014 hunting ban.

The concerns about the lack of local consultation expressed by DWNP officials, especially those regional-level staffers working on the conservation estate, stemmed from their awareness of the local-level perceptions of wildlife and conservation in communities. A junior-level DWNP research official in Maun expressed frustration about the disjuncture between the high-level discussion around wildlife pitched at a continental and global audience, compared with the daily grind of dealing with communities impacted by human-elephant conflict.[16] In this instance, he believed the approach to charismatic animal conservation in particular was alienating and failed to adequately address the concerns of human populations sharing land, water, and other resources with wildlife. He noted that Botswana's number of elephants "makes for a good story. It looks like a conservation success in New York City,

London, or Manchester. But for the person on the ground, this is forcing a very dangerous environment."[17]

Throughout my fieldwork, respondents with incredibly diverse backgrounds and positionalities, including local residents of the conservation estate and even duly elected MPs,[18] reported not being consulted about wide-ranging and impactful policies like the hunting ban or conservation enforcement policies. Many asserted that they should have been made part of the decision-making process.[19] What this indicates in these instances is the subtle conversion of the kgotla from a venue of consultation to an arena for dissemination, wherein it becomes a unidirectional conduit for government to inform of policy rather than an imagined space of exchange. This has far-reaching impacts not only for how state authority is viewed locally on the conservation estate but also for how the practices of state are enacted across the country.

Take for example, the 2014 hunting ban decision. When the issue was finally addressed in dikgotla in villages on the conservation estate, it was not for consultation but rather for dissemination. People in these communities expressed the sentiment that the decisions had already been taken before the meetings, and they were expected not to consent after participation and consultation but to acquiesce to a fait accompli. One respondent described the policies arriving in the community predetermined and not up for debate in the community.[20] Therefore, while the institution of the kgotla is vital to the discourse of democratic governance propagated by state agents, there is a significant disconnect from the practice on the ground where kgotla meetings are most typically used as places to deliver "policy pronouncements ... [, where] people [are] not being engaged, stakeholders not being engaged" and where "unilateral decisions" are announced.[21]

Officials, at times as high-ranking as the president or government ministers, attend kgotla meetings to announce a decision rather than to ask for views. The vignettes attesting to this from my fieldwork all occurred during the Khama presidency, but this is relatively commonplace on the conservation estate and should not be construed as a feature of only one presidential administration, being rather evident across several decades of state interventions on the conservation estate. As an example, Sapignoli (2018) and other scholars of the Central Kalahari noted this precise mode of state use of the kgotla in the 1980s when these forums were used to announce decisions to communities in Central Kalahari Game Reserve, rather than hear the opinions and preferences of the citizenry. In discussions with a prominent community activist from the CKGR resettlement communities, he described those early kgotla meetings not as open spaces of dialogue with the state but as catalyzing events in the long chain of causation leading up to the evictions and forced removals from the protected area.[22] Decades later during my fieldwork in a conservation-adjacent communities in this area, and to the north as well, I heard echoes of this same dynamic.

A group of women in the village of Sankuyo, a community well known for its proximity to lucrative conservation areas and with a historical involvement in the tourism industry, recalled the then-president's visit to their kgotla in the weeks leading up to the

FIGURE 3.1. *Kgotla* building in the village of Khwai. Author's photograph.

January 2014 hunting ban. They described how President Khama did not come to seek their views about the hunting ban: "The problem is that when they come to the people, they have already made a decision.... The government doesn't consult us. We will just hear that there are meetings, and we will be told that the final decision has been made without taking our opinions and ideas. We will love if the government can consult us before making the decision."[23]

The political space that local residents believe operates as a two-way channel between the rulers and the ruled is, in reality, often an institution facilitating the dissemination of government decisions to local levels. This mechanism of dissemination is unlike the mythical space of indigenous democratic traditions praised in state-sponsored discourse, though neither does the historical reality of the kgotla fully match its current idealization (Gulbrandsen 2012).[24] For the most part, as the above quote illustrates, local residents have bought into the notion of the kgotla as a principal metaphor for how the exercise of authority should be manifest. This, in fact, is a testament to the effectiveness of the postcolonial efforts at uniform state building around the traditions of Tswana society and its ability to create a political institution imbued with legitimate authority across a culturally heterogeneous population. This is all the more notable when considering that most of the conservation-adjacent communities are inhabited by ethnolinguistic minorities who have—to various levels of enthusiasm—embraced the Tswana institution of the kgotla as a symbol of postcolonial civic participation. However, these very same residents are frustrated when they believe adequate consultation has not been done appropriately. They argue that the due diligence of "consultation," which pervades so much of the discursive culture of government in Botswana, is lacking. During the lead-up to the national hunting ban and the early days of its implementation in 2014, local residents and traditional authorities alike conveyed frustration that they first heard of the ban not through a kgotla but hearsay, rumors, and media outlets. The village *kgosi* in Kacgae in Ghanzi District noted: "We heard about the hunting ban through rumors, the newspaper, the radio. Professionally, as a kgosi, [I feel that] these things are supposed to be addressed in the kgotla. No official came to tell us what was happening. I am still not sure why. . . . Government should be done at the kgotla level. But instead they just changed things, bringing a complete idea without explaining the reason for the change."[25] By arguing that "government should be done at the kgotla level," the respondent is attempting to negotiate the enactment of authority and the responsiveness of state authorities to the citizenry, especially for communities like his that exist on the conservation estate. The potentialities for the imposition of direct state control, often through the presence of the military, heightens the stakes for maintaining the integrity of kgotla traditions on the conservation estate.

Moreover, the above quote is additionally insightful because it demonstrates the degree to which the state has been extremely effective at getting buy-in from local people (especially non-Tswana) concerning the kgotla. This is not trivial. Rather, it has immense implications for the state-building process in these parts of the country that are inhabited by non-Tswana ethnic groups but have nonetheless adopted this form of social and political organization as a means of direct dialogue with central state actors and is demonstrative of the power of postcolonial state building. It is also a rebuke to the arguments that ethnic identity politics are divisive, when non-Tswana communities have embraced an originally Tswana institution (albeit with plenty of historical baggage) as a symbol of unified postcolonial citizenship and state authority. However, the problem arises when these very communities on the conservation estate begin to believe—with some credible experiential evidence—that the articulated promise of a responsive and accountable state authority is not being upheld. In short, the state is failing to uphold its side of the bargain.

The work of bypassing or downplaying the kgotla's potential capacity for dialogue shows the detrimental impact on local perceptions of legitimate authority when the institution is ignored, as is often the case with decisions made about the securitized conservation estate. Beyond illustrating the specific frustration at the way communities were informed about the hunting ban, the above quote from a village kgosi is also a critique of a central fiction of the kgotla model: while it is articulated as a space of intersection between equal stakeholders—the people and the state—in large part it only functions as a mechanism of the state. The differentials in power at the kgotla level are substantial, impacting the ideal functioning of the institution as a site to temper state authority. It is open as a venue for consultation, when the state deems it necessary.

State authorities set the terms of when the kgotla is used, by whom, and how. Local people are not empowered to summon or demand attendance of their national leaders at the kgotla when there is discontent regarding a policy, and consequently it functions as an arm of the state. This dynamic can be seen across the board—and not limited to the conservation estate. However, the often life-and-death policy stakes of the conservation estate does make the conditions for its residents unique. This is not to downplay the importance of state policy on non-conservation areas but to reemphasize the exceptionality of lived experiences of those residing on the conservation estate. When conservation-adjacent citizens lack the chance to express their opinions on policies, they perceive themselves to be ignored and neglected by the authorities, especially considering the singular magnitude with which conservation policies directly impact their lives. Recall the manner in which conservation policies implicate a whole host of behaviors—such as the ability to move freely around one's ancestral home or use land and resources necessary for basic survival—that are deeply embodied and impactful to people's subjective understanding of themselves in relation to the state. Moreover, the imbricated marginalities of the class of citizens resident on the conservation estate has led scholars to categorize them as subalterns, highlighting the power differentials in this context (Mbaiwa and Hambira 2023).

Respondents viewed government policies as brought to the conservation estate in their final form—not subject to renegotiation or further consideration. A young man involved with the community trust in Khwai described the hunting ban as "brought to us as a solid stone.... It was a complete thing that we were handed."[26] Despite the fact that many respondents felt they *should* have been consulted prior to this decision (as seen earlier in this section), they also believed that there was very little they could have done to alter the situation as it now stands. An older Bayei man from Sankuyo further characterized this "finality" in a martial context: "The decision is final, and there is nothing we can do about it. The problem is that this is a military government. By its nature, a military government does not listen to the people."[27] For him, the lack of consultation is not a failure of Botswana's democratic norms but indicative that the very nature of authority on Botswana's conservation estate is overtly coercive. For this respondent, the mask of participation has been pulled away. This cannot be disentangled from the long-standing presence of the BDF and other armed agents of the state on the conservation estate. While Botswana is quite obviously not run by a military junta, from his perspective, as a resident on the conservation estate, the primary state agents he sees are military or law enforcement personnel. In the respondent's context, the principal mode through which bureaucrats and elected officials communicate is via dictates. From his lived experience, Botswana is more akin to a military government, and, importantly, his lived experience is not outweighed by the macro-level indicators of Botswana's democracy. His belief is clearly grounded in and on the securitized conservation estate.

When the local traditional authorities took umbrage not only at the fact that they were not consulted about the hunting ban but also that the community was not even officially informed of the change in any proactive manner, they had no recourse to demand an audience with decision-makers. National politicians cannot be summoned to the kgotla. Instead, the kgotla is used when and how the state sees fit. Therefore, the institution of the kgotla continues to serve a vital political purpose for those in power, as it provides the veneer of consultation and deliberation, even if the ultimate policies are set and finalized before the officials leave Gaborone. However, even if central authorities do seek input from the citizenry, it is done on the state's terms and timeline, not necessarily corresponding to local demands, which may go years unheard, if ever acknowledged. An instructive example is the decision to *use* the kgotla system and widespread consultation at the end of the hunting ban in 2018 and 2019 (see Mbaiwa and Hambira 2023 for a detailed accounting). Local people had been demanding to be heard on this issue for years, but only the state could initiate this kind of outreach. This, in turn, can result in state authorities getting the type of feedback and consultation that they want, coalescing with a predetermined set of priorities. When it became clear that the new president wanted to end the hunting ban, the consultation process was used to bolster the state position. This does not suggest that the kgotla could never be used in a responsive manner but rather that the massive gulf in power differentials for actors engaging in kgotla dialogue render the use of the space to manufacture consent a possibility.

Ultimately the ambivalence of state narratives around consultation works to construct a widespread belief on the conservation estate that the residents are a subset of citizens uniquely lacking substantive voice and political agency touted in national imaginaries. Decisions related to antipoaching and other resource-use restrictions work to structure a system wherein local people of the conservation estate feel untethered from the set of rules and modes of authority that they have been told to recognize for their whole lives—the promise of consultation articulated in the state's own narration of itself. A middle-aged man expressed this sense of confusion in relation to conservation, stating, "Government keeps on abruptly changing rules and regulations on the utilization of natural resources but in a contradictory manner."[28] This encapsulates a greater disruption felt when the norms of consultation are discarded, as is commonplace in the securitized landscape of the conservation estate. In postcolonial Botswana, all Batswana (even those from non-Tswana backgrounds) are familiar with state authorities who emphasize the kgotla as a spatial and institutional interlocutor between the rulers and ruled. As such, the kgotla has been invested with significance not only by those in power but also by those they seek to rule, who see it as a mechanism through which to be heard. And while in the past the kgotla has perhaps been overidealized, and at times manipulated, the frequent decision over the years to bypass it with regard to certain conservation policies contributes to fractures in the participatory consensus in which many local people still believe.

Who Counts? Expertise on the Conservation Estate

> They [the government] always concern themselves with what the international community says about Botswana. . . . They don't pay attention to how the ordinary Motswana is impacted.
>
> —Resident of Xuoxao[29]

Some respondents explicitly expressed resentment at the fact that, as they viewed it, people from outside their area were making conservation decisions regarding land and resources to which they felt intimately connected. This positioning constructs a moral and political universe wherein the local supersedes the idea of the nation that sits at the heart of securitization discourse discussed in the previous chapter. One of the central and unique characteristics of the conservation estate is the way in which it renders previously marginal territories places of intense interest on the part of national and international actors. Garland suggests that conservation is what she calls a "translocal social field," through which subjectivities and reputations can be defined, articulated, and contested and through which relationships at a variety of scales are manifest in international and domestic systems (2008, 64). She urges that scholars attend to the "tradeoffs and calculations that get made at the level of African nation-states when a decision to pursue a conservationist strategy is taken, or how such a strategy could affect both the nation-state's standing in an international context and its relationship with rural populations on the ground in the areas where the programs are to be implemented" (65). Interviewees throughout the conservation estate utilized repertoires of local participation, an ideal espoused in state discourse, to contest decisions seen as led by the central state, drawing their authority from local expertise and knowledge rather than the emergency discourses used to justify securitized state authority. One respondent directly encapsulated this view of state interventions: "Instead of banning hunting [in 2014], government should engage us to figure out and solve any problems concerning hunting activities. We live alongside these animals. We know them better than people from Gaborone or further afield who want to tell us how to live with them."[30] This man is invoking the legitimate authority to speak for animals and rejecting the notion of state authority used to justify the securitization of conservation spaces in service of animal protection. Moreover, here he defines expertise as a signal that consultation is necessary. Yet, in his telling, the label of "expert" is not given to government officials or technocrats who have formal markers of expertise—degrees, professional qualifications, and the like—but live away from the conservation estate. Rather, it is the local people who are best equipped to "do conservation." Similarly, many interviewees see consultation as a means to work with the government, not strictly as a means to express an antigovernment stance, a participatory model of citizen-state relations where authority is coproduced rather than asserted through coercion. This perspective notes how consultation can be used to solve problems relating to wildlife and resource management because of their local knowledge, arguing that people of the conservation estate have valuable skills to contribute to the policymaking realm. They can be, in fact, a net positive for resource management, and by extension the state as a whole, rather than merely a hindrance or threat. Consultation, in this rendering, is presented as an avenue to ameliorate localnational tensions, to bridge the perceived gulf, and to participate in state endeavors rather than being viewed as an obstacle. People living on the conservation estate view the failure of the government to recognize their conservation bona fides as a disregard for, or even outright denial of, their grievances.[31] Nonetheless, there are some interviewees who take the line of argumentation even further, suggesting that this failure to meaningfully consult and engage their communities constitutes a denial of their rights as Batswana, which is something that does not occur with other communities, making their experience unique and exceptional among Botswana's citizens. A middle-aged man living in the village of Boro in Northwest District articulated this position: "One feels like government is denying us rights which we are entitled to like the rest of Batswana. It breeds mistrust between government and the community. Even if the president was to come here, we will regard him as a threat to our lifestyle."[32] Very directly, this respondent is describing his subjective understanding of how he experiences state authority. He perceives himself as a different kind of citizen due to the political conditions of conservation. By contrasting his position to "the rest of Batswana," he is making a claim that life on the conservation estate is exceptional and outside the normal experiences of his fellow countrymen living elsewhere across the state's territory. However, his exceptionality is not that of Agamben's state of exception as recounted in the previous chapter but rather (somewhat ironically as an ethnic minority) that the exceptionality of his citizenship is out of step with the postcolonial state-building project predicated upon equality and uniform citizenship. He is using the state's own project to show its contradictions on the conservation estate.

At their core, failures of consultation are not merely technical but also work to orient the ways in which conservation-adjacent people imagine themselves within the state system: Are they subjects of state authority or engaged citizens? Many continue to forcefully argue that despite being shut out of the key decision-making processes impacting their lives and livelihoods, that legitimate authority remains invested with them. A young man encapsulated this view by saying, "The community is the rightful decision-maker. Government should consult the community."[33] When consultation is removed, local people view political decisions such as the use of force in antipoaching and other resource-use restrictions as illegitimate. Yet the perceived illegitimacy does not temper the policies' significance; they still impact day-to-day existence on the conservation estate. This is a powerful assertion of local authority grounded not in state institutions or practices but rather in locally legitimate notions of governance, consent, and authority. As such, policies made without local perspectives are viewed as illegitimate, and many believe that unlike in other areas of Botswana, policy decisions with day-to-day ramifications are made with foreigners, not locals, in mind.[34]

As the conservation estate becomes a site of international interest in an exceptional manner compared with other rural spaces in Botswana, the relationship between citizens and the state is mediated by the international system and various international interlocutors including tourists, conservation advocates, and safari company operators. This disrupts citizen-state relationships by seemingly privileging the conservation imperatives of these groups, especially regarding charismatic megafauna like elephants. This dynamic is not found elsewhere in the country. The Western conservation gaze is entirely uninterested in the rural Tswana cattle post, the focal point of the non-conservation countryside, for example. Non-local people, often consumers or creators of a very particular kind of wildlife experience, exert a significant amount of power with regard to the way conservation is enacted in Botswana. This outwardly focused orientation works to displace the connection between the state and its citizens residing on the conservation estate. This disruption is felt unevenly over Botswana's territory, creating a uniquely disenfranchising experience of citizenship for those living in conservation areas.

Duffy suggests that policies that may deter foreign "ecotourists" or that are not favored by the "experts" in influential environmental NGOs are sublimated by domestic elites in order to maintain the state's position as a site of wildlife tourism. What Duffy (2002) calls "marketing the nation state" is the deliberate shaping of an image of a place for the international tourism market in a way that may bear little relationship to the lived experiences of local people. While the cultivation of imaginaries of state is incumbent in every state-building process, Duffy argues that these dynamics are omnipresent in the context of wildlife tourism because of the ways in which national and international actors are central to the creation and exportation of a national imaginary "primarily intended to appeal to visitors rather than residents" (2002, 72).

The tourist industries that buoy the Botswana state and economy remain highly dependent on external relationships and international visitors. In an interview with the park management team of Moremi Game Reserve (one of the most popular protected areas in Botswana), the staff recounted seeing at most a dozen Batswana tourists in a year. They explained this dearth in cultural terms, noting that "Batswana do not go to the protected areas a lot because we have *moraka* [cattle post], *masimo* [crop fields] where we go there maybe also to relax. . . . Some people have never even gone to protected areas even though they have money."[35] Those Batswana who can afford the expense of a wildlife safari seem to be less enthusiastic, on aggregate, about this type of leisure activity.[36] To many Batswana, holidays are still often associated with the rural homestead, the moraka, at the heart of Tswana cattle culture. The cattle post—not the wildlife sanctuary—remains the primary rural experience of most Batswana not native to the conservation estate, reproducing the divide between what is viewed as a typical "rural experience" and what is considered a "wilderness experience."[37] This unfamiliarity and the distinction it creates perpetuate the stereotypical perceptions of areas of "the bush" as wild, untamed, and outside the geographical space of mainstream society. These spaces are separate from the moral universe constructed as "normal" and "ordered," and most Batswana, though certainly not all, with the means to travel for pleasure choose to eschew wilderness experiences. This has two effects: the wilderness appeal is viewed as a somewhat odd preoccupation of those from the Global North,[38] further illustrating the industry's dependence on external consumers, and it creates a distinction between the type of Batswana who consider themselves "rural" and those who live in the "wilderness" of the conservation estate. Therefore, Botswana's core tourism industries are highly dependent on foreign consumption, the state may proactively produce the very conditions to keep Western tourists "buying" Botswana's conservation, even in the face of local opposition.

Reflecting on the daily logistics of getting local people on the conservation estate to talk to me about my research clearly illuminates the way in which they understood their relationship to the state as mediated to an extent by foreigners. Interview participants frequently argued that decisions impacting daily life on the conservation estate were made in response to the needs and desires of people who look and sound like me (an educated, relatively wealthy white foreigner from the Global North) and who embody the same privileges that I do. In light of this, many seemed to view me as a potential conduit to connect them to the halls of power, to a state system by which they feel paradoxically both alienated and ignored as well as surveilled and controlled. Many respondents seemed to view our conversations as acts of negotiation or resistance—a means through which to assert a position of expertise and authority based on their communities' long-standing ability to live side by side with wildlife and hopefully have that message conveyed to those in power. A man in the village of Sankuyo ended our conversation with a call to action. He had been frustrated and confused by what he saw as contradictory state pronouncements and lack of answers regarding how the government would help his community weather the impacts of the hunting ban. He said, "Government will give you answers because of you being white. I plead with you to take our concerns to government. Foreigners are [more] listened to than locals.... Go tell your fellow nationals that the communities of Sankuyo, Mababe and Khwai are having it hard."[39] Pragmatically, engaging in an interview with me was viewed as an innovative way to express opposition to the hunting ban, the most stinging of the state's restrictive policies during the time of my fieldwork and a policy whose justification was framed around certain "expert" opinions about wildlife protection. A man in New Xade expressly connected his time spent with me to the end-goal of government officials hearing his position and recognizing his expertise: "I have given you a lot of information. We conserved for a long time; we stayed for a long time without extincting [sic] animals. The government should go and read what I have given you and should do something to change policies."[40]

Perhaps in recognition of the disconnect between the local, national, and global scales, narratives of resistance, in order to claim their own kind of authority, utilized discourses of participatory conservation and local knowledge, articulating historical and contemporary proximity to wildlife as a means to argue that conservation-adjacent Batswana are best suited to determine how resources are used. While the appeal to regionally and spatially specific knowledge is not an explicitly ethnic claim (though later chapters will examine that type of claim), these calls do stress the point that there is a lack of understanding of what it means to live with co-local wildlife, and on the conservation estate generally, by other Batswana. This divide exists not only between the urban dwellers and conservation-adjacent communities but also between rural people who do not live on the conservation estate.

In a practical, quotidian sense, most wildlife management and resource-use policies do not impact the urban dwellers of Gaborone or Francistown or even residents of eastern Botswana's rural villages but rather those Batswana living on the conservation estate. This is, in some ways, obvious. For the people of the conservation estate, unlike other Batswana, wildlife management are issues central to their quality of life and ability to make a living, as well as the way in which they view themselves in relation to the wider social polity. When a prominent San activist said quite pithily, "We need to be given a chance to have a say in how we will live,"[41] he was saying that people on the conservation estate are not only seeking to secure an economic strategy or resource-use plan but are also endeavoring to secure a modicum of self-determination and democratic citizenship within a polity that overtly expresses these ideals in speeches, position papers, and on the radio. By evoking these differences and subtly highlighting the hypocrisy, the distinct contours of citizen-state relations that exist on the conservation estate become apparent. Local people perceive themselves as exceptionally left out of the supposed mainstream consensus around therisanyo and the other ideals embedded in the national mythology. While assimilation to mainstream sociopolitical norms and institutions goes on, they are still denied the same set of rights as other Batswana. This exposes the embedded tensions of an assimilationist state-building project enacted in a unique and exceptional sociopolitical space, the conservation estate. In part III, I will examine the double bind that people on the conservation estate find themselves in—their specifically ethnolinguistic claims of difference and indigeneity are rejected, but, as this chapter notes, often their invocations of mainstream citizenship and belonging are ignored too.

Who Is Counted? Electoral Politics and the Conservation Estate

> They did not come to get our opinion on the that issue.
> They simply make decisions for us without consulting us.
>
> —Resident of the village of Mababe[42]

While the proclaimed ideals of the kgotla may be illusory and their attempts to count as experts unsuccessful, people on the conservation estate still cast a ballot every five years. Recognizing that politicians come to their communities in the hopes of winning their votes,[43] local people want (and try) to leverage one of the few things in their possession they view as potentially valuable—their ability to go to the ballot box. As one participant in a group interview in Qabo noted, "When they do a law, they have to come and consult the community first. We are the ones who vote them in. When they want to do something that will impact us, they must consult before they do the decision. They just can't take a decision from themselves."[44] This interview participant is invoking notions of democratic accountability, which adhere to the idea that elected officials should be responsive to the needs of their constituents. When decisions are made that are contrary to their needs and even appear to value the needs of wildlife over people, interviewees on the conservation estate are quick to explain why this is incongruous with Botswana's self-imagining as a democracy. An older man in the Ghanzi resettlement village Bere noted, "Government should also protect us. It should know that we are its people. Government prioritizes wild animals over people. Animals can't be taken from the bush to come and cast votes."[45] The respondent here is subtly playing on the idea of citizenship. Who are the citizens—the animals or the people? And who does the government serve, if not the voters in a democracy? Who gets counted?

As noted in the previous chapter, Botswana's resident wildlife populations become anthropomorphized to the point where they are imbued with political subjectivities, often to the detriment of the co-local human populations of the conservation estate. The restructuring of the moral and political universe to include animals-cum-citizens also leads to a conservation position that downgrades the predicament of human-wildlife conflict and envisions "a wild nature that poses no threat beyond the threat of disappearing" (Neumann 2004b, 212). The primary beneficiaries of this reordering are animal populations themselves but also those people able to capitalize on marketing of animals as live commodities through safari experiences to visitors from the Global North. Very infrequently are they people living on the conservation estate (Mbaiwa and Hambira 2020).

The conservation estate creates qualitatively different experiences of citizenship within the state, despite an adamant rhetoric of equality and unity on the part of the authorities. The experiences of rural people in Botswana are not uniformly different from those of the urban dwellers but are varied by the way in which the imperatives of the conservation estate structure the experiences of a particular segment of rural people who live alongside one of Botswana's most important natural resources: wildlife. While human-wildlife conflict is identified as a major challenge by many DWNP officials,[46] on the ground local Batswana feel ignored and neglected by the authorities responsible for wildlife, especially elephants. This is borne out by the widespread feeling that "they [DWNP] are quick[er] to respond to poaching than they are to problem animals."[47] There is a pervasive view that state conservation policy privileges the needs of wildlife over the needs and aspirations of the citizens of the conservation estate. There is a clear recognition among the residents of the conservation estate that the commodification of co-local wildlife fills the national coffers, but they vehemently question whether this benefits them in any material sense. A woman in Xuoxao recalled candidly, "I am of the view that the lives of the people, who live in a tourism area that generates a lot of money like ours, should be better. The financial success of the wild animal tourism industry should be reflected through the standard of living of its residents. There shouldn't be a mismatch."[48] Beyond simply the perceived injustice of living with co-local wildlife without reaping the rewards, residents also asserted a spatially differentiated experience of their relationship to the state due to the copresence of wildlife. Living in day-to-day contact with wildlife produces an articulation of difference as an act of claim-making to specific, particularized rights as human residents—and voting constituents—of the conservation estate. A former MP, a native son of the Northwest District but a resident in Gaborone for many decades, made this case by arguing categorically that if an animal, such as an elephant, made its way to the capital city, it would be shot, "whereas people living in the Chobe, the people living in Ngamiland [Northwest District], they *are expected* to live with elephants" (emphasis mine).[49] The privileging of wildlife—as political refugees, for example—has a distorting effect on the relation of the state to citizens, and, importantly, this distortion is different and varied across the breadth of Botswana. This transforms what it means to be a citizen and the social relations that constitute it. As certain charismatic species begin to be perceived as moral subjects in their own right, the question of who or what deserves the protection and consideration of the state becomes apparent. The umbrella of "citizenship" and security is rhetorically expanded in such a way that the presence of wildlife alongside conservation-adjacent citizens fundamentally mediates, alters, and reorders their relationship to authority.

Local people see the act of voting as creating a relationship of obligation between the elected official and the community—they expect their MPs should advocate for them regardless of the presence of co-local wildlife in their constituency. Yet the logic of this classic resistance to an unwanted policy (petitioning one's elected representative) begins to fray with regard to many environmental policies in Botswana because of the "emergency" logics applied to conservation and wildlife. The securitizing speech acts described in the previous chapter lift certain policies out of and beyond the strictly political realm. The occluded nature of policymaking in a securitized environment makes it difficult for local people to realize that even the seemingly straightforward approach of issue-based voting is problematized by the way in which these sets of issues are dealt with on the national stage, primarily by "emergency" or firmly within the realm of the security establishment, which tends to be opaque to the average citizen.

Local respondents use this situation to call into the question the democratic bona fides Botswana has often touted domestically and internationally as an "African miracle" (see chapter 1). An interviewee in the village of Khwai explicitly invoked Botswana's democratic standing and the seeming hypocrisy of the lack of consultation: "We are living in a democratic country. Democracy should be done and followed thoroughly, and not being consulted is . . . another way of ignoring the democracy. . . . Because obviously if you suggest something, you should give people . . . time to think of it and see how it affects their life. That's how you should take a decision, collectively not just individually."[50] There is a savvy, tactical use of Botswana's much-touted democratic reputation in order to contest what is seen by conservation-adjacent citizens as authoritative overreach, using the very institutions and discourses promoted by the state in order to resist state action. When the state falls short of this idealized discourse that has been made readily available for public consumption, these same citizens attempt to invoke the government's own focus on consensus-driven politics as a means of protest and resistance and as a rejection of decisions made without their consultation. It is a rational attempt at resistance when a lack of consultation occurs. A man in the village of Boro encapsulated this approach by saying, "These kind of decisions are the opposite of democracy. Democracy is about trust and fairness."[51] By equating democracy not just with the act of filling out a ballot paper every five years, he is harking back to a broader definition of democracy that the state refers to when invoking the kgotla and Vision 2016 and somewhat ironically demonstrating the effectiveness of the state's educative project. In doing so, he is arguing that the state's top-down mode of securitized implementation of policy on the conservation estate is a direct contradiction of the idealized rhetoric used to describe its historical and contemporary democratic systems.

Throughout my fieldwork, respondents on the conservation estate equated their lack of consultation with a derogation of their rights as democratic citizens, often explicitly invoking the norms of a democratic social contract between constituent voter and elected official as a rationale for why their concerns and anxieties should not be sublimated to the needs of co-local wildlife. Failures of consultation at the kgotla, top-down dictates, the predominance of state coercive agents, and the overall alienating dynamics of the policies on the conservation estate coincides with the areas of the conservation estate largely being friendly electoral terrain for various opposition parties. While I am not suggesting a direct causal link (and there have been members of the ruling Botswana Democratic Party elected in constituencies on the conservation estate), the conservation estate differs from other rural areas of the country by its general lack of support for the BDP.

When President Khama stepped down after two terms in April 2018, his loyal vice president, Mokgweetsi Masisi, became president under the constitution's automatic succession rule. However, President Masisi would have to face the voters in his own right in the upcoming October 2019 general election. In the months after Masisi's accession to the presidency, the upcoming electoral contest was widely seen as likely to be the most competitive in Botswana's history, and there was concern within the BDP that the party could lose its parliamentary majority for the first time. It is from within this context that Masisi undertook series of decisions related to conservation policy, including major reversals of Botswana's stance on the ivory trade and the ending of President Khama's signature hunting ban (LaRocco and Mogende 2022). Observers, analysts, and politicians inside and outside of the country understood these moves, especially the systematic use of kgotla meetings and community dialogue leading up to the cessation of the hunting ban, as a way to generate goodwill in areas of historical opposition strength, thus bringing the electorally exceptional conservation estate into the fold of the BDP's other rural strongholds to the east.[52]

However, the political geography of the 2019 election results presents an intriguing paradox that counters some of the conventional wisdom associated with the changes in conservation under President Masisi. While constituencies on the conservation estate, especially in the areas north near the Okavango Delta and Chobe National Park, have historically been opposition strongholds, the general sentiment leading up to election day assumed the changes to conservation policy might redound to the BDP's benefit and allow the party to shed some of its associations with unpopular policies in the region. Yet these predictions did not come to pass. Rural voters, particularly in Ngamiland, voted for the main opposition party, the Umbrella for Democratic Change (UDC), largely in keeping with past electoral choice.

While the changes in conservation policies did move in the direction of the preferences of many communities on the conservation estate and the BDP was ultimately victorious in the 2019 contest on a national level, the parliamentary constituencies of the conservation estate remain for the most part in opposition control (Brown 2020). The paradox demands interrogation of the commentary in the lead-up to the election, which cast the changes to conservation policy, especially with regard to hunting, as a ploy to sway voters.[53] If this was the intent behind these policies changes, it was relatively unsuccessful on the conservation estate, whereas the BDP did make substantial improvements in the country's urban constituencies, which have also been typically associated with the opposition.

There are several potential explanations for this. The first is that after decades of marginalization, even the dramatic changes made in 2018 and 2019 by President Masisi could not sway populations to the ruling party long associated with locally unpopular conservation policies, even after the reappearance of consultative mechanisms. The BDP-led government, which has continually been in power for five decades, was readily associated with the conditions of the conservation estate by people living there. The feelings of marginalization, alienation, and injustice were strongly felt, and this historical memory of insufficient consultation was not displaced by efforts made in the eighteen-month period leading up to the 2019 election. Second, it is possible that analysts simply underestimated the depths of loyalty to the opposition in these areas. Even despite the specific overtures in conservation policy (such as the rolling back of the hunting ban), the UDC's policy manifesto was seen as more credible and appealing than the BDP's (Makgala 2019). The opposition promised to reform the Community-Based Natural Resource Management (CBNRM) program to address some of the systemic recentralization seen since the enactment of the 2007 policy (for a description of this process, see DeMotts and Hoon 2012; Poteete 2009a; Rihoy and Maguranyanga 2010). The opposition manifesto promised to give communities more decision-making powers, in keeping with the spirit, if not the past implementation, of CBNRM. In doing so, it sought to restructure the decision-making processes on the conservation estate. This was a possible contrast to the BDP, which, though willing to enact piecemeal policy changes in line with popular sentiment, did not propose structural changes to decision-making on the conservation estate. In fact, the opposition's reference to the shortcomings of the 2007 CBNRM

Policy signaled a broader commitment to notions of participation and consensus on the conservation estate. This can perhaps explain the enduring appeal of the opposition. Moreover, this is coupled with observers' overestimation of the ability of stand-alone policy changes made in the immediate run-up to an election to disrupt years of partisan alignment. The failure of this strategy to move votes in the opposition's conservation strongholds dispels some of the tropes of African elections and voters as simply transactional. Third, Masisi's discourse around his administration's decision to reverse a series of conservation policies promulgated under his predecessor framed the issue largely in contrast to the preferences of international community, the global conservation movement, and large tourism multinationals. He deployed a mode of nationalist rhetoric with regard to Botswana's sovereignty and control over its natural resources, which was apparently more impactful in urban areas than on the conservation estate. By making the issue not only about the day-to-day dangers of human-wildlife conflict and the impact of conservation policies but rather by pitching it in a valence of rebuking neocolonial control over Botswana's ecosystem and resources and contesting the international media narratives often leveraged by the former president, Masisi widened the appeal of the changes beyond those who actually live in conservation areas.

Finally, it is possible that despite overt changes in policy, the day-to-day conditions for many living in the impacted areas have not changed substantially (see chapter 7), thus diminishing the potential electoral impacts of planned policy changes. This suggests that even amid one of the most turbulent presidential transitions in Botswana's history (Brown 2020; Seabo and Nyenhuis 2021), much of the political and electoral terrain of the conservation estate remained the same.

This chapter interrogated how people attempt to adopt, contest, or resist the securitization of the conservation estate using the state's own imaginary about democracy, participation, and consultation. In line with a core argument of this book, there are limitations on deploying the language of democracy as a form of resistance to securitization. In Botswana's securitized environment, the state is not seeking the consent of those citizens it is governing. Botswana's assertion of its democratic authenticity, particularly at home, is often derived from the kgotla as a cultural institution. The kgotla is emphasized and articulated by the state as an indigenous African institution that predates colonialism and is characterized by many in government as more genuine, broad-based, and legitimate than electoral politics alone. It is presented on the public stage as a reason for Botswana's democratic success (notwithstanding the long-standing potential limitations of this institution). The seeming derogation of the institution of the kgotla when it comes to much conservation policy is viewed as deeply perplexing by many people living on the conservation estate. The exceptionality of the conservation estate stands out here, as decisions regarding the daily life on the conservation estate are not made at the kgotla or even widely discussed at the kgotla beforehand but rather are embedded in the logic of securitization.

Residents of the conservation estate are told through mechanisms like Vision 2016 to invest in the institution of the kgotla as a form of indigenous participation, alongside Botswana's postcolonial electoral democracy. This is all the more powerful in areas where Tswana political structures are imported—the adoption of the kgotla system is part of assimilation and has been emphasized by government authorities as *the* way to interact with the state. At the same time, people of the conservation estate—again, often non-Tswana—have attempted to instrumentalize the kgotla as a means of communication of local positions to those in power. Yet they find themselves ignored by the very state that promotes the kgotla and the ideals of consensus and consent or partaking in a somewhat performative pantomime of participation when the state chooses to consult them on its own terms.

Through a discursive closure, people on the conservation estate claim that avenues for contestation have been shut down, and in the process the democratic nature of consultative authority is lost. This is a recognition that on the conservation estate the logics of securitization lie just below the state mythologies of democracy and participation. Sentiments of futility animate the ways in which local residents appear to acquiesce to what they view as credible threats of force. One middle-aged woman in East Hanahai noted, "We just agree with everything because we don't want to go to jail."[54] Local acceptance of the presence of military actors or resource restrictions is not cultivated because state actors have won local approval for these measures or because communities view these measures as legitimate trade-offs in conservation but rather because of the top-down commands they receive and the manner in which these commands are embedded in the state system. These commands, backed up by the implicit and explicit use of state power in enforcement, lead to compliance through attrition rather than genuine consent built over the years.

This chapter has also contended with the fact that very often there are two other categories of actors in the dance of democratic accountability on the conservation estate—co-local wildlife populations and the international community. My very presence conducting research was indicative and productive of this. The conversations that form the empirical basis of this book became a mechanism through which residents on the conservation estate believed they could communicate and convey their positions to the state, as other channels like the kgotla or electoral politics seemed to stymie them. Local people viewed their position as so marginal that they saw me as a potentially valuable interlocutor with the state on their behalf. Not even a citizen of Botswana, in their eyes I stood a greater chance of being recognized and heard by the state, further evincing the extent of their perceived, and perhaps actual, marginality to the structures of authority under which they live. This internationalization of the citizen-state relationship is all the more noteworthy in light of Botswana's professed emphasis on democracy and participation. As local people perceive that government policy is influenced to a greater extent by "foreigners," they begin to view this constituency as the one upon which to make claims, rather than their own government. Finding little success in the consultative process or the expression of grievances, they view the idea of bringing outsiders on their side as potentially more fruitful. This speaks to the marginality of these communities within the state and their limited ability to mobilize national political actors in response to their predicament because they occupy a site of local conservation that is highly informed by international dimensions.[55]

A coda for this section, which has encompassed the two previous chapters, is the observation that securitization produces qualitatively different experiences of citizenship and state authority on the conservation estate compared with elsewhere in Botswana, especially in relation to the bypassing of consultative forums like the kgotla and the emphasis on the coercive use of state power in order to achieve compliance with conservation policies. This places the citizens of the conservation estate in a situation unlike their compatriots. While the local recognition and repetition of state participatory discourses appears to be a reasonable strategy for resistance, it becomes more complicated on the conservation estate. Both the state's professed valorization of consent and its dependence on modes of coercion produce outcomes that shut down contestation—first through the depoliticization of the kgotla and its circumvention and then in the deployment of a securitizing discourse, which puts the environment in the realm of national security and therefore not up for debate. This operates to foreclose the potentialities of what issues are rendered "political" and determine the setting of the political agenda. The contradictions of state building do not make it a less powerful force in the lives of conservation-adjacent Batswana, but they do disrupt the ability for resistance, negotiation, and contestation. State building and the exercise of authority therein is not driven by a single logic, but it is still real and impactful, producing an environment wherein resistance is difficult.

Part II

Territory

4

Land and Ownership on the Conservation Estate

The drive from Ghanzi Town, Ghanzi District's capital and administrative center, to the settlement of New Xade, one of the villages where many people relocated from Central Kalahari Game Reserve reside today, takes several hours depending on the road conditions and the weather. On one of my trips to the community during fieldwork, I was accompanied a prominent community member who had written and spoken extensively about his experiences leaving the CKGR, his recollections of the landmark *Sesana and Others v. the Attorney General* trial, and his various roles in civil society and San advocacy. As we drove down long stretches of highway and the time and scenery passed, our conversations meandered. Periodically we would drive by the gated entrances of private farms still owned in freehold by the descendants of early white settlers. One of these visual cues turned our conversation to ownership, land, and belonging. He described the role of the land in his community, the feelings of alienation I would shortly come to observe myself in New Xade, the fundamentally vexed relationship of the state's territorialization of the CKGR, and the deeply held local notions of ownership unrecognized by the state. My informant said how he wished that half of the protected area could be degazetted and returned to its owners, the original inhabitants of the CKGR, so they could have the same rights to land as other Batswana. I was somewhat taken aback by his striking statement, which must have been apparent on my face. He responded, with a slight smile, "It is generous to only take back half—it is all ours."[1]

This conversation echoed many others throughout my fieldwork and reaffirmed the centrality of the land of the conservation estate to state building. Death frames this explicitly, noting that "green states in Africa are brought into being through the governance of land" (2016b, 13). Moreover, the governance and state-building capacities described by Death are bound up with the grounded terrain of the conservation estate. Protected areas, especially flagship parks, are symbolically and practically powerful in this regard, as they become crucibles in which questions of state, territorial sovereignty, and resource control are manifest in politically salient ways (Gissibl, Hohler, and Kupper 2012; Lunstrum 2014). Thirty-nine percent of Botswana's territory is covered by protected areas or Wildlife Management Areas (WMAs) (Barnes 2001).[2] In the context of Botswana, alongside the flagship protected areas, there is expansive growth in the discourses and practices associated with the conservation estate occurring outside of the national parks in more banal and quotidian conservation spaces where biodiversity conservation must share space with human residency. The spaces of everyday conservation are of most interest in the state-building process. The areas outside and just adjacent to national parks are primary sites of territoriality—the spatial organization of a state that allows for the control over the access and rights to land and resources (Vandergeest and Peluso 1995). This is due to the pervasiveness of human settlements in these areas and the complex interplay that results from the intersection of human and animal spaces.

This chapter is presented in two sections that investigate the manner by which the dynamics of land and territorial control play out on the conservation estate and in the state-building process. Both sections deal with the book's central arguments: (1) that the particular nature of the conservation estate produces a unique class of citizen experiencing vastly different relations to the state than their co-nationals and (2) that core imaginaries of the state become tested, fraught, and begin to fray on the conservation estate due to a host of conflicting and contradictory logics apparent in the state-building process, often frustrating resistance on the part of those residents. The first section begins by interrogating the processes of land alienation on the conservation estate and subsequent state maneuvers aimed at relocating dispossessed populations. It does so while contextualizing the history of land tenure in Botswana and focusing on the singular case of the CKGR. The next section then trains its attention on the discourses of property and the manner in which the state's ability to enact territorial control is curtailed by regimes of private property, opening up avenues of resistance for citizens. However, I argue that on the conservation estate citizens are differentially capable of invoking narratives of ownership, a variation that uncovers racial and class tensions obscured by the discourse of Botswana as a nonracial state. Using the contrast of the 2014–19 hunting ban's implementation across privately held versus communal or state land, the second section of this chapter deals with questions articulated by Sikor and Lund: "How and why some actors benefit from resources by way of property and others do not" (2009, 8).

History, Land, and "Tswanadom"

The conservation estate is embedded in land politics. Therefore, a foundation in Botswana's precolonial and colonial history is needed in order to engage with the current context of land and territory through which the core arguments of this book are made. The physical terrain of a postcolonial state—its land—is a canvas upon which its state-building process is drawn because, as Ramutsindela and Büscher note, "the centrality of land in state making in Africa has deep colonial roots that have huge implications for building the postcolonial state" (2019, 9). In the precolonial era, centralized Tswana chieftaincies known as *merafe* (singular *morafe*) arose, primarily in what is now eastern Botswana; they were highly structured and centralized kingdoms ruled by a chief or king, the *kgosi*. Though the colonial footprint of the Bechuanaland Protectorate, which began in 1885, was comparatively light, it was through these Tswana merafe that the area that would become contemporary Botswana was incorporated into the British Empire. The political systems of most merafe remained intact and relatively autonomous even as they were incorporated into the protectorate as tribal reserves (Bennett 2002; Gulbrandsen 2012; Maundeni 2002; Molomo 2008; Zips-Mairitsch 2013).

The British declared most land outside of direct territorial control of the eight centralized Tswana chiefdoms as either freehold or Crown land. The so-called tribal reserves, which constituted the political center of the protectorate, "were the successors to the pre-colonial proto-states" (Bennett 2002, 6). In these areas, Tswana groups were dominant and viewed as the relevant political interlocutor by the colonial government. In tribal reserves, non-Tswana residents often occupied a less-than-equal relationship vis-à-vis the political and land authority, sometimes even as members of a servant class lacking distinct rights or abilities to make claims on their own behalf. For example, the colonial-era Tagart Commission characterized the situation of the San people in Bamangwato Reserve in the early twentieth century as akin to slavery (Hermans 1977). Land held directly by the Crown, which forms the backbone of today's conservation estate, was drawn exclusively from areas not directly under control of the Tswana. This fact helps to historicize the overlap between non-Tswana areas and the conservation estate (see figure 4.1).

Independence codified Tswana approaches to land tenure, ownership, and occupation, privileging Tswana conceptions of residency and production into policy. A government official in charge of land-use planning at the Ghanzi Land Board described Tswana modes of spatial organization as a series of concentric circles. First and at the center was the *motse*, or village. Surrounding the village most adjacently was *masimo*, or farm land. The final

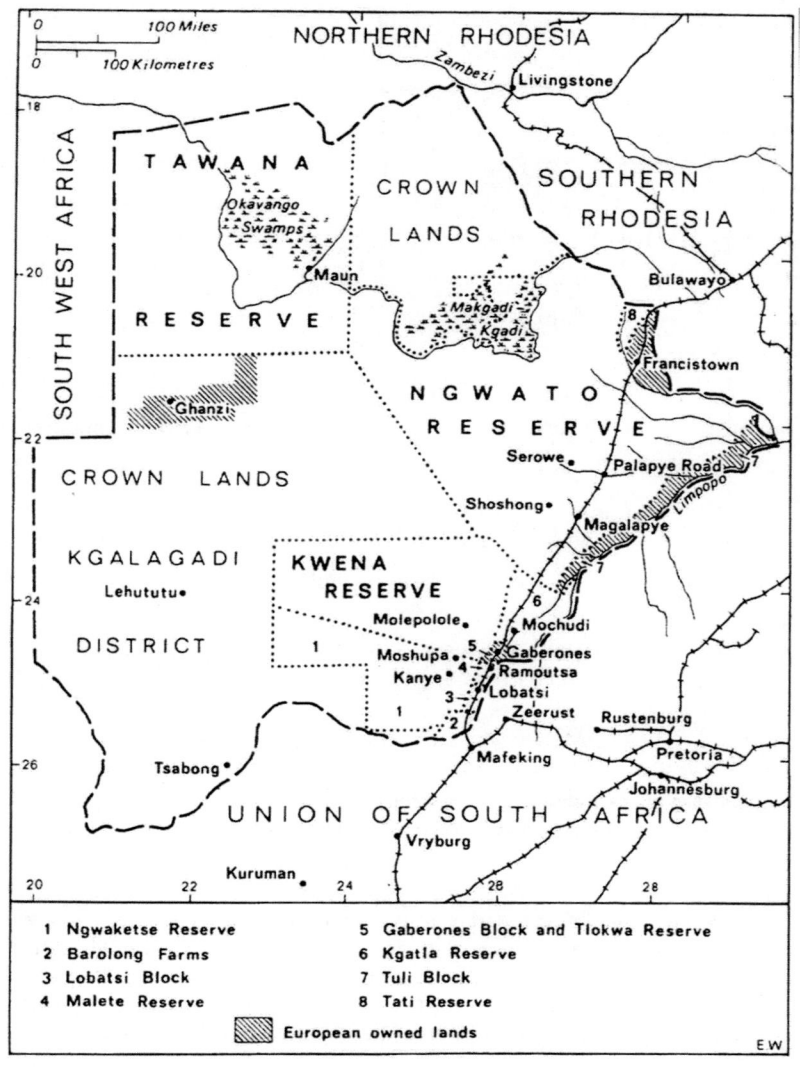

FIGURE 4.1. Map of the Bechuanaland Protectorate in 1940. Source: Schapera (1970) 2021.

concentric circle was the *moraka,* or cattle post. She identified the area beyond the cattle post, and outside of the realm of Tswana social order, as *naga,* or bush/wilderness. Implicit in this description are assumptions not only about how and where people should live but also how people should go about pursuing various livelihood endeavors.[3] Currently land in Botswana is divided into three categories: (1) communal or tribal land, (2) state land, and (3) freehold or private land. These categorizations have roots in the precolonial and colonial eras and are of great significance for the way in which conservation is enacted as a project of the contemporary postcolonial state.

Communal Land

Communal land is derived from the colonial-era tribal reserves described at the beginning of this section. The Tribal Land Act of 1968 moved allocation of land from traditional authorities, the *dikgosi,* to district land boards. Under this statute, communal land was deemed reserved for "tribesmen" until 1993, when the land legislation was amended to remove this discriminatory phrase (Molomo 2008). Despite removing land from tribal authority, the association of the chieftaincy with land allocation remains strong, as eight of the twelve land boards in the country are named after Tswana merafe. For example, the land board in Northwest District is called the Tawana Land Board despite the fact that this area is Botswana's most ethnically diverse, and the Batawana namesake may not even make up a plurality of the region's citizens (Molomo 2008; Solway and Nyati-Ramahobo 2004).

State Land

At independence, Crown land was converted into state land. Importantly, state land is most common in the north and west and has now mostly become protected areas for biodiversity conservation or the surrounding buffer zones and migratory channels (Campbell 2004; Magole 2009; Molomo 2008). While conservation predates colonialism—Botswana's first game reserves were hunting areas reserved for the use of Tswana chiefs—much of the architecture of the contemporary conservation estate derives from the colonial period. This is due to the fact that protected areas were overwhelmingly created from parcels of land held directly by the Crown (Campbell 2004). There is a comparatively small conservation estate in the east of the country. There are exceptions, like small private reserves such as Mokolodi Game Reserve outside Gaborone, Khama Rhino Sanctuary located about thirty minutes by car from the village of Serowe, and freehold farms converted into conservation ranches in the Tuli Block. The bulk of the conservation estate remains to this day in the sparsely populated north and west of the country, away from the Tswana areas (Campbell 2004). Of the conservation estate's 39 percent of land area, protected areas account for 17 percent and for the most part strictly exclude human occupation. As will be discussed in later sections, the CKGR is the only exception, and no other protected area in Botswana permits residency of any kind.

The remaining 22 percent of the conservation estate is made up of WMAs. Established in 1986 by the Wildlife Conservation Policy, WMAs give priority to wildlife and wildlife-related economic activities but, importantly, unlike national parks and game reserves, they do not preclude human residents (Taylor 2004). WMAs act as buffer zones and migration corridors in and around Botswana's protected areas. They are monitored and maintained by the Department of Wildlife and National Parks and are located in Botswana's northern and western districts. WMAs are further subdivided into Controlled Hunting Areas (CHAs) (Atlhopheng and Mulale 2009; Parry and Campbell 1990). WMAs are pervasive in the rural periphery, have a high level of state discretion in administration, and have been explicitly established to expand the conservation estate beyond formally demarcated parks and reserves.

Freehold Land

Although European settlement in the Bechuanaland Protectorate was not widely encouraged, especially in comparison to neighboring

Namibia, South Africa, and Zimbabwe, freehold land still accounts for 6 percent of Botswana's total area. It was originally given to white settlers and concessionary companies like Cecil Rhodes's British South Africa Company, which then acquired the rights to large blocks of land and sold farms to individual owners. Freehold land includes rural agricultural land and some residential plots in Botswana's major urban areas, like Gaborone and Francistown. The agricultural lands given to European settlers in the Protectorate era include the farm blocks of Ghanzi, the Tati Concession (Northeast District), Tuli, and Lobatse, which consist of some of the country's best arable and grazing land (Moyo, O'Keefe, and Sill 1993). On these parcels the owners have unlimited rights to the land and its terrestrial resources (Molomo 2008).[4] This is a detail central to arguments about ownership and territory presented in this chapter. While no new freehold land has been sold since 1978, existing freehold land remains privately owned (Magole 2009).

The Case of the CKGR

Dispossession and land alienation on the African continent, and especially in southern Africa, is often thought to be related to private ownership and a relic of colonial-era expropriations. Yet in Botswana conservation-related dispossession does not fit neatly with these criteria. The amount of land alienated to private white landowners is a mere fraction of what occurred in neighboring South Africa, Namibia, and Zimbabwe, but the impact of conservation-related removal is significant. Moreover, the timescale of this process is instructive. There are numerous examples of postcolonial removals related to the upkeep, and at times expansion, of the conservation estate (Chatty and Colchester 2002; Sapignoli 2018). In these conservation-related dispossessions, human occupancy is rendered invisible, either through complete removal from the area or through strict limitations on continued access to territory or resource use therein (Brockington 2002; Neumann 1998; Nustad 2015).

The establishment of Botswana's protected areas required the eviction of people in almost every instance, including Moremi Game

Reserve (Bolaane 2013), Chobe National Park (Taylor 2000), and Nxai Pan National Park and Makgadikgadi Pans National Park (Magole 2009). The most noteworthy instance of conservation-related removal is of the CKGR, in that the eviction process took place fully under the postcolonial government and was the impetus for the longest legal battle in Botswana's history, *Sesana and Others v. the Attorney General*. As the empirical backdrop for much of the field research conducted in Ghanzi District, a fulsome discussion of the CKGR is warranted. What I present below is a general summary of the issues and events related to the park and its inhabitants. However, longer monographs such as Sapignoli (2018) and Zips-Mairitsch (2013) are valuable resources for further analysis.

When the CKGR was first established, its original function was to provide a haven for human practices of hunting and gathering as well as for wildlife (Good 2002). In 1961, when the reserve was officially demarcated, around four thousand people lived there. While Botswana's first president, Sir Seretse Khama, vowed to recognize the colonially established arrangement as a space for the San and Bakgalagadi residents (Armstrong and Bennett 2002), it soon became a major point of contention. As a creation of the British protectorate, in the years since independence the CKGR was deemed by some a colonial project protecting—and even fetishizing—"backward" behavior of certain groups, largely the resident San and Bakgalagadi communities, at the expense of modernization (Taylor 2004). Efforts were made to resettle populations found therein as a means to "prepare" them for integration into mainstream society (Hitchcock 1991). By the mid-1980s, the number of residents still in the CKGR was about thirteen hundred. From 1986 to 1997 state authorities exerted indirect pressures to incentivize emigration, like freezing development, neglecting existing infrastructure, and hobbling service delivery mechanisms (Hitchcock, Sapignoli, and Babchuk 2011; Sapignoli 2018). By 1997 the government had cut off services (pensions, water provision, mobile health clinics, food rations, and distribution of Special Game Licences for subsistence hunting), and most residents were moved to resettlement villages at New Xade and Kaudwane. Another round of removals occurred in 2001, and in January 2002 the borehole wells were sealed permanently (Taylor and Mokhawa 2003). The official justification for the removal from the CKGR was threefold: (1) it was too expensive to provide services within the reserve, (2) people and wildlife are incompatible, and (3) more effective development could occur elsewhere (Hitchcock, Sapignoli, and Babchuk 2011; Taylor and Mokhawa 2003; Saugestad 2001; Zips-Mairitsch 2013). Others, notably the London-based NGO Survival International (SI), have ascribed more sinister motives to the government of Botswana related to antagonisms toward hunter-gathering people and believe that relocations were to make way for mineral extraction in the reserve (Solway 2009; Taylor and Mokhawa 2003). Irrespective of motive, the process of removal became subject of a protracted court battle in the first years of the twenty-first century.

Sesana and Others v. the Attorney General began in February 2002 as an urgent action to reestablish services in the CKGR. The proceedings eventually morphed into handling much more complex legal questions and dragged on until the final judgment was handed down on December 13, 2006 (see Sapignoli 2018 and Zips-Mairitsch 2013 for detailed accounts). Botswana's High Court eventually ruled in favor of the San plaintiffs, but the government's interpretation of the ruling has been greatly criticized for limiting the application of the decision to only the named plaintiffs rather than the whole impacted class. For example, in 2010 the UN special rapporteur on the rights of indigenous peoples, James Anaya, criticized the government, stating, "The Sesana decision would seem to suggest that all former residents of the game reserve who were relocated should be permitted to return without having to obtain entry permits and should be able to subsist and maintain a dignified life within the reserve" (quoted in Zips-Mairitsch 2013, 357–58). The government's interpretation does not recognize the underlying premise that all former residents should be able to return to live freely in the reserve. The government has continued to deny provision of services to the inhabitants of CKGR as well as implement bureaucratic barriers to those who legally have the right to reside there. Key issues related to the CKGR removal raised in academic literature include the rights of people to reside within the protected areas and use resources, local say in decision-making, rights to make livelihood decisions and access social services, the ability to determine development priorities, and questions of culture and identity in the wider Botswana polity (Good 2008; Hitchcock, Sapignoli, and Babchuk 2011; Molomo 2008; Sapignoli 2012, 2018; Zips-Mairitsch 2013).

The CKGR controversy and court case galvanized San communities in unexpected ways. The CKGR is a potent symbol; it acts as an imagined contrast to the dependent conditions of living in government resettlement villages or squatting on freehold farms. These wider reverberations are important because the specific case of the CKGR only directly impacted around thirteen hundred of Botswana's fifty thousand San citizens. Yet Saugestad (2011) cautions that while the CKGR issue has become emblematic of wider marginalizations facing San people, it can overpower other concerns facing these communities as well as antagonize the state. That "this matter gained dynamic media attention as well as symbolic value in international politics and far beyond the borders of the Kalahari" (Zips-Mairitsch 2013, 317) may very well be both a blessing and a curse to Botswana's San population. For instance, Solway (2009) argues that SI's involvement weakened local San organizations and ultimately created a worse outcome for the San population. Some scholars interpret the CKGR case as a pyrrhic victory for the San because of the way in which the transnational dimensions of activism hardened the state and contributed little in terms of material improvements to the lives of the San, resulting in the government's very narrow interpretation of its legal obligations under the ruling (Sapignoli 2018). The conceptualization of SI's activist tactics as fundamentally threatening to the stability and prosperity of the state resulted in the state's hard-line application of the court's ruling regarding the CKGR (Saugestad 2011).

For the government of Botswana, the CKGR removals and the subsequent international backlash to the state's actions were revelatory. The eviction of populations from the CKGR opened Botswana up to international criticism for the first time in its history. The attempts of activists and international NGOs to connect the evictions to Botswana's diamond industry and well-honed slogan—"diamonds for development"—were interpreted as an existential threat to the state (Taylor and Mokhawa 2003). Moreover, the controversy stoked by SI's push for a diamond and tourism boycott laid bare some of the structural issues of Botswana's economy—the precariousness of an "economic miracle" that depended largely on luxury commodities like diamonds and tourist experiences, the sensitivity to outside forces, and failures of economic diversification.

The widespread condemnation surrounding the CKGR removals expressed by the international community was unprecedented for a country that was not only on the right side of history with regard to racial politics in southern Africa but also has been Africa's political and economic darling for most of its time as an independent nation-state. Unaccustomed to international scrutiny, Botswana has been hypervigilant since the height of the CKGR controversy about how it is perceived in the international system and highly attuned to the external perceptions of the state. The state's policing of its image has ranged from things as simple as attentiveness to its official social media presence to actions as extreme as the deportation of academics and journalists critical of government actions, as noted earlier.

Relocation and Resettlement:
The CKGR and Contemporary Citizen-State Relations

> We've come a hell of a long way since the 1960s, and that's why we hope [the San] will catch up with the rest of us. They belong in towns and cities like you and me. They are not animals, they are not a tourist attraction.
>
> —Sidney Pilane, Botswana's attorney general during
> *Sesana and Others v. Attorney General*[5]

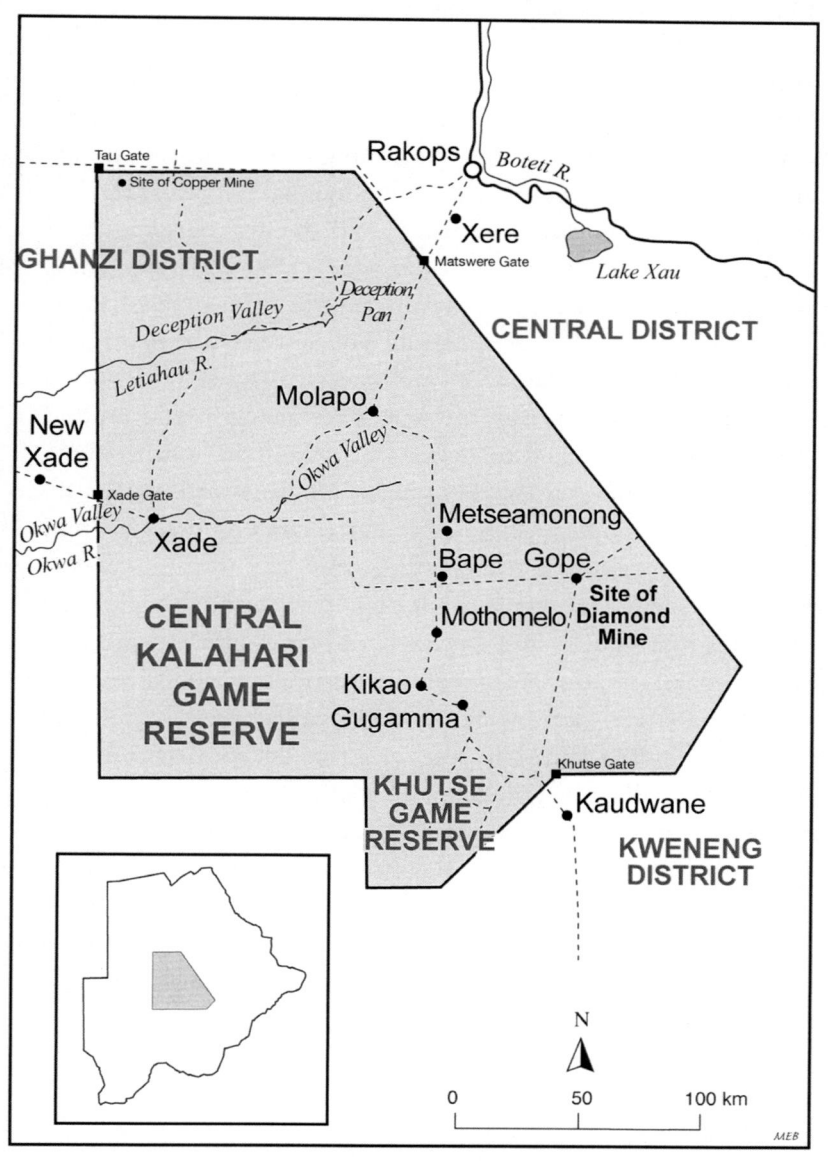

FIGURE 4.2. Map of the Central Kalahari Game Reserve. *Source:* Hitchcock, Sapignoli, and Babchuk 2011.

Sidney Pilane was tasked with defending the government's position during the CKGR court case, which adjudicated the legality of the government's removal of San and Bakgalagadi Batswana from the country's largest protected area (Sapignoli 2018). Embedded in his statement at the beginning of this section are assumptions related to where and how individual Batswana can live that are tied to identity, citizenship, and the appropriateness of various forms of land-use strategies across state territory. These assumptions cannot be divorced from the processes of state building, as conservation policies, like all policies, are not neutral or apolitical. As the above quote implies, for many state actors in Botswana the phenomenon of human residency in and around protected areas is linked to notions of primitivity and the proverbial naga of Tswana social organization. This works to justify the absence of people in these areas in the contemporary era and makes those individuals still claiming residency, use, and ownership rights seem aberrant and out of step with the modernizing consensus that "they belong in towns and cities like you and me." This links conservation, resource-use restrictions, and the rise of protected areas to notions of spatial organization. These logics align with Tswana cultural values that are deeply tied to life in a centralized village as an anchor of political belonging, identity, and order and the urge to mandate that citizens who exist outside of this consensus must "catch up with the rest of us."

Displacement and relocation from protected areas are often justified in the name of both conservation and progress, supposing at least a correlation, if not a direct causal link, between the two concepts. Protected areas in Botswana were carved out from places inhabited by people who were "more often than not San" (Taylor 2004, 161). This holds true for the creation of Moremi Game Reserve, Nxai Pan National Park, Makgadikgadi Pans National Park, and Chobe National Park in the north and Khutse Game Reserve and Kgalagadi Transfrontier Park in the south (Magole 2009).

Throughout my fieldwork a consistent theme was reiterated by interview respondents. They often argued that the practice of removal and relocation was reserved solely for San populations. Many interviewees linked the political act of state-mandated relocation directly to their identity as San people, discursively connecting the events of the CKGR removal to other instances of relocation (and perceived possibility of future relocation) throughout the country. A young man in the village of Khwai, a community originally moved from Moremi Game Reserve and periodically threatened with further displacement, noted: "We haven't heard of any tribe [sic] being relocated apart from the Basarwa [San]. So, we saw this relocation issue with the people of New Xade. It happened once more with the Khwai residents here, long before I was born. So, now they [the government] are trying to bring it for the second time or the third time. So, this practice is only forwarded for Basarwa [San]. Why? The question is why?"[6] With this statement, the respondent is tracing a long history of removals of San people from conservation areas, directly invoking the exceptionality of these spaces in Botswana as sites occupied predominantly by national ethnolinguistic minorities. He connects the conservation estate, as a spatial category of land, with the presence of non-Tswana people. He uses this connection to question the ostensible equality of the state and policymaking in Botswana by noting that it appears "this practice [relocation] is only forwarded for Basarwa [San]." The final clause of his statement is similarly indicative of the misalignment between articulated state mythologies and the lived experiences of state policies on the conservation estate. He asks why this occurs, as it is seemingly out of step with the ideals of consultation and equality promoted by the government and described earlier chapters.

The San kgosi of Khwai touched on this issue as well: "Relocation issues in our country is [sic] an issue of concern to most communities like us. There have been a lot of rumors going around that we were threatened to have that relocation. . . . It creates a lot of conflict. We understand issues of CKGR."[7] His insistence that the community of Khwai, a predominantly San community, "understands [the] issues of [the] CKGR" is a powerful expression of the use of ethnic identity politics in attempts to reject the state's ability to unilaterally regulate rural territory. This is all the more powerful when considering that the Khwai community in Northwest District is hundreds of kilometers away from the CKGR and the relocation villages where many former residents now live. This evokes a pan-San solidarity that transcends the internal diversity of San groups. (The community at Khwai is Bugakhwe San, whereas those relocated from the CKGR are primarily G//ana and G/wi.)[8] The CKGR casts a long shadow of influence, even within communities that are geographically very distant from it. In this manner, San people across the country discursively utilize the only instance of San-state interaction where the state's position was successfully rebuked—the landmark CKGR court decision in favor of San plaintiffs—in order to contest and negotiate their own positions regarding spatial organization and recognition on the conservation estate.[9]

However, this strategy can be problematic on two counts. The first is that the CKGR case is a less than ideal analogy for a victorious David-and-Goliath scenario on the part of the San. Even while the letter of the decision was written in favor of Roy Sesana and his fellow complainants, in practice the state's interpretation of the ruling has been highly circumscribed and limits the practical conferral of land and residency rights to the CKGR San (Sapignoli 2018). The second issue with this strategy of solidarity is the fact that the state views overtly ethnic politics as hostile and tends to perceive ethnic organizing, particularly on the part of San people, as threatening to the state project.[10] Because San populations are relatively marginalized, the state is well positioned to dismiss and reject this style of contestation, compared with other minority groups (such as Kalanga Batswana) that have been more successful at ethnic organizing (Werbner 2004). Nonetheless, many respondents both in the north and west of Botswana articulated a connection between geographically separate San communities living on the conservation estate as "the same family"[11] and subject to a particular and distinct set of interactions between themselves and the state over land politics. A middle-aged man in Khwai noted, "We have seen people being relocated from CKGR, and they are from the same family [San people]. Just because the government has powers, they decided to move them, but they didn't want to move at all because this is where they were raised and their culture—they know everything. In the past we used to stay in what is Moremi Game Reserve, but we were moved from there. I think we were moved three times, so it is a problem for us."[12]

His statement provides several insights to be unpacked. The CKGR is held up as a demonstrative case of dispossession—directly related to the respondent's own position of marginality and insecurity of land tenure in relation to Moremi Game Reserve. These same sentiments of the forced nature of removals are very apparent in Khwai's neighboring village, Mababe. The community at Mababe is also predominantly San,[13] and its residents had previously occupied a much more expansive area than where the village now sits. They were removed from Chobe National Park during the colonial era and have since struggled to assert their claims to the area. An elderly man recollecting the park's founding stated, "The government stole that land from us. They used dirty tricks claiming that they were making a firebreak and then changing to making it into the park. They did not consult us about that before transferring part of our land into the park. We had refused to have our land made into our park, and the land [was] forcefully taken from us."[14] There are several important points articulated by this respondent. By using the term "stole," he strongly conveys a notion of ownership and a conceptualization of the community's belief that they were the rightful owners of the land. His type of ownership is not recognized in the same manner as the rights of owners of private, freehold property (discussed in the following section), further drawing distinctions to the variable characteristics of citizenship produced by the variable land tenure regimes on which conservation practices are overlaid. The malice with which state actions are characterized—using "dirty tricks" and "forcefully" taking the land—indicates the tensions inherent in the citizen-state relationship on the conservation estate. The state is perceived as undeterred by local discontent, all-powerful, and unmoved by expressions of grievance. Furthermore, the interviewee made no distinction between the actions regarding land made by the colonial state and the postcolonial state. This man, while unsure of his exact age, believed he was in his eighties, was an adult at independence in 1966 and "remembered the time before Seretse." For him, the state behavior that characterized the founding of Chobe during the Protectorate period was not limited to the colonial era but remained true for "Seretse's son,"[15] the president at the time of our discussion, Ian Khama. This indicates a trajectory of spatial regulation of the conservation estate that spans beyond the colonial era and into the contemporary state.

Despite decades of settled residency in state-sanctioned villages, many San respondents continued to express an expansive idea of territory and ownership out of step with the state conception of land tenure and at odds with the state's apparent impulse to regulate movement over space. For example, while some residents relocated from the CKGR conveyed a wish to move back permanently, other saw the right to access the CKGR freely as paramount, even while still retaining a more permanent residence in New Xade (see figure 4.2). A man in his early thirties residing in New Xade said, "We should be allowed entry into the CKGR at any time so that we could spend some time in there without being required to carry a permit. Our wish is to move between New Xade and CKGR as we please without any restrictions."[16] With this statement he seeks to collapse the importance of the state's cartographical knowledge production—for him the divide between his current place of residence and the CKGR is simply a line on a map. It is not a social reality that exists organically in his community but rather a top-down state regulation of space that is perceived as artificial. His rejection of the requirement to carry a permit is another discursive contestation of the trappings of state authority that are made material on the conservation estate through regulation, ordering, and categorization. The requirement of seeking a permit from the DWNP in order to access the CKGR is viewed as misaligned with local concepts of spatial organization but also as counterintuitive to the CKGR ruling. Local people often speak of the ruling as a recognition that the CKGR is theirs even if the legal situation is far more complex. The government's continued insistence on monitoring, regulation, and enforcement of a border already regarded as spurious exacerbates the local view of government's illegitimacy as the only arbiter of space.

On a practical level, access to the terrain of the conservation estate throughout the country is often restricted based on who can afford to pay for entry. For example, when meeting with the CKGR parks liaison office in Ghanzi, my DWNP interviewees encouraged me to take some time off from my research to visit the CKGR as a tourist. They assured me that upon payment of the visitor fee, I could receive my permit by the end of the day and be free to experience the unique environment of the Central Kalahari.[17] Access to the reserve was a commodity that could be sold. The harsh line that exists even for legal residents of the reserve was made immaterial from the perspective of the tourist experience. This relative freedom for prospective tourists to move across the conservation estate occurs alongside the state's strict interpretation of the CKGR ruling as well as other limitations that structure citizen access to parks throughout the country. This contrast shows the prioritization of the use of conservation spaces as a tourism commodity rather than for their recognition as a place of residence, a source of livelihoods, or site of spiritual connection for people with long-standing claims on the territory. Local users become defined as transgressors of protected areas but largely not the foreign actors who access this space. This is a phenomenon by no means limited to Botswana. In his book project analyzing continental trends connecting environment and state building, Death observes this same dynamic. He says of protected areas, "The communities who live, farm, harvest, hunt, worship, and work in these lands are separated from conservation areas by fences, fined when they trespass or hunt or harvest in these areas, and in general excluded from the land. By contrast, scientists, researchers, park officials, and tourists are allowed access to the parks and even encouraged to enter them as part of the conservation project" (Death 2016b, 83).

Having outlined in broad strokes the historical and contemporary saliency of removals and relocations on the conservation estate, I delve in the following section into the way in which the regime of private property operates across the state's territory. It examines how characteristics of land tenure—notably private ownership on freehold land—generate complications regarding territorial control and illuminate the class and racial fault lines apparent in various citizens' abilities to contest state practice.

Property, Ownership, and Land Tenure

> In a way, the government does not see the game ranches as part of conservation.... They are primarily concerned with what happens on state land, with the animals considered government property.
>
> —Private landowner, Ghanzi District[18]

Lund (2013) distinguishes between land as territory and land as property. He argues that land can be conceptualized as "territory," which has a political connotation and is governed but not owned, or as "property," which has both spiritual and legal connotations and can be owned but not governed. The definition of territory versus property is foundational to the structuring of social relations and the grievances that emanate therein. In the postcolonial context, the application and superimposition of certain kinds of property regimes remain salient as, Ramutsindela and Sinthumule note, "at the core of private property, in its Western sense, is a construction of exclusive property relations between people and things, which is made possible by individuals holding 'things' in formal and explicit ways" (2017, 418). Property regimes shape sociopolitical relations and structure axes of inequality. In the context of postcolonial southern Africa, Ramutsindela notes, "dichotomies of land tenure regime in Africa arise from the colonial allocation of property rights and the inability of postindependent states to radically transform agrarian and land relations" (Ramutsindela 2017, 110). More broadly, the dynamics of private property and land ownership intersect with the conservation estate across the region. The leveraging of conservation in spaces of private ownership allows freehold owners, who otherwise may face calls for redistribution, to deflect. Ramutsindela notes that in South Africa, private nature reserves and game ranch owners use their conservation roles "to push back land claims" (2015, 2260). Ramutsindela and Sinthumule specifically examine this phenomenon in transfrontier conservation areas (TFCA), such as the Greater Mapungubwe TFCA, which encompasses areas of Botswana where variegated property rights established mostly along racial lines "laid the foundation for a racialized participatory process in which some have more choices than others," creating power imbalances and "vulnerability of local people and their land" (Ramutsindela and Sinthumule 2017, 429).

Owners of freehold land are able to interact with conservation and the associated tourism industry on their own terms, while still having their property rights, in distinct contrast to other communities on the conservation estate discussed below. The racial connotations of freehold land cannot be understated, as the "predominantly racial character of freehold land in the region, and the 'superiority' associated with private property were inherited by the post-independence state" (Ramutsindela 2017, 111). Conservation becomes a politically acceptable means of entrenching communities descended from settlers into the landscapes and postcolonial polities (Fox 2018; Gressier 2015; Hughes 2010). In the case of peace park initiatives in southern Africa, Ramutsindela argues that these conservation efforts further strengthen and entrench the land rights of predominantly white landowners. This contrasts with the situation of rural communities living on communal or state land, which become subject to greater state power as this land is incorporated into the conservation estate. Nor is this limited to southern Africa. Further afield in Kenya, Fox (2018) argues that conservation has allowed white landowners to consolidate power and influence into the postcolonial era despite largely abstaining from formal politics. This occurs alongside and in contrast to adjacent communities, wherein "conservation has masked and depoliticized the systemic marginalization of pastoralists" (Fox 2018, 213).

The dynamics of land tenure and ownership (or lack thereof) figure to a great degree in attempts at political-spatial organization on the conservation estate and can account for the multifaceted nature of state building across its territory. This section is concerned with the interplay between spaces of "property" and spaces of "territory," which coexist, and are often contiguous, on the conservation estate. It examines the varied impact of the hunting ban across Botswana, focusing on the institution of private property and the manner in which certain conceptions of ownership transfigured the hunting ban's reach and the ability of the state to reorder social and ecological arrangements on the conservation estate. The prevalence of "property" on the conservation estate does open up areas of negotiation when it comes to citizen-state interactions but only for certain types of citizens—those who own freehold land as property. When local residents who are not owners of property, but rather dwellers on territory, attempt to utilize the discourse of ownership, their ability to contest state practices are curtailed.

Throughout southern Africa there is reluctance to upend rights regimes related to private property, even when they were founded in the colonial era and resulted in widespread dispossession (Murombedzi 2003). Though unsurprising due to the relatively conservative nature of Botswana's decolonization process, the wealth and stature of the decolonizing Batswana elites, and the country's nearly total encirclement by minority-ruled regimes, the government chose not to disrupt the tenets of private property ownership at independence.

The often underappreciated politics of race in Botswana become more salient and immediate on the conservation estate due to a variety of factors but perhaps most importantly resulting from the apparent outsized influence of white citizens (as well as white foreigners) in the lucrative tourism industry. With low rates of European migration and only 6 percent of land held privately,

Botswana's land issues are different from its formerly white-ruled neighbors. There is no significant history of settler colonialism, and Botswana prides itself on a racial legacy tied to tolerance, opposition to apartheid, and citizenship based on civic, rather than ethnic, criteria. Botswana has been both critical and wary of explicit racial politics adopted by some in the region, like Zimbabwe. Nonetheless, Botswana's unique racial politics cannot be ignored (Alden and Anseeuw 2009). This is of great relevance on the conservation estate, where racial stratifications in both land ownership and the tourism industry produce a kind of politics of color that is specific to Botswana's state-building process.

While Botswana is certainly unique in southern Africa, it is on the conservation estate where its proclamations of a nonracial democracy most deserve scrutiny. In her ethnography of the white citizens in northern Botswana, Gressier (2011, 2014) notes that this group of Batswana generally avoids any politics of recognition. As a small group of relatively economically empowered citizens with access to land, whites have sufficient individual rights and political citizenship to see no need to agitate for further recognition under the current political system. In Northwest District, white citizens downplay their ethnic or racial background as minorities in favor of the label "Motswana" in order to differentiate themselves from the many white expatriates working in the tourism industry (Gressier 2011). Furthermore, "white Batswana tend to emphasise the difference of Botswana's political history from neighbouring South Africa, Namibia, and Zimbabwe, suggesting that interracial relationships have been, and continue to be, for the most part positive" (Gressier 2014, 2). This divide plays out differently in Ghanzi District, where my research shows a greater social and political allegiance between white Batswana and white African counterparts living and working on the district's freehold farms, who quickly pivot toward their experiences (often in Zimbabwe) as a cautionary tale.

The difference in the land tenure regimes found in the country's north and west is key. White citizens in Ghanzi, unlike their counterparts in Northwest, are largely owners of private property. Unlike the freehold farmers, those living in the Okavango must seek land through the Tawana Land Board like all other citizens, which makes the erasure of a settler mentality among the population more credible (see table 4.1). The social and spatial organization of the Ghanzi farms—stand-alone homesteads on privately owned land—differs greatly from the way in which Maun acts as a multiethnic and multiracial hub in the north. The white citizen population in Ghanzi is less integrated into the wider community than the population in Northwest, which has lived under the Batawana chieftaincy, with some white Batswana men from the area even opting to undergo initiation into the Tawana regiment, a cultural rite of passage into adulthood common throughout Tswana-speaking communities (Gressier 2015).

Table 4.1. Land characteristics in Ghanzi and Northwest Districts

	Ghanzi District	Northwest District
Land tenure	Freehold land, state land	Communal land
Land authority	Individual private owners, Ghanzi Land Board, Ministry of Lands	Tawana Land Board
Tswana morafe	N/A	Batawana Tribal Authority
Primary industry	Cattle	Photographic tourism

The situation of private property and land ownership is complexly imbricated over "whiteness" and citizenship on the conservation estate, so it is worth considering the overlapping dynamics of freehold land and wildlife. In Botswana, as in much of southern Africa, the ability to own wildlife resources, like the ability to own land, is tied to dynamics of race and increasingly class (Snijders 2012). Wildlife is often construed in state discourses as a *national* resource, akin to the country's mineral deposits. State authorities like to emphasize that there is no private ownership of wildlife and that all wildlife is held in trust by the state on behalf of Batswana, frequently invoking the fact that "the animals belong to us all,"[19] yet this is not entirely true. While the bulk of the country's wildlife is held in trust by the government, animals that are found on privately held game farms are, in fact, the property of the landowner. For example, prior to the relocation of several South African rhinos to northern Botswana, some of the very few rhinos within the country resided on a large game farm in Ghanzi, making them the property of the ranch owner.[20] In an interview, this landowner was quick to point out, and reiterated several times, that these were his private property and that the state had been reluctant to take any responsibility for them, necessitating significant out-of-pocket expenses for their maintenance, protection, and veterinary care.[21] Even prior to the imposition of the hunting ban, private landowners could choose whether or not to hunt on their wildlife property (for example, in the Tuli Block area where many landowners adopted a non-use stance for wildlife). Landowners were able to make these decisions for themselves, without significant government interference. The decision for some private landowners to cease hunting on their own property was made independently from the policy dictates of the state. In this context, the locus of decision-making sits with the landowner.

Though described in this book as a nationwide hunting ban, the 2014–19 moratorium is more complex and qualified. In a September 2013 press release by the then Ministry of Environment, Wildlife and Tourism, the noted exception to Botswana's "national" hunting ban was described: "Hunting in registered game ranches will not be affected by the ban."[22] This one line of text belies significant political implications of this policy caveat, which exposes tensions around race, property, and recognition among Botswana's various citizens on the conservation estate. Indeed, if the logics at work on the conservation estate were directed in an overarching and coherent manner, it would follow that hunting would have been banned everywhere (as much of the government's public relations on the matter seemed to imply at the time).[23]

However, the hunting ban in this context serves as a prime example of the geographical and legal exceptions that exist in the top-down propagation of laws, policies, and practices related to conservation. When taking private property such as game ranches into account, the state seemingly relinquished much of its authority over the animals and resources existing on freehold land, in pursuit of an accommodating orientation toward private ownership and capital investment.[24] These spaces of private property are characterized by greater freedom in the face of conservation laws, and they are overwhelmingly owned by a small, discrete constituency that appears to operate outside the otherwise top-down imposition of state authority. The bulk of privately held freehold land is owned by white farmers, often, though not always, descendants of Afrikaner trekkers who purchased the land in the early twentieth century. While many of the original parcels of land remain agricultural cattle farms, a number have either been fully or partially converted to operate as game farms.

The exceptionality of game ranches with regard to the hunting ban was a result of both the manner of the ban's implementation and the notion of property—as opposed to territory—in the land tenure regime. As the hunting ban was instituted through the zeroing-out of hunting quotas, it had no impact on institutional spaces not governed by the state-issued quotas from the wildlife department, like game ranches, and, because of the conception of game ranches as private property, the state was either unwilling or unable to exert its authority regarding conservation in these spaces. Respondents from the DWNP characterized game ranches on freehold land as outside their purview. One DWNP interviewee noted that game ranchers "own the land, so we can't do anything,"[25] and the director of the department characterized these spaces primarily as "private property," despite the fact that they are also part of the conservation estate.[26] This is a recognition of the limitations imposed on conservation by the dynamics of private ownership (in a Western legal-rational sense) and the manner in which the DWNP's authority stops at gate of a game farm unless the state chooses to contravene the tenets of the private property regime. Such a proposition would fundamentally upend core foundations of the postcolonial state.

The implications of ending hunting on game farms would have deeply impacted the tenets of private ownership, the perception of Botswana's orientation to capital, the racial dynamics of land ownership across southern Africa, and, importantly, the way in which Botswana portrays itself as exceptional, especially in comparison to its neighbors.

White landowners in Ghanzi are political cognizant of this and quick to make comparisons (which may stretch credulity) of Botswana to Zimbabwe if it suits their argument.[27] During fieldwork, the incumbent Khama administration was outspoken in its criticism of Robert Mugabe and was an outlier in the Southern African Development Community because of its public positions toward his Zimbabwe African National Union–Patriotic Front (ZANU-PF) regime.[28] During this time period, rumors flew in public discourse that Khama and Mugabe had an acrimonious working relationship. This perception colored most local reporting on Zimbabwe-Botswana relations at the time and had a direct bearing on the strategic deployment of the specter of Zimbabwe by landowners in Ghanzi.[29] And Botswana's coolness toward regional political actors was not limited to Zimbabwe. The Khama government was also wary of South Africa's Economic Freedom Fighters—denying the party's leader, Julius Malema, the right to enter the country—evincing Botswana's skepticism about redistributionary politics aimed at privately owned land.[30]

Interviewees from the white community in Ghanzi District recognized that the government was concerned about how white citizens, and landowners in particular, are perceived to be treated and used that to their advantage in subtle negotiations with the state. This community articulates itself as well connected to wider regional networks and keenly observant of continental political trends as they relate to private property ownership.[31] While many in this constituency have roots in Ghanzi going back over a century, several of the newer white families left Zimbabwe in the early 2000s after ZANU-PF's Fast Track Land Reform.[32] This positioning creates political subjects, a mix of citizens and non-citizen residents, who are simultaneously very appreciative of the government's concern for the regime of private property but also quick to criticize any perceived or potential encroachment on the institution of ownership and their status therein. In managing this multifaceted orientation to the state, one interviewee (a Zimbabwean national resident in Botswana), recalling his peripatetic lifestyle after leaving Zimbabwe, referred to his family and friends as the "white tribe" of southern Africa, a rhetorical position that claims both insider and outsider qualities.[33]

Both relatively new arrivals as well as Batswana citizens descended from early settlers noted how they believed Botswana would protect their private property rights but also intimated that perceived state incursions into the private property regime would be articulated by their community as political behavior akin to Zimbabwe's Fast Track Land Reform.[34] This potential analogy is an implicit threat to Botswana's exceptional national image and recognized the state's own anxiety around the ZANU-PF regime. By staking out a position that state interference on freehold land would prompt this community to draw a comparison to ZANU-PF—a government of which the BDP had been critical, especially during the later Mugabe years[35]—they leverage the state's concern with international image to solidify their own ability to negotiate the terms of their relationship to policies on the conservation estate. Their interconnectedness to regional networks, as well as their ability to gauge the global temperature with regard to the reception of land reform of privately held land, allows for a considerably advantageous position in negotiations with the state, in stark contrast to other Batswana living in Ghanzi's conservation estate (to be evaluated later in this section). The Ghanzi landowning constituency has a unique ability to maneuver when it comes to conservation restrictions imposed upon the rest of the country.

It is worth considering what sets this group of game ranch owners apart from commercial safari hunters. While commercial safari hunters are also a relatively wealthy constituency plugged into the same social and political circles described above, the dynamics of land tenure matter here. Negotiation is not simply about wealth, race, or savvy political positioning. The government had more or less full reign on conservation concessions—WMAs and CHAs—because they are ultimately owned by the state. Hunting concessions were allocated from either state or communal land, thus under the purview of government structures, either district land boards or the Ministry of Land directly in the case of state land. Hunting concessions were effectively rented from the state, which holds land in perpetuity. The actual quotas that permitted safari hunting on concessions to take place in the first place were also allocated by the DWNP.[36] Neither of these facts hold true for game ranches, which operate on private land and allow the hunting of animals according to their own calculus. The state imperative to end hunting during Khama's presidency, while highly unpopular, could not be easily derailed by the commercial safari hunting sector because of these conditions. Yet when the ambition to end hunting throughout the entire country ran up against a constituency more institutionally and discursively empowered—private landowners—the state had to back away from what would have been a revolutionary reordering of the private property regime. This is, of course, notwithstanding the way in which the ban on hunting was deeply disruptive to the more marginalized communities on which it impacted. This demonstrates a state-building project that is impactful certainly but not all-encompassing. It is most expansive in the face of weak or fragmented resistance, avoiding clashes with politically and economically empowered constituencies and showing reluctance or inability to disturb the operations of private property.

People who have successfully converted their old cattle farms into large game estates have been able to reap the benefits of tourism, capitalizing on commercial hunting, a market that they exclusively dominated during the period of the hunting ban.[37] This situation led to local resentment and commonplace accusations that game farmers lured animals onto their land to benefit from them exclusively. While there was no way to verify these claims during my fieldwork, rumors and displeasure with regard to game farms were persistent among neighboring communities, particularly in Ghanzi District. A participant in a focus group in Qabo, a resettlement community that abuts a nearby game farm, said, "The white farmers took the animals to put them on their farms to begin with. Maybe that's why there are few left? So, the farmers are left to benefit, and we are just left like that."[38] The description of the farmers as white was evocative of the dynamics that undergird the tensions incumbent in the land tenure regime. By and large people living in the Ghanzi resettlement communities have been alienated from the land that became private property—land they perceive as taken from them.[39] Moreover, those people owning the contemporary spaces from which Ghanzi's San population was removed, frequently the descendants of the families involved in the initial displacement, are believed to continue to benefit from the wildlife populations resident on their farms, at the expense of the area's original inhabitants. Though not uniformly wealthy, this disproportionately white community is vastly better resourced than the local people of the area. Beyond their comparative economic privilege, private landowners live relatively free from government intervention compared with those people removed and resettled from freehold land and protected areas, who now reside almost exclusively in communities created and maintained by the state. Landowners are seen, rightfully, as a privileged class, occupying a unique social, economic, and political situation on the conservation estate. The continuation of hunting on game farms alone—as the only place in the country where this activity was still permitted during the period of the ban—frustrated local people, activists,[40] and elected officials alike. An opposition MP from the Okavango region expressed one of the most common grievances associated with this situation: "Government says hunting will only be allowed in registered game farms. Now the question is, who owns these farms? I was saying to the minister, are you saying poor people cannot eat game meat? It is now only for the elite? Because these farms are owned by the elite and game meat from these farms does not come cheap. So, we've conserved our animals for the elite."[41]

This MP highlighted the perception in which "elites" are not subject to the same conservation-related restrictions as the general population. He conveyed the manner in which it appears to local people that the government is playing favorites and choosing to privilege one set of constituents over another, in a way that applies a different set of rights and recognitions upon game farmers and only further obligations and restrictions on others. By evoking a social justice critique—that poor people are bearing the greatest and disproportionate burden of conservation efforts—he was impugning the development credentials of the government and taking issue with the state-promoted narratives of participation and equality.

However, he made this critique from within the bounds of another important state imaginary–the nonracial state. Most, though certainly not all, game farm owners are white Batswana, but the interviewee, in this case an MP, assiduously avoided a racial framing, opting for the terminology of "elite." Of course, my positionality as a white woman is important here. While my racial identity came up periodically in interviews in a variety of contexts, it was almost never explicitly referred to in conversations with elected officials and senior government bureaucrats, in part reflecting a broad elite consensus that such direct discussion of racial identity is impolite and counter to valorized state norms. Nevertheless, this MP's use of the term "elite" hints at the way in which local people created non-overlapping circles of "white" and "Batswana," as a man in the village of Bere noted, "Only those on the Afrikaner farms can eat game. As Batswana we don't get to, and it is not good."[42] This respondent's rhetorical construction implies a kind of favoritism, and an unwarranted one at that, because of this community's questionable claim to insider status. This statement creates an opposition—Afrikaners *or* Batswana, as categories that are separate. In this proposition, white citizens are perceived as outsiders, even if Batswana by birth and nationality, notwithstanding that this is complicated by the great number of non-citizen white residents in lucrative tourism and agricultural industries.[43] While perhaps not intentional, this interviewee internalized the grievances created by the exceptionality of private land on the conservation estate as a rejection of the state's explicitly nonracial self-image. This is demonstrative of the latent racial politics that are often sublimated in the public discourse in Botswana and also indicts the government for presumably being more attentive to "outsiders," however problematically construed, than "insiders." Local residents of the conservation estate find themselves contesting their own positions of marginality by decrying the apparent insider status afforded to game farmers over themselves. This is done in order to resist the unfairness with which they viewed the one exception to the hunting ban—the fact that animals will still be sold and consumed on game farms. One Motswana conservation practitioner expressed this complaint: "What's happened now is the hunting will continue only in private game farms, which basically means you've made hunting an elitist occupation. Because the people who own the game farms, who are they? It's mostly foreigners. It's not our local communities."[44] Here he blurs the line between foreigners and white landowners. By creating a juxtaposition between "local communities" and "foreigners," he collapses the possibility that game farm owners could be white Motswana citizens, rejecting the state's nonracial conception of citizenship in favor of a discourse that highlights the injustice generated by the state's attention to private landowners over other local populations on the conservation estate.

Local Conceptions of Ownership

> I refuse to believe that it is a wildlife area; we consider it our home.
>
> —Resident of the village of Bere[45]

At the heart of local grievances and frustrations with the predominantly white landowning community in Ghanzi District is a disjuncture between the types of land tenure and ownership recognized by the state and that recognized by most people on the conservation estate. This dichotomy is amplified by the population demographics of the conservation estate. Most people living in and around Botswana's protected areas are non-Tswana and descend from individuals who organized their lives in a spatially divergent manner from the rest of "mainstream" society. In light of this, people on the conservation estate attempt to normalize their ideas of ownership within the status quo. San territoriality and land tenure systems are deeply complex but nearly entirely overlooked by state institutions, which often looked through the terra nullius lens. Historically, this misreading of San land-use systems led to their areas of historical residency to be seen "as unoccupied and as ideal candidates for designation of conservation areas" (Magole 2009, 601).[46] The view of land as "vacant" and unowned is a myth that derives from a disconnect between San notions of ownership and the mainstream conceptualization (Bolaane 2013). One San activist directly linked this to the privileging of Tswana norms of territory and land-use patterns: "How land is distributed in Botswana is determined by the Tswana-speaking people. For example, you can't be allocated land for hunting and gathering—this land-use activity is not recognized by the government of Botswana."[47] Perhaps unsurprisingly, an activist dedicated to the issues of his ethnic community sees this as a concern of political identity and argues that the exclusion of traditional San activities from the system of territorialization and land regulation and allocation is part of a state strategy that disempowers this population. His statement demonstrates the power to create sociopolitical realities through categorization: because there is no land tenure arrangement recognizing hunting and gathering as a legitimate land-use strategy, these activities exist outside of "normal" and acceptable behaviors.

While most prominent in Ghanzi, where people are surrounded by privileged freehold landowners, these sentiments were echoed in Botswana's north. An elderly woman in the village of Mababe in Northwest District recalled the previous livelihood strategies of her community that included the collection of wild foods. When Chobe National Park was first established in 1960 as a game reserve, areas previously used for wild food gathering by Mababe's San population became part of the protected area (see Taylor 2001). When asked if her life had changed since the gazettement of the park, the elderly woman responded:

> Respondent: There are challenges because at first we used to gather food in the area that is now occupied by the park. But nowadays if you go there you will find a soldier who can shoot you.
>
> Author: A soldier can shoot you for collecting food?
>
> Respondent: Yes, he will be killing you for trespassing in his land. It's his land now.[48]

The securitization of the conservation estate has the ramifications beyond law enforcement (see chapter 2) and the reordering of subsistence behaviors. As the exchange above indicates, the material presence of the military in the territory devoted to conservation also accounts for the way land is inhabited, managed, and owned. From her perspective, the legitimate occupation of space is done through the barrel of a gun—those who are armed agents of the state "own" the land. These processes work to reconfigure local ideas of ownership and belonging and reterritorialize land as purview of the state, superseding on-the-ground perceptions of ownership and enforcing the strength of the state's tenure regime at the expense of locally derived concepts of ownership, autochthony, and, for San respondents, indigeneity. This is particularly powerful in and among communities removed from land in order to make way for a protected area (see this chapter's first section), as the presence of armed soldiers, in a practical sense, dispels the myth that the community still "owns" their former territory, even if they continue to adamantly make such claims. The prevalence of soldiers throughout the conservation estate is a physical manifestation of the failure of local concepts of ownership. This is in stark contrast to the apparent strength of the private property regime of freehold land and the wide latitude for the exercise of authority on the part of landowners recognized by the government.[49]

The abnegation of San "ownership" has not been achieved through force alone but also by the absence of San territorial realities on the practical technologies, such as mapping, that create social categories. Historically San territoriality was not limited to the people's place of occupation at any given moment but included the larger swath of land within which they seasonally migrated. Derived from this history, contemporary San communities have much more expansive notions of territory than the current political cartography suggests. An extensive community-mapping program inside the CKGR illustrated San territoriality that conventional maps often fail to capture. Inside the reserve, practitioners worked with former and current residents to account for the details left out of most cartographical exercises. One of the consultants working on the community-mapping program said that residents of the CKGR have "very complex territorial structures over vast areas. They've got hundreds of named units of land, and they have very detailed knowledge of each of those areas. They [DWNP] see Molapo [a community inside the CKGR] as a dot on the map, and until all this work was done the department never actually realized that, well, that's just the point that the department knows and that all of the surrounding areas is very much the focus [of the territory]."[50]

This brings to the fore the ways in which local conceptions of place, territory, and ownership are often lost in technocratic exercises of delineation and boundary-crafting, especially related to protected areas. These community-based exercises aim to re-embed the lived experiences of people onto territory to which they feel connected and give value to the emotional resonance of land claims. In many conservation-adjacent communities, the territory around them, and perhaps inaccessible to them, is a forum through which they seek to assert rights and insist on ownership in a manner relevant to their social world.

Community-mapping exercises are often related to a suite of policy proposals influenced by participatory ideas, like community-based conservation, that have been prominently used by conservation-adjacent people in Botswana to claim ownership.

When the first participatory conservation program, known in Botswana as the Community-Based Natural Resource Management (CBNRM), was introduced in the 1990s, many government elites were concerned that an expansion of the state's recognition of user rights would morph into calls for owner rights (Hitchcock 2006; Poteete 2009a). This was prescient and perceptive; many conservation-adjacent populations *do* view CBNRM arrangements as a means to exert rights over not just wildlife but also land, in a way reimagining the state consensus on territory and gaining a modicum of ownership akin to what they believe nearby private landowners (as well as other Batswana) have.

Many young San, particularly those educated to the secondary level and living in communities that have been relocated out of protected areas, often insist that CBNRM must recognize their rights as owners and original inhabitants of the land.[51] The assumption is that they could exert the same modes of contestation and resistance available to private landowners if they were recognized as such. One young man recounting community dialogue with DWNP noted, "We do not agree to anything that does not give us back our rights."[52] For these individuals, "rights" are afforded to those who own land. Specifically, in the case of the community relocated from the CKGR, this segment of younger individuals is adamant that the state should acknowledge their "tribal" rights to the CKGR (which is state land) as their historical territory, akin to the manner in which Tswana merafe are implicitly recognized as such for their Tswana residents. Their claim, in short, is that other Batswana living in various places throughout the country are accepted as having rights to land either as owners or members of a merafe. The presence of protected areas superimposed on their historical territories should not impede a similar set of recognitions for their community. In this context, land- and resource-use rights do political work—they convey a sense of dignity and recognition within Batswana state and society and highlight the fact that many people on the conservation estate perceive these basic tenets of citizenship and inclusion in the national project as lacking. The calls for land rights and ownership among people of the conservation estate also do cultural work, producing a sense of cohesion and identity heretofore inaccessible to many San people within Botswana.

Political recognition of San peoples is discursively tied to the legal status of the land they once occupied, especially in cases where land has become part of the conservation estate or sold as freehold land. This argument is well summed up by San writer and activist Kuela Kiema, who said in his memoir, "The Tswana live on tribal territory whereas the Kua [San] live on 'state' property. Our children are socialised at an early age to believe that they do not have any tribal land and that we cannot claim any land as a tribal territory" (Kiema 2010, 61). While the allocation of local ownership rights on the conservation estate appears to be a nonstarter for the government for several reasons, not the least of which is they reject the overtly identity-based political claims being made, residents continue to attempt to use the institutional levers of CBNRM to negotiate and contest the terms of resource governance.[53] A decades-long process of recentralizing CBNRM policy (LaRocco 2016; Rihoy and Maguranyanga 2010) can be understood against this backdrop of local attempts to use the program to instantiate ownership rights. The persistent deployment of ownership claims by local people has caused significant discomfort to government officials tasked with overseeing the conservation estate. DWNP employees frequently pushed back against any expansion of the category of "ownership." For example, the team responsible for the management of the CKGR conveyed the government's reluctance to allow the tenets of CBNRM to morph into rhetorical or actual ownership: "Many communities around Ghanzi, and especially in New Xade, are expecting to own the land, but that is not how the program [CBNRM] works."[54] They and their colleagues are adamant about the fact that CBNRM only offers communities the ability to benefit from certain parcels of land and does not confer ownership or the incumbent ability to contest or block state policies that ownership implies. As one official in the Ghanzi regional office put it, the communities must understand that the arrangements of CBNRM and community-use zones does not constitute "ownership" before any meaningful concession in terms of resource beneficiation would be agreed to by the government.[55]

Officials seem to recognize the potency with which communities take up this line of argumentation and the potentially detrimental effects on the state project. Some have even used the analogy of mineral-wealth distribution in an attempt to diminish these local claims to ownership and contestations regarding authority over this territory, demonstrating an anxiety about the differential precedents potentially established by CBNRM (Poteete 2009a; DeMotts and Hoon 2012). A senior official in Ghanzi said, "With the CKGR people they prefer for the money to go straight to their coffers. But it does not work like that. Look at diamonds. It is not just Orapa or Jwaneng that benefits."[56] The reference to Jwaneng and Orapa is telling. These are towns close to Botswana's lucrative diamond mines. By drawing up these communities as places of contrast to conservation-adjacent communities, the state official was making the point that diamond revenues are not linked to a specific locality but rather are nationalized, as should conservation resources. Nonetheless, local people see the state's discursive commitment to CBNRM as a means of contestation, as a way to create a legal relationship of ownership of a territory they already believe is theirs. In reality CBNRM is a highly circumscribed program that mostly reflects and reinforces state claims and positions, as references to the use of national resources like the mineral deposits are frequently used to deflate local claims to ownership. While local people view the state's discursive emphasis on CBNRM as a potential avenue for resistance, this is limited because of the low level of practical state commitment to the program and the diminishment of participatory conservation (see part I).

The assertions of ownership described above are not universal. Even despite frequent attempts to reclaim rights to the reserve through participatory conservation programs, many in the resettlement village of New Xade expressed a sense of resignation. A middle-aged man in the village noted, "The only way we can benefit from the CKGR is by stealing, not publicly."⁵⁷ The notion of "stealing" provides insights into how some in this community view their ownership rights as diminished in practice and subjectively self-ascribe resource use as theft. This is perhaps compounded by the fact that many in the community believe that government officials only view them as poachers (see chapter 2), as one respondent suggested, "Government said that we had to move because the area was a game reserve and did not want the animals to be disturbed. I don't think the government recognizes our knowledge about conservation. They just see us as poachers."⁵⁸ This belief that the state views people of the conservation estate as thieves or poachers illustrates the way in which many local people have internalized that the state is unable or unwilling to recognize their concepts of ownership of land and resources. As the comment above suggests, some people have begun to relate to this position, saying they can only benefit from the reserve by "stealing." The expansion of this subjectivity is noteworthy as it suggests that the social reality of surveillance, separation, and state scrutiny created by the control of land has worked to reorient some local peoples' self-conceptualization in their environment. As one cannot "steal" what one already "owns," this subjectivity suggests that conservation-adjacent people have been circumscribed in their ability to deploy "ownership" as a means of claim-making, especially in comparison with the well-positioned constituency of private freeholders, whom the government accepts and recognizes as legitimate owners of their property.

There is a tale of two kinds of ownership on the conservation estate. One, private property, is recognized and embedded in the legal system. The other, a kind of indigenous ownership tied up in notions of autochthony, locality, and ethnicity, attempts to harness the evident power of the former in order to negotiate with the state. Yet the avenues for contestation and recognition open to freehold landowners are not readily available to other actors on the conservation estate. Following from Lund's distinction between territory and property outlined at the beginning of this section, when land is not "owned" in the proprietary sense, it is subject to being governed as territory by state authorities. There is a stark contrast between the way state-recognized landowners interact with the state, compared with local people who dwell on land fundamentally governed by the central authorities.

The far-reaching impacts of the intersection between conservation and land tenure regimes can produce what Bluwstein and Lund call the "double territorialization—of landscape and of mind" (2018, 453). Where one sits upon the conservation estate—on territory or on property—shapes individual subjectivities as well as the way in which communities attempt to interact with the state. The calls for ownership are attempts to meaningfully inscribe local people on a map that has not accounted for their social reality in the official cartography and to make real attempts at contestation, negotiation, and resistance. However, the residents of the conservation estate are among the most marginalized citizens of Botswana, and arriving at a moment where their political claims are recognized at the same level as those of the tourist industry or Botswana's private landowners has heretofore been illusory. They lack a vital tool in a repertoire of resistance—a claim of ownership accepted beyond their communities. Local people of the conservation estate, usually San, attempt to seek recognition of their concepts of ownership and have had little success. As residents of state "territory," they are subject to the dictates of central control to a far greater extent that those who reside on their own "property."

This chapter has illustrated the manner in which conservation policies, while articulated as uniform and national, can and do fluctuate in response to myriad logics, interests, and imperatives at work in the state-building project. It has explored the way contestation, negotiation, and resistance are fragmented and limited on the conservation estate—that the unique confluence of conflicting logics of "property" and "territory" on Botswana's conservation estate lays bare the racial and class tensions that tend to be masked by the state's overt nonracial imaginary.

5

Infrastructure and the Contours of Settlement, Tourism, and Conservation

In 2009 as a young budget tourist on a mobile safari through the Okavango Delta, I recall being told that the Okavango, the "jewel of the Kalahari" (Ross 1987), was uninhabited by people and untouched by development, that this was one of the few places in Africa where animals were wholly unaccustomed to the presence of humans—a last bit of totally unclaimed and pristine remote wilderness.[1] I was slightly perplexed by this assertion. Were not the very people telling me this—the young Batswana leading me through the complex channels and waterways in dugout canoes called *mokoros*,[2] guiding an unwieldy group of tourists through the bush on early-morning walking safaris—clear evidence that people were, in fact, an integral part of this landscape? I remember thinking that if no one lives here, then who are these people who so clearly know every inlet and island in the delta? The paradox was clear.

What is most often omitted from glossy tourism marketing materials is the historical context explaining that protected areas around the world are unpopulated patches of wilderness because of purposeful policy intended to make them so. The "untouched wilderness" that I, and many others like me, encountered was a product of centuries of interactions between people and their environments. Yet the presentation of parcels of remote land as pristine and unoccupied, bereft of the trappings of modernity, is a political endeavor that devalues and delegitimizes claims of residency and local ideas of ownership (Bolaane 2013; Brockington 2002; Dowie 2009; Neumann 1998; Nustad 2015). Moreover, this presentation of unpeopled and undeveloped land directly limits the physical and social mobility of conservation-adjacent people and strengthens the state authorities and capital interests that maintain, control, and profit from rural nature-based tourism and the protected area system upon which it depends.

The second chapter of this section on territory and state building shifts gears and focuses on the material and instrumental technologies that shape the contours of territorial control on the conservation estate—examining the dispensation of state infrastructure and the perceptions, subjectivities, and relationships produced therein. This chapter argues that distinct logics of tourism and pervasive tropes of peopleless wilderness substantially alter the relationship between the state and its citizens on the conservation estate and creates a deeper differentiation in the state-building project that cannot be accounted for by only thinking about divisions between "rural" and "urban." As the vignette opening this chapter suggests, interrogation of state building on the conservation estate is also an examination of the politics of spatial reorganization more broadly. Shifts in the use of space and territory transform what it means to be a citizen in Botswana and the social relations that constitute it.

The previous chapter was primarily concerned with the ways in which variegated ideas of ownership impact spatial organization and territorialization on the conservation estate. This chapter, in turn, focuses on material aspects of spatial organization by interrogating how the provision or absence of infrastructure on the conservation estate is linked to the manner in which the state controls and regulates the use of space within its territory and organizes the residency patterns of its citizens through government interventions. It does so by interrogating the ways in which ambiguous, and seemingly contradictory, government expansions and retractions of state infrastructure function as mechanisms of state building.

Analysis of state infrastructure provision, or the lack thereof, can provide a window into how and why these "unpeopled" parcels of land are created and packaged for tourist audiences. Through this chapter, I utilize the dialectic of legibility and illegibility as a framing heuristic in the analysis. It interrogates how the provision (or absence) of state infrastructure such as all-weather roads, bridges, permanent buildings, water reticulation, electricity, and transportation facilities in regions of the conservation estate that host the bulk of Botswana's lucrative tourism industry are linked to state control and regulation of the use of space within its territory and the manner in which it organizes residency, migration, and mobility patterns of its citizens living adjacent to sites of tourism. It examines how ambiguous and seemingly contradictory government expansions and retractions of infrastructure function in concert with Botswana's vital but highly stratified tourism industry. The presence or absence of infrastructure is tied closely to the needs, perceptions, and landscapes sought by tourist visitors.

The importance of infrastructure is twofold, giving credence to Neumann's argument that "both wilderness and concentrated settlement are products of a single process, the creation of the modern territorial state" (Neumann 2004b, 212). The provision of infrastructure in a central location is a carrot to entice centralization and "modernization," in accordance with a developmentalist agenda that seeks to territorialize space and people. In Botswana's western region, the provision of infrastructure acts as a means through which to draw out previously sparsely populated and seasonally mobile people from "the bush" to live in state-sanctioned villages, pulling them into a relationship of "legibility" with the state, much like the processes articulated by Scott (1998). Conversely, in the north of the country, where the bulk of the tourism industry is based, the calculus is different. The denial of infrastructure is a stick to compel people to leave, or at least remain invisible, on the conservation estate, which is deemed more valuable without people. The allocation of infrastructure is delayed or denied in order to maintain the fiction of a peoplefree wilderness that appeals to tourist consumers—occluding the presence of local people, limiting their mobility, and shrinking their infrastructural footprint on the land to near imperceptibility on the part of tourist visitors and state authorities. This renders these populations "illegible."

While drawing from Scott's concept, I suggest that illegibility need not only be understood as a form of resistance to or avoidance of state power (Scott 2009) but that in the unique context produced by the imperatives of wildlife tourism on the conservation estate it operates an alternative manifestation of state power. By assessing various axes of diversity within two regions of Botswana's conservation estate, this chapter highlights how the myth of a peopleless wilderness (a perception buoying Botswana's tourism industry) produces highly differentiated modes of state intervention, shifting local peoples' ability to interact with the state, the tourism industry, and other citizens. The management of conservation spaces in western Botswana is imbricated upon histories of eviction and sedentarization (see chapter 4). This explains the juxtaposition of the more robust provision of infrastructure in western Botswana with the relative neglect in the north. Preferences and expectations of foreign tourist consumers generate differentiated incentives for the Botswana state across its territory on the conservation estate, in some places necessitating legible citizens, while in others producing illegibility.

Infrastructure as Statecraft

Control over space plays a key role in defining, constituting, and operationalizing state power (Badiey 2013; Boone 2013; Engel and Nugent 2010; Maclean 2010). Importantly, how infrastructure is deployed throughout space impacts the production of a normative political and social order, which is of particular relevance in marginal or frontier spaces where extension of infrastructure may be a vector of state and capital control. Infrastructure can provide insight into social relations, state power, and citizen-state relations (Anand 2017; Gohain 2019; Gupta 2015; Harvey 2006; Mann 1984; Marijnen and Schouten 2019). Roads in particular hold significant resonance in analysis of the sociopolitical importance of infrastructure provision (Harvey and Knox 2015; Death 2016b). Selective infrastructure provision and access provide a window into how states incorporate or exclude people and spaces from the national imaginary (Gohain 2019). Moreover, often articulated as a modernizing endeavor, especially for those living at the margins of state control, the act of "infrastructuring" is a primary vector for development (Nugent 2018, 30; Chalfin 2010; Das and Poole 2004; Mosley and Watson 2016). Large-scale infrastructure projects and ambitious development plans have come back into fashion on the African continent, tied to the "Africa rising" narrative and presented as key vehicles for social and economic uplift. This has reinvigorated the use of Scottian framing in the analysis of infrastructure and growth in Africa (see, e.g., the 2016 special collection edited by Mosley and Watson in the *Journal of East African Studies*).

Scott's concept of legibility highlights citizen mobility as a key anxiety of modern states and the processes that attempt to make societies more legible—categorized, simplified, sedentarized, measured, and controlled—as key logics of statecraft and state capacity (1998). It is a modality of simplification and standardization that reorganizes space, nature, and social practice. Legibility allows for systematic governance and is understood to be a core tenet of high-modernist technocratic developmentalism. Through these grand schemes, aimed at achieving legibility of peoples and environments, states seek to make themselves governable and, importantly, profitable. Legibility is viewed here as an impulse of states. The inversion of this, illegibility, is conceptualized in his later work as the purview of people. Scott's 2009 book *The Art of Not Being Governed* envisions illegibility as a mechanism for escaping the overbearing state. In his analysis of upland Southeast Asia, in the mountainous region he defines as "Zomia," locals use their relative inaccessibility, remoteness, and presence in "wilderness" as a means to evade state control, avoid oppressive state policies, and take refuge. Illegibility, in this configuration is a strategy of resistance, wherein populations may make themselves illegible, absenting themselves from political governability and thus seeking to avoid the control of the state and exploitations of capital. Damonte argues that illegibility is the "lack of data and social knowledge required for fostering state control over territories and populations" (2016, 957). However, the empirical case of Botswana's conservation estate suggests that illegibility may not simply be a lack of capacity to "see" local complexity but also the purposeful obscuring of these spaces for the sake of capital accumulation. Uribe's analysis of road infrastructure in the Colombian Amazon is instructive here. He suggests an alternative framing of illegibility not simply as a synonym for "ungoverned" or "uncaptured" but also "an ambiguous and volatile terrain in which infrastructure's techno-political and social worlds are constantly co-produced" (2018, 7). As such, the illegible spaces are not absent, beyond, or resistant to the state but rather are coproduced. This is further reflected by the ways in which the use of infrastructure is never uniform or coherent across whole swaths of state territory but instead fragmented and ambiguous. In reckoning with these contextual and spatially differentiated analyses of infrastructure, Uribe calls for a "dialectical understanding of state-society interactions produced by infrastructure" (2018, 3). When taking into account the global political economy of tourism, specifically wildlife and nature tourism in many countries in Africa, illegibility of people in nature may also serve state interests rather than just being a form of resistance to state building. Responding to the global tourist gaze on the conservation estate that tends to valorize the aesthetics of primitivity, Edenic pristineness, and rusticity, states may in fact have an incentive to mask their populations and present an image of wilderness spaces as devoid of people—making their own citizens illegible. This takes seriously empirical scenarios wherein capital extraction is bound up with the lack of infrastructure and development and the seeming absence of concomitant populations. This is increasingly relevant in wildlife tourism–based economies that premise capital accumulation on the commodification of an undeveloped, people-free wilderness (Brockington, Duffy, and Igoe 2008; Brockington and Duffy 2011; Kelly 2011; Neumann 1998, 2004b, 2000).

Wilderness, Tourism, and Conservation in Botswana

> Even the residential plots we occupy have not been registered officially because apparently we are living in a tourism area. We are regarded as *bomaipaahela* [illegal settlers].
>
> —*Kgosana* (headman), village of Boro[3]

Wildlife-based tourism is premised on commoditizing a particular vision of nature separate from culture that resonates with tourists. This nature/culture divide is curated and reinforced by design in the tourist experience, often in tourism "circuits" that obscure the presence of people and any hints of so-called modernity (Butt 2012). This creates spatial enclaves of tourism, which Igoe argues enact a "representational order that is commonly experienced through controlled motion in safari vehicles. They cater to consumptive tourist desires, but have also become increasingly significant to the management of people, wildlife, and related modes of development" (2017, 14). Therefore, wilderness and remoteness are "social construction[s], resulting not from state inaction but from state intervention of a selective kind" (Gohain 2019, 206). Saxer and Andersson identify three features of remoteness that are analytically resonant. First, they argue that areas deemed remote are, in fact, entangled with connectivity "wiring them to the world economy and into global politics and mediascapes" (2019, 143) in a "patchwork of distance and proximity" (2019, 144). Next, they identify the economic usefulness of remoteness, which can be seen in the ways that lacking "development" acts as authenticator of ecological and cultural heritage in the tourism industry. The areas "off the grid" of legibility are not excluded from the global economy but are important nodes of extraction in their own right. Finally, they observe that remoteness amplifies the likelihood of "remote control" of these spaces (2019, 149).

Botswana's sizable conservation estate is intimately connected to the tourism industry, which is almost entirely based on wildlife safaris and other "wilderness" experiences. The previous chapter explored how this endowment is intimately connected to historical evictions (often of non-Tswana communities) and premised upon a stratified land tenure system. While centered around the country's protected area network, Botswana's tourism product is spatially and experientially diverse across the conservation estate. There are ecological and touristic differences between the Okavango/Chobe region and the Kalahari (Barnes 1991). Though neither region is monolithic in either ecological or social features, there are some broad characteristics that define each. The northern areas of the country have larger wildlife populations and riverine ecologies, whereas the western Kalahari is more arid and features desert ecosystems. Botswana's north (including Northwest and Chobe Districts) is home to Botswana's most well-known and sought-after protected areas, Moremi Game Reserve and Chobe National Park. The main ecological and landscape feature of the north is the Okavango Delta, a recently inscribed UNESCO World Heritage Site, a Ramsar wetland of global importance,[4] and the proverbial golden goose of Botswana's tourism industry. It features prominently in travel publications and documentaries aimed at Western audiences and attracts much attention in developed countries as a favorite destination of members of the British royal family. The desert ecosystem is dominated by the massive Central Kalahari Game Reserve. While less obviously lucrative than the popular high-end destinations in the north, the CKGR occupies a unique space in Botswana's conservation portfolio and is enjoyed by self-drive tourists. Approximately the size of Belgium, the CKGR is the second-largest terrestrial protected area in the world after Selous Game Reserve in Tanzania.

Botswana's increasing reliance on tourism reflects the trajectory of economic development in the country over the past several decades (Pfotenhauer 1991). By 2007 tourism was the country's second-largest industry (Mbaiwa and Darkoh 2009). Looking toward a future when the country's diamond reserves are exhausted, Botswana's national development plans emphasize tourism as an essential avenue for continued economic growth at the national level (Atlhopheng and Mulale 2009). The government has emphasized a "high-value, low-volume" model of tourism development, which favors fewer tourists but who pay a premium for more luxury guest experiences predicated on remoteness, exclusivity, and the absence of human occupation. The illusion of untouched space is a key selling point. High-end international tourists (usually from the Global North) typically fly into Maun, the north's transportation hub and Northwest District's capital, and then take small aircraft directly to four- and five-star lodges in the heart of the Okavango Delta. Self-drive tourists and mobile safaris make up a substantially different sector and are more likely to be found throughout the conservation estate (including in the Kalahari), whereas high-end clients are more common in the north. Tourism, like diamonds before it, is a luxury good with a highly elastic demand that relies upon international tourists. It is an experiential rather than a material commodity, and because of this, foreigners' perceptions and preferences often drive demand and shape local realities. The presence of people or signs of contemporary human residency like paved roads or electrical infrastructure have little place in this imagined landscape.

Tourism in Botswana has been defined as an enclave industry. It is dominated by large multinational corporations. Many of the investors and owners are foreign, and there is little citizen involvement at higher levels of the sector. Most Batswana in the industry are employed in low-wage service jobs, with management positions commonly held by expatriates (Mbaiwa 2005). When there is citizen involvement in the industry, it is typically by well-connected elites, often non-local to the conservation estate, who possess connections to political power (Mbaiwa and Hambira 2020). More broadly, the industry is poorly linked to the local economy, and rural poverty in and around the Okavango Delta has increased even as tourism has grown rapidly. Enclave tourism reflects the needs and preferences of the clients, not the host communities, is dependent on demand from developed countries, and engenders resentment and alienation at the local level (Mbaiwa 2005). Predicated on the securing of undeveloped hotspots, enclave tourism bears relevance to Ferguson's 2005 analysis of Scott's oeuvre. He refines Scott's concept of high-modernist developmentalism "by reviewing some of the ways that recent capital investment in Africa has been territorialized, and some of the new forms of order and disorder that have accompanied that selectively territorialized investment" (2005, 378). Ferguson argues that rather than the highly legible nationalized projects of Scott's *Seeing Like a State*, the era of globalized capital had brought a hotspot, or enclave approach, seen through intense mineral resource extraction or, as he puts it, "seeing like an oil company." Wildlife tourism is a kind of in situ hotspot on the conservation estate—resource exploitation, which like mineral extraction is highly capitalized but dependent on the absence of development for that exploitation.

Western Botswana: Ghanzi District and the CKGR

> When I was a young man, before we were removed from Central [the CKGR], there were many animals. We didn't finish the animals, because we know better. . . . The Tswana killed off their animals and then came to take ours. Now the government says the animals belong to the government and to the lekgoa [white people, meaning tourists].
>
> —Resident of New Xade[5]

The landscape of Ghanzi District is dominated by freehold cattle farms mostly owned by descendants of early European settlers, Wildlife Management Areas (WMAs), and the CKGR. The Botswana government does not enumerate census information by ethnicity; however, scholars estimate that around half of the region's population are San—descendants of the original inhabitants who were dispossessed or moved off the land to make way for the commercial cattle industry and wildlife reserves (see chapter 4). Postcolonial Botswana has privileged development approaches that seek to reorient the spatial organization and land-use practices of San people. The state initiated a series of policies, now collectively known as the Remote Area Development Programme, aimed at settling these communities in government-sanctioned villages and limiting access to natural resources, while also utilizing populations barred from traditional economies as a cheap labor reserve for commercial cattle farms in Ghanzi and elsewhere (Hitchcock and Holm 1993; Nthomang 2004).

The history of state anxiety caused by nonsedentary populations, mobility restrictions, relocation, and resettlement looms large across this region, especially with regard to the CKGR, as discussed at length in the previous chapter. The CKGR removals and subsequent legal case are relevant contexts for analyzing the state distribution and dissemination of infrastructure across this part of the conservation estate. Dating back to the period before, during, and after relocation, government officials explicitly drew upon modernization and legibility as the legitimizing logic for state action and directly contrasted spaces serviced by built infrastructure with spaces deemed appropriate for wildlife and tourism. The government's narrow interpretation of the ruling is intimately tied to infrastructure provision and delivery of social services. Those remaining within the reserve must travel to resettlement villages like New Xade in order to access services and infrastructure, a strategy that has continued to draw out the remaining population since the court ruling. However, Sapignoli notes that the prohibition on infrastructure within the CKGR is more nuanced and fraught. While the removed communities were told they could not be provided with infrastructure and services because that would clash with the conservation imperative, "permanent infrastructures were present [in the park] that *embody state interests*, such as roads, camping sites for tourists and wildlife scouts, elegant tourist lodges, new boreholes for wildlife, a working diamond mine, and camps for police and game scouts" (2018, 257, emphasis mine).

Infrastructure Provision in Ghanzi District

With the exception of the Transkalahari Highway (which facilitates long-distance travel through the district and is utilized by self-drive tourists), Ghanzi has a limited road network linking a series of remote communities. Settlements in Ghanzi tend to be eighty to one hundred kilometers away from the next village or community.[6] These are resettlement villages established in the 1970s and 1980s (with New Xade being the most recent) to bring San communities in from mobile lifestyles "out in the bush" as well as relocate the families of those working as low-wage laborers on commercial freehold farms in the district. Various resettlement communities are isolated from each other as well as from the district capital, Ghanzi Town. The rudimentary road infrastructure limits mobility in and out of these communities. However, within the resettlement villages themselves, the government has invested significant resources to the provision of infrastructure and services. The state has a visible presence in these remote areas, ostensibly to serve the relocated citizenry. Villages in Ghanzi typically have, at a minimum, a primary school, a health clinic, a *kgotla* and office for the traditional authorities, and often other state-provided buildings. Electricity is provided to some of the government buildings, such as the school, and water is made available at several publicly accessible wells and boreholes. By June 2017 some communities even featured the innovation of solar-powered streetlights. While quite basic compared with more urban districts in Botswana, the average settlement in Ghanzi boasts far more of these amenities than similarly isolated communities in the northern part of the country.[7] In fact, my research assistant, herself from a small village on the Okavango panhandle, remarked several times that the Ghanzi resettlement communities appear well resourced and substantially built-up in comparison to her home area. Many local interview respondents suggested that the prevalence of this infrastructure is an inducement or reward for their acquiescence to government relocation programs, as a way to incentivize continued sedentarized living as well as promote the so-called modern orientation of village life, away from historically mobile modes of being associated with life in the WMAs or the CKGR.[8]

These resettlement villages become sites of necessity for the survival of those relocated. No longer able to move freely and use the resources and local environments as they once did (see chapter 6), residents are dependent on the services provided at these nodes of state intervention. For example, in Ghanzi District's arid ecosystem, the availability of water often limits where sedentarized human settlement can occur. Previous mobility patterns meant that human movement followed water supplies. However, as the restrictive topographies of parks and other protected areas became enacted, these seasonal movements were curtailed. If people are unable to move freely throughout protected areas in response to the changing availability of water supplies, they need to avail themselves of water where it is present—in the villages, not out in the bush. Moreover, as restrictions on the gathering or hunting of food coalesced into a sharp regime of non-use, people of Ghanzi's settlement villages, who have little historical experience with husbandry or agriculture and live in a place where the ecosystem does not support much crop production, became more and more dependent on food handouts and government welfare payments disbursed by the state in the places where it meets its citizens. Since resettlement began in earnest in the 1970s, first from freehold farms and later from wildlife areas, Ghanzi's population has been made legible to the government by both removing them from the bush and by creating infrastructure as nodes of control for the basic necessities of life—water and food—that can no longer be obtained from the environment due to limitations on mobility and subsistence produced by "people-free" protected areas and associated regimes of resource non-use.

Notably, in these communities the infrastructure provision often went above and beyond the mere subsistence level to include other items of state intervention, like kgotla buildings and community structures. Despite these seemingly benevolent investments in infrastructure and services, state efforts often fall flat in communities where meaningful consultation with the local residents is lacking. A Gaborone-based NGO worker with experience in several Ghanzi settlement villages noted: "Get there, and you will see government structures, very beautiful structures, there for its people. It [the government] is visible, but they always fail when it comes to communication. Whenever they have to communicate to Basarwa [San] and their needs, there is a failure somewhere."[9] It is as if these structures become an empty shell of the promise of more consultative relationships between the government and its citizens on the conservation estate. State actors view the allocation of modern, permanent buildings as an evident commitment to the development of people relocated on the conservation estate.[10] As the above interviewee noted, this is not enough to constitute a productive, enduring relationship between the state and its conservation-adjacent citizens. In New Xade the government built a permanent structure meant to act as a preschool for children still too young to attend the local primary school. When I arrived in the village in March 2014, it had been largely repurposed as an informal kraal for goats and other small stock. The government had failed to grasp that the local community had well-established social networks for childcare and saw the building as having an alternative function from the original state-intended purpose.[11] No one had asked what kind of formal infrastructure would serve a locally relevant need, but rather the act of building a structure in the resettlement community was viewed by state actors as a valuable project, regardless of end-user preference. These infrastructure projects cannot simply be interpreted as public services provided by an altruistic government for the benefit of the people. They reflect the normative values of how and where people are supposed to live and reveal the kinds of priorities the state has in mind for its resettled citizens.

Many citizens on the conservation estate argued that the state model has not accounted for their day-to-day needs once their land-use and residency patterns were altered. Respondents noted that since being moved into villages and placed under strict conservation restrictions, they lack the ability to obtain household-level subsistence, often feeling hemmed in and unable to access mobility-based economies like food gathering (see part III). Sapignoli, an anthropologist with years of ethnographic experience among the communities removed from the CKGR, observed a similar phenomenon of resignation and destitution. She noted of the community of New Xade, "It is only when I spent time with the residents of the village that another reality became apparent, a reality in which people had few jobs and depended mainly on government destitute rations, in which they 'do not know what to do' because the land is poor and unfamiliar, and in which they often get arrested while hunting or in possession of wild meat" (Sapignoli 2018, 67). Respondents during my fieldwork further described how their geographic remoteness precluded them from taking advantage of employment in the tourism industry, as the district does not support a high density of lodges or campsites and the resettlement villages are distant from those that do exist. The provision of communal services at resettlement nodes—clinics, schools, a kgotla—did not make up for the changes in spatial arrangements and livelihood opportunities brought about by living in the village. Government authorities pointed to the increased provision of services and infrastructure as evidence of upliftment, but many residents remained aggrieved:

> Author: So, what would you say to someone that says, look, here in New Xade you have a school, a clinic, and social services?
>
> Respondent: The school is there, but it is not meant for me but children. Will I eat that school?[12]

Local residents regarded the provision of infrastructure as inadequate in terms of providing them with holistic well-being. In the case of the most high-profile resettlement village, the government appears to be trying to make New Xade as attractive a place as possible for those people removed from the CKGR. In fact, many government officials earnestly described their endeavors there with pride. Yet, despite good-faith efforts, this policy focus on infrastructure is done according to the state's modernist visions of what is needed in these areas—not in response to local concepts of settlement, mobility, and territory—and their connections to locally significant ideas around well-being. The presence of government-built public buildings did not override the general sense of discontent that pervaded the community, as one man said curtly, "I never loved to be relocated."[13] People in these resettled communities frequently recounted with dissatisfaction the fact that they were told they *must* relocate away from the conservation estate in order to access the much-touted state services. In contesting this, relocated people explicitly drew upon what they see as contradictory practices occurring elsewhere in Botswana. A man working for a small San advocacy organization in Gaborone characterized the situation thus: "As far as development happens, for most groups development comes to the people, but with the San we are expected to have to go to the development."[14] Here he highlighted the perception that some Batswana are treated differently in interactions with the state across territory, calling into question the notions of equality in citizenship promoted in state discourse. Government officials reject this thinking, suggesting that concentration of infrastructure in particular state-sanctioned localities is a technical matter of monetary or administrative resources available, rather than an overt strategy of concentration and removal of people from the conservation estate. The Ghanzi District development officer tasked with the disbursement of projects in the area noted, "We have limited resources, so it is good to be within one area to access services, especially if there is one area that is already serviced."[15]

This is, of course, a credible position from the point of view of the state. Without delving into the merits of the financial argument, it is apparent that people in western Botswana interpret the concentration of services through the lens of regional and ethnic difference rather than accept the rationale of technocratic limitations offered by government. The long history of sedentarization, the knowledge of which is very much alive in San communities, colors their willingness to accept the government's stated rationales—whether credible or not. They perceive a world in which other Batswana do not have to choose between living and moving where they please and having access to government-provided infrastructure and services. For people in the rural conservation estate in the Kalahari region, the emphatic provision of resources at discrete, concentrated locations is viewed as a continuation of the logics of removal from the protected areas and indicative of the state's control over territory they understand as their own.

Northern Botswana: Northwest District and the Okavango Delta

> We have long talked about the road, but they say the road will not be constructed because it is next to the park. They also say that electricity would not erected because animals will destroy the electricity.
> —Residents of Sankuyo[16]

Local discontent with the state's top-down model of infrastructure provision in Ghanzi District might lead one to wonder how citizens view infrastructure policy in regions that have not been subject to the government's same impulses. The situation in Northwest District, the hub of Botswana's lucrative protected areas, provides an interesting point of comparison across the conservation estate. Transportation infrastructure is a good place to begin this analysis.

Livingston's interrogation of Botswana's fraught and complicated relationship to economic growth argues that "roads are the *sine qua non* of development" (Livingston 2019, 87). Death writes at length about the role of roads as an analytical window into the conservation estate: "It is a visceral incision into a landscape, governing lived space through the movement of peoples and representational spaces through maps and imagined geographies. It is also a socially and politically ambivalent technology: associated with progress, speed, modernization, and opportunity but also with danger, fear, hazards, and the prospect of increased environmental degradation on local and global scales" (Death 2016b, 71–72). We see that these twinned, contradictory impulses can be found in the citizen-state contestation over road infrastructure in Botswana. The paved road network in the northern part of the country was largely nonexistent before the 1990s, when infrastructure improvements were made to facilitate the growth of the tourism industry (Mbaiwa and Darkoh 2009). Despite these changes, rural communities still consistently complain that the improvements have not transformed their lives but rather have only allowed tourists to efficiently reach the outskirts of the Okavango Delta, specifically to the town of Maun, and then venture farther afield into the wetland to experience "wilderness" via aircraft or specially equipped safari vehicle. All sites visited for this project in the delta were accessible only by poorly maintained gravel or dirt roads—in many cases being merely a faint track in the bush. Concern about road accessibility and infrastructure was constantly expressed to me in the villages of Sankuyo, Khwai, and Mababe—all located inside the veterinary cordon fence and home to significant populations of game. The road leading to these communities is paved for approximately twenty-five kilometers outside of Maun and then is made of gravel until it reaches the buffalo fence. Deeper into the delta, the road becomes a sandy track, frequently susceptible to being washed out by the heavy storms and flooding that accompany Botswana's short but intense rainy season. These instances of heavy flooding or washouts sometimes necessitate long, circuitous detours that add several hours to trips to and from Maun. Despite decades of requests for upgrades to the road, it remains neither fully graveled nor paved.

Some in these communities attribute this failure to a lack of government funds or their low population size, but the overwhelming majority of interviewees associated the unpaved roads with their location within a lucrative wildlife tourism area of the conservation estate. Sankuyo's *kgosi* suggested, "There are some certain developments that when they do them, they have to consider the wildlife in these areas. For example, the road. Talking about the road, some people don't think that it's a good idea to have a tarmac road because some people will speed up and kill animals."[17] An embedded contradiction is that while wildlife-based tourism, most often in the form of the safari or the game drive, has mobility as its central logic, this experience is predicated upon the immobility of local populations and limited provision of basic transportation infrastructure on the conservation estate, as Gardner notes in his analysis of the global opposition to a proposed road in Tanzania's Serengeti (2017). Many residents explicitly connected this lack of infrastructure to the tourism industry and the particular visions of "wilderness" associated with wildlife safaris. Poor roads become coded to tourist visitors as part of the charm and adventure of the experience and reiterate to them that the delta is a place for animals, not people, making their travel there more unique and exhilarating. A man involved on his community's village development committee argued, "Tourist clients are complaining that they don't want a tarred road."[18] This respondent demonstrated the manner in which the government rationale of fiscal limitations is generally not accepted in these communities, even if it may very well be true. The perception that the protection of animals preempts residents' calls for infrastructure improvements reaffirms the locally held idea that wildlife species are valued above the human residents of the conservation estate. The belief that decisions are made with animals or tourists as the referent, rather than local residents, is commonplace no matter how emphatically the state argues otherwise. Despite government officials saying delays in infrastructure are attributable to a lack of money, people continue to believe that it is related to the presence of wildlife and the state's predominant interest in maintaining those populations for the tourism industry. This demonstrates the state's difficulty in being seen as a credible broker on the conservation estate and the manner in which the legitimacy and transparency of state decisions are questioned consistently by conservation-adjacent people. Local people, feeling remote from the consultation process (see chapter 3) are reluctant to take the state's word in good faith. Even strenuous assertions to the contrary do not dispel rumors about why the state has failed to deliver.

Issues with roads notwithstanding, many high-end tourists, especially clients at the most expensive lodges, are able to fly into Maun from Johannesburg or Gaborone and almost immediately fly out again deep into the heart of the delta in helicopters or six- to twelve-seat planes that can land on private airstrips operated by luxury lodges. This enclave experience is juxtaposed with the daily lives of those on the conservation estate who struggle with the lack of transportation infrastructure. Conservation-adjacent residents, many of whom are the descendants of those evicted during the colonial era, highlight the poor roads as exacerbating their condition of marginality and limited mobility. Moreover, rather than seek to make themselves unseen as an act of resistance or avoidance of the state, their illegibility in the eyes of the state is a key grievance. In numerous interviews, the issue of the roads was given as an example of the relationship between local people and the state. A middle-aged woman in the village of Mababe recounted a meeting with government officials where the community expressed dismay at the quality of their surrounding infrastructure: "We talked about the state of the road. The president once came here, and he said he needed a plane to get from Sankuyo to Maun because the road leading there was in a very bad state. It has been long since we complained about this road, and up to today we haven't seen any response, let alone any efforts to fix it."[19]

In the minds of conservation-adjacent people, air travel is almost exclusively associated with wealthy tourists or government officials who bypass and fly over them. The fact that representatives of the state often visit their areas via plane or helicopter is symbolically resonant for local people—government officials literally have not traveled their roads and cannot relate to the hardship that the lack of infrastructure brings; the people remain unseen. Instead, elected officials and administrators opt for the mode of transportation preferred by the *makgoa*, or tourists.[20] Air travel (and air power) within the conservation context, what Massé (2018) calls "verticality," becomes synonymous with state actors. Local residents, on the other hand, are subject to the vagaries of their poorly maintained and not infrequently impassable dirt roads. The physical disconnect between the realities of living without reliable transportation infrastructure and watching government elites fly in and out of remote and inaccessible areas of the conservation estate exacerbates the divide between the rulers and the ruled and generates resentment toward tourist visitors. Conservation-adjacent residents perceive that what infrastructure development has been put in place, such as improvements of the road network to reach Maun from the south and high-profile expansions of the Maun airport, are not meant for them. The continued poor state of the roads is related directly to the residents' place on the conservation estate, where a premium is put on an imagined rusticity sought after by international visitors. In her history of Moremi Game Reserve, Bolaane (2013) recounts how certain makeshift bridges have been left intact because of the rustic "charm" they provide for visitors. In a similar vein, a research informant recalled the long lines of self-drive and lodge vehicles waiting to cross a single, rough-hewn wooden bridge near the Khwai gate. He attributed the delay not to the volume of people entering the park but rather the time each vehicle required for guests to get out and take photographs on the bridge for their social media profiles.

Infrastructure Provision in Northwest

The lack of road improvement is not the only infrastructural constraint placed on people living in the northern conservation estate. Several villages on the outskirts of the delta, as well as a few remaining communities closer to the core area, require infrastructure above and beyond roadways to facilitate accessibility and mobility. For example, to travel to the village of Ditshiping from Maun, you must drive a four-by-four approximately an hour along a dirt track. From there, you will be offloaded at a mokoro station (see figure 5.1) to wait for local polers to transport you several kilometers farther into the delta and past a well-known hippo pool, the occupants of which the polers circuitously and steadfastly avoid (see figure 5.2). Once reaching the other side of

FIGURE 5.1. Mokoro station, Ditshiping. Author's photograph.

FIGURE 5.2. Traveling to Ditshiping via mokoro. The hippo pool is to the left. Polers must hug the bank in order to avoid disturbing the animals. Author's photograph.

this route, it is a thirty-minute walk through the bush to finally arrive at the center of the village. Even this route is sometimes further blocked due to flooding that disrupts these connections.

The building of a bridge over a single delta channel would make this route more directly accessible via four-by-four, something the residents have called for over many years. Without such a bridge, people of the community feel their developmental options are limited. A young man from Ditshiping said, "I wish the bridge could be completed because more developments would follow given the accessibility of the village."[21] During my most recent fieldwork the community was still not visited by a mobile clinic or other government services because it could not be reached by motor vehicle alone.

However, the residents of this community have not simply accepted the government's reluctance to embark on infrastructure development. Along with neighboring Xuoxao,[22] the residents of Ditshiping, under the auspices of their community trust,[23] have begun to build bridges themselves. "We are in an inaccessible area," one resident told me. "The trust is trying by all means to improve our lives, as they are trying to build a bridge right now."[24] In this context, the community trust was viewed as the central institution providing for the community and one of their main sources of well-being. Nonetheless, local residents insisted that the trust was not a substitute for the government but rather a means through which to collectively organize their contestation of the state's neglect of their areas. They have taken it upon themselves to construct and maintain bridges on their own, cobbling them together with whatever materials are accessible and affordable—logs, wire, corrugated roofing sheets, rope, even a few Coca-Cola bottles—thus marking their presence on the land with infrastructure despite the disinterest of the authorities. This do-it-yourself engineering is a kind of legibility as resistance, an inversion of usual theoretical framing that sees illegibility as a key tool for expressing discontent with state behavior. It stands as a rebuke to government delays in infrastructure delivery as well as a call by the local residents for the state to meet them halfway in their pursuit of further infrastructure development. Rather than trying to absent themselves, they are making claims on the land and on the state, inscribing their community into the landscape with the materiality of infrastructure. As of June 2017, the trust had built and maintained seven of the eight bridges needed to access the village of Xuoxao (the government built one), though heavy rains made Ditshiping still inaccessible. A young man noted, "The government gave us an excuse that there is no accessibility to this area, and we built the bridge ourselves as a community to see what excuse the government would give now."[25] With the construction of the bridge, the community is now marginally more accessible and indeed legible, and from the point of view of local people the government must no longer delay infrastructure and greater service provision to the community. Residents consistently reiterated the fact that they had met the government halfway and demonstrated the self-reliance promoted in the national ethos (by

FIGURE 5.3. Unfinished community-built bridge, Ditshiping. Author's photograph.

the Setswana term *boipelego*) and in the Vision 2016 document. As they perceive themselves as meeting state-emphasized benchmarks, people in conservation-adjacent communities attempt to leverage this position into concrete partnerships.

It is notable that despite the disappointment generated by the lack of state-sponsored infrastructure and service provision, the communities in the delta retained the tendency to view the government as a partner and sought to negotiate with it from a position of equals. Within these attempts it appears that local residents recognize and buy into the state rhetoric of self-reliance and then proceed to meet those expectations, only to be ignored. This creates a frustration that begins to fragment the relationship between the state and its citizens in these localities. For their efforts, conservation-adjacent people hope to see some sort of compromise from the government. In fact, at the time of my fieldwork there was much anxiety related to their ability to maintain the finished bridges as well as complete the work on those still under construction. The government decision to end hunting had ripple effects here, as the income for the community trust, the institution funding and organizing the voluntary work, had greatly decreased. One of the local residents involved in the Ditshiping construction effort noted, "We built bridges using money collected from the hunting operator by the trust. Now since hunting is stopped that means no hunting operator will give us anything, and the government is also not helping us with developments here."[26] Without the trust's income or a renewed commitment from the government, it was unclear to them whether these bridges could be maintained, let alone completed.

The observations made around the example of the bridges shed light on three important points linking the role of infrastructure to the larger arguments of this book. First, in a space where government is conspicuously distant or even absent, conservation-adjacent communities have opted out of looking only toward the center and instead turned to their local institutions to undertake relatively large infrastructure projects. These attempts rebut government rhetoric that associates people on the conservation estate with unproductive lifestyles, dependence on handouts, and disinterest in communal uplift.[27] Community leaders have tried to use this collective action to leverage cooperation from district and national figures and sought redress for what they see as an unfair lack of government involvement. Even as they attempted to address their situation locally, the use of discursive comparison between those areas outside and inside the conservation estate was fairly typical. These juxtapositions are often used to frame the argument of neglect and disinterest for these areas—the production of a purposeful illegibility—on the part of the government. The MP for the Okavango area in 2014 was from an ethnic minority group and a member of the political opposition. In our conversations he directly contrasted the situation in his constituency area with that of Central District, the heartland of the Botswana Democratic Party and the tribal home of the Khama family. He asked, "Why there is a hospital in Palapye, forty kilometers away in Mahalapye there's another, sixty kilometers away in Serowe there is another, when there is no hospital in Okavango?"[28] These three large villages in Botswana's east are all within two to three hours' driving distance from Gaborone and situated along the Gaborone–Francistown road. They are the core of the old Bamangwato *morafe* (kingdom) and viewed by many residing on the conservation estate as receiving outsized favoritism in development and infrastructure provision due to their historical connection with the ruling BDP and Botswana's first president, Seretse Khama. Regardless of the merits of this belief or of the efficacy of a direct comparison between two distinct regions, the use of these towns in Central District as a point of reference is noteworthy. It constructs those Batswana living in the southeastern populations centers as favored insiders set against the self-ascribed outsiders of the conservation estate. Perhaps counterintuitive given familiar analyses of the rural-urban divide, the places with which the articulation of difference is drawn are not the main urban centers of Botswana—Gaborone or Francistown—but instead traditional Tswana villages of the rural heartland. Locations like Palapye, Mahalapye, and Serowe are most relevant to the daily lives of Botswana's rural residents, not urban elites.[29] This makes apparent the observable differences that exist within the concept of "the rural": the conservation estate functions in such a way that its citizens view themselves as having experiences of citizenship substantively different from not only those in the urban areas but also their counterparts in rural non-conservation spaces.

Second, in the north, many respondents believed the limits of government infrastructure developments were derived from an overriding goal of removal and the creation of an entirely people-free wilderness, readily packaged and sold to willing tourists. A young man from Sankuyo argued, "They delay developments because they want to relocate us. So maybe they want us to give up and say 'Okay, now you can relocate us to where you guys think you want us to be.'"[30] He described a slow attritional approach to citizen relocation, which was certainly evident elsewhere in the country, such as in the years leading up to the more forceful removal of communities from the CKGR. This statement demonstrated the manner in which the failure of infrastructure provision in these conservation areas was able to generate a subjectivity and positionality on the part of local people vis-à-vis the government. Residents perceived the lack of infrastructure development as instrumental and almost punitive, as a way to create despondency and complacency among those living on the conservation estate. The lack of modern infrastructure cause residents to question their status, as a young man noted, "There are rumors flying thick and fast that we might be relocated from this place. We fully reject that relocation. If anything, government should gravel our road and erect a bridge structure."[31] This respondent regards the imposition of permanent, government-sponsored infrastructure as sign of longevity of tenure and a right to occupy land; without it the insecurity remains. Without infrastructure to make their claims material, and in a sense legible, they fear they are easily

FIGURE 5.4. Community-constructed bridge, Xuoxao. Author's photograph.

removed—another set of people disappeared from the map and the landscape in order to set the stage for tourism. As a result, the delay in service provision was highlighted as evidence of potential future relocation. "I suspect why they haven't been bringing amenities here is because they have relocation on their mind-sets, long before we even heard of," a resident of Khwai told me. "So that is the reason why developments are being trapped."[32] The collective historical memory of colonial-era relocations as well as the recent CKGR controversy loom large, with informants frequently invoking the specter of these past removals.[33]

Finally, some believe that the slow to nonexistent provision of infrastructure is directly linked to the tourism industry.[34] Tourism operators note that Botswana's comparative advantage is in its "Edenic" wilderness, an aesthetic made a key selling point in tourism marketing materials, with remoteness touted as a kind of ultimate luxury. Operators say that tourists revel in the unbridled nature they seem to observe in Botswana's Kalahari Desert and Okavango Delta and reiterate these notions in their marketing materials.³⁵ The lack of infrastructure—dirt roads, makeshift bridges, limited permanent structures—work to produce a primitive pristineness that appeals to many tourist audiences. The limited infrastructural footprint is not seen as a problem but instead directly linked to the area's appeal. This in turn devalues the conservation estate as a human space. In keeping with a "rustic" image of wilderness, building policy within the Okavango Delta and the surrounding areas is strictly for non-permanent structures made of wood, canvas, and thatch—no brick and mortar or concrete.³⁶ While this most obviously applies to new buildings related to the tourism industry—lodges and camps—and was a regulation promulgated by the Botswana Tourism Organisation (BTO), it has also limited new infrastructural developments in those communities inside and immediately adjacent to the core areas of the delta.³⁷ Villagers in Ditshiping—one of the few remaining settlements close to the core delta—understand their development prospects through this lens, believing that only non-permanent structures can be hoped for while they remain at their settlement.³⁸ The emphasis on "nature tourism," and its incumbent views of wilderness, comes into direct conflict with local aspirations for infrastructure and service development. The conservation estate in this region becomes an enclave of capital exploitation but not through "development" as such but rather through the purposeful underdevelopment of pristine and "untouched" wilderness. The appearance of primitivity is what allows these spaces to be intense nodes of capital exploitation. This culminates, ultimately, in local people believing relocation is both connected to tourism and imminent. An interviewee in Xuoxao suggested, "We are going to be relocated to make a place where guests are hosted [a tourist lodge] and a park."³⁹

During a community meeting in the village of Khwai, the local MP said the residents should not "spoil" the wilderness by trying to overdevelop it or make it look like Maun because "by so doing you are spoiling the wilderness and that would mean tourists not coming here."⁴⁰ This is asking residents to absent themselves from their landscape so as to not inconvenience the perceptions of Botswana's fee-paying visitors or disrupt the workings of enclave tourism. The creation of the conservation estate is not solely an ecological endeavor of spatial organization but also a social one—as the conservation estate becomes a receptacle in which particular expectations are managed and attended to and in which experiences of wilderness are contrived.

Infrastructure and the Dialectic of Legibility and Illegibility

> I suspect we will be relocated due to this World Heritage listing. Government can never let people live alongside animals forever. We think they might expand the frontiers of the delta and make this area to be exclusively for wildlife.
>
> —Resident of Xuoxao[41]

In Botswana the state's dispensation of infrastructure on the conservation estate varies widely between the north and the west. Though both regions are vast and diverse, overarching trends in the provision of infrastructure in each area provide fertile ground for analytical comparison. In the west of the country, in the settlement villages of Ghanzi District, the provision of infrastructure operates as a means through which to draw out previously scattered and seasonally mobile people from the sparsely populated bush to live in state-sanctioned and monitored villages, pulling them into a relationship of "legibility" with the state. In the north of the country, particularly around the Okavango Delta where the bulk of the tourism industry is based, the calculus is different. The allocation of infrastructure is delayed or denied in order to maintain the fiction of a people-free wilderness that appeals to tourist consumers—pushing local people into a kind of "illegibility" wherein neither foreign visitors or state actors "see" their existence on the land. This runs counter to earlier theorization around marginal spaces and peoples that suggests it is in the state's interest to make these populations more legible, when their aim is to remain illegible and unincorporated. Contrastingly, the provision of infrastructure in standardized locations in the west of the country is a carrot to entice centralization and "modernization." The denial of infrastructure in the north is a stick to compel people to leave, or at the very least remain invisible, in an environment deemed more valuable and lucrative without people. The policies that dictate the provision (or lack) of infrastructure around Botswana's conservation estate are felt in highly differentiated ways in the north and the west, though they are consistent with the same project of spatial control of citizens in the state. The preferred outcome differs in each region. There is an inclination to settle citizens in assimilated modes of residency and promote agropastoralism in the west (see part III) versus the need to perpetuate a myth of a peopleless wilderness in order to buoy a vital economic sector in the north. The lack of infrastructure in Northwest District serves to render this population invisible. Unlike their compatriots in the western part of the country, they are not relocated, and they are only provided with minimal infrastructure, making the "modern" footprint in the northern part of the country small and appealing to visitors who purchase the myth of uninhabited wilderness. In this way, state interest in "legibility" and "illegibility" may be held simultaneously across a territory, evidence of the complicated constellation of logics that fall under the umbrella of state building and structure citizen-state relations.

Conservation and tourism-adjacent citizens in Botswana's north and west evinced diametrically opposed grievances regarding the provision of state services and infrastructure. In the northern conservation estate, where the bulk of the ecotourism industry occurs, local residents felt their development needs were dismissed in order to create and maintain the myth of vast expanses of pristine and people-free wilderness, not only stranding them but camouflaging their very presence. In interviews, these residents repeatedly called for better, all-weather roads, concrete and metal bridges, and permanent health and education infrastructure, which they currently lack. They believe their calls are ignored and their persistent illegibility did not manifest as a form of resistance but rather another mechanism of state control.

Moreover, they attributed their unseen status to the preferences and pressures of another, more favored constituency—the tourist operators of the Okavango and their wealthy Western clientele. On the other hand, in Botswana's western conservation estate, infrastructure development has been provided to a much greater extent, especially to communities recently and controversially removed from the CKGR. However, these communities do not look upon this infrastructure provision glowingly. They tend to regard these buildings and services as part of a larger process meant to coax them into abandoning their former mobile land-use practices in favor of a centralized, sedentary lifestyle, absenting them from the territory. Throughout my fieldwork, they argued that the services and structures provided do not coincide with their development goals or needs. Yet by centralizing legible populations in purpose-built villages that appear well-serviced or in some cases even privileged, the state limits the ability for these communities to articulate land claims over nearby commercial cattle farms or parts of the conservation estate.

While displaying opposite orientations toward government provision of conservation-adjacent infrastructure—the people of the north claim there is not enough, and in those of the west say there is too much or not the right kind—both regions demonstrate the manner in which local preferences in marginal areas are sublimated to larger state interests. These projects are related to the manner in which land is made productive (through tourist and capital exploitation) and the way in which people are made to be modern citizens permitted to participate in the life of the nation (through sedentarized, centrally organized settlements). The former is related to the state's economic interest in capital accumulation through the freezing of environments as untouched and undeveloped. Ironically, these tourism spaces that are intentionally devoid of "development" are equally representations of the modern(izing) state-building process.

The question remains: Why not attempt the same sort of centralizing relocations in the north as were enacted in the west, in order to make this space truly "peopleless"? There are two possible reasons why the state must settle for simply making the residents of the northern conservation estate less visible rather than entirely removed and relocated, as had been common practice in the past. The first is that a widespread relocation project is no longer politically feasible. With the international attention given to the CKGR removals and subsequent court battle, any large-scale move to evict residents from lucrative spaces of wildlife tourism could be a public relations disaster for Botswana, particularly if it began to impact the perspectives of potential tourist clients.

Second, the residents of the northern conservation estate are highly politicized and agitated against such a possibility. Many of the current residents experienced historical relocations out of Moremi Game Reserve and Chobe National Park in the late colonial period and contemporarily use a wide variety of strategies noted above in order to legitimately emplace themselves in their current locations. They are politically savvy in this regard and are quick to make analogies to the situation with the CKGR. Explicit relocations may no longer be politically possible, so long as Botswana wants to maintain its reputation as an "African miracle." Instead, the people of the northern conservation estate have been made purposefully illegible by the state—beyond the sphere where "normal" development occurs—and virtually unknown to the thousands of visitors who come to view the protected areas every year. These tourists often leave with the impression that the Okavango Delta, in particular, is truly a people-free "haven." By limiting the prevalence of permanent and conspicuously modern non-tourist infrastructure, the state is able to sustain the illusion of a pristine, untouched wilderness without incurring the political and reputational damage that would result from further relocations.

The state's provision of infrastructure is not bounded by a single grand plan about the nature and scope of rural life across

Botswana's conservation estate but rather is influenced by contingent interests and objectives. Capital extraction through conservation produces the contours of citizen-state relations across the breadth of rural land in often paradoxical and contradictory ways. Importantly, these dynamics are not found in Botswana alone. In their study of Mozambique, Witter and Satterfield (2019) recount the ways in which incentivizing state infrastructure in resettlement communities is coupled with the purposeful divestment in areas with latent potential in wildlife and tourism. The distinct logics of tourism and peopleless wilderness substantially alter the relationship between the state and its citizens on the conservation estate, in some places generating legible citizens, while in others producing illegibility. The provision of infrastructure acts as a way to induce state preferences in settlement patterns, either enticing or disincentivizing citizens to live in particular places or adopt particular patterns of residency. However, the assimilatory impulses of a uniform high modernism in the Scottian sense are not the only logics at work. In areas close to the Okavango, communities go to extraordinary lengths to make themselves legible, to write their presence on the maps and grids of the region, and to solidify their presence with the material imposition of infrastructure built by their own hands. Due to imperatives dictated by the global tourism industry and the assumptions related to unpeopled wildernesses, the differentiated deployment of infrastructure coproduces so-called primitivity and modernity simultaneously. In pursuit of "authentic" wilderness experiences, tourists get something that is not very authentic at all but rather highly choreographed and curated to suit their preconceived notions. Of course, it is ironic that in the continent where humans first evolved and have lived uninterrupted for millennia notions of an untouched, unpeopled wilderness still persist.

This section has focused extensively on the ways in which the conservation estate is an exceptional sociopolitical category within Botswana's territory, illustrating the significant level of differentiation across "rural" space and landscapes. The lack of uniformity in the manner in which service provision and infrastructure manifest on the conservation estate implies that there may be room for negotiation and contestation at the local level. It is clear that the state is responding to other simultaneous and overlapping imperatives—the tourism industry or private property rights—to enact policies in a differentiated manner throughout the country. With this there is the potential of negotiation or resistance on the part of local people on the conservation estate, and people on the ground attempt to articulate themselves in such a manner to make their positions central to the concerns of the state. It is demonstrative of the fact that state policies do not *have* to be implemented in a uniform manner, despite the fact that they often are (see part III). When context-specific policies are apparent, like the exceptionality of game farms or the distinct disbursement of infrastructure, they are not taking account of the locally constituted needs of the resident population but instead are bending the implementation of state policy to meet divergent goals. Conservation decisions that are ostensibly uniform but highly differentiated in practice—like the hunting ban and the maintenance of a vision of wilderness—are not constitutive of an overarching design but reflective of the various power discrepancies and parochial interests that influence the exercise of state power.

Part III

Identity

6

Conservation Restrictions and the Construction of Criminalized Identities

As I approached the compound of the *kgosi* of West Hanahai for the first interview of the day, I noticed that a half dozen women had also convened there and were sorting through small piles of what looked, to me, like bits of shrubbery. As the kgosi, an amiable man in his midforties, became more comfortable with my presence, he began to explain the flurry of activity. The women—ranging from a teenager to an elderly grandmother—were his relatives and, just back from an early-morning gathering trip, were beginning to process their collection. He rattled off the names of the plants, first in Naro, then Setswana, and finally English—brandy bush, spiny cucumber, wild raisin. They did not gather wild fruits often, he said, but the rains had been good lately, and they did not want to miss the opportunity. He did not wish to talk about whether it was legal to collect without a permit from the government, but by way of explanation he said, "I am kgosi, but I am also Basarwa [San]."[1] With this statement, he captured the intersecting dynamics at play for residents of Botswana's conservation estate—many of them ethnolinguistic minorities—in terms of resource use, livelihoods, state development objectives, and identity within the state.

This chapter probes questions of identity, development, and livelihoods. It is concerned with how conservation intersects with who citizens are and how the logics and imperatives of conservation may shape, construct, or distort these subjectivities within the national project. It examines the clash between conservation practices related to resource use and the logic of rural development in Botswana, wherein the unique and spatially contingent restrictions experienced on the conservation estate result in citizens who cannot take advantage of state development programs. The central point of this chapter is that the state curtails various livelihood (and identity) approaches in the hope of shaping subjectivities and behaviors toward the Tswana "mainstream." Yet the particularities of conservation itself cause this transformative project to fail; the state's emphasis on difference-blind development cannot recognize the differentiation generated by the conservation estate. In fact, the identity-formation project of the difference-blind state produces a contradictory result: a segment of Botswana's population that lives on the conservation estate sees itself as *more* different and often internalizes subjectivities that render its resource-use and cultural practices criminal and transgressive.

Empirically this chapter is concerned with conservation policies related to gathering of natural resources, with a particular attention to the gathering of ostrich eggshells. It will be followed in the subsequent chapter by an analysis of hunting. These entry points allow for the interrogation of the Botswana state's discursive and material attempts to use biodiversity conservation to shape identities and behaviors of its citizens in particular ways. This chapter takes seriously the starting point in the literature that argues that the state uses development processes as an attempt to shape, discipline, and reorient the behavior and livelihood patterns of its conservation-adjacent people in order to render them "mainstream" citizens in Botswana's postcolonial nation-state. However, the overlapping, though not always aligning, logics of conservation and development complicate the intentionality of this project. I argue that the process is not neat or straightforward but fraught, ambiguous, and at times contradictory, resulting in local negotiations and the deepening of differentiation between those citizens living on and off the conservation estate, rather than further incorporation into the state's "mainstream" project.

Ethnicity, Identity, and the San

While San people share challenges with many other residents of the conservation estate who do not describe themselves as San, they are given extra attention in this book for three reasons: (1) their preponderance in Botswana's rural conservation estate, (2) their status as political, social, and cultural outsiders, and (3) their experience as the subjects of the bulk of the evictions from protected areas.

San communities have been the focus of much academic, literary, and media scrutiny for nearly a century. The San are particularly studied in anthropology—so much so that some scholars have characterized the "anthropological cult" of the Bushmen (Gupta and Ferguson 1992, 15; Wilmsen 1989). Academics and activists have struggled to agree on one common, nonpejorative term to use to encompass the entirety of former hunter-gatherer peoples speaking Khoesan languages in southern Africa, the majority of whom reside in Botswana. There is no unified terminology and no agreement upon an appropriate overarching term (Hitchcock et al. 2006; Sapignoli 2018; Saugestad 2001; Zips-Mairitsch 2013). Many people living in conservation-adjacent communities are considered "Remote Area Dwellers" (RADs). While the term is technically neutral, the bulk are non-Tswana minorities like the San, Bakgalagadi, Hambukushu, and Bayei. Most RADs self-identify as San, and "RAD" is often used colloquially as a euphemism for San. *Basarwa* (singular *Mosarwa*) is the Setswana term, though also not without its detractors. "Basarwa" is used in official government statements and is the appellation most widely used by other Batswana. The term roughly derives from a Setswana phrase, *ba-sa-rua dikgomo*, which means "those who do not rear cattle" (Armstrong and Bennett 2002, 192–93; Zips-Mairitsch 2013, 157; see also Mogwe 1992). This group of people, therefore, is generally defined by their dearth of Tswana qualities: Setswana is not their mother tongue, they do not typically raise cattle on a large scale, they historically lived outside traditional villages, they did not utilize Tswana institutions like the *kgotla*, and so on (Saugestad 2001, 65). While in Botswana this group is commonly referred to as RADs and Basarwa, in this book I use the appellation "San" because this was the most common way interviewees requested to be referred to in English text.[2]

Without a census that enumerates ethnicity, exact figures are hard to come by, but estimates suggest the San make up about 3 percent of the total population of Botswana—around fifty thousand people (Hitchcock, Sapignoli, and Babchuk 2011; Taylor 2004). Their status is that of a "distinct minority amongst minorities" in that they tend to sit on the lowest rungs of Botswana society, beneath all other groups in terms of economic, political, and social power (Taylor 2004, 153; see also Good 1992; Mazonde 2004). While the government of Botswana does not recognize indigeneity,[3] this discourse is frequently deployed by San in Botswana, who often adopt the politically charged moniker of "First People" (Hitchcock 2006). An emphasis on indigeneity often relies on a kind of primordialism, or strategic essentialism, that is subject to intense academic debates but is nonetheless the manner in which many San describe themselves, along with many allies (Sylvain 2014). Many of the San's most fervent supporters, such as the British NGO Survival International, often express essentialist arguments about San people's "natural" connections to the environment (see Chebanne 2003) and, intentionally or not, tend to perpetuate problematic notions of the "noble savage."

Social scientific assessments of the San have been similarly fraught. The so-called Kalahari debate in anthropology can be roughly divided into two camps: "the traditionalists," associated with the Harvard Kalahari Research Group,[4] and "the revisionists," led by the former's critic, Edwin Wilmsen.[5] The traditionalists regard environment and ecology as the primary determinants of the San lifestyle of hunting and gathering, while the revisionists emphasize political economy as the primary determinant of San livelihood strategies. Traditionalists tend to focus on the San as isolated and highly attuned to their environment, while revisionists understand them to be part of an economic underclass existing within a larger and more integrated economy (Barnard 2006; Saugestad 2001; Sylvain 2014; Zips-Mairitsch 2013). Within this debate, social scientists are in agreement that San peoples were the first inhabitants of southern Africa but diverge in their thinking about how San communities coped with successive waves of "immigrants."

This has relevance for the contemporary political contestations over the state in Botswana in that "each side of the Kalahari debate claims better [and different] politics" (Sylvain 2014, 254): the traditionalists, the politics of recognition, and the revisionists, the politics of class. This debate has evolved into a wider debate about the way positions of indigeneity are used in political activism and ethnic identification (Barnard 2006; Kuper 2003). Much of the Kalahari debate appears to be concerned with the "actual": attempts to determine the historical material conditions of these groups of people found throughout southern Africa. Yet the debate runs the risk of missing the forest for the trees. Whatever their historical origins, communities of San people today perceive themselves in distinct ways, deploying particular imaginaries and constructed positions from within their social context. Barnard recalls that "simply because a community may be of recent invention does not mean that it is not real. Real 'traditions' can be invented, just as 'imagined communities' can be real communities—assuming we recognise social reality as a social construct (cf. Hobsbawm 1983)" (Barnard 2006, 7). Indigeneity, like ethnicity, is a political concept and is malleable, constructed, and relational. While they may not be "real" in any primordial sense, identities can structure relationships and vice versa (Saugestad 2001). This is perhaps the most relevant point for considering various identity claims that result from interactions with state- and nation-building processes. Despite the proverbial battle lines drawn by the Kalahari debate, actors on the ground often operate from positions of flexibility: San informants "often insist they can be both modern and traditional at the same time" (Sylvain 2014, 257).

The identity context is a substrate upon which Botswana's state-building and development policy are instantiated. There is a linear thinking when it comes to ideas of development and natural resource use related to Botswana's conservation-adjacent population and for San people in particular. The aversion toward livelihood strategies such as gathering and hunting on the part of the Tswana-dominated postcolonial government has its origins in "Victorian evolutionary schemata that placed hunting societies at a lower rung on the evolutionary scale than pastoralists and agriculturalists" (Nustad 2015, 66; MacKenzie 1988). The state-led development approach for residents on the conservation estate, based on assumptions that compare Tswana and San economies and lifestyles on a hierarchical scale, has privileged assimilation into mainstream resource-use strategies (Taylor 2002; Saugestad 2001). Gathering and hunting are understood by many government officials to be *only* temporary activities employed to cope with hardship (Zips-Mairitsch 2013). For the average Motswana, San communities are seen as an unwelcome reminder of Botswana's not-too-distant past of economic adversity, and the persistence of lifestyles "of the bush" is thought of as incompatible with the country's hard-won economic prosperity in the postcolonial era (Saugestad 2001). A retired civil servant encapsulated the manner in which particular relationships to the environment are viewed as failures of development from within the mainstream paradigm and as representative of Botswana's history of material poverty: "Our grandparents lived like Basarwa—all Batswana lived like Basarwa. But we left that lifestyle behind and moved on. It is a tedious life and they must be brought out of it to live like us" (quoted in Taylor 2004, 153). It is unsurprising that there are people in positions of authority who still regard San livelihood and cultural practices with skepticism, and many, though certainly not all, rural extension workers have expressed negative and even disdainful feelings toward their San clients, in part because the policies they are tasked with enacting are "embedded in a framework of attitudes and perceptions that could best be described with terms like contempt, condescension and ambivalence" (Zips-Mairitsch 2013, 241). A conservation and development practitioner who has worked with San communities in northern and western Botswana for over two decades made a similar observation:

> The problem is that hunting and gathering is seen as a backward—it's not seen as a valid form of land-use because it's associated with being in a "primitive state" quite literally. But it misses the very important point that it is a practical form of land use and it generates immediate benefits and it reduces the levels of dependency on other people and government. . . . It is very much an identity issue as well, where they [the government of Botswana] see themselves as needing to emulate the West and a perceived Western ideal in terms of lifestyle and where they think they should be [developmentally]. I think that they literally feel embarrassed about having been "backward" or [when] anyone . . . reminds them of being in an "uncivilized state," as they see it. So the hunter-gatherers are an embarrassment. And the problem is twofold. One is a deep-seated resentment culturally of the hunter-gatherers and, secondly, of wanting to sort of measure up to everyone else and feeling that, well, these people are sort of holding us back.[6]

This is a point that is echoed in much of the existing literature related to the ways in which conservation and development processes are perceived in Botswana, particularly by government elites (Madzwamuse 2010; Magole 2009; Rihoy and Maguranyanga 2010; Twyman 1998). It distills a core imaginary about the state, citizens' place in it, and the manner in which certain conservation policies may be used to produce a set of desired developmental outcomes. Former vice president Mompati Merafhe made a similarly strong statement when he said of Batswana, "We all aspire to Cadillacs and would be concerned with any tribe to remain in the bush communing with flora and fauna" (quoted in Good 2008, 124). This orientation is highly relevant to the ways in which conservation policy is exercised as a state project—a vehicle for a state-led construction of appropriate citizenship in the national polity and the promotion of assimilation to that ideal.

This chapter explores the way in which livelihood approaches tied to conceptualizations of non-Tswana identity are routinely sidelined by conservation restrictions. While the subsequent chapter will examine the way hunting has been regulated as part of the state-building project, this chapter focuses on gathering. The collection of wild fruits and other plant products from the surrounding veldt is seemingly less politicized, in part because it does not invoke the concern (and at times revulsion) around the hunting of animals. It is also direct, primary subsistence for some of the most food-insecure communities in the country. However, gathering also implicates aspects of identity, heritage, and cultural practice, as this chapter will examine in relationship to ostrich eggshells. It examines the ways in which subsistence gathering practices have been altered in response to state preferences for a people-free wilderness and the commercial use of resources, highlighting the kinds of limitations placed on citizens that are unique to the conservation estate alone. It explores how local people attempt to adopt the state-promoted paradigm of commercial use of wildlife products. Yet, even in this instance, the state's impulses for commercialization are enacted ambiguously, as concurrent conservation regulations prevent local people from meeting the state's ideal vision of commercialized resource use.

Counterintuitively, the Botswana state attempts to integrate its rural populations into the cash economy through conservation have the opposite result of the intended policy pronouncement, making people on the conservation estate *more* dependent on state welfare programs. By disrupting the subsistence practices and livelihood activities of conservation-adjacent people through policies meant to bring them into the "mainstream" and "out of the bush," the state fundamentally reorders the relationship of these citizens to the state and vice versa. A second key line of argumentation is that the commonplace strategy of resistance to the state-building process on the conservation estate—appeals to ethnic identity—may be limiting on two fronts: (1) the state is overtly hostile to identity-based claims, and (2) this discourse relies on stereotypical and at times primordial constructions of identity. Local residents often contest the state's identity-shaping policies using self-essentializing rhetoric that may be problematically configured and, in turn, is easily rejected by state authorities' emphasis on Botswana's long-standing claims of non-ethnic citizenship.

Gathering on the Conservation Estate

> I don't know what conservation is, but I know when people say it, I can't eat brandy bush. That is my life.
>
> —Resident of New Xade[7]

The lives and lifeworlds of people on the conservation estate differ from their compatriots living on rural land not dominated by the logics of biodiversity conservation, a differentiation cognizable when looking to mundane and seemingly apolitical activities, such as the gathering of firewood. In many conservation-adjacent areas of Botswana, residents have a long history of utilizing gathered veldt products as part of their daily activities. This holds true not only among the formerly hunter-gatherer San groups who inhabit much of the Kalahari landscape but also among many other rural dwellers such as the Bayei, who gather wild fruits such as the *twsii* plant found throughout the Okavango Delta.

Interviewees in both Northwest and Ghanzi Districts recounted myriad ways their lives were dependent on the surrounding environment. Indeed, there are numerous of reasons why people may engage in gathering activities to varying degrees outside of the geographic confines of their settlement, including collecting food, gathering building materials like reeds and thatching grass, collecting firewood essential for cooking and warmth, and

FIGURE 6.1. Collected thatching grass, Boro. Author's photograph.

gathering for medicinal or crafting purposes (see figure 6.1). Respondents frequently recounted use of wild foods (or the desire to do so) as a part of their daily subsistence. There are a wide variety of edible fruits, nuts, and plants that are historically and contemporarily collected from the veldt. They include the morama bean (*Tylosema esculentum*), tsamma melon (*Citrullus lanatus*), brandy bush (*mogwana / Grewia bicolor*, or *moretlwa / Grewia flava*), sandpaper raisin (*mogkomphatha / Grewia flavescens*), mongongo nut (*Ricinodendron rantanenii*), and bird plum (*motsintsela / Berchemia discolor*) (Roodt 1993). While gathering activities are primarily associated with women, both men and women participate, though often for men gathering occurs opportunistically during hunting trips (Twyman 2000).

Gathering is not limited to the conservation estate, though the practice is most often associated with the non-Tswana people living there. When gathering is thought of expansively, nearly all rural people undertake some gathering activities, especially related to firewood and building materials. What draws the distinction, therefore, is not the activity itself but the category of sociopolitical space upon which these activities occur. Those living on the conservation estate must approach these practices from within a regime of greater state restrictions and scrutiny than their counterparts in other rural communities. Despite cultural valence of these activities for many San people and their direct ability to supplement nutrition, on the conservation estate much of this subsistence gathering behavior has been curtailed due to conservation efforts or at least because of common (mis)understanding of conservation efforts on the part of local people.

Gathering and Boundaries: Physical, Ecological, and Psychological

A resource's availability is not simply dependent on the environment's fecundity but rather is also impacted by other social processes (Twyman 2000; Ribot and Peluso 2003). In each village where I conducted interviews for this project, gathering practices had been historically practiced. In some areas these practices continued, albeit in modified forms, whereas in other villages restrictions, as well as local perceptions of these restrictions, rendered gathering completely impossible. The boundaries of accessibility to resources may be more perceived than real in a material sense. In Botswana the boundaries put up between conservation-adjacent residents and their environments are varied. There are three fundamental ways in which interviewees in Northwest and Ghanzi Districts characterized their relationship to the surrounding environment in the context of gathering. There are "real" boundaries, ecological boundaries, and perceived boundaries, all of which are unique to the conservation estate.

Real boundaries exist where a protected area has been created and adjacent residents can no longer engage in gathering practices within the confines of the park, as may have been their historical practice. For example, this was the case in the village of Mababe in Northwest District, where residents recounted their historical eviction from Chobe National Park and their inability to collect plant resources from their former territory (Taylor 2000).

Ecological barriers are commonplace when formerly transhumant people have been resettled into villages wherein residents are unfamiliar with the surroundings and the local environment no longer can support widespread gathering activities, as is often the case in Ghanzi's resettlement villages.[8] Sapignoli observed this in her fieldwork as well, where she noted that "none of the remote area settlements was large enough to support even a group of fifteen full-time foragers" (2018, 95). The concentration of previously mobile populations, as a matter of state policy, is often implemented based on the ability to provide services, infrastructure, and "development" at central nodes. However, this diminishes the ability of these resettled communities to use and access surrounding plant resources because the environment cannot support the concentrated levels of population. Perceived boundaries exist where the environmental conditions are good and can support wild food collection and communities theoretically have access to resources from subsistence, but, in practice, gathering is greatly proscribed due to widespread fear of repercussions for being found "out in the bush," especially by armed state agents tasked with conservation enforcement. These are uniquely created on the conservation estate and are based on the broader sociopolitical impacts of these spaces.

These local boundaries, both theoretical and actual, limit gathering behaviors that other rural people can undertake with less scrutiny, and they structure the nature of life on the conservation estate. They create conservation-adjacent people as particular types of Batswana, limiting certain kinds of behaviors regarded as out of step with the national consensus of citizenship. In all three gathering scenarios, boundaries of varying impermeability on the conservation estate keep people from accessing resources; some relate to the strictly defined delineations of national parks, while others relate to the fear of potential violent encounters resulting from the ever-broadening category of "poacher." Many wildlife officers readily equate gathering with illegal access, with one saying, "What is happening with veldt products is also poaching."[9] The conceptual stretching of the word "poacher" leads to people commonly believing, with good reason, that the category is rapidly expanding to encompass a whole host of practices unrelated to the illegal use of wildlife resources. A young man in the northern village of Xuoxao remarked, "We are going to be treated in the same way as poachers. One will land in trouble when caught with a stack or pile of grasses or reeds at a wrong time."[10] Certainly the gathering behaviors that would have citizens out in the bush are not limited to the conservation estate, as rural people throughout the country rely on their environments for building materials and energy needs. However, state conceptualizations about the identity and economies of their non-Tswana citizens and the widespread anxiety about the presence of people on the conservation estate create a situation where conservation-adjacent residents become subjects of surveillance even for commonplace activities like gathering firewood.

These kinds of restrictions are further underpinned by local misunderstandings of regulations regarding gathering as they are written into Botswana's conservation law, which has either been inadequately explained or willfully misrepresented. The government agency tasked with monitoring the use of wild products confirmed that licensing is only required for *commercial* harvesting of floral products.[11] Officially, no permission is needed for subsistence use of non-animal natural resources found in Botswana.[12] Yet confusion and fear of the negative consequences for being found out in the bush remain common in conservation areas, which are surveilled and patrolled to a greater extent than in other rural areas. On the ground among interviewees, including some prominent community members like traditional authorities and members of village development committees, there is tremendous uncertainty about regulations related to the gathering of wild fruit, firewood, and other veldt products. While subsistence use may be within the letter of the law, the pervasive anxiety that being found out gathering may lead to violent repercussions or even meeting one's end as a "poacher" (see chapter 2) makes legal behavior seem proscribed, as residents fear the consequences of breaking a law they do not fully understand. As a practical matter, de jure permission transforms into a de facto ban.

The disjuncture between local people and state authorities on the conservation estate is particularly noteworthy because it elevates questions of positionality in the rendering of seemingly neutral or uniform legal regimes around resource use. It matters that the citizens on the conservation estate may feel remote, disconnected, or marginalized from officialdom, and their ability to use resources to which they are legally entitled depends on how well or poorly they interact with state institutions (see Shinn and Hall-Reinhard 2019 for a similar discussion about fishing and permitting in the Okavango Delta). They are also physically remote from the regional centers of power—Maun and Ghanzi Town—where the relevant authorities are located on a daily basis. Even if people living on the conservation estate felt comfortable in engaging the relevant state authorities regarding these issues, few members of these communities possess the material resources to do so. Ultimately these (mis)perceptions and material limitations result in the diminished ability of conservation-adjacent people to claim their resource-use rights that exist on paper, if not in practice. An interviewee involved with the San development organization, Kuru Trust, suggested that "hunting and gathering is basically banned; we are contained and controlled,"[13] indicating the way restrictions reserved for the conservation estate are directly generative of political subjectivities therein. Real or otherwise, conservation-adjacent communities are concerned that every activity in which they interact with the environment—from collecting firewood to gathering food for subsistence—is subject to state inquiry and scrutiny in a way not apparent elsewhere.[14] As two women said to me, "When we are out gathering, we are out stealing. I am afraid to be caught because it is unlawful."[15] This certitude of the unlawfulness of their activities goes beyond simple confusion: they are actively reproducing the subordinate subjectivity they experience on a daily basis. They are self-policing in response to unwritten rules of life on the conservation estate. It is perceptive in that, for all intents and purposes, these activities are "unlawful" from a practical standpoint. Despite the official legality of subsistence gathering, these conservation-adjacent citizens live in an exceptional space within the state project. They are remote from and subordinate to centers of power that dictate permissible and impermissible behavior on the conservation estate, such that it is difficult—nearly impossible—to make the official reality of unencumbered subsistence a lived reality.

Gathering as Identity Practice

Despite barriers, people are invested in the practice of gathering for reasons that go beyond subsistence alone. It would be disingenuous to claim that many San in Botswana express a preference to remain exclusively hunters and gatherers. In fact, almost no Batswana have been strictly hunter-gatherers in decades; just the opposite is true. Most interviewees wish to see some significant changes in their lifestyles but on their own terms, taking into account practices they deem culturally important. Respondents talked about practice of gathering in a variety of ways and gave reasons for its importance ranging from necessity in order to meet daily food needs to their own preferences and tastes. The traditional leader described at the beginning of this chapter spoke enthusiastically about the different flavors and preparations of wild foods he remembered from his childhood and how the relishes that his family was still able to make from gathered plants made the foodstuffs provided in government food baskets (often maize meal or pasta) palatable to his taste. My research strongly suggests that gathering remains important in two key ways: as one viable economic strategy for attaining food security among many and as an important cultural and identity marker in a diverse and heterogeneous Batswana society.

In arguing that gathering is a cultural practice, local residents rejected the idea that conservation authorities should be the primary actors setting the priorities for how resources are used. They did this by staking a claim over the governance of the conservation estate, based primarily on discourses of identity and local expertise.

Respondents recounted local social controls and taboos around resource use that worked to inculcate sustainable use and policed reckless abuse in the past. Despite the widespread internalization of the poacher category, many in these communities forcefully pushed back against the perception that they were transgressive or criminal in their use of veldt products. The appointed headman of West Hanahai found this characterization particularly objectionable, stating, "We know when to harvest [wild fruits]; we don't just go out into the veldt to harvest whenever. We know when to let it grow. . . . Basarwa people—almost all of us—rely on these products, know them, know where they are and how to use and conserve them. When you gather, you only take the part you want. You leave the root and don't take the whole plant."[16] By invoking his own Basarwa/San ethnic background, he used the very discourse that is viewed problematically by the state in order to contest the restrictions mandated by conservation. He embeds both "use" and "conservation" as areas of ethnic expertise, as a manner of counteracting what is seen locally as the state's concept of conservation-as-non-use (even if some commercial utilization is promoted). This man, the same introduced at the outset of this chapter, insistently referred back to his extended family separating out the edible fruits gathered early that morning. He pointed to them when describing his frustration with the conservation permitting system as he understood it, saying, "The government doesn't believe I will use resources wisely. I need to get a permit for collection. They don't think we can use wisely, but we've been here for long and the wild fruits are still here. To get a permit, I have to pay for it. I have to travel to Ghanzi, and I have to fill out a form. And the permit is only good for some time."[17] Because the formal difference between subsistence and commercial permitting requirements has never been clarified, most conservation-adjacent people, including many locally prominent individuals, operate under the assumption that they are required to obtain permission even for subsistence. However, though not legally required, a permit may indeed be needed in practice as a type of insurance mechanism to avoid uncomfortable and potentially dangerous interactions with wildlife authorities. Nonetheless, on the conservation estate, permitting is a fraught notion for several reasons. First, conservation-adjacent residents most usually view these resources as already "owned" by their community (see chapter 4). Second, they feel as if the ability for anybody with enough money to purchase a permit opens the area to outsiders not local to their area, thus diluting their own claims.[18] A respondent in the village of Bere described how the Department of Wildlife and National Parks requires permits, despite gathering being "how we are supposed to live" and "part of my culture."[19] There is a third dimension to consider: that the bureaucratic process of obtaining a permit is opaque and intimidating for conservation-adjacent people, often pushing them away from any subsistence use because of lack of clarity around the process.

The process of obtaining a permit is a bureaucratic interaction that can provide insight into how the state and people interact on the conservation estate. The physical distance between conservation areas and district capitals, the limited transportation infrastructure, and the lack of clear information all create disincentives in the process. One respondent reported, "Just traveling to Ghanzi to try to get a license is very challenging."[20] The centralized bureaucratic control of resource use overlaid on the geographical remoteness of the conservation estate renders the possibility of seeking this kind of proactive approval problematic, if not impossible. Residents recounted feeling alienated and confused by policies and did not know where to go to get clarification or advice.[21] When asked about the general perception of the illegality of subsistence gathering among conservation-adjacent people, the wildlife officer tasked with community outreach in Ghanzi District told me the following, rather than address the source of the confusion:

> When thinking about gathering, about things like wild fruits and veldt foods, the aim is not for the individual but for the

> community. We don't want them to use these for subsistence, for everyday, but commercialized. Gathering shouldn't be for subsistence but as a poverty-eradication method that the community benefits from through commercialization. Subsistence is not a way to move forward. There is a good market for these wild products like grass and wild fruits, but the benefits should go to the whole community, not to the individual. Through this they can move away from subsistence to the cash economy, so the community—not the individual, every day—can get the maximum benefit from these resources.[22]

State agents tasked with determining the use or non-use of resources in line with conservation policy promote a particular approach to resource exploitation—that of marketing, commoditizing, and commercializing resources, even those typically used for subsistence. The above statement demonstrates a bias against subsistence use that is undergirded by the assumptions of what kind of behaviors inculcate economic "progress" ("subsistence is not a way to move forward") and the use of policy nominally enacted for biodiversity management to reconfigure local people's relationship to the environment and the market ("through this they can move away from subsistence to the cash economy"). This respondent highlighted how there is a "good market" for wild products—not that veldt products actually have nutritional or subsistence value that can be tapped. The commercialization of these resources is seen as the only acceptable utilization, where the consumption of wild products is replaced by the sale of wild products to commercial buyers and presumably followed by the purchase of foodstuffs to meet nutritional needs. In this case, the focus on assimilation into the cash economy through commercialization is presented as a means of bringing people on the conservation estate—constructed as outsiders to a certain extent—into the mainstream.[23] This also indicates that the conservation policy is not primarily concerned with the *ecological* outcomes of these rules—commercialization is more likely unsustainable from an ecosystems perspective than community-level subsistence—but its aims are focused on the social, political, economic, and cultural impacts of "conservation" policies. The commercializing process of conservation is intimately tied into notions of how one is viewed as a proper citizen of Botswana, in which livelihood and economic approaches are viewed as "modern" and "appropriate" on the evolutionary scale that predominates government thinking, and how specific behaviors like gathering are deemed permissible only within a limited, paradigmatic approach to conservation, development, and resource use—for sale, not consumption. Despite subsistence economic behaviors falling within the letter of the conservation law, these activities are nonetheless being discouraged in favor of a commodified and commercialized approach to resource utilization.

Using the example of ostrich eggshells, the next section examines the ways in which rural people are often keenly aware of the commercial opportunities their location on the conservation estate may provide. Even when the state's preference for non-subsistence use of resources overlap with the skills and goals of conservation-adjacent citizens, the unique characteristics and limitations of life on the conservation estate proscribe their ability to make a living according to state-sanctioned economic modes.

Gathering Ostrich Eggshells: Criminalizing Development

We don't know how we can get money from tourists if we cannot make our crafts.

—Resident of Kacgae[24]

In light of the previous section's consideration of the dynamics of gathering, the restrictions and limitations around the collection and utilization of ostrich eggshells on the conservation estate are particularly illuminating. They demonstrate the conflicting discourses around conservation and development at odds on the conservation estate. Rather than resisting calls for commercialization, local people enthusiastically adopt this approach, only to be stymied by the unique set of conditions around resource use that are produced by the conservation estate and by assumptions about the way conservation-adjacent people interact with the state.

Unlike the wild fruit and plant products described in the previous section, ostrich eggshells have no basic subsistence use. Obviously, they are not food for humans. Unlike firewood, reeds, and thatching grass, they have no fundamental value in energy production or building material. However, this belies the importance of this natural resource—both in cultural terms and in commercial potential. Ostrich eggshells are sought after primarily as source material for beads that are used to make necklaces, bracelets, and earrings and to ornament traditional bags and aprons. Beadwork is primarily a female occupation and has become a craft industry highlighted as a mechanism for poor women to engage in the cash economy. This is done in recognition that women, and female-headed households, tend to be among the poorest segments of Batswana society. This is a potentially lucrative, culturally specialized, and relatively small-scale industry. The beads produced from one average-sized ostrich eggshell can make a simple bracelet. For a large item of jewelry, such as a necklace, two to three eggshells' worth of beads are required, depending on the complexity of the pattern and design (see figure 6.2).[25]

In Botswana, San people are particularly well known for this beadwork as a unique cultural skillset. They have been encouraged by the government to use these traditional skills for income generation, through the sale of cultural commodities (beaded jewelry, beaded hunting bags, decorative beaded cloth) to tourists for cash. In addition to commercial possibilities, the jewelry and decorative items made using ostrich eggshell beads, skins, and leather are important pieces of San material culture and central to traditional systems of exchange and gift-giving (Good 2002, 51).

In the context of a discussion about employment and economic opportunities on the conservation estate, the Ghanzi District development officer noted the potential of beadwork, saying, "The San people of Ghanzi are very talented in making

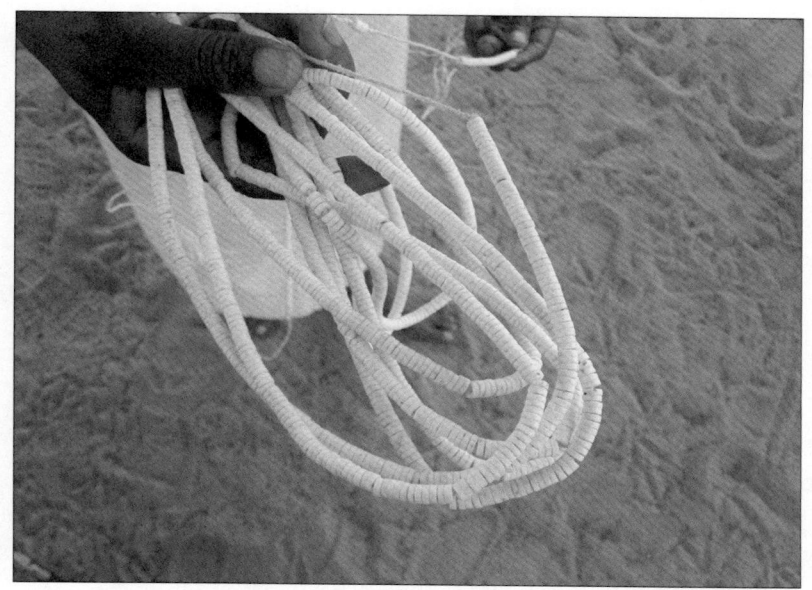

Conservation Restrictions and the Construction of Criminalized Identities 249

FIGURE 6.2. Ostrich eggshell beads made by a woman in West Hanahai able to secure external donor funding for the purchase of the raw materials. Author's photograph.

crafts using skins and beads."²⁶ In San-predominant villages in the district, residents are frequently told to use their crafts and cultural skills as marketable commodities, often in light of limited economic opportunities available in remote resettlement communities. But this enthusiasm is not facilitated by the conservation policies on the ground. One woman directly addressed this disconnect, saying, "I don't understand regulations around eggshells. They tell us they want to eradicate poverty but won't let us use the resources we need to do so."²⁷ As the woman suggested, despite state rhetoric lauding this particular approach, commercial resource exploitation is far from straightforward. Counter to the apparent availability of naturally occurring ostrich eggshell fragments, in Ghanzi there is a severe shortage of the raw materials necessary for these crafting ventures. This is not because of a lack of raw materials from the environment. As with other gathered products, the issue is not availability but access.

In the past, while out in the bush on gathering trips, women would come across and collect the broken eggshells from recently hatched ostrich chicks. These broken shells would then be used to make beads for traditional crafting. This is no longer the case, for reasons explained below. Reflecting on the past, an older woman who had collected eggshells for much of her life emphasized her specific local knowledge around collecting, saying, "People would only just collect the empty shells. We don't collect when there are young still inside. Please understand that we are telling the truth, and we want future use."[28] It is noteworthy that this interviewee deployed the claim of "future use," a discourse highly valued in mainstream discussions of conservation policy—it is the language of sustainability and sustainable development—in order to negotiate for improved access. The current regime against which she articulated her own expertise was established by the government's 1994 Ostrich Management Plan, which is the specific legislation legally empowered by the 1992 Wildlife Conservation and National Parks Act. The Ostrich Management Plan requires the purchase and possession of a trophy dealer's license in order to collect, process, or sell ostrich shells (Hitchcock, Johnson, and Haney 2004, 176). The regulation persists despite ostriches not being endangered. There is no discernible ecological reason for classifying and regulating ostrich eggshells as wildlife trophies—akin to elephant tusks and rhino horns.[29]

As with most regulations relating to gathering, there was widespread confusion among those on the conservation estate about the procedures for obtaining a license, the timing of collection permitted under a license, and the rights of people to collect products for subsistence versus commercial use. A woman in West Hanahai said, "The Wildlife Act doesn't make sense to me. They don't allow us to collect eggshells, which are all over the area in abundance.... Our living standards are low, and we can't afford to travel all the way to Ghanzi to get a permit. Our people have no choice but to resort to illegal collection."[30] Conservation-adjacent women, in particular, viewed these restrictions as fundamentally illogical. From their point of view, ostrich eggshells are abundant; to the ostrich itself, the eggshells are simply a waste product, and the collection does not harm the animal at all.

In the face of these circumstances, local people felt compelled to either abandon their traditional (and potentially lucrative) practice or find themselves transmuted from craftspeople into criminals. Echoing the subjective identification with poachers noted above, a woman in the village of Bere noted, "If you just go and collect ostrich [eggshells], you are punished for being a poacher."[31] Under the existing regulation, any person who collects abandoned shell fragments is illegally in possession of an animal trophy and subject to heavy fines and potential jail time, a prospect that has led many to abandon the practice altogether. Whether one is a "poacher" or not is particularly fraught when injected into the contestations between the state and its indigenous citizens. These environmental questions become, then, "not straightforwardly a matter of resources, but instead they raise questions about particular histories and relations of domination and resistance that have been enacted in processes defining what the law is, how property is to be conceived of and regulated, and how resources are to be conserved" (Gombay 2014, 10). Very often respondents living in conservation-adjacent communities took on the description assigned to them by this discourse: "Everyone is becoming thieves. To restrict things totally makes us all poachers. It is us, the people, who are used to conservation, who are being pushed into poaching. The government is taking people and making them into poachers."[32] In saying this, the respondent shifts responsibility, and ultimately blame, for "making them into poachers" onto the state. This highlights the manner in which the institutional and discursive context of the conservation estate shapes identities and subjectivities on the part of citizens. While a stated goal of the conservation restrictions ranging from limitations on movement and residency to proscriptions on certain types of primary resource use may have been to encourage more tourism-oriented use of natural resources and wildlife, the consequence of these decisions has been to convert otherwise law-abiding citizens into perpetrators of a deviant practice. The dividing line of transgression has been moved, and long-standing behaviors transfigured into crimes worthy of state intervention, often seen as dangerous to the security of the state (see chapter 2).

Women reported still often seeing broken eggshells on gathering trips and simply walking past them for fear of encountering wildlife officers and military personnel, despite the commercial demand the shells elicit in the village and beyond. The perception among respondents is that the conservation restrictions make any ad hoc collection of eggshells from the bush not only illegal but dangerous. Two women in Kacgae recalled the way in which the monitoring and enforcement of resource use is embedded in dehumanizing interactions with the state. They said, "If you are found with a shell, they don't talk to you like you are a person but just harshly harass you."[33] Many interviewees suggested that being found in possession of eggshell fragments could result in violent confrontations with wildlife officers, and all of the women I spoke with were too afraid to collect eggshells as they had done in years past.

Bureaucratic Hurdles: Permitting and Inequality

The state continues to encourage beadwork as a means of reducing poverty and as an income-generating opportunity for poor women, in particular. Moreover, without stating it overtly (in keeping with the aversion to identity-based claims), government officials obliquely note that this is a potential source of revenue for poor *San* women in particular. How, then, are these women supposed to take advantage of the natural and cultural capital around them? Wildlife authorities based in Ghanzi District provided two solutions. The first is for these women to acquire the necessary trophy licenses themselves. The second, if the first is unattainable, is for these women to buy eggshells from existing licensed trophy dealers.

Both of these "solutions" are flawed and yet revealing about the nature of citizen-state interactions on the conservation estate.

Conservation Restrictions and the Construction of Criminalized Identities 253

When asked about the ability of predominantly poor women on the conservation estate to obtain the appropriate trophy dealer's license from his office, the regional wildlife officer in Ghanzi said, "Oh, it is easy to gain a license. You just come into the office [of the DWNP], fill in the form, and pay the small fee, and you will get one."[34] This does, of course, seem straightforward. However, when this statement is unpacked, it quickly becomes clear that it is rife with misunderstanding and miscommunication, problems that demonstrate the difficulties of certain citizens in accessing state institutions and navigating development programs as they manifest in the unique sociopolitical environments of the conservation estate.

First, the individuals living in conservation-adjacent villages often reside hundreds of kilometers from the district wildlife office in Ghanzi Town. These communities are typically quite marginalized, lacking both private and public transportation, and are often only accessible via poorly maintained dirt roads through the bush (see chapter 5). Private vehicle ownership is very rare, and state transportation provided by the district council is often limited to people needing medical attention in the town center or the ferrying of children to boarding schools for secondary education. To simply "come into the office" is not a realistic option for most people. And the act of filling out a form to obtain a license requires basic Setswana and English literacy skills, which a substantial majority of those who would need this permission lack. The communities with the beading skills are non-Tswana, and those most likely to retain the cultural knowledge tend to be older and less exposed to formal education.

Finally, the wildlife officer implied in an offhand manner that paying "a small fee" is an easy task rather than an overbearing obstacle that would prevent most San women from receiving a license. The communities that have been targeted as having beadwork potential are among the most impoverished in the country; most residents have little means of obtaining cash other than through government-sponsored welfare programs for the destitute or through state-sponsored public works initiatives like the Ipelegeng program, which provides a small monthly cash stipend for light manual labor projects like picking up litter or clearing small shrubs and weeds from public spaces. These communities operate on the fringes of the cash economy, without formal employment opportunities, making a permit expensive. Naturally, women on the conservation estate worry about the prohibitive cost. I spoke to two skilled beaders in East Hanahai who were unable to purchase the permit. One woman said, "I've heard the license for eggshells is 150 pula. That is too much."[35] Despite the wildlife officer's assurance of the ease with which women can access the state-sponsored permissions in order to embark on an income-generating endeavor using local natural resources, this process remains very difficult.

Many women cited the complexity and logistical difficulty of obtaining the license as a reason they have opted out of beadwork, though one further avenue for securing the necessary raw materials remains. It illustrates the vastly uneven access and ability of various citizens of Botswana to exploit natural resources. If a woman is still intent on embarking on commercial beadwork, she can buy the ostrich eggshell raw materials from a licensed trophy dealer. This person is most often the owner of a privately held, freehold game farm. These game farms, some of which breed ostriches and produce eggshells as a by-product, collect the shells from their hatchlings and process them for private sale to beadworkers throughout southern Africa. But this situation did not sit well with most women interviewed. A middle-aged woman in East Hanahai forcefully noted, "People on farms, the *maBuru* [Afrikaners], can collect within their farms and then sell it to us. How is that fair?"[36] Here she is invoking the unfairness of the privileging of another class of citizen on the conservation estate, Ghanzi's nearby population of white landowners (see chapter 4). Without a permit of their own, relatively poor women are required by conservation regulations to purchase raw materials from relatively wealthy game farm owners, despite the fact that these women may have theoretical access to naturally occurring eggshells in their own areas. While on the surface this transaction may appear less cumbersome than obtaining a trophy dealer's license outright, the cost is prohibitive without significant donor or governmental support.[37] Thus, even those women who *want* to embark on some form of resource commercialization rather than for local consumption or subsistence—an approach considered ideal by state authorities—are subject to nearly insurmountable obstacles.

Conservation regulations around ostrich eggshells create a gulf of misunderstanding between the women on the conservation estate and the government, perpetuating their sense of alienation and dispossession and seen as yet another way wherein state authorities have co-opted the patrimony of the San for the benefit of others. "They saw Basarwa [San] making a living from beads," I was told, "so that's why they came up with the rule. And not everyone can go and get a permit—only a few."[38] This perspective demonstrates the manner in which differentiation of citizenship and opportunity on the conservation estate occludes the state's own developmental imaginary. Local attempts to utilize ostrich shells commercially is not a form of overt resistance to state norms but instead an adoption of these norms. Nonetheless, even accepting the government's position appears likely to fail on the conservation estate. As observed in chapter 5, people on the conservation estate are often willing to meet the terms set by the state. In this they are working with state priorities, rather than against them, although, as the limits of ostrich shell commercialization demonstrate, this too is a vexed proposition.

Women on the conservation estate are provided with deeply contradictory signals. On one hand, the discursive message from government officials is dominated by the rhetoric of commercialization—entrepreneurial self-help, of using their unique cultural and natural capital to lift themselves out of poverty. On the other, the lived reality is that in this expressly commercialized system of resource utilization, the poor—who often live in closest contact with the natural resources—are the least equipped to take advantage of the environment around them, regardless of the rhetoric of locally (and culturally) specific resource beneficiation. The talk of economic empowerment through resource commercialization is viewed on the conservation estate as disingenuous. Barriers to entry keep the poor out of the commercial market while simultaneously preventing them from adopting subsistence livelihood approaches instead. A woman in West Hanahai conveyed this frustration with remarkable candor: "We Basarwa are beadmakers, but we cannot pick up eggshells without a permit. It is hard to earn a living from beads. It is difficult without access."[39] San/Basarwa women recognize their unique ability to market commercially appealing artifacts of their material culture and express a preference to meet the development goals laid out by state actors as ideal—to be self-starting, industrious Batswana engaged in the cash economy. While they earnestly attempt to align themselves to the state's development priorities, the conditions that are exceptional to life on the conservation estate impede this change. San craftswomen are left in a state of limbo—regulated out of traditional economies of subsistence gathering and still unable to make a livelihood in line with the state's mainstream expectations.

Identity and Image: The Ambiguity of San Culture in the State Project

> It is ironic, to say the least, that the same people who deny us the right to use our traditional hunting skills and dances to generate income happily display our pictures as tourist icons in lodges, hotels and on television.
>
> —Kuela Kiema, *Tears for My Land*[40]

Assertions of identity within Botswana are ambiguous because of the unique way in which certain cultural communities like the San continue to be prominently featured in the visual representations of the state, further complicating the picture of identity and citizenship in Botswana's postcolonial polity. As with the gathering dynamics examined above, even if the overwhelming majority of San people in Botswana do not want to live as hunter-gatherers, many still see the importance of maintaining cultural awareness and skills required for their traditional economies, particularly as a means to tap into a tourism market they view as dominated by outsiders co-opting their cultural heritage.[41] Interviewees recognized the commonplace appropriation of San cultural symbols, practices, and images, often for the profit of others: "Our culture is very popular and likable. With our culture comes familiarity with natural resources and their wise utilization. Those foreign to our culture will not know any of that. But you see, as we speak, Batswana [non-San citizens of Botswana] are showcasing our traditional dance that is part of our culture as Basarwa [San]. That would not happen if I had it my way."[42] The respondent observes the state's enthusiastic emphasis on his culture when it suits a particular interest. He is arguing this is unfair to his community, which perceives its everyday and mundane practices of cultural enactment (like the gathering of eggshells) as proscribed by state entities. Intriguingly, though the state tends to privilege livelihood activities and social arrangements associated with the Tswana majority, it still heavily relies on the evocative visual imagery of San culture in its own marketing. The tourism industry and the government itself have used vivid and at times stereotypical images of San people and cultural practices in its public materials.[43] Though simultaneously anxious about the presence of materially poor former hunter-gatherers, state institutions continue to actively appropriate San cultural images, though often in deeply essentializing ways, relying on highly choreographed scenes of San people in skins and with traditional bows and arrows.[44] While wildlife is certainly the top draw, San culture is important in the promotion of Botswana as a tourism destination, particularly in the western parts of the country.[45] Many San respondents viewed this perceived appropriation as insulting, particularly as most people on the conservation estate see few benefits from the representation of their cultural practices.

The imagery of apparently "timeless" San people (akin to the problematic trope of the "noble savage") is deployed in capitalist endeavors, but no recourse is made for the real, contemporary individuals who constitute this visually distinctive cultural group. The limitations felt by beadworkers extend to other artisans. For example, tourist brochures, online marketing, and luxury lodges utilize the images of San people wearing traditional skins, but the actual practice of an individual San Batswana engaging in the necessary activity to obtain said skin—hunting—was forbidden during the period of the hunting ban and remains heavily proscribed even with the reintroduction of some trophy hunting across the country (see chapter 7). This has particular relevance for craftspeople working in niche markets and with very specific materials. An elderly man in Kacgae who worked with leather for decades described the barriers created by the hunting ban: "The hunting ban hurts me because during hunting I was getting skins to make leatherwork and traditional attire. The schools would buy this to compete in traditional dancing competitions, but since the hunting ban I do not know how to get leather."[46]

There was no clear solution to his predicament, nor was it evident that these downstream effects of the ban had been seriously contemplated. After our conversation the man asked me to try to find him an answer. I spoke with DWNP officials in Ghanzi Town who said that leather could be purchased from licensed game farmers (the only group exempt from the hunting ban) or cattle producers, though this craftsman rejected the idea of using cattle leather in his work. In light of the material and practical limitations experienced by craftworkers unable to access ostrich eggshells, it became clear to me that this would not be a viable solution for those artisans working with other animal materials. The message this conveyed was that San identity is valued only as a simulacrum of a culture of a time gone by, with no room in the narrative for those contemporary individuals who still identify with a culture that has, for the most part, been quite crudely instrumentalized in tourism marketing, or for specific San individuals seeking to engage in market-based commercialization of their cultural skills.

———

This chapter explored the intersections between identity claims and development paradigms within the state-building process on the conservation estate. It articulated the ways in which people who consider themselves non-dominant within the state—rural and non-Tswana—view livelihood approaches and ethnic identification as overlapping categories in the broader state-building process. Conservation and development decisions that alter the livelihood options available on the conservation estate are not perceived as value-neutral but rather as purposeful attempts by the state to replace local notions of belonging and identity with a connection to the larger project of nation, premised upon Tswana modes of being. Yet these assimilatory practices embedded in development programs are not neat or straightforward but instead fraught, ambiguous, and at times contradictory, leading to a deepening differentiation of conservation-adjacent citizens rather than heightened incorporation.

Interview participants saw conservation-related policies as related to a long-term process throughout postcolonial Botswana that has promoted Tswana sociocultural and economic norms while devaluing alternatives, especially from Botswana's marginal non-Tswana communities. Regardless of whether this is an intentional aim of policy, this is the way these policies are overwhelmingly perceived and percolate through the conservation estate. Consequently, changes in the relationship between conservation-adjacent people and the environment are believed to operate within a web of state mechanisms used to bring perceived outliers into the dominant, majoritarian culture. Generated from this anxiety is a commonplace strategy of resistance to the state-building process on the conservation estate—appeals to ethnic identity. However, despite its widespread purchase on the conservation estate, these strategies may be limiting on two fronts: (1) the state is overtly hostile to identity-based claims, and (2) this discourse relies on stereotypical and at times primordial constructions of identity. This local discourse of identity runs the possibility of being self-essentializing and problematically draws upon stereotypical notions about the "noble savage," which further pigeonhole and disadvantage San people who believe their cultural practice is a constituent part of their identities in modern, contemporary Botswana.

7

Promises of Modernity and Failures of Development on the Conservation Estate

In the run-up to the October 2019 national election in Botswana, former president Ian Khama broke with the long-standing tradition of an apolitical retirement and actively campaigned against his own handpicked vice president and current incumbent president, Mokgweetsi Masisi.[1] The acrimonious relationship between Khama and Masisi is multifaceted, but a key dispute relates to environmental policy.[2] Botswana's hunting ban, which prohibited commercial safari hunting and suspended subsistence Special Game Licences (SGLs), was operational from 2014 until 2019 (Mbaiwa 2005; Selby 1991). It was closely associated with the tenure of President Khama, who stepped down in 2018 and was succeeded by Masisi. While the two men served together and were both members of the ruling Botswana Democratic Party, upon taking office President Masisi opted to reverse a series of controversial conservation policies associated with the Khama administration, including reinstituting trophy hunting after a five-year moratorium,[3] disarming some antipoaching forces,[4] and lobbying the Convention on International Trade in Endangered Species of Wild Fauna and Flora (CITES) to allow for legal ivory sales.[5]

While much attention has been paid to the reinstitution of the commercial safari hunting of charismatic animals like elephants, comparatively little analysis has considered the government's decision not to restore the SGL program to its pre-2014 status. The maintenance of the Khama-era phase-out of SGLs demonstrates a policy coherence between the Khama and Masisi administrations that is not seen in most other natural resource–use policies. This continuity is worth probing within the context of hegemonic understandings of resource use, development, and economic modernities widely held by many political elite, civil servants, and policymakers in Botswana. Ongoing discursive contestations about conservation and development involve a whole host of values, normative positions, and symbolic meanings that are attached to particular resources or environmental practices, such as hunting. This chapter focuses on the way narratives of development, identity, and belonging are simultaneously challenged, contested, and reinforced on the conservation estate. It traces the history of resource-use restrictions related to the consumption of wildlife and in doing so articulates the state's overarching vision for the practice. It examines how over the years, and across several presidential administrations, particular economies have been deemed "primitive" and subject to restriction.

While all Batswana have histories of game meat consumption, the decisions made around wildlife management have particular impact on Botswana's diverse San communities, which have long consumed game meat harvested through various government-sanctioned hunting regimes. These patterns of meat consumption are tied to notions of identity, citizenship, and belonging within the wider Botswana state. San people frequently articulate their perceived difference from mainstream society based on their contrasting meat-consumption cultures, compared with dominant Tswana cultural and economic norms associated with cattle production. Cattle, which Gulbrandsen argues occupy a place of "immense symbolic, economic and political importance" in Tswana cultural practice (2012, 112), also played a crucial role in the early period of Botswana's postindependence developmental state policy (Gulbrandsen 2012; Peters 1994; Samatar 1999). While the cattle-dominated economy of the postindependence period has been superseded in national importance by the diamond and tourism industries, agropastoralism occupies a more-than-economic place in the national imagination, especially among the politically and culturally dominant Tswana, and husbandry remains a focal point of contemporary rural development strategies.[6] Botswana's sweeping hunting ban fundamentally upended and criminalized the game meat culture common to most San groups, especially those in the western Kalahari region. Concerted efforts to end commercial hunting, the continued prohibition of non-commercial hunting practices, and the promotion of cattle farming are all interpreted by San communities as policies of forced assimilation into Tswana culture and society. Cattle production and beef consumption are promoted as development approaches that are "modern" and contrasted with supposedly "primitive" and "profligate" hunting practices. Nonetheless, a developmental meat transition is justified in government discourse along ecological and conservation lines without fully engaging with the environmental impact of a widespread transition away from game meat and toward cattle production in an arid, desert region dependent on boreholes for its water supply.

In 1966 newly independent Botswana set about constructing a unitary nation-state across the politically and ethnically heterogeneous territory that once was the Bechuanaland Protectorate, in a clear rejection of the governing orientations of the surrounding minority-ruled states. However, as noted earlier, the effect of building a supposedly non-ethnic state was to elevate the culture, language, and status of the largest and most politically powerful group, the Tswana (Datta and Murray 1989; Nyamnjoh 2004; Roberts 1985; Solway 2002; Zips-Mairitsch 2013). The Tswana-dominated postcolonial government's aversion to non-commercial resource-use strategies, such as subsistence hunting and gathering, and the accompanying reliance on game meat entailed in such lifestyles, is based on assumptions that privilege assimilation into mainstream resource-use strategies, like cattle rearing and other forms of agropastoralism (Saugestad 2001; Taylor 2002). This perspective fails to consider the potential of alternative meat cultures. As will be discussed at length below, many government officials believe non-commercial hunting to be *only* a temporary economic activity employed to cope with hardship rather than an approach suited to local environmental conditions and steeped in particular historical and cultural contexts (Zips-Mairitsch 2013).

The question of how citizens are authorized or barred from using natural resources is not simply ecological or economic but also social and political. Thus, the reauthorization of commercial safari hunting with no concomitant return to the pre-2014 system of SGLs requires consideration. This chapter centers on questions about the dynamics of non-commercial hunting in contemporary Botswana, with specific emphasis on the ban's continued consequences for non-commercial hunting. I use the term "non-commercial hunting" to account for the more-than-economic dimensions of the hunting practices typically glossed as "subsistence."[7] While policies related to this mode of hunting are less headline-grabbing than commercial safari hunting of charismatic species, investigating the lack of change in this area illuminates long-standing policy trajectories with regard to the environment, development, and identity within contemporary Botswana, even across presidential administrations perceived as starkly divergent in their approaches to natural resource use.

Continuity and Change in Botswana's Hunting Regime

Old life was the way of the bush. New life is the Motswana way.

—Resident of West Hanahai[8]

There has been sustained scholarship on hunting as a socioeconomic and cultural practice across Africa.[9] In southern Africa, empirical examinations of trophy hunting (Koot 2019; Wright 2016), game farms (Brandt 2016),[10] and "canned" hunting (Schroeder

2018) are common. In the context of Botswana, much of the recent scholarship on hunting examines the impact of the moratorium on the safari hunting industry, with an empirical focus on the country's north (Mbaiwa 2018). However, the systematic hemming in of non-commercial hunting predated the implementation of the 2014 moratorium. Historically, Botswana was the only country in southern Africa to have national legislation regarding subsistence hunting (Spinage 1991; von Richter and Butynski 1973). Although long regulated in various ways, hunting existed as a customary right among the largest Tswana-speaking groups in the precolonial era, and various communities across the country consumed game meat. During the period of the Bechuanaland Protectorate (1885–1966), colonial authorities and traditional leaders slowly began to curtail hunting rights and systematize access to wildlife. Thereafter, the postcolonial government introduced SGLs as part of the 1979 Unified Hunting Regulations (Hitchcock 1996, 2001).[11] The SGLs had existed as a provision for rural subsistence hunters mostly living in the western part of the country since the 1970s. They were not a universal policy; rather they were limited to a small slice of the population, more often than not rural dwellers who identified as San. These licenses permitted their holders to continue practicing subsistence hunting within a strictly regulated regime (Hitchcock 1996). The main objectives of the SGL were developmental: to concretize the legal framework for hunting among the poorest segments of Botswana's population and to provide food security or a cash income through the direct consumption or sale of meat. While some in the government have suggested that the SGLs were always meant to be a temporary poverty-eradication measure,[12] by the mid-1990s over two thousand SGLs had been issued throughout Botswana's remote areas. Some recipients received them every year for nearly two decades.

Despite its longevity, the SGL program faced significant headwind as a development initiative. Officials voiced a variety of reservations about the program. Some politicians argued that SGLs were conferring special rights to a specific class of people along ethnic lines at the expense of all citizens, thereby invoking Botswana's "non-ethnic" postcolonial project to highlight the incompatibility of SGLs with the country's "difference-blind" orientation (Hitchcock 2001). While less common than concerns over the program's particularistic nature, some interviewees invoked moral and animal rights–based arguments, suggesting that the kind of hunting authorized by the SGL system was inhumane since some license holders use traps or snares.[13] Another view commonly expressed by interviewees from government circles was that hunting was a backwards activity, the practice of which reflected badly on Botswana's reputation as an "African miracle."[14] These informants favored the discontinuation of the program and its replacement with other social welfare projects more compatible with Botswana's national image.[15] Indeed, by 1996 the SGL system had fallen out of favor and had been replaced by the Community-Based Natural Resource Management program, which had become paradigmatic throughout the region (Murombedzi 2003; Neumann 2005; Rihoy and Maguranyanga 2010; Swatuk 2005). CBNRM brought a quota system that exchanged individual hunting rights for communal access to wildlife resources through community conservation trusts. Notwithstanding this broad policy transition, some SGLs remained valid until the January 2014 hunting ban, mostly in the districts of Ghanzi and Kgalagadi, where there was comparatively little safari hunting and sizable communities of San RADs.[16]

Beginning in 2011 the Khama government phased out all hunting, both commercial and subsistence, in areas within a twenty-five-kilometer radius of national parks and game reserves, eliminating safari hunting in many Wildlife Management Areas on the conservation estate (Mbaiwa, Stronza, and Kreuter 2011). In late 2012 the government announced a nationwide ban on hunting both commercially and for subsistence purposes to begin in January 2014.[17] Rather than reworking the statute that legislates natural resource use—the Wildlife Conservation and National Parks Act of 1992[18]—the hunting ban was enacted via presidential directive. The lack of legislative framework perhaps eased the way for its reversal five years later. At the close of 2013, hunting quotas set at the discretion of the Ministry of Environment, Natural Resources Conservation and Tourism were reduced to zero rather than fully dismantling the legal architecture of hunting.[19] SGLs were not reauthorized as they had been in previous years.[20] The director of the Department of Wildlife and National Parks at the time of my field work characterized the way in which SGLs, though still existing on paper in 2014, were viewed at the time to be irrelevant to the well-being of conservation-adjacent citizens: "Special Game Licences exist in the law [the 1992 act]. The law was not amended. They were specifically meant to assist those who were hunter-gatherers. Over the years, we've experienced a significant decrease in requests for SGLs. Those applying are often not the original recipients, and there are other social programs they can benefit from. The program was fading away because of disuse. Nobody is dependent on hunting and gathering anymore because they are using other social grants and benefits."[21]

The director's comments were in keeping with the thinking that hunting is, first, merely an economic strategy and, second, a primitive and no longer acceptable strategy at that. In line with this, most government employees described the SGL program as obsolete and anachronistic. The regional wildlife officer for Ghanzi and Kgalagadi Districts said, "There was no reason to continue issuing SGLs because there are now other options. They were given to those unable to work as a way to alleviate poverty and destitution, but now they can access other social services and supports."[22] His response presented a rather rose-colored view of the prevalence of social programs and the ways in which the state is able to support conservation-adjacent citizens. However, as was demonstrated in the previous chapter, there is often a substantial disconnect between these support systems in theory and in practice. In fact, many people on the conservation estate believe state interventions do not make up for the shortfall in their subsistence that has occurred from the cessation of both individual hunting rights. Accounting for what they view as deprivation, local residents of the conservation estate draw a clear and logical line through the history of the resource-use restrictions placed upon them. A woman in Mababe recounted the past forty years of conservation regulations brought to her community: "In the past, our former president, Seretse, gave us Special Game Licences, and these we gave back to government in exchange to being given a trust [CBNRM]. Now that hunting is banned, it's the end of our trust because the trust depended on hunting to make money. How are we going to survive now?"[23] Local people believed that government policy on the conservation estate was directed in such a way to incentivize particular kinds of livelihood approaches. Many viewed the hunting ban as merely the culmination of a longer process to disincentivize, devalue, and ultimately end hunting as a practice in Botswana. A safari operator noted, "The impact [of the hunting ban] will be big, but this process began earlier, slowly. The government has been slowly cutting the hunting quotas until many concessions just weren't [financially or commercially] viable."[24] This interviewee used to buy hunting quotas given to the resettlement villages in Ghanzi to then sell on to safari clients from abroad. Beginning in the early 2000s, he slowly began to shut down this portion of his business and focus exclusively on bringing clients to his private game farm for hunting trips (see chapter 4). His decision was a result of the low quotas and undesirable species given to these communities by the DWNP, making it impossible to sell viable hunting trips. Typically hunting quotas in these areas of western Botswana were made up of small numbers of jackals, baboons, and springhares and could not be marketed profitably in a commercial context. He simply pulled out of those operations long before the 2014 ban was implemented.

Government interviewees echoed the intentional logic of the trajectory of diminished quotas over several years. One senior official based in Ghanzi said, "Hunting is not the best way to generate money from wildlife, so that is why we've given them low quotas for many years. We need to move away from this issue of killing."²⁵ This demonstrates a clear position that hunting is not the ideal or preferred way for citizens of Botswana to earn a living, tied to notions of what kind of human-environment interactions are appropriate. The tone of the official above is clear—when he says "we need to move away from this issue of killing," his distaste for the practice of hunting is evident. In this conceptualization, hunting is "killing"—destructive and brutal—and local people must be instructed in the proper way to exploit, or not exploit, Botswana's natural resources.

During the tenure of the ban, journalistic reporting and scholarly assessments tended to focus on communities in the northern conservation estate that had previously relied on commercial safari hunting income.²⁶ After his ascent to the presidency in April 2018, Masisi authorized a cabinet subcommittee to study the ban, which reported its findings in May 2019. The report of the Cabinet Sub Committee on Hunting Ban and Social Dialogue was primarily centered on human-elephant conflict and livelihood concerns related to community-based organizations losing revenue from safari hunting. Several recommended policy changes were highlighted in this process, including reinvigorating the safari hunting industry, managing the elephant population (specifically dealing with human-elephant conflict), renewed attention to Botswana's system of wildlife fences, demarcation of new game ranches to act as buffer zones, revision of the compensation scheme for wildlife damage, closure of migratory routes deemed not to be beneficial, and the consideration of elephant culling and commercial processing of their meat. All but the suggestion regarding the canning of elephant meat were taken up by the government.²⁷ Commercial safari hunting for international clients would be reopened through the previous system, whereby hunting quotas in Controlled Hunting Areas were marketed via commercial hunting operators and community-based organizations. These quotas would include permits to hunt elephants, a fact that has dominated national and international discussion of the rollback.[28] The changes made to the hunting regime in 2019 were based on the assumption that the primary and appropriate mode of resource utilization is commodification (much like the policy logic of gathering described last chapter) and the connection of hunting to market imperatives. The set of recommended policy changes did not include reopening SGLs, nor did it address subsistence hunting, with this aspect of the ban nearly absent from the national (and indeed global) conversations that have accompanied the reversal of the commercial restrictions. The justification given for this decision was a familiar one: government now provides social safety nets and empowerment programs aimed at the country's most impoverished, making subsistence hunting obsolete.[29] This orientation shares continuity with earlier modernist assumptions about how resources should be used for development, the emphasis on a cash economy, and citizens' expected modes of participation in it.

If hunting is just one livelihood strategy among many, then the series of restrictions described above is conceived of very differently than if the act of hunting is articulated as central to the formation of one's identity. San interview respondents on the conservation estate described the activity of hunting and the practice of consuming game meat as part of their cultural heritage. Conservation restrictions are not interpreted by local populations merely as targeting their livelihoods but also targeting their ways of life and self-conceptions of identity within the larger nation-state and state-building project. In this sense, the hunting ban, the most recent of a long series of restrictions, was seen not merely as a technical, dispassionate decision about wildlife management but also perceived in a deeply corporeal manner by those most affected by it on the conservation estate. A woman in Kacgae described the situation in dire terms: "[The hunting ban] is like a big tree has been cut [felled] between us and our lives eating meat."[30]

Citizen Hunting: A Compromise on the Horizon?

> I am happy that I have "won" an elephant. I had hoped I would be able to sell the tusks. I don't eat elephant meat so I do not know what I am going to do with it. I think as citizens we should be allowed to sell the licenses to commercial hunters or export the tusks to improve our livelihoods.
>
> —Hunting lottery winner, Maun[31]

While the restoration of SGLs was not listed as a policy option by the Masisi administration, in a break from previous policy the government did reintroduce citizen hunting licenses, which had been phased out with the advent of CBNRM. At first blush this appeared to signal a recognition of non-commercial hunting as a legitimate practice. However, it is markedly different from the previous regime in ways that essentially make it irrelevant for communities and individuals who previously accessed game meat through the SGL system, especially in the country's western conservation estate. September 2019 saw the allocation of citizen hunting licenses for the first time in over a decade.[32] Although they are non-commercial in nature, they are deeply embedded in market logics and utilize a fee-for-service model for environmental access and resource use.[33] They are also difference-blind, in keeping with the state's professed development project, conferring no particular priority on groups with historical or cultural connections to hunting, and they are allocated through a lottery system. The demand for licenses proved very high. In Maun in the north of the country, for example, 5,990 people entered the raffle for just eight elephant licenses.[34] The citizen hunting lottery, like other difference-blind policy approaches, is in theory open to all Batswana. However, in practice the barriers to entry are prohibitive to many, particularly among those most marginalized on the conservation estate. The lucky few among the lottery entrants win the privilege of paying for their license (which for sought-after animals like elephants is 8,000 Botswana pula, approximately $800). Moreover, the winner bears all the costs of the hunt beyond the license fee. The license requires the lottery recipient to be accompanied by a professional hunter and guide as well as officials from the wildlife department. The citizen hunter must provide for transportation and accommodation costs of the hunt.[35] This is markedly different from the logistics and practices permitted by the SGL system. In addition to the high cost of holding a license, unlike other reinstated hunting permits the new citizen hunting licenses have no commercial value because they are nontransferable (i.e., they cannot be sold to safari tourists), nor can the hunter sell the trophy. As the winner of a much sought-after elephant license quoted at the beginning of this section notes, the only material value is the meat, which he does not consume. Thus, in practice, this mode of non-commercial hunting represents a recreational luxury that is out of reach for most Batswana and certainly for the previous recipients of SGLs. Moreover, its universal nature means that winners of the license may not have any particular prior connection to game meat consumption or the practice of hunting as a traditional mode of human-environment interactions.

Reporting in the local press has provided perspectives from lottery winners that shed light on some of the inherent contradictions of this policy. In the September 2019 lottery, a Motswana woman in Maun won the right to hunt an impala. She said in an interview with the newspaper *Mmegi*, "It will be my first time to eat an impala. We have never seen or eaten the meat of these animals. I think it's commendable that the government has reintroduced hunting because this will boost food security in our impoverished areas."[36] The invocation of food security is particularly notable. The SGL was expressly aimed at food security in Botswana's most remote rural communities on the conservation estate. However, with the lottery system and its attendant financial requirements, it is unlikely that citizen hunting licenses will reach food-insecure citizens. While citizen licenses nominally provide for a post-ban opportunity to access game meat again and reinscribe hunting as a permitted activity for the citizens of the country, with its uniform application, reliance on a difference-blind lottery method of distribution, and fee-for-service model, it is consistent with some of the assumptions around resource use that characterized previous developmental policies in Botswana.

Proteins and Progress:
Linear Assumptions about Development in Contemporary Botswana

> If people know the value of the wildlife, they won't then look at wildlife as, you know, meals on hooves.
>
> —Former president Ian Khama[37]

The practice of hunting in non-commercial settings, including as the primary mode of protein procurement, is for some an unwelcome reminder of Botswana's not-too-distant past of economic adversity. Former president Khama expressed this position in a thirty-five-minute televised special on Botswana Television (BTV) that aired in the early months of the ban's implementation in 2014. In the course of a wide-ranging interview about conservation policy, the illegal wildlife trade, and the newly operational hunting moratorium, he said: "Don't forget that your ancestors [gestures to off-camera interviewer] like mine, like others sitting around here, they used to hunt, as well, wildlife for their subsistence. They used to hunt wildlife. But over time we have divorced ourselves from that kind as this country has developed. About Survival [International], ... they would like to see Basarwa living that kind of existence, which is backward, and not allow them to come into mainstream society."[38] His comment encapsulates the manner in which particular relationships to the environment, especially for those citizens living on the conservation estate, are viewed as evidence of a failure to develop from within the mainstream modernization paradigm. Hunting, and the lifestyles "of the bush" that the practice connotes, are thought to be incompatible with the country's hard-won economic prosperity in the postcolonial era and citizens' abilities to be part of the mainstream

(Saugestad 2001). While the above quote is notable because it comes from a senior political leader speaking on the state broadcaster, it is not unique. Scholars have noted similar perspectives from frontline bureaucrats as well (Taylor 2004). Given the pervasiveness of these norms, it is unsurprising that there are people in local and national positions of authority who regard San livelihood and cultural practices with skepticism.

The implicit contrast with development in the Global North was present throughout President Khama's 2014 BTV interview, wherein he argued that any support for, or promotion of, hunting was the result of an untoward and voyeuristic "fascination," often on the part of Westerners who no longer have subsistence economies but who "want to impose that on us when we are trying to develop our people."[39] This emphasis on foreign actors as the primary proponents of subsistence discourages sympathetic local responses to the practice. These comments can be seen within a much longer context of high-level government statements equating hunting with ancestral practices that must be shed in order to achieve development. The oppositional binary of hunting-or-development is a point echoed in much of the existing literature related to the ways in which conservation and development processes are perceived in Botswana, particularly by government elites (Madzwamuse 2010; Magole 2009; Twyman 1998). Good (2008) cites similar statements made by half a dozen political leaders and officials dating back to the early 1990s. Similarly, Kuela Kiema, a Kua San, recounts in his memoir how former president Festus Mogae (in office 1998–2008) came to the New Xade *kgotla* in 2007 and told the assembled community, "All Batswana were once hunter-gatherers but with the introduction of modern economic practices, they have abandoned such ways" (2010, 139). The 2019 decision not to reinstate the primary mechanism through which most Batswana, primarily of San descent, had been able to continue hunting—the SGL—suggests that the current policy is, to some extent, in keeping with these earlier orientations. With the designation of SGLs as unnecessary or obsolete, the current orientation reinforces the clear binary, according to which certain relationships to the environment and resources on the conservation estate are antithetical to developmentalist visions of modern Botswana (Chebanne 2003; Molomo 2008).

Whereas government officials equate hunting and game meat consumption with backward practices, destitution, and lack of integration into mainstream society, many in Botswana's San communities on the conservation estate view them as practices imbued with cultural significance: tied to their individual and communal identity, of symbolic and cosmological importance, and, crucially, entirely compatible with "modern" lifestyles (Hitchcock 2002; Twyman 1998). Moreover, San respondents rejected the characterization of hunting as destructive or profligate, a designation that is prominent in both colonial and contemporary evaluations of their hunting practices. One respondent noted, "[Hunting] is part of our culture. Hunting doesn't only mean killing; it teaches you a lot of things."[40] The cultural didacticism described by this respondent reinforces the notion that hunting is not something to progress beyond but rather that the activity of hunting, and the practice of consuming game meat, should be understood in terms of cultural heritage. Policies such as the 2014–19 hunting ban and the continued prohibition of SGLs are not interpreted as simply restricting their menu of possible livelihood strategies but are also seen as targeting their identity and way of life—a much broader interpretation than hunting as an economic strategy alone. Game meat was consistently described by informants as the "staple food" of San peoples, both in terms of nutrition and identity.[41] San respondents regularly utilized analogies of consumption in their discursive contestation of state environmental and development policies. This was commonly done by associating various ethnolinguistic communities with different primary sources of nutrition, symbolic of cultural identity and not just livelihood strategy: "People have different backgrounds; some have been raised off meat while others off sorghum. We the Basarwa [San] rely on hunting."[42] In local discourse, game meat occupies an important place as an ethnic signifier. The implications of hunting restrictions embedded on the conservation estate, up to and including the national moratorium, were seen as unfairly targeting their cultural and subsistence practices, more so than any other group in the country, and further differentiating this subset of citizens in significant ways from other communities. Overturning the ban's commercial limitations alone does not address these concerns.

Game Meat: A Marker of Deprivation or a Staple Food?

> Hunting is our culture as Basarwa. Cattle farming, which is the mainstay of Black [Tswana-speaking] people's livelihood, has not been stopped. So why hunting?
>
> —Resident of Groot Laagte[43]

During its tenure, the hunting ban essentially closed off the only two practical, legal avenues for access to game meat for San communities: through licensed subsistence hunting or the receipt of meat from safari hunters (as their clients only keep the trophy) (Mbaiwa 2018). However, even prior to the ban, outside of the game farm industry, community-based safari hunting tourism was not practical in much of the western conservation estate due to low quotas and commercially undesirable species.[44] Game meat was still available for purchase from privately owned game farms, but this was exorbitantly expensive for the average household in the western Kalahari and not a viable strategy for access to protein and a "staple food." Illegal hunting, while clandestinely practiced, was and is risky due to Botswana's securitized enforcement-first paradigm (see chapter 2) and the often years-long prison sentences meted out to those deemed poachers. As such, the hunting ban was of a piece with a succession of policies that necessitated the transformation of daily livelihood practices on the conservation estate and may indeed facilitate a broader transition to cattle rearing. Many San respondents regarded the hunting ban as simply the most recent iteration of a long process of disincentivizing and devaluing hunting, with the ultimate goal of undermining the practical and cultural significance of both hunting and the consumption of game meat as a staple food.[45] Effectively, the state's orientation to this mode of resource use on the conservation estate is premised on the assumption that it only ever was a stopgap measure in moments of economic crisis. This was affirmed by President Khama in the early days of the moratorium:

> You know in the past when Basarwa were living in the CKGR [Central Kalahari Game Reserve], we admit we knew that they were allowed to [hunt] by the previous colonial government.... Here we are, we have a game park, and we are saying to people, Look in those days the government was not able to have social welfare programs like we do now where we are able to help people who are poor.... We couldn't afford that soon after independence. So, it was convenient maybe for those people to be able to look after themselves. Now we are saying we are able to look after them, and we do. We make interventions. We give them livestock, as you know, for people living in those situations.[46]

From this perspective, hunting was something permissible only until the government could step in and provide other forms of social welfare for its citizens on the conservation estate. Once alternative livelihood forms, in this case the provision of cattle, could be facilitated by a developmental state, hunting was considered aberrant. Even after the substantial changes to the hunting regime brought about in 2019, these rationales remained commonplace and were used to justify the continued prohibition on SGLs.[47] Policymakers describe SGLs as a relic of another time, one before the state was able to fill the void and provide for each citizen within the mainstream state-building project of development. Despite the confident assessment of government officials, state interventions do not make up for the shortfall in subsistence across the conservation estate, largely related to the unique set of conditions created by the category of space itself.

The historical trajectory limiting non-commercial hunting rights, culminating in the 2014 ban and beyond, cannot be understood simply as a technical policy enacted in response to a set of ecological criteria, evidenced by the way in which seemingly scientifically grounded requests for modifications to the uniform moratorium were unsuccessful throughout the five years of its tenure. At the announcement of the hunting ban, several prominent San activists hoped it would be possible to win an exception for their communities to continue to hunt for the non-commercial purpose of obtaining game meat. Recognizing both the stated government rationale for the ban (a wildlife decrease) and the international distaste for the hunting of specific species like elephants, these activists sought an exception for nonendangered animals such the springhare, tortoise, and kudu. They argued that these species had utility as sources of game meat and were valued in cultural practices but not "charismatic" and unlikely to invoke international outrage if hunted.[48] This request fell on deaf ears.[49] From 2014 to 2019 the prohibition remained a blanket ban across all species, with the only exceptions generated from the regime of private property present on freehold game farms (see chapter 4). The refusal to consider modifying the ban to accommodate culturally and ecologically specific requests for game meat from nonendangered animals is quite telling. The ban was more about ensuring certain citizens did not hunt than it was about not hunting in order to meet an ecological imperative. The logic, therefore, becomes untethered from conservation (as a technical practice), even if conservation remained the ban's primary justification. This illustrates that this policy, while ostensibly driven by conservation, is also one inherently linked to the exercise of state building, seeking to create Batswana who adhere to a particular idealized vision of citizenship within the national project.

While deemed necessary based on claims of wildlife decline, the hunting ban cannot be understood solely as a "conservation" policy. By disrupting subsistence practices and livelihood activities through policies meant to bring people into the "mainstream" and "out of the bush," the state fundamentally reordered its relationship with certain citizens. If San populations on the conservation estate cannot legally continue to source protein from the hunting of game meat, then what will they do? State development practitioners see this policy as hastening a long sought-after transition to a cattle-based economy, despite substantial existing barriers.

Cattle versus Game Meat: A False Choice?

> The government is on about promoting the Botswana culture, but by ending hunting our culture as the San people will be endangered.
>
> —Resident of New Xade[50]

State rhetoric places the transition to cattle rearing on a modernist continuum of progression and utilizes quasi-naturalistic language to suggest the "evolution" of populations toward economies where hunting and the consumption of game meat become obsolete.[51] The adoption of a cattle-based economy is seen as a self-evident developmental goal,[52] which represents one pole of the "primitive"/"modern" dichotomy in contemporary Botswana. This binary is embedded in the conception of two discrete, and largely incompatible, meat cultures representing distinct ways of ordering human-environment interactions.

However, many San people view the issue of non-commercial hunting, game meat, and the adoption of cattle rearing with greater nuance and fluidity than is often afforded to them in state discourse. This includes seeing integration into a modern, livestock-driven economy as compatible and complementary with cultural identities related to hunting and continued game meat consumption, in direct contrast with the claims that developmental progress necessitates abandoning these practices. Take, for example, one of my interview respondents, a man in his late twenties who fully embraced government livestock initiatives in West Hanahai. As part of the resettlement process that moved Naro San from nearby freehold farms in the 1970s, the village was given a farmer's trust and land for rearing cattle. At the time of our conversation, the young man was the chairman of the trust and responsible for over five hundred head of cattle owned collectively by the San community of West Hanahai. On the surface, he is precisely the kind of young San to which government officials refer in development initiatives: highly proficient in Setswana, entrepreneurial, engaged in the cash economy, and dedicated to the model of livestock for development. Yet one quickly realizes that shifting attitudes toward hunting and the consumption of game meat do not inevitably follow his embrace of cattle-based livelihoods. He said, "I think, very much, that we here in West Hanahai need to continue to hunt. The government must let us. I have an idea: They let us hunt once a month. Each month the old men take out some young ones and teach us these skills. Because this is our culture. How will our sons know how to hunt? How will our daughters know how to make beads? If the government would let us do these things for our culture, it would be much better."[53] This articulates less of a transition and more of a fusion of two modes, akin to what Robins (2003) identifies as "indigenous modernities." The hunting practice the young San man envisions for West Hanahai is one that would occur with much greater regularity than is possible under the regime of post-ban, citizen-licensed, one-off hunts: hunts under the auspices of local social control rather than state agencies. Additionally, unlike these licensed hunts, the respondent conceptualized the behavior as having potential as a community activity. For him, hunting is not simply a way to put game meat on the table but also a cultural activity that must be actively maintained in contemporary Botswana, even alongside other livelihood approaches. Moreover, mainstream society and non-commercial hunting are not contradictory, despite the fact that he is precisely the demographic to which the government looks to prove that hunting is a relic of a bygone age.[54]

Another San young man from the village of Khwai in the north of the country said, "You cannot tell a Tswana man not to teach his children about their cattle. You cannot tell a Moyei not to build *mekoro* [traditional dugout canoes used in the Okavango Delta]. But why can you tell a Basarwa not to hunt? We Basarwa are looked at as inferior. We are disrespected. We are not poachers. We do not finish the animals. We are hunters. It is our culture, and we know the animals best. They are ours."[55] These men demonstrate that many ethnic minorities on the conservation estate see hunting as a way to continually enact what they consider to be their unique culture within a nation-state where assimilation into Tswanadom has been paramount. Whereas government officials equate hunting with backward practices, destitution, and being outside mainstream society, many San people view hunting as a practice imbued with cultural significance, tied to their individual and communal identity and of symbolic and cosmological importance, and, crucially, fully compatible with "modern" lifestyles. While livelihoods remain a key point of grievance, many San respondents reframed the debate beyond the matter of the economy.[56] This directly opposes the government orientation that understood subsistence hunting as just one livelihood strategy among many and the least desirable one at that. Shifts toward a cattle economy, the government claims, can be brought in to substitute for the financial and calorific losses enforced by the five-year hunting ban and continued mothballing of SGLs. By making their grievance not only about the basic necessities of life but also about intangible cultural values, San respondents argue hunting is an irreplaceable cultural practice and that resource-use modalities like the consumption of game meat have a place in their version of modernity and therefore ought to be compatible with contemporary Batswana subjectivities.

As noted in the previous chapter, very few San people express a desire to return to hunting and gathering alone. Most interviewees wish to see some significant changes in their lifestyles, which may include incorporating agropastoralism into their economies but on their own terms and taking into account practices they deem culturally important. For them to replace non-commercial hunting would be to replace their identities, making them into a different kind of people and into a different kind of citizenry.

Local Claims of Environmental Knowledge

> When I was born, I found these animals here. Now I am an old man as you can see, and they are still here. My parents died and left these animals. They are just like our livestock.
>
> —Resident of Mababe[57]

Perhaps in light of the perceived (and actual) state preference for assimilation, San interviewees attempted to deploy identity-based claims as a means to contest state discourses and policies regarding hunting and other resource use. This frequently resulted in the adoption of self-essentializing rhetorics that claim environmental stewardship is "inherent" to conservation-adjacent people in general and San people in particular. Interviewees would point to the pervasiveness of wildlife populations in areas inhabited by minority groups to bolster their claims. An older San man, resident in the Ghanzi resettlement village, Qabo, said, "Historically, and naturally so, we the Basarwa have been living off wild animals, but they have not been wiped away. Look, our forefathers having [sic] been consuming these animals, but we our generation has found them, and so will future generations even if hunting was to continue."[58] This type of statement attempts to directly negate the claims that hunting is detrimental. This is done by deploying histories of sustainable resource use as evidence of this community's good stewardship. In this, wildlife is not threatened by hunting but rather protected through his community's claims of inherent knowledge and harmony with the local environment. This point was reiterated by those who argued that their communities are unique wellsprings of deeply held knowledge that is both legitimate and valuable to the effective management of the nation's resources as a whole. A well-known San activist asked rhetorically, "Go and talk about an eland, and see who knows more—an old woman or a biologist? Let's use their [elders'] knowledge."[59] By directly comparing an old woman—presumably uneducated in the conventional sense—to a biologist, the interviewee repudiated the dominance of "scientific fact" in conservation policy and made a claim to authority based not on education or technical expertise but rather based on a historical and contemporary proximity to wildlife, cultural regard for wildlife, and his claims that the community has a kind of innate ability to act as knowledgeable stewards of the ecosystem.

Stewardship-based claim-making requires an essentializing perspective that links identity to behavior in an inborn manner and veers close to the trope of the "noble savage" and other kinds of eco-primordialisms. This is problematically reminiscent of state assumptions about San "primitivity." Notwithstanding, this discourse contests the types of knowledge upon which authoritative claims are made and upon which definitive policies are built, enacted, and maintained from within the state-building project. Beyond simply asserting that copresence with wildlife indicates a historical stewardship of the conservation estate, respondents used the persistence of biodiversity in their areas as a mechanism through which to discount the authority held by the state over conservation decisions. An older man in New Xade noted, "We used to eat wild animals for a long time but never finished or extincted [sic] them. When we lived in the Central [the CKGR], some Tswana-speaking people would come to our area to hunt. Where the Tswana people were staying, there were no more animals left. But we never finished our animals, so they preferred to come to our place to hunt."[60] This worldview is attempting to weaken the state's unequivocal claim over the authority to enact conservation restrictions by appealing to logics of local history and ethnic identity and the rights of local people to assert authority over their environment. These rhetorical imaginaries of resistance utilize their contemporary proximity to wildlife to argue that they, conservation-adjacent communities, are more fit to determine how resources are used than decision-makers in far-off, urban Gaborone.[61] By equating the failure of "Tswana-speaking people" to protect and maintain their own local biodiversity, the respondent is critiquing mainstream society for their loss of wildlife—the same mainstream society seen now shaping their lives, livelihoods, and territories in the name of conservation. This man, like many others, suggested that the copresence of wildlife in their areas was due, in fact, to their long-term attention to conservation as a cultural norm. Those state agents dictating national conservation policy—in their eyes, the "Tswana-speaking people"—had been derelict in their own environmental stewardship yet now set the terms of national resource management impacting the respondents' historical territory. This was viewed by interviewees in the conservation areas as not only counterintuitive but also dismissive of their good practices and a failure to recognize the specificity of life on the conservation estate.

Local communities rely on various repertoires to protest conservation decisions, such as claims of autochthony, discourses of belonging, and indigeneity. These call on local ethnic identities and histories and are juxtaposed against the dominant national paradigm of a homogenous state organized around Tswana language and culture, presented by the central government. The deployment of identity and regional politics is a particularly fraught strategy because of Botswana's postcolonial nation-building project around Tswana identity and the state's reluctance to accept notions of indigeneity for discrete populations. This is seen as a potential assault on the postcolonial consensus, which many officials believe to be at the heart of Botswana's economic growth and internal tranquility since independence. While this positioning is strategic in terms of tapping into a politically salient set of issues within many San communities, it is viewed with suspicion by state actors invested in the status quo. Activists employ a geographically sensitive critique to top-down, state-led conservation policies, one noting, "The people making these decisions have no wildlife in their area."[62] Apparent here is the direct discursive juxtaposition between the conservation estate and the rest of the country. This is all the more potent because of the way the presence of valuable wildlife populations tends to centralize policymaking away from the areas where people coexist with it to the national capital.

Consistently throughout my fieldwork, residents of the conservation estate argued that conservation policies, especially those related to the possible hunting and consumption of game meat, were mandated upon their areas and communities by outsiders who did not share the burden nor were required to sacrifice—materially and culturally—as a result of the decisions taken.

Transition to Cattle: Potential Ecological and Economic Impacts

> Government has given cattle to each family, but I think that that is a waste of money because there was no consultation, and we don't even have syndicates and kraals to keep the cattle.
> —Resident of West Hanahai[63]

Despite the renewal of commercial safari hunting and the implementation of a citizen hunting lottery since 2019, the practical limitations on accessing game meat that were commonplace during the ban continue apace. Game meat is available for those citizens able to purchase it at market rates or lucky enough to win a rare license and able to pay for the privilege of a recreational hunt. As an answer to the near total abolition of game meat consumption, the government of Botswana has offered the prospect of a substantial reordering of meat culture in the western conservation estate. This is of a piece with existing development policy (Twyman 2000). A cornerstone of Botswana's postcolonial development ethos, especially at the local level, has been an emphasis on cattle rearing—viewed as the backbone of rural Tswana society—as a means of wealth creation and modernization. Yet despite this long-standing developmental emphasis on cattle, various ecological and economic features, and citizen preferences, limit their ability to avail themselves of cattle.

State authorities are dismissive of the notion that game meat for protein consumption might be more ecological and economically suitable to the Kalahari environment.[64] However, it is unclear whether a widespread transition to a cattle-based economy is ecologically sustainable in an arid and drought-prone environment.[65] As an example, Ghanzi's current beef production is reliant on a system of aquifer-fed boreholes. This typically requires intensive capital and infrastructure investment from commercial farmers. From a hydrological perspective, it is unclear how an expansion of a water-intensive industry will intersect with the unknowns of climate change in a region that is regarded as highly susceptible to deleterious consequences (Hambira, Saarinen, and Moses 2020).[66] Development practitioners have noted that subsistence hunting, rather than animal husbandry, may be a longstanding adaptation to the vagaries of a harsh and unpredictable ecosystem where access to water is the key limiting factor to survival.[67] The state's enthusiasm for cattle rearing and the denigration of game meat consumption have not seriously reckoned with the potential ecological consequences of the transition across the various ecosystems of the conservation estate.

Moreover, the top-down emphasis on cattle rearing, to the exclusion of other livelihood options, remains controversial, notwithstanding those members of San communities who have actively incorporated cattle rearing into a diverse portfolio of economic strategies. Many San respondents continue to express disinterest in fully exchanging one meat regime for another. Their reluctance may be warranted. Small-scale producers have limited access to this hierarchical, highly competitive, and well-established market. Beef production is dominated by the country's Tswana "cattle barons" as well as by Afrikaner farmers in the Ghanzi District.[68] Legislative frameworks such as the Tribal Grazing Land Policy and institutional structures such as borehole syndicates make it difficult to nearly impossible for cash-strapped, politically marginalized people to thrive in the cattle industry (Magole 2009; Malope and Batisani 2008; Molomo 2008; Peters 1994). Rosy government projections about the uplift associated with cattle ownership fail to take into account the structural barriers and marginalities faced by San communities on the conservation estate.

As an example, cattle disbursements have been the primary mode of rural development and state-led financial compensation offered to people removed from protected areas like the CKGR (Hitchcock 1999; Hitchcock and Vinding 2001).[69] However, as was seen in the CKGR case, disbursements were slow to arrive, and when they did many recipients were prone to exploitation.[70] Numerous informants, especially women, older respondents, and those with little to no formal education, recounted personal difficulties in their own experiences with cattle rearing.[71] Many had sold their cattle in return for a much-needed but short-term cash injection to cope with a sudden crisis or hardship. Some had been unable to care for their cattle due to lack of training in, and community knowledge of, animal husbandry, and others still had seen them become victims of predation by wild animals, which frequently goes uncompensated by wildlife authorities.[72] As noted above, many women expressed unease about the male-dominated cattle industry, which they viewed as potentially hostile to female-headed households (see Must and Hovorka 2019).

Finally, the state-led transition from game meat to cattle consumption has potential pitfalls from a food-security perspective. San respondents believe game meat to be a healthier option than domesticated protein sources. Numerous interviewees argued that the consumption of beef made them feel ill.[73] They attributed a whole host of gastrointestinal discomforts to a protein diet now made up primarily of beef, with others highlighting the association of hitherto unheard-of lifestyle diseases like diabetes and heart disease with less healthy eating habits. There is a pervasive belief in these communities that beef contains more chemicals, hormones, and other additives than game meat, and the majority of respondents continued to express a preference for game over domesticated protein sources.[74] Of course, such claims are medically unverified and warrant skepticism until confirmed with scientific rigor. While it was well beyond the scope of my project to adjudicate these health and wellness claims, the pervasiveness of this discourse among San respondents speaks to a deep apprehension toward domesticated protein sources that is prevalent in these communities and provides insight into a widespread reluctance to embrace an assimilationist meat transition.

A group of middle-aged residents gathered in Qabo in Ghanzi District said that the implementation of the hunting ban meant "We do not have the right to feed ourselves."[75] Their use of both the discourse of rights and the discourse of consumption illustrates the manner in which the conservation and development decisions of the state are uniquely embodied by San people from the conservation estate. The hunting ban was not abstract but directly impacted what people put in their bodies to sustain themselves and their right to make determinations about these fundamental processes. Any policy that limits their ability to make choices regarding this most basic function of life is regarded as "violating our rights."[76] This discourse of rights contrasts with the position of the wildlife authorities. Despite local invocations of rights-based claims, government officials argued that access to game meat was "never guaranteed" and that its availability was determined on a yearly basis. "It [is] just that people got used to it. But it was never guaranteed to be forever."[77] This is fundamentally in opposition to those local residents who view hunting not only as their cultural birthright but also as a legal right to which they are entitled. Nonetheless, the policy changes brought about by the Masisi administration did not meaningfully address the kinds of hunting practices most relevant in these spaces. Despite the rollback around commercial hunting restrictions, the policy inertia with respect to SGLs and non-commercial hunting continues to move in one direction—toward prohibition.

Blanket conservation and development policies, overwhelmingly made by government officials based in Gaborone, are typically based on hierarchical assumptions that result in the adoption of one-size-fits-all policies across the breadth of national territory. Many key decision-makers lack firsthand experience with impacted communities and environments. Without taking into account locally specific ecological or social constraints (or opportunities), top-down policy frameworks emphasize national priorities and often promote conformity with "modernizing" or assimilationist end-goals. As one local resident observed, "conservation used to differ according to local culture and tradition, but today it is similar all over the country."[78] The majority of Botswana's state interventions do not seem to take into account the unique perspectives created by the varied ecologies and cultures of the country, especially on the conservation estate (Shinn 2018). As another illustrative example, DWNP staff members tasked with implementing and monitoring national conservation policy rotate regularly between district offices. Very few officials are local to their assigned districts, often producing steep learning curves in each new context.[79] A senior wildlife officer bristled at the suggestion that wildlife officers should be recruited from the conservation estate, thus utilizing local knowledge and leveraging embeddedness in the community for policy ends. He rejected the idea of local deployments as ethnic favoritism, arguing that such preferential treatment would amount to special privileges and be detrimental to national unity.[80] Similarly, the country's 2014 hunting ban, implemented in a uniform way, despite diverse conservation, economic, and cultural imperatives, was a clear example of top-down, unitary policymaking. The hunting ban had particular impact for San communities, who articulate a continued preference for game meat consumption that is largely ignored by policymakers. As a result, across the conservation estate, many San informants view the hunting ban not as a resource-management policy but as an extension of a long-standing government concern to incentivize, cajole, and at times enforce an identity-based transition in meat consumption practices from game meat to cattle.

For all their many differences with respect to conservation, environmental, and natural resource-use policies, the Khama and Masisi administrations appear to be in agreement that widespread non-commercial hunting and the practices regulated by SGLs are outmoded, reiterating support for government social welfare programs as viable substitutes for a behavior understood to be simply economic. Even the ban's partial reversal with respect to citizen hunting is built on universalist assumptions that do not capture the differentials in social capital and financial resources available to individuals hoping to attain licenses. After the seemingly substantial changes in environmental governance by the Masisi government, in the realm of conservation policy certain communities will face more of the same. The maintenance of a system that in practice prohibits non-commercial hunting for this population, in concert with the long-standing promotion of cattle farming, acts as a mechanism of forced assimilation into Tswana culture and society. The underlying linear conception of development—transition from hunting and gathering to agropastoralism—obscures a more subtle understanding often expressed on the ground, wherein cattle and game meat can be seen as compatible and contemporaneous sources of subsistence and livelihood. This nuance is often lost in the pursuit of a uniform policy framework, which also masks the relative marginality of the communities that articulate alternative models of development and modernity.

Conservation as a Source of Dependency

> They have made peace with poverty, and they are so comfortable with it, you cannot blame the government, which provides all sorts of handouts.
>
> —Social and community development officer, West Hanahai[81]

Thus far, the two chapters of this section have dealt at length with the practices of gathering and hunting as cultural phenomena tied to political identity claims and examined how a suite of livelihood strategies associated with these behaviors have been restricted on the conservation estate. In the absence of these strategies, the state argues there are myriad alternative economic approaches and social programs upon which conservation-adjacent people can rely. This section is concerned with the ways in which the initiatives meant to create conservation-adjacent people as mainstream citizens by reconfiguring their relationship to resource use and the environment have the perverse effect of rendering them heavily dependent on government for their daily subsistence. State assumptions based on mythologies of modernity, development, and linear progress collapse under the specific conditions produced by the conservation estate. The particularized constraints of the conservation estate impede government development initiatives proposed uniformly throughout the country. This section focuses on the one-size-fits-all manner of development approaches, a premise that envisions an ideal kind of rural individual, with contradictory impacts on people who fall outside the "default" norm. This section concludes by examining the ways in which assumptions of mainstream "modernity" have resulted in limited livelihood options for people on the conservation estate, inculcating a citizenry almost entirely reliant on food handouts and low-level cash welfare inputs in order to survive, a situation that structures the citizen-state relationship on the conservation estate.

For many within the DWNP, development is viewed as essential to a holistic conservation approach because, as one midlevel official based in Maun said, "poverty is one thing that stops people from wildlife management and conservation."[82] Yet the majority of Botswana's state interventions in poverty reduction do not seem to take into account the unique contexts and restraints created by the logic of biodiversity conservation. Development projects are often totally unsuitable for poor people living on the conservation estate, due to the specific characteristics of this category of political space. Botswana's development interventions—which are optimistically called "poverty eradication" programs by the government—are largely uniform throughout the country,[83] despite the fact that both conservation initiatives and human-wildlife interactions make the viability and feasibility of these projects widely variable across the breadth and width of Botswana. In fact, the early experiments in CBNRM, with their decentralized approach and place-based beneficiation structure, have largely been recentralized and brought under government control precisely due to state reticence regarding differentiated development (see Rihoy and Maguranyanga 2010; Poteete 2009a). Rural areas—conservation estate or not—are subsumed under the same umbrella, and the central government defines both the "problem" of underdevelopment and the "solution," often failing to consider the ways in which simultaneous top-down conservation processes conflict with its own development policies. The restrictions of conservation create dependent clients because social programs do not take into account the unique limitations and conditions placed on the citizens of the conservation estate. Two so-called poverty-eradication policies in particular—livestock disbursements and promotion of arable farming—are severely or completely disrupted in conservation-adjacent areas.

As noted in the previous section, a cornerstone of Botswana's development ethos has been an emphasis on cattle rearing—viewed as the backbone of rural society—as a means of wealth creation and modernization. Yet it is not only in the western conservation estate where various structures put in place to manage and protect wildlife limit citizens' ability to avail themselves of cattle.

Veterinary Fences

While Botswana's national parks are famously unfenced, the country is transected by a series of veterinary cordon fences meant to prevent the transmission of disease from wild game species such as buffalo to the domestic cattle population (McGahey 2008). This system dates back to the colonial era but has been expanded and maintained by the postcolonial government. The fences sit along key sites of wilderness/agriculture interface, primarily in the north of the country. In addition to the immediate result of limiting veterinary disease, they also extend state control over resources and weaken local access to land, grazing rights, and water resources (McGahey 2008). Under the 1975 Lomé Convention, Botswana can sell its beef exports to the European Union at an advantageous price above the global market rate but only on the condition of abiding by the strict EU cattle disease regulations, which mandate fencing and vaccination in order to control

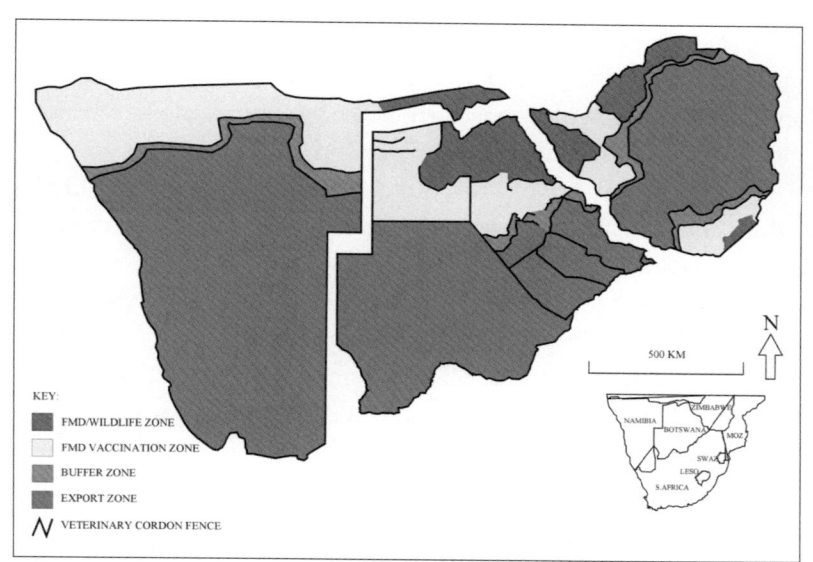

Modernity Promises and Development Failures on the Conservation Estate   293

FIGURE 7.1. Map of veterinary fences across southern Africa. *Source:* McGahey 2008.

outbreaks.[84] Outbreaks of cattle disease overwhelmingly occur in the country's north where there is greater possibility for contact between wild game populations and livestock. For example, the main vector of foot-and-mouth disease is the wild African buffalo (*Syncerus caffer*). In 1995–96 there was an outbreak of another wild-borne cattle disease, contagious bovine pleuropneumonia, which resulted in the culling of 320,000 head of cattle, the entire herd of Northwest District. It also prompted the emergency erection of 1,130 kilometers of new fencing and the closure of the Maun abattoir (Bolaane 2013; McGahey 2008).

This fencing protocol has established northern Botswana as a "red zone" due to these disease outbreaks. Cattle raised within the red zone cannot be transported to other parts of Botswana or exported for the international market. In addition, inside the red zone there is another series of fences known as the "buffalo fence," which encloses the core areas of the Okavango Delta and creates a cordon sanitaire between the wild game species and livestock. People living in villages located inside the buffalo fence—such as

Sankuyo, Khwai, Mababe, and Ditshiping—are not permitted to rear any cattle whatsoever. Essentially the fences create a series of concentric circles, with the innermost communities closest to the delta prohibited from livestock ownership.

Whereas those within the buffalo fence are mostly resigned to their inability to own cattle, the communities living just adjacent to it—such as Boro and Xuoxao—live with the perpetual anxiety that the boundaries of the buffalo fence may be expanded to permit greater freedom for wild game, while making cattle rearing illegal in their areas.[85] The expansion of the buffalo fence has been suggested in the past and is a constant on conservation practitioners' wish list.[86] Importantly, the buffalo fence and the veterinary cordon fences play a significant role in the way in which conservation-adjacent communities may access state-sponsored development programs. Cattle disbursements are a primary mode of state-led rural development and usually the promised method of financial compensation offered to people relocated out of the conservation spaces like the CKGR.[87] Respondents directly link their location to their different incorporation into state-led programs: "Because we are inside the buffalo fence there is less development and opportunities."[88] Even those outside of the buffalo fence, but still within the red zone, see comparatively little return on cattle rearing because of their geographical location closest to large game populations and predators. Cattle predation in Northwest District also makes the receipt of livestock a fraught development proposition for those permitted to keep livestock in the first place. The MP representing the Okavango constituency, just outside the buffalo fence but within the red zone, noted, "You give people cattle one day; the other day the wildlife takes the cattle away. The aim now of trying to help people eliminate poverty becomes a vicious circle."[89] The application of this national strategy of poverty eradication in his constituency fails to recognize the local concerns generated by another national strategy—the preference for wildlife conservation. Similarly, the *kgosi* of Sankuyo described the predicament of his village:

> I think the biggest challenge is that the natural resources that we have are hindering the community to make other income-generating activities like *other people in some areas* [italics mine]. For example, the government has a lot of initiatives regarding the poverty eradication—things which the Sankuyo village does not benefit from because of the location of the village in the wildlife area. Some people get goats and stuff; some people get free seeds from the government. But in Sankuyo you cannot get that. That's a big challenge because the natural resources that we live with is [sic] hindering us from getting other assistance from the government. Then that becomes a problem. It becomes a problem also because we are 100 percent [sure] that we own those resources, [but] we cannot use those resources fully to substitute for what we should be getting.[90]

This quote demonstrates the compounding frustration of their location on the conservation estate making them ineligible for national development programs combined with the fact that his community cannot use their local resources to make up for the absence of state support. As he puts it, they cannot "fully substitute" the shortfall in government support because of conservation restrictions on resources that they as a community believe they "own" (see chapter 4). While other rural people, and even some of those living in the conservation areas in the west, can anticipate a level of government development support in the form of cattle provision, those within the buffalo fence cannot avail themselves of the program, nor can they sell or consume game meat absent a commercial hunting quota. As became clear during the years of the hunting ban, hunting quotas can be zeroed out by policymakers with little recourse for communities to object. Those outside of the buffalo fence but within the red zone cannot be confident that any investment in cattle will bring them economic benefits. In Botswana's northern conservation areas, the proximity of game and predator species creates a direct limitation that frustrates the local people's ability to avail themselves of support that is obtainable by citizens who live elsewhere, while they also have a hard time carving out specific rights to the resources and environmental conditions that surround only them.[91]

Arable Farming

Having interrogated the way in which cattle-based development programs face obstacles across large swaths of the northern conservation estate, it is worthwhile to consider how other state-led rural development projects fare. A similarly frustrated situation arises in relation to government support for arable farming through the Integrated Support Programme for Arable Agricultural Development (ISPAAD) and the "backyard gardens" initiative. ISPAAD is an arable farming measure that is aimed at rural smallholders. It provides free or subsidized seed, fertilizers, and basic equipment for planting and harvesting crops, primarily maize and sorghum, throughout the country. In northern Botswana, seed recipients face a nearly hopeless task. An MP from a northern constituency noted, "People's fields have now turned into grazelands for these herds of elephants. Even if government talks about the seed program, it has never worked in my area. If you assist with the seeds, they plough for the elephants. So, it has not worked in terms of trying to alleviate people in abject poverty."[92] Despite the north of Botswana boasting some of the best hydrological conditions for crop farming, the population of large herbivores, especially elephants but also game species, make this subsistence livelihood activity nearly impossible and farming as a development initiative impracticable. While some still attempt to avail themselves of the program,[93] many people throughout the north have abandoned the practice all together, citing frustration with tending their fields for elephants' benefit.[94] Again, the copresence of wildlife and the dominant logic of conservation creates direct and apparent developmental trade-offs that are unique to the conservation estate.

An elephant can destroy an entire field in a night, and for those depending on subsistence agriculture this has devastating and long-lasting effects.[95] Local inhabitants described elephants to me as pests that graze in their fields, destroy their storage huts, and eat already harvested grain, all of which has significant impacts on food security over the long term.[96]

Batswana living on the conservation estate have tried a plethora of approaches to secure their fields from animals. They employ a variety of human-elephant conflict-mediation strategies in an attempt to drive elephants away from their crops, ranging from fencing and making noise with drums to lining fields with ground chili pepper.[97] Some ignite "chili bombs"—dung mixed with chili pepper—to deter elephants.[98] All of these require a mixture of time, money, and effort, and even then there is no guarantee of success. This burden is largely carried by remote and often marginalized communities. A local wildlife officer noted, "People try to keep them [elephants] off, and they use all means—wire strings, chili peppers, drums, and noise. People spend sleepless nights trying to keep elephants at bay."[99] These time- and labor-intensive strategies to scare away herds from crop fields are not always successful,[100] nor are all households capable of engaging in such mitigation tactics.[101] These are emotional, physical, and financial investments that are not required of Botswana's other rural citizens living away from the conservation estate, further drawing distinction between conservation-adjacent Batswana and their countrymen outside of this socioeconomic habitat.

Most other rural dwellers never have to contemplate a scenario wherein their entire harvest is lost in one evening, yet this is a persistent reality for conservation-adjacent communities in Botswana—a slow kind of violence imbued with anxiety and precarity. A midlevel staffer in Maun relayed the ways in which the local clients he serves in northern Botswana are disadvantaged compared with those rural people not residing on the conservation estate. He noted, "They live with the wrath of elephants. I am from forty kilometers outside of Gaborone [in Molepolole], my home village. There are no elephants [there], but just look around here. There are too many."[102] By invoking his home village, he drew attention to the ways in which there is a qualitative difference between those Batswana who live on the conservation estate and,

FIGURE 7.2. Elephant-control sign in the village of Sankuyo: "Use chili pepper to scare elephants away from the crop fields instead of resorting to lethal means." Author's photograph.

seemingly, everyone else. The distinction between life in his home village and life in Gaborone paled in comparison to the spatially contingent impacts of living on the conservation estate. Nowhere else in Botswana, outside of the conservation estate, are the modes of life, livelihoods, and behaviors so shaped by the imperatives of co-local wildlife and their protection. A respondent encapsulated this differentiation by saying, "We live with things which they [other Batswana] only see on television."[103]

Backyard Gardens

The backyard garden initiative was of particular interest to government authorities during my fieldwork.[104] Rural households throughout the country were encouraged to cultivate small vegetable gardens on backyard plots in order to supplement their diets and potentially sell excess on the local market. This program was strongly encouraged at kgotla meetings, on the radio, and in the state-run print media.[105]

Remarkably, this highly water-intensive initiative was promoted uniformly throughout arid Botswana, which periodically faces drought and water shortages.[106] Interviewees in Ghanzi District demurred at the promotion of this particular poverty-eradication measure in their area. One man on the local village development committee in Kacgae said, "Many poverty-eradication programs fail here because they are not suited for the people or the place. The backyard gardens program doesn't work because water is very scarce, and people don't like eating these vegetables as their staple [food]."[107] Those who did heed government advice found themselves in a difficult position. The promotion of the backyard garden initiative coincided with the pay-for-service model of water provision in many rural settlements, a concept not fully or adequately explained to local residents. Those households in Ghanzi that attempted to make use of the backyard gardening program ended up using a significant volume of water growing (or attempting to grow) crops unsuitable to the Kalahari Desert and then were left with a large, and often unpayable, bill from the water utility. Even if enough vegetables were produced to be sold as a surplus, the income would not outweigh the cost of the water needed to grow them in the first place.[108] One development practitioner observed this national, top-down orientation as a failing, saying, "One has to look at local conditions and move these planning decisions in the right kind of way because it's a reoccurring theme. [You] have decisions made at a national level completely and utterly out of sync with what's happening on the ground."[109] Both the approach to backyard gardening and the provision of support for cereals farming show a disconnect between the local social and ecological context and the policies set at a national level. They demonstrate how the policy regimes of the conservation estate can counterintuitively result in development initiatives producing more dependency, not less.

Conservation policies also have the effect of shutting down other potential livelihood options. Though this varies in the northern Okavango ecosystem and western Kalahari conservation areas due to local social and ecological conditions, people in these regions face similar challenges in carrying out autonomous economic activities related to diverse livelihood strategies, including subsistence hunting, gathering wildlife products, crop or livestock farming, and even commercialization of the traditional craft industry (see chapter 6). The restrictions that are incumbent in conservation have limited the menu of practicable livelihood choices of those people living in the conservation estate. As a young man in Khwai, Northwest District, said, "You bring your goats here or your cattle here, the lions will take them. You grow anything, the elephants will come around."[110] Beyond constraining the options available, this engenders a sense of dependence on government programs, a new reality that is often viewed with resignation by those most impacted. A middle-aged woman from a Ghanzi settlement village noted, "Everything from the bush needs a permit. It feels like I can't go anywhere and I am not independent. In the old days we could hunt with SGLs and gather as we went. But now I need assistance at every turn."[111] This respondent created a stark dichotomy: the environment brought welfare; the government brings assistance and a life of dependence. This contrast was one that I heard echoed across the varied socio-ecological systems of the conservation estate, in the arid resettlement villages in the Kalahari and in the communities situated along watery channels and green floodplains of the delta. The constraints of conservation consist not only of material poverty but also a poverty of choice, which limits how she could earn a living. Conservation restrictions—the rules that dictate that everything "needs a permit"—constrain her options to the point where she no longer felt able to use resources productively and described herself as entirely dependent on small welfare supports. Conservation has not brought benefits but rather reliance on state assistance for basic survival.

Some local residents drew a direct correlation between environmental policies, social welfare programs, and their (former) subsistence activities. An older woman in Bere noted, "The government introduced the food rations so that we would not go and kill those animals."[112] This is illuminating because in her worldview, government-designed social supports are not seen as coming from a place of state obligation to its citizens but rather as a means to protect wildlife. In fact, another respondent further inverts this relationship, arguing that social welfare is derived from resource use and what the government provides is something different: "Our social welfare is in using the environment. But now people have to depend on the government."[113] Botswana's development strategy offers an interesting paradox: while structuring livelihood activities to render conservation-adjacent people "mainstream," the people also become dependent on the government for survival.

Conservation in the Face of Difference-Blind Development

By examining the limitations of cattle rearing in the north and the failures of promotion of farming in the north and west, it is apparent that government rural development policy has a tendency to be one-size-fits-all, enveloping the conservation estate in a development regime that does not recognize the social, political, and ecological peculiarities of this category of space. Nonetheless, officials often claim that if particular areas are targeted in different ways, the policy then becomes discriminatory and unfair. This is tied up with notions of the unitary state and is clearly reflective of the anxiety around "separate development" inculcated in apartheid South Africa, the legacy against which much of Botswana's development policy is oriented even today. While this justification is perhaps admirable in that regard, its logic is somewhat flawed. Because rural development policy is uniform throughout the countryside, it takes the areas not predominated by the conservation estate as its default. The emphasis on difference-blind development fails to account for how state-enforced conservation policy does make life in these areas qualitatively different, particularly compared with rural areas in eastern Botswana, which are more distant from the protected areas and wildlife populations. This particular imaginary of the unitary state capable of delivering even, effective, and undifferentiated programs begin to fray in the conservation estate.

Rural developmental policy is difference-blind despite the fact that people living on the conservation estate are subject to a fundamentally different set of ecological and policy restrictions. This means programs that are unsuitable continue to be promoted for people who cannot benefit from them, counterintuitively producing bias when the intent is to be difference-blind. It does not allow for the consideration of locally specific ecological, political, or social constraints or opportunities but rather conforms to the promotion of blanket policies. More important, it fails to recognize the facts that people in these areas do see themselves as different and that these subjectivities of difference are often forged directly in relationship to resource use, or lack thereof, in the other rural areas of the country. Programs that bring people on the conservation estate into the cash economy by restricting use of natural resources end up transforming these individuals into dependent clients. Conservation limits access to local natural resources, and many of the centrally developed replacement programs like cattle or farming are ill-matched to the context, leaving local people in a bind not of their own creation.

People living on Botswana's conservation estate characterize their cultural practices as just as valuable to the national heritage and worthy of protection as the country's wildlife. By using cultural discourse to register their grievance, they try to reinscribe their value as human inhabitants of Botswana and insist that the needs of copresent wildlife should not supersede their own. Young San people, even those who are most adept at integrating into the mainstream, enthusiastically state that they do not want to practice hunting and gathering full-time but that they deeply appreciate the cultural value of these skills and wish to maintain this set of practices for further generations. This pushes back against the state narratives introduced in this and previous chapters that conceive of hunting and gathering practices as strategies of last resort. These discursive and material positions allow people to adopt the mantle of "hunter-gatherer," which in this context is an important self-ascribed label used by San to assert an independent and politically charged identity within the Botswana national project, as a means of asserting the differentiation felt on the conservation estate. By emphasizing gathering and hunting as cultural activities—not merely economic choices—San people reject the government's preference for commercialization as the sole mechanism for resource use, though this does not mean that respondents uniformly resist commercialization or are averse to participation in the cash economy.

This chapter has demonstrated the myriad ways in which the mythologies of the state-building project are stretched, tested, and often called into question on the conservation estate. As argued in the final section, when the uniform approach to development is deployed in areas where the priorities of conservation predominate, the two state logics contradict one another. Botswana's uniform rural development policies mask and ignore the unique conditions created by the conservation estate, constructing not rural citizens but dependent subjects, further differentiating people on the conservation estate from their counterparts in other rural and urban localities in the country. This results in the paradoxical effect of nominally "equal" one-size-fits-all programs producing and exacerbating differentiation and inequality. The failure of a whole host of developmental strategies in light of socio-ecological constraints in the conservation estate begs the question as to whether the type of livelihood approaches emphasizing non-use of wildlife and gathered products favored by the state can be productive in the spaces of the conservation estate marked by ecological limitations (such as difficult hydrological conditions) and human-made limitations (such as the creation of veterinary cordon fences). It also suggests that locally relevant livelihood approaches remain legitimate in the eyes of the residents because they offer the best chance at economic autonomy within the particular socio-ecological setting of the conservation estate.

Conclusion

One of the first interviews I conducted during the research for this project was at the headquarters of the Department of Wildlife and National Parks in Gaborone. Early as it was in my fieldwork, I had yet to grasp the scale and scope of what this project would become, but I listened eagerly to all the busy civil servants who took time out of their day to talk to me. There was one conversation that at the time did not seem particularly noteworthy or revelatory, but I found myself coming back to it after nearly every village visit I made over the next several months. A senior DWNP official stated, "When a police officer puts on his nice uniform, he should think to himself that wildlife got him the uniform. Without wildlife there wouldn't be roads, schools, or clinics."[1]

What the official was describing was the fundamental premise upon which conservation policy is justified in Botswana—that it benefits the state, and implicitly all of the citizens of the state, in line with the imaginary of unitary governance, development, and citizenship. This is the logic applied to the country's diamond wealth and also the rationale for a series of policy reforms that centralized revenue, decision-making, and national control over Community-Based Natural Resource Management programs since the mid-2000s. Citizens are encouraged to support conservation initiatives because of the welfare it brings to society. As the government's reasoning goes, if a conservation policy is good for tourism, it is good for Batswana as a whole, reiterating a key element of the state's mythology around unitary national development. This is an expression of the social contract upon which the state expects—and at times demands—consent from the populations living among animals and in landscape of value to the tourism industry.

It was not until my fieldwork in these communities, speaking with the people directly impacted on a daily basis by the state's project of conservation, that was I able to discern the ways this argument's logic begins to fragment on the conservation estate. Local people regard everyone but themselves as recipients of the windfalls of Botswana's environmental state building. But this is more than simply a subjective understanding—it is borne out in their material realities. Despite the official's statement, throughout my fieldwork I observed many of the places on the conservation estate where there are no roads, schools, or clinics—often to adhere to tourist imaginaries of an "untouched wilderness" (see chapter 5). Nor are they patrolled by regular police officers but rather by wildlife rangers and military personnel (see chapter 3). The unifying rhetoric of national development, legitimate authority, and shared identity falls flat in spaces of persistent economic, social, and political marginality brought about, in part, by conservation. Interviewees living on the conservation estate believe their needs and interests are sublimated to a variety of actors, including foreign tourists, expatriate tour operators, and government elites profiting from conservation, with scholarly research supporting their intuition (Mbaiwa and Hambira 2020). This happens while they are left to deal with the daily impact of decisions largely made in Gaborone, often without their input (see chapter 3), despite repeated protestations. A young man in the village of Boro described this disconnect succinctly: "They [tourists] get to derive pleasure from viewing the animals while we are residents don't reap anything but destruction of our crops. . . . Now *makgoa* [tourists] are going to take pictures, which are of no benefit to me."[2]

This book began from the premise that if we want to more fully understand African states in the postcolonial era, we can and should examine conservation policies. This positioning, while drawing from the literature of political ecology, is its logical inverse. This approach takes seriously the fact that strategies that underpin conservation—monitoring, categorization, policing, and ordering of people, territories, and resources—are also connected to the politics of state building. The central research question examined concerned the ways in which the logics and strategies of conservation function as part of the postcolonial state building in Botswana and how the contestations over this shape the relationships between the state and its citizens.

Throughout this book I have attempted to enrich the theoretical perspective that without an "end point," the state is always undergoing a process of change and transformation. State building is an ongoing construction project, the process of which—rather than any end product—is the relevant empirical phenomenon. I have sought to do this by using the unique analytical framing of the "conservation estate" as the terrain on which the arguments about the state builds. I suggest that the particularities of the conservation estate allow for it to be an especially apt empirical venue for studying the nature of the state, state building, and citizen-state relations.

The environment cannot be neatly cleaved from other social and political functions. State-led environmental projects, such as biodiversity conservation, impact different segments of the population in starkly different manners. Examining or evaluating a policy's "success" or "failure" is not analytically helpful with conservation, as the most significant impacts of any given program or policy may be entirely unrelated to the environmental imperative invoked as its justification. Instead, research should turn toward interrogating what these policies do in an empirical sense at their target locations and among the local populations found therein.

In this conclusion, I return to the three central arguments threaded throughout this book's three empirical sections. The first is the theorization of the conservation estate itself, a conceptualization that assists in the examination of two nested arguments about rural differentiation and the limits of rural resistance on the conservation estate. After this presentation of the substantive findings, I consider avenues for further research informed by this book.

Key Arguments

The Conservation Estate as a Social and Political Category of Land

This book advanced a definition of conservation that is tied to its political elements. The component parts of conservation—control over land, policing of human behavior, the structuring of the authority that allows or disallows certain subjectivities—render conservation a political phenomenon that may be analyzed separate from considerations of "nature" or wildlife.

Across the three thematic parts—"Authority," "Territory," and "Identity"—the idea that the conservation estate is a social and political category of land has been omnipresent. What divides the conservation estate from other types of rural land is not a prima facie environmental condition but rather the structuring of power and authority in such a way as to render the space different from other, at times contiguous, areas of the rural geography of the state.

Using the conservation estate as an empirical vantage point also gives credence to existing analytical narratives focused on the uneven, contingent, and multivalent aspects of the state. The theorization of the conservation estate provides a productive, and new, way to observe this phenomenon. The conservation estate is home to differentiated experiences not only because of the prevalence of the logics of conservation but also due to the fact that it is a category of land wherein the multiple and varied narratives and interests of the state intersect. Section I, for example, probed the way in which two contradictory logics—securitization and democracy—share a home on the conservation estate and highlighted the fraught and ambiguous nature of the state. Similarly, part II observed an analogous phenomenon with regard to the clashing logics of conservation on one hand and development on the other. In both cases, the state is revealed not to be constitutive of an overarching design but reflective of the various concurrent imaginaries, power discrepancies, and parochial interests that influence the exercise of state power in open-ended ways. Another dynamic of state building captured on the conservation estate is the role of the international. The global system trains attention onto the conservation estate in a manner highly differentiated from other spaces of rural territory. As a site of international scrutiny, the conservation estate brings to the fore the imbricated influences of local/national/international that operate in specific instances of state building and highlights that these interactions are not uniform across a state's territory.

Citizenship on the Conservation Estate

The particularities that are characteristic of the conservation estate alone alter the relationship between the state, its citizens living on or adjacent to this category of space, and their compatriots living elsewhere across Botswana's territory. This has relevance for the nature of citizenship on the conservation estate and cannot be accounted for only through bifurcation of territory into rural/urban.

The state-building project produces an outcome where conservation-adjacent people experience a vastly different set of lived circumstances from other Batswana, including those living in rural areas that are not dominated by the logic of conservation. These differences include not only the presence of wildlife as an intermediary in citizen-state relations but are also constituted in varying ability to move freely, in spatial organization, in livelihood opportunities, in the role of state surveillance and scrutiny, and in the importance of the conservation estate to the international system.

Two salient features that characterize the nature of citizenship in the conservation estate are (1) the mediation of the citizen-state relationship created by the copresence of wildlife and (2) the intersection between the logics of conservation and simultaneously held but countervalent state narratives like democracy, participation, and development. The first feature creates a political category of person—a political subjectivity produced by the proximity to conservation and wildlife. Co-residency with wildlife is not simply an ecological reality but also generates unique conditions and positionalities on the conservation estate, which work to construct conservation-adjacent people as "outsiders" to the state-building project. The relationship between conservation-adjacent humans and the state is mediated by the proximity of wildlife such that their status as either citizens or subjects is deeply problematic and manifests in the widespread perception held by local people that they are less important to the state than wildlife. Their position as political subjects exists alongside, and in the shadow of, animals. The second feature is generative of differentiation of citizenship between those who live on the conservation estate and those who do not.

Chapter 2 examined the way in which the process of securitization operates in a particularized manner in the conservation estate, with scrutiny, suspicion, and potential violence reserved for conservation-adjacent citizens. The residents of the conservation estate become different as their subjectivities are elided with that of "poachers"—as foreign, criminal, and dangerous to the integrity and stability of the state. This is a construction that precariously differentiates conservation-adjacent people from other rural dwellers as a type of fifth column of poaching and consequently results in the fraying of Botswana's widespread democratic narratives in this setting.

The conservation estate uniquely structures the contours of citizen-state relations across the breadth of rural land in often paradoxical and contradictory ways. Indeed, chapter 4 showed that land-control processes on the conservation estate inculcate differentiation. Relocation is perceived as a policy singularly applied to those on the conservation estate, a strategy that renders invisible conservation-adjacent populations. The subsequent chapter argued that the distinct logics of tourism and peopleless wilderness substantially alter the relationship between the state and its citizens on the conservation estate, in some places generating "legible" citizens, while in others producing "illegibility," creating paradoxes both within the conservation estate and without.

Chapters 6 and 7 interrogated the manner in which limits on livelihoods and rural development render conservation-adjacent citizens differentially unable to utilize state-led development processes. The state's one-size-fits-all approach to development policy is deployed in areas where the priorities of conservation predominate, and the two state logics contradict one another. This results in assimilationist and integrative rural development programs that produce the opposite outcome from the intended and overt policy pronouncement—making people on the conservation estate more dependent on state welfare programs rather than less.

Negotiation, Contestation, and Resistance

The state-building project is ambiguous even if it appears coherent, which creates limitations and difficulties in contestation. On one hand, the apparent inconsistency of state action that results from the multivalent nature of the state-building process leaves it open for critique. Yet on the other, this muddled condition also works to confound resistance, as the would-be subjects of state projects have difficulty in determining where to focus their opposition. There is no guarantee of a relationship between the articulated logics and the actual policies on the ground, as such local resistance strategies are often aimed at co-opting and redeploying a state logic that is mythical or imaginary and not actually manifest in the quotidian processes of the state. While contradictions present opportunities for negotiation, they also work to vex resistance. This argument has been evidenced by the myriad strategies of negotiation, contestation, and resistance on the part of conservation-adjacent citizens. One prevalent strategy used by local people is what I term "recognition, repetition, and resistance." In this triad, conservation-adjacent people absorb state rhetoric (recognition) and attempt to utilize the state's own rhetorical positions (repetition) to draw attention to their grievances (resistance). However rational this tactic may be, it assumes the state's positions are uniform and coherent, which is its downfall.

The analysis in chapter 3 explored how local people rely on appeals to the *kgotla* and democratic relationships of voting in their attempts to contest conservation policies like the hunting ban and enforcement-first antipoaching. This strategy rearticulates the state's professed valorization of consent and consultation. While the local recognition and adoption of state participatory discourses appears to be a reasonable strategy for resistance, it fails on the conservation estate because of the deployment of a securitizing discourse that puts the environment in the realm of national security and therefore not up for debate.

Chapter 4 recounted a similar strategy of recognition, repetition, and resistance that utilizes the discourse around private ownership as a means of contestation. Discursive emphasis on "ownership" of conservation territories is a recognition of both past land alienation and the potential benefits afforded to those recognized as "owners." Local people observe the apparent flexibility and maneuver afforded to private landowners on the conservation estate and attempt to co-opt this for themselves through ownership-based claim-making. Yet because these conceptions exist outside of the officially recognized tenure regime promulgated by the state, these calls are rejected.

Not all approaches to contestation adopt the state's narratives. Chapters 6 and 7 explored the use of ethnic subjectivities and local claims of identity as resistance strategies, in contrast to the state's preference for downplaying ethnic diversity and cultural specificity. In addition to the limitations of using rhetoric deemed suspicious by state authorities, the local discourse of identity runs the possibility of being self-essentializing and problematically draws upon stereotypical notions about inherent and inborn behaviors, which can liken these modes of resistance to regressive and retrograde notions of identity.

An important facet of the way recognition and repetition play out on the conservation estate is that this process is not always done to resist but rather at times attempts to adapt to the state's prerogatives. This was seen in chapter 5 with the way local people build their own infrastructure in order to bridge, literally, the gap between themselves and the state and in chapter 6 where conservation-adjacent people enthusiastically attempt to adhere to the state's commercialized approach to ostrich eggshells. Regardless, these apparently earnest attempts to align to the state's goals fail. This, perhaps, further alienates and differentiates conservation-adjacent people from the state and may contribute to the adversarial relationship that so often exists between the state and many of its conservation-adjacent citizens.

The failure of this kind of recognition and adoption indicates that the multifaceted nature of the state and state imaginaries does not necessarily lead to more equitable outcomes. While the discourses and institutions of conservation may be somewhat fluid, in this fluctuation there is inequality. Some actors and institutions are better placed to make claims, dispelling the romanticization of hybridity, flexibility, and negotiation that is commonplace in much contemporary scholarly discussion of state building in postcolonial Africa. Growing out of this, some actors and institutions—be they state agents, private entities, or members of the global conservation movement—are better placed to set narratives, craft the parameters of the debate, and (re)produce relationships of power even in the face of resistance.

Where to Go from Here

One of the last interviews I conducted for this project almost never happened. In 2017 I traveled back to Botswana to the communities where I had conducted research, in order to disseminate my initial findings. In addition, I deposited a copy of my doctoral thesis with the National Archives and with the DWNP's departmental library. I was also scheduled to have a debriefing meeting with wildlife officials in that same department.

When I arrived on the day of the appointment, there was an unusual buzz of activity in the typically staid office. Amid this backdrop, one of the receptionists apologetically told me the meeting would have to be rescheduled because my counterparts were attending to an emergency. When I returned a few days later, the equally apologetic staff explained that there had been an unprecedented incursion of an elephant into the village of Molepolole on the day of our originally scheduled meeting. The staff had rushed to the community to assess the impact and damage and tried to determine how and why an elephant had wandered so far from its usual terrain.[3] Molepolole is a growing peri-urban village approximately an hour's drive from Gaborone. It is well connected to the capital city and one of the towns commonplace in Tswana political geography described in Chapter One. It is not part of the space that I had conceptualized as the conservation estate. Yet, this incident remained with me for two distinct reasons. First, the sudden—and shocking—appearance of an elephant so far removed from the "wild" spaces where it "belongs" elucidated that the boundaries of the conservation estate are not necessarily permanently fixed but instead dynamic and in flux. As ecosystems and climate change, as human populations grow, the spaces home to wildlife and integral to biodiversity will also change, perhaps in unexpected or counterintuitive ways. This will potentially draw heretofore unimpacted populations, geographies, and political contexts into the conservation estate.

Second, this incident highlighted what happens when the impacts on the conservation estate expand into spaces long central to the mainstream state. I could not help but compare the frenzied flurry of activity in response to the elephant finding its way to the outskirts of Gaborone with the many times informants across Botswana's northern conservation estate had lamented the department's lack of engagement about their own concerns of wildlife encroachment. Would the same level of concern and attention be afforded to those communities long exposed to these kinds of human-wildlife conflicts, or did Molepolole's proximity to the center of state power render it a different case altogether? Would communities in the Tswana heartland be told to accept the increasing copresence of wildlife, with all that entails, as their counterparts in the north and west of the country have long been expected? Or was that a mandate reserved for some populations only? The brief interlude I witnessed at DWNP headquarters provides some insights into these questions, but further research will be needed to disentangle what will happen as populations continue to expand into the human-wildlife interface of the conservation estate or as a changing climate facilitates (or even necessitates) wildlife populations venturing into geographical, ecological, and political zones from which they have long been absent.

Having reiterated the major arguments of this book, I will now discuss three further lines of inquiry opened up by this research. This will include considering how the conservation estate may be, or become, a sociopolitical concept relevant to urban and other non-rural spaces, considering how broadly generalizable the analysis of the conservation estate is to other regions and geographic contexts, and, finally, outlining potential future research in light of the climate crisis and nascent debates about the nature of conservation and environmental policymaking.

The Conservation Estate in Urban Contexts

For this single case study, I have developed the concept of the conservation estate from within the context of Botswana. In this setting, the breadth of scope of this sociopolitical space is decidedly rural, and many of the arguments of this book are specifically focused on how the lens of the conservation estate allows scholars to more robustly examine differentiation across rural space. However, the logics, practices, discourses, and politics of conservation are by no means limited to rural contexts alone. This leaves open to further investigation the manner in which the theoretical concepts presented in this book may be adapted and utilized in other contexts such as urban and peri-urban geographies.

As the above anecdote about the unexpected human-wildlife interface near the capital city suggests, assessing the portability of the concept will be a fruitful avenue of further research.

Moreover, this expansion can help refine the theoretical claims beyond the rural spatial bias in the case of Botswana. The concept of the conservation estate can be applicable to diverse kinds of environments—those that are found around the world and attract international attention while placing restrictions on human residency and resource use. These spaces also exhibit the potential for economic commodification of the environment, a characteristic of the conservation estate that may make it useful in a broad range of empirical arenas, including those in urban contexts, and for scholars across various disciplines concerned with the intersection between social, ecological, and economic dynamics.

The Conservation Estate in Other Regional Contexts

In the study of environmental politics, I suggest that the analytical category of the "conservation estate" may have purchase in other empirical cases—certainly elsewhere in Africa but also throughout the world. The concept of the conservation estate is useful broadly across the Global South, where most of the world's endowment of conservation and wildlife spaces are located. Botswana, with a substantial percentage of its land area set aside for conservation and expansive endowment of wildlife species, was an ideal case study for the aims of this research. However, it is not completely idiosyncratic in the size, scope, and global importance of its conservation estate. The analysis of this sociopolitical category of land can be apt in a variety of other contexts across Africa as well as the wider Global South. The application of the conservation estate lens within Africa may be intriguing and analytically productive. Africa, as a whole, is a demographically young continent, with much of the projected global population growth of the twenty-first century expected to take place in that region. With Africa already home to burgeoning megacities and the expansive "wildlife spaces" that I have rendered as the conservation estate, how these sociopolitical contexts meet, merge, and interact will be vital empirical venues for analyzing African state practice, state building, and citizen-state relations moving forward.

Moreover, the "hotspot" logic that dominates global biodiversity conservation implicates similarly situated geographic contexts in South America, Southeast Asia, and elsewhere in the Global South. I have already noted how the global footprint of protected areas over-indexes countries and regions that share certain attributes—namely, experiencing conditions of post- and/or neocoloniality—while also being least culpable in the global environmental, climactic, and biodiversity crises currently unfolding. The analytical attention to the political role of conservation in these spaces will be a valuable addition to the work presented here and can test the portability and generalizability from a single case to countries within Africa and beyond to other regional contexts.

The Conservation Estate in the Climate Crisis

From the empirical vantage point of Botswana, this book presented theoretical arguments about the political impacts of biodiversity conservation on state building, state practice, and citizen-state relations. Botswana's endowment of national parks, game reserves, and other areas set aside for biodiversity conservation elicit global attention. Policies surrounding their management are central to both domestic state building and the country's international relations.

However, biodiversity conservation is not the only environmental mechanism that we can assess for its social and political effects. In a time where the global ecosphere is in flux and we are experiencing dynamic and unpredictable impacts of anthropogenic climate change, it is possible to widen the aperture. Amid the fits and starts of international efforts to address the crisis, institutional arrangements and policy structures such as carbon offsets, payment for ecosystem services, and REDD+ programs have become highly relevant to the arguments of this book. While distinct from the context of Botswana, where the conservation estate is primarily focused on traditional wildlife management and the associated tourism industry, the suite of policies that direct attention to carbon sinks and other regions integral for climate mitigation render these similarly situated spaces part of the conservation estate. This establishes a valuable future trajectory for this line of research. If we take more seriously the political and social impacts of conservation, as this book argues, the theoretical insights developed from spaces primarily associated with biodiversity conservation can, for example, act as a useful entry to assessing the political processes of citizen-state relations in and around globally important carbon sinks. The claims of this book may also further analysis of the role of state building and state practice in managing REDD+ and other payment-for-ecosystem-services initiatives. Further research regarding the nature of politics will be germane to land that is set aside not for wildlife alone but also for the development of renewable energy production like solar farms. Moreover, as extractive processes such as the mining of rare earth minerals needed for the renewable energy transition become framed as within the scope of "environmental" or "green development," these efforts at climate mitigation and adaption can benefit from insights developed here.

I began this book with a lengthy discussion of the literature on the state and land politics in Africa. Throughout I have endeavored to take the existing scholarship seriously and expand upon it in enriching and illuminating ways to highlight the contingent nature of the state and demonstrate how this plays out on a new empirical venue—the conservation estate. Focusing on this particular category of political and environmental space contributes to a greater understanding of the nature of the postcolonial state, the multivalent state-building process, and differentiated citizen-state relationships. It provides greater understanding of rural space within the state, moves beyond simple binaries of rural/urban, and improves upon literature that accounts for rural differentiation but fails to fully capture the conservation estate as a category of space in its own right. By proposing that the conservation estate is a relevant site in the study of rural politics and land politics, I have sought to connect more fully the insights of political ecology to the interrogation of the postcolonial state. The concept of the conservation estate adds another heuristic tool for thinking about the intersections between people, territory, and authority. The creation and maintenance of the conservation estate have the potential to operate as means through which a state can construct its own "stateness" via the exercise of authority, territorial legitimacy, and the inculcation of belonging. This also may exacerbate and expose the inherent contradictions embedded in the state project.

Appendix
Primary Source Interviews

CEG	Community Escort Guide
DEA	Department of Environmental Affairs
DFRR	Department of Forestry and Range Resources
DOT	Department of Tourism
DNM	Department of National Monuments
DWNP	Department of Wildlife and National Parks
GDC	Ghanzi District Council
GLB	Ghanzi Land Board
NWDC	Northwest District Council
SET	Settlement Extension Team
TLB	Tawana Land Board
VDC	Village Development Committee

Interview number	Participant(s)	Date	Location	Participant description
1	1	Sept. 4, 2013	Gaborone	NGO–conservation
2	1	Sept. 9, 2013	Gaborone	NGO–conservation
3	1	Sept. 10, 2013	Gaborone	NGO–conservation
4	1	Sept. 17, 2013	Gaborone	NGO–development
5	1	Sept. 23, 2013	Gaborone	NGO–conservation
6	1	Sept. 25, 2013	Gaborone	Civil servant–DWNP
7	1	Sept. 25, 2013	Gaborone	Elected official
8	1	Sept. 25, 2013	Gaborone	Elected official
9	1	Sept. 25, 2013	Gaborone	Elected official

Interview number	Participant(s)	Date	Location	Participant description
10	1	Sept. 26, 2013	Gaborone	NGO–conservation
11	1	Oct. 7, 2013	Gaborone	Civil servant–DEA
12	1	Oct. 8, 2013	Gaborone	Multilateral donor practitioner
13	1	Oct. 11, 2013	Gaborone	Civil servant–DWNP
14	1	Oct. 11, 2013	Gaborone	Civil servant–DWNP
15	1	Oct. 14, 2013	Gaborone	Civil servant–DWNP
16	1	Oct. 16, 2013	Gaborone	Civil servant–DWNP
17	1	Oct. 16, 2013	Gaborone	Civil servant–DWNP
18	1	Oct. 21, 2013	Gaborone	Civil servant–DEA
19	1	Oct. 24, 2013	Maun	NGO–conservation
20	1	Oct. 24, 2013	Maun	Elected official
21	1	Oct. 25, 2013	Maun	Multilateral donor practitioner
22	1	Oct. 25, 2013	Maun	Civil servant–DEA
23	1	Oct. 29, 2013	Shakawe	Elected official
24	1	Oct. 29, 2013	Shakawe	Traditional leader
25	1	Oct. 29, 2013	Shakawe	NGO–conservation and development
26	1	Oct. 29, 2013	Shakawe	Resident
27	1	Oct. 29, 2013	Shakawe	Resident
28	1	Oct. 29, 2013	Shakawe	Resident
29	1	Oct. 29, 2013	Shakawe	Resident
30	1	Oct. 30, 2013	Shakawe	Resident
31	1	Oct. 30, 2013	Shakawe	Resident
32	1	Oct. 30, 2013	Shakawe	Resident
33	2	Oct. 30, 2013	Shakawe	Residents
34	6	Oct. 30, 2013	Shakawe	Residents
35	1	Oct. 31, 2013	Shakawe	Civil servant–NWDC
36	2	Oct. 31, 2013	Shakawe	Residents
37	1	Nov. 1, 2013	Maun	NGO–conservation
38	1	Nov. 1, 2013	Maun	Civil servant–TLB
39	1	Nov. 4, 2013	Maun	NGO–conservation
40	1	Nov. 4, 2013	Maun	NGO–development
41	1	Nov. 5, 2013	Maun	Multilateral donor practitioner
42	1	Nov. 6, 2013	Maun	Multilateral donor practitioner
43	1	Nov. 6, 2013	Maun	Photographic tourism
44	1	Nov. 6, 2013	Maun	Photographic tourism
45	1	Nov. 7, 2013	Maun	Civil servant–DWNP
46	1	Nov. 7, 2013	Maun	Civil servant–DWNP
47	2	Nov. 8, 2013	Maun	Parastatal employees
48	1	Nov. 9, 2013	Maun	Photographic tourism
49	1	Nov. 11, 2013	Maun	Civil servant–DNM

Appendix

Interview number	Participant(s)	Date	Location	Participant description
50	1	Nov. 11, 2013	Maun	Civil servant–DWNP
51	3	Nov. 11, 2013	Maun	Civil servants–DWNP
52	2	Nov. 11, 2013	Maun	Civil servants–DWNP
53	1	Nov. 12, 2013	Maun	Civil servant–DOT
54	1	Nov. 13, 2013	Maun	Commercial safari hunter
55	1	Nov. 13, 2013	Maun	Multilateral donor practitioner
56	1	Nov. 15, 2013	Maun	NGO–conservation and development
57	1	Nov. 15, 2013	Maun	Civil servant–NWDC
58	1	Nov. 15, 2013	Maun	Civil servant–DWNP
59	1	Nov. 16, 2013	Maun	Photographic tourism
60	1	Nov. 18, 2013	Maun	Resident
61	1	Nov. 19, 2013	Maun	Traditional leader
62	1	Nov. 20, 2013	Sankuyo	Resident
63	4	Nov. 20, 2013	Sankuyo	Residents
64	3	Nov. 20, 2013	Sankuyo	Residents
65	2	Nov. 20, 2013	Sankuyo	Residents
66	1	Nov. 21, 2013	Sankuyo	Resident
67	1	Nov. 21, 2013	Sankuyo	Resident
68	1	Nov. 21, 2013	Sankuyo	Resident
69	5	Nov. 21, 2013	Sankuyo	Residents
70	1	Nov. 21, 2013	Sankuyo	Resident
71	1	Nov. 21, 2013	Sankuyo	Resident–CEG
72	1	Nov. 21, 2013	Sankuyo	Resident
73	1	Nov. 21, 2013	Sankuyo	Resident
74	1	Nov. 21, 2013	Sankuyo	Resident
75	1	Nov. 22, 2013	Sankuyo	Resident
76	1	Nov. 22, 2013	Sankuyo	Resident
77	1	Nov. 22, 2013	Sankuyo	Resident
78	1	Nov. 22, 2013	Sankuyo	Resident
79	1	Nov. 22, 2013	Sankuyo	Resident
80	1	Nov. 22, 2013	Sankuyo	Resident–VDC
81	1	Nov. 22, 2013	Sankuyo	Resident–CEG
82	1	Nov. 25, 2013	Boro	Traditional leader
83	1	Nov. 25, 2013	Boro	Traditional leader
84	1	Nov. 25, 2013	Boro	Resident–VDC
85	1	Nov. 25, 2013	Boro	Resident
86	1	Nov. 25, 2013	Boro	Resident
87	1	Nov. 25, 2013	Boro	Resident
88	1	Nov. 25, 2013	Boro	Resident
89	2	Nov. 25, 2013	Boro	Residents

Interview number	Participant(s)	Date	Location	Participant description
90	1	Nov. 25, 2013	Boro	Resident
91	1	Nov. 26, 2013	Ditshiping	Resident–VDC
92	1	Nov. 26, 2013	Ditshiping	Traditional leader
93	1	Nov. 26, 2013	Ditshiping	Resident
94	2	Nov. 26, 2013	Ditshiping	Residents
95	1	Nov. 26, 2013	Ditshiping	Resident
96	1	Nov. 26, 2013	Ditshiping	Resident
97	2	Nov. 26, 2013	Ditshiping	Residents
98	3	Nov. 26, 2013	Ditshiping	Residents
99	1	Nov. 26, 2013	Ditshiping	Resident–CEG
100	1	Nov. 27, 2013	Xuoxao	Resident
101	1	Nov. 27, 2013	Xuoxao	Resident
102	1	Nov. 27, 2013	Xuoxao	Resident
103	1	Nov. 27, 2013	Xuoxao	Resident
104	1	Nov. 27, 2013	Xuoxao	Resident
105	3	Nov. 27, 2013	Xuoxao	Residents
106	3	Nov. 27, 2013	Xuoxao	Residents
107	1	Nov. 28, 2013	Maun	Civil servant–DWNP
108	1	Nov. 28, 2013	Maun	Civil servant–DWNP
109	1	Nov. 28, 2013	Maun	NGO–conservation and development
110	1	Nov. 28, 2013	Maun	NGO–conservation and development
111	1	Nov. 30, 2013	Maun	Photographic tourism
112	1	Dec. 2, 2013	Mababe	Resident–CEG
113	1	Dec. 3, 2013	Mababe	Resident
114	1	Dec. 3, 2013	Mababe	Resident
115	5	Dec. 3, 2013	Mababe	Residents
116	1	Dec. 3, 2013	Mababe	Resident
117	1	Dec. 3, 2013	Mababe	Resident
118	1	Dec. 3, 2013	Mababe	Resident
119	5	Dec. 4, 2013	Mababe	Residents
120	4	Dec. 4, 2013	Mababe	Residents
121	1	Dec. 4, 2013	Mababe	Commercial safari hunter
122	1	Dec. 4, 2013	Mababe	Resident
123	1	Dec. 4, 2013	Mababe	Resident
124	1	Dec. 4, 2013	Mababe	Photographic tourism
125	1	Dec. 5, 2013	Mababe	Resident
126	1	Dec. 5, 2013	Mababe	Resident
127	1	Dec. 5, 2013	Mababe	Resident
128	1	Dec. 5, 2013	Mababe	Resident
129	1	Dec. 5, 2013	Mababe	Resident

Appendix

Interview number	Participant(s)	Date	Location	Participant description
130	1	Dec. 9, 2013	Khwai	Resident–CEG
131	1	Dec. 9, 2013	Khwai	Resident
132	1	Dec. 9, 2013	Khwai	Resident
133	1	Dec. 10, 2013	Khwai	Resident
134	1	Dec. 10, 2013	Khwai	Resident
135	1	Dec. 10, 2013	Khwai	Resident
136	1	Dec. 11, 2013	Khwai	Resident
137	1	Dec. 11, 2013	Khwai	Resident–VDC
138	1	Dec. 11, 2013	Khwai	Resident
139	1	Dec. 12, 2013	Khwai	Resident
140	1	Dec. 12, 2013	Khwai	Resident
141	1	Dec. 12, 2013	Khwai	Resident
142	1	Dec. 12, 2013	Khwai	Resident
143	3	Dec. 12, 2013	Khwai	Residents
144	1	Dec. 12, 2013	Khwai	Traditional leader
145	4	Dec. 12, 2013	Khwai	Residents
146	1	Dec. 16, 2013	Maun	NGO–development
147	1	Jan. 22, 2014	Gaborone	Multilateral donor practitioner
148	1	Jan. 23, 2014	Gaborone	NGO–development
149	1	Jan. 24, 2014	Gaborone	NGO–development
150	2	Jan. 28, 2014	Gaborone	Parastatal employees
151	1	Jan. 28, 2014	Gaborone	Civil servant–DOT
152	1	Jan. 30, 2014	Gaborone	Elected official
153	1	Feb. 3, 2014	Ghanzi	Civil servant–DOT
154	1	Feb. 4, 2014	Ghanzi	Civil servant–DWNP
155	1	Feb. 4, 2014	Ghanzi	NGO–conservation and development
156	1	Feb. 5, 2014	Ghanzi	Civil servant–GDC
157	2	Feb. 6, 2014	Ghanzi	Civil servants–DWNP
158	1	Feb. 8, 2014	Maun	NGO–conservation and development
159	1	Feb. 10, 2014	Ghanzi	Civil servant–DWNP
160	1	Feb. 10, 2014	Ghanzi	Civil servant–DFRR
161	1	Feb. 10, 2014	Ghanzi	Parastatal employee
162	1	Feb. 11, 2014	Ghanzi	Traditional leader
163	1	Feb. 11, 2014	Ghanzi	Civil servant–DWNP
164	1	Feb. 11, 2014	Ghanzi	Elected official
165	2	Feb. 11, 2014	Ghanzi	Civil servants–DWNP
166	2	Feb. 12, 2014	Ghanzi	Civil servants–GLB
167	1	Feb. 12, 2014	D'Kar	NGO–development
168	1	Feb. 12, 2014	D'Kar	NGO–development
169	1	Feb. 13, 2014	D'Kar	NGO–development

Interview number	Participant(s)	Date	Location	Participant description
170	1	Feb. 14, 2014	Ghanzi	Private landowner
171	2	Feb. 17, 2014	Ghanzi	NGO-conservation
172	1	Feb. 17, 2014	Ghanzi	Private landowner
173	2	Feb. 17, 2014	Ghanzi	Private landowners
174	2	Feb. 18, 2014	West Hanahai	Traditional leaders
175	1	Feb. 18, 2014	West Hanahai	Civil servant-SET
176	1	Feb. 18, 2014	West Hanahai	Civil servant-SET
177	2	Feb. 18, 2014	West Hanahai	Residents
178	3	Feb. 18, 2014	West Hanahai	Residents
179	1	Feb. 19, 2014	West Hanahai	Resident
180	1	Feb. 19, 2014	West Hanahai	Resident
181	4	Feb. 19, 2014	West Hanahai	Residents
182	1	Feb. 19, 2014	West Hanahai	Resident
183	2	Feb. 19, 2014	West Hanahai	Residents
184	1	Feb. 19, 2014	West Hanahai	Resident
185	1	Feb. 19, 2014	West Hanahai	Resident
186	1	Feb. 19, 2014	West Hanahai	Resident
187	2	Feb. 19, 2014	West Hanahai	Residents
188	1	Feb. 20, 2014	East Hanahai	Civil servant-SET
189	1	Feb. 20, 2014	East Hanahai	Civil servant-SET
190	1	Feb. 20, 2014	East Hanahai	Resident
191	1	Feb. 20, 2014	East Hanahai	Resident
192	2	Feb. 20, 2014	East Hanahai	Residents
193	3	Feb. 20, 2014	East Hanahai	Residents
194	1	Feb. 20, 2014	East Hanahai	Traditional leader
195	1	Feb. 21, 2014	Kacgae	Resident
196	1	Feb. 21, 2014	Kacgae	Resident
197	1	Feb. 21, 2014	Kacgae	Resident
198	2	Feb. 21, 2014	Kacgae	Residents
199	3	Feb. 22, 2014	Kacgae	Residents
200	1	Feb. 22, 2014	Kacgae	Resident
201	1	Feb. 22, 2014	Kacgae	Resident-VDC
202	1	Feb. 22, 2014	Kacgae	Civil servant-SET
203	2	Feb. 22, 2014	Kacgae	Residents
204	1	Feb. 22, 2014	Kacgae	Resident
205	2	Feb. 22, 2014	Kacgae	Residents
206	1	Feb. 23, 2014	Kacgae	Traditional leader
207	1	Feb. 23, 2014	Kacgae	Resident
208	1	Feb. 24, 2014	Ghanzi	Commercial safari hunter
209	1	Feb. 25, 2014	Groot Laagte	Resident

Appendix

Interview number	Participant(s)	Date	Location	Participant description
210	1	Feb. 25, 2014	Groot Laagte	Resident
211	1	Feb. 26, 2014	Groot Laagte	Traditional leader
212	1	Feb. 26, 2014	Groot Laagte	Civil servant–SET
213	4	Feb. 26, 2014	Groot Laagte	Residents
214	1	Feb. 26, 2014	Groot Laagte	Resident
215	2	Feb. 26, 2014	Groot Laagte	Residents
216	3	Feb. 27, 2014	Groot Laagte	Residents–VDC
217	1	Feb. 27, 2014	Groot Laagte	Resident
218	3	Feb. 27, 2014	Groot Laagte	Residents
219	2	Feb. 27, 2014	Groot Laagte	Residents
220	2	Feb. 27, 2014	Groot Laagte	Residents
221	4	Feb. 28, 2014	Qabo	Residents
222	1	Feb. 28, 2014	Qabo	Resident–VDC
223	1	Feb. 28, 2014	Qabo	Resident
224	2	Feb. 28, 2014	Qabo	Residents
225	1	Feb. 28, 2014	Qabo	Resident
226	4	Feb. 28, 2014	Qabo	Residents
227	1	Mar. 1, 2014	Ghanzi	Private landowner
228	1	Mar. 3, 2014	Ghanzi	Resident
229	1	Mar. 3, 2014	Ghanzi	Photographic tourism
230	2	Mar. 4, 2014	New Xade	Residents
231	1	Mar. 4, 2014	New Xade	Resident
232	1	Mar. 4, 2014	New Xade	Resident
233	1	Mar. 4, 2014	New Xade	Resident
234	1	Mar. 5, 2014	New Xade	Civil servant–SET
235	1	Mar. 5, 2014	New Xade	Resident
236	2	Mar. 5, 2014	New Xade	Residents
237	1	Mar. 5, 2014	New Xade	Resident
238	1	Mar. 5, 2014	New Xade	Resident
239	1	Mar. 5, 2014	New Xade	Resident
240	2	Mar. 5, 2014	New Xade	Residents
241	1	Mar. 5, 2014	New Xade	Traditional leader
242	1	Mar. 6, 2014	New Xade	Resident
243	1	Mar. 6, 2014	New Xade	Resident
244	2	Mar. 6, 2014	New Xade	Residents
245	1	Mar. 6, 2014	New Xade	Resident–CKGR plaintiff
246	1	Mar. 6, 2014	New Xade	Resident
247	1	Mar. 6, 2014	New Xade	Resident
248	1	Mar. 6, 2014	New Xade	Resident
249	1	Mar. 10, 2014	Ghanzi	Private landowner

Interview number	Participant(s)	Date	Location	Participant description
250	1	Mar. 11, 2014	Bere	Resident
251	1	Mar. 11, 2014	Bere	Resident
252	1	Mar. 11, 2014	Bere	Resident
253	1	Mar. 11, 2014	Bere	Traditional leader
254	1	Mar. 12, 2014	Bere	Resident
255	1	Mar. 12, 2014	Bere	Resident
256	2	Mar. 12, 2014	Bere	Residents
257	2	Mar. 12, 2014	Bere	Residents
258	1	Mar. 12, 2014	Bere	Resident
259	1	Mar. 12, 2014	Bere	Resident
260	1	Mar. 12, 2014	Bere	Resident
261	1	Mar. 12, 2014	Bere	Resident
262	2	Mar. 13, 2014	Bere	Residents
263	1	Mar. 13, 2014	Bere	Civil servant–SET
264	1	Mar. 13, 2014	Bere	Resident
265	2	Mar. 13, 2014	Bere	Residents
266	2	Mar. 13, 2014	Bere	Residents
267	1	Mar. 15, 2014	Ghanzi	Civil servant–GDC
268	4	Mar. 16, 2014	Ghanzi	Private landowners
269	1	Mar. 18, 2014	D'Kar	Traditional leader
270	1	Mar. 18, 2014	D'Kar	Resident
271	1	Mar. 18, 2014	D'Kar	Resident
272	2	Mar. 18, 2014	D'Kar	Residents
273	1	Mar. 18, 2014	Ghanzi	Civil servant–DWNP
274	2	Mar. 18, 2014	Ghanzi	Civil servants–DWNP
275	1	Mar. 19, 2014	D'Kar	Resident
276	1	Mar. 19, 2014	D'Kar	Resident
277	1	Mar. 19, 2014	D'Kar	Resident
278	1	Mar. 19, 2014	D'Kar	Resident
279	1	Mar. 20, 2014	Ghanzi	Civil servant–GLB
280	1	Mar. 20, 2014	Ghanzi	Civil servant–DWNP
281	2	Mar. 20, 2014	Ghanzi	Commercial safari hunters
282	1	Mar. 24, 2014	Gaborone	Civil servant–DWNP
283	1	Mar. 28, 2014	Gaborone	Civil servant–DWNP
284	1	Mar. 31, 2014	Gaborone	Civil servant–DWNP

Glossary of Setswana Terms

Batswana Demonym referring to all nationals of Botswana. This is often a source of confusion because officially all citizens, regardless of descent, are referred to as Batswana. Singular *Motswana*.

Kgosi Chief. Plural *dikgosi*.

Kgosana Headman.

Kgotla Traditional Tswana public meetings held in the villages of Botswana. The word can refer to the physical location of the kgotla building, as well as the cultural institution.

Makgoa White people. Used interchangeably with "tourist." Singular *lekgoa*.

Merafe Precolonial centralized Tswana kingdoms. Singular *morafe*.

Tswana The culture and traditions of the Setswana-speaking groups: Bakgatla, Bakwena, Bamangwato, Bamalete, Bangwaketse, Barolong, Batawana, and Batlokwa.

Notes

Introduction

1. This was the name of the ministry at the time of my research. It has since changed to the Ministry of Environment, Natural Resources Conservation and Tourism (MENT), which is sometimes referred to simply as the Ministry of Environment and Tourism, but the institutional functions remain the same.
2. Author's personal conversation, August 2013, Gaborone.
3. In his article "Green States in Africa: Beyond the Usual Suspects," in *Environmental Politics*, Death introduced the argument he expanded to monograph length in *The Green State in Africa*. Both were published in 2016.
4. See Büscher and Fletcher's 2020 monograph *The Conservation Revolution: Radical Ideas for Saving Nature beyond the Anthropocene* for further analysis of the Half-Earth model of conservation.
5. Botswana is home to the largest population of African bush elephants (*Loxodonta africana*), over two hundred thousand individuals—approximately one-quarter of the entire population of the species (DWNP 2012).
6. The *Daily News* (Gaborone), the government-run state newspaper, was a valuable source in this respect.
7. I employed one man from August until December 2013, after which he was offered a full-time post at the University of Botswana's Okavango Research Institute. My second assistant was a woman whom I employed from January until March 2014 and again in 2017. Both had university-level educations and were fluent in English and Setswana, and my second research assistant was fluent in Thimbukushu as well.
8. Both transcribers were fluent in English and Setswana. One had two master's degrees, and the other was enrolled in a master's program at the University of Botswana at the time of data collection and has since graduated.

Chapter 1: Lay of the Land

1. The year 2019 was the last prior to the global coronavirus pandemic, so these figures reflect the more typical importance of Botswana's tourism industry. "Botswana 2021 Annual Research: Key Highlights," https://wttc.org/Research/Economic-Impact.
2. Most tourists in Botswana are international visitors, in part as a result of the country's high-value, low-volume approach to the industry, which privileges the luxury and high-end sector.
3. Linfield, M., Berlowitz, V., and Fothergill, A., dirs., *Elephant* (Los Angeles: Disney+, 2020).
4. Setswana and English are the only official languages used in state-run institutions. Citizens need primary proficiency in either one in order to secure access to state services. This accounts for language shifts in non-Tswana speakers, especially San people (Mafela 2009).
5. This "Tswanafication" resembles the Russification/Japanization/Magyarization described by Anderson (1982) in *Imagined Communities*.
6. The kgotla is both the name of the building where these meetings take place (a physical location in a community) as well as the social institution itself, a kgotla meeting.
7. The Kalanga are the most politically and economically powerful of the non-Tswana groups in the country. Well placed in institutions of higher education, government, and the private sector, Kalanga individuals have promoted their cultural and linguistic identity within the nation-state (Werbner 2004).
8. In this context a Farm Block is an area where large tracts of land were sold as freehold farms primarily to white settlers during the colonial period.
9. "Okavango Delta," UNESCO, World Heritage Convention, http://whc.unesco.org/en/list/1432.
10. Archaeological evidence, including San rock art at the Tsodilo Hills site, suggests the progenitors of Botswana's contemporary San population have been resident in this area for tens of thousands of years.

Chapter 2: Coercion on Botswana's Conservation Estate

1. E. Thompson, dir., *Poaching Wars with Tom Hardy*, aired August 29, 2013, on ITV, Burning Bright Productions.
2. "UN Secretary-General Ban Ki-moon's Message for 2015 World Wildlife Day," UN Office on Drugs and Crime, February 27, 2015.
3. For example, assertions such as this are typical of Western reporting on elephant poaching: "Moreover, profits reaped by the poachers have helped to fund organisations such as the Lord's Resistance Army, which kidnaps and mutilates children. Or al-Shabaab, which kills elephants to help pay

for the weapons it needs to conduct atrocities such as the Westgate mall massacre. Or Boko Haram, which sent supporters across the border into Cameroon to trade ivory to fund its terrorist network. There is a lot more at stake than the survival of a single species." E. Lebedev, "Giants Club: We Must Unite to Fight the Elephant Poachers—and We Must Win," *The Independent*, August 2, 2015. It is worth noting that there is little to no empirical evidence of this link of poaching to international terrorism, but it fits neatly into a wider narrative about African states, security, and global insecurity.

4. L. Chube, "MP Calls for Reduction of Demand for Illegal Products," *Daily News* (Botswana), March 8, 2015.
5. Thompson, *Poaching Wars with Tom Hardy*.
6. J. Sejabosigo, "Botswana Hopes for US Help," *Daily News* (Botswana), February 22, 2016.
7. Interview with DWNP official, September 25, 2013, Gaborone, no. 6.
8. Interview with head of Anti-Poaching, March 31, 2014, Gaborone, no. 284.
9. Occasionally reports of incidents will be released in an ad hoc manner through state media or in the private press, but there is no comprehensive accounting, reporting, or publicly accessible database. Interview with director of the DWNP, March 28, 2014, Gaborone, no. 283; media accounts during fieldwork, August 2013–April 2014.
10. Interview with UN official, January 22, 2014, Gaborone, no. 147.
11. Interview with photographic tourism operator, November 6, 2013, Gaborone, no. 43.
12. Interview with DWNP deputy director, October 14, 2013, Gaborone, no. 15.
13. Interview with DWNP official, September 25, 2013, Gaborone, no. 6.
14. Referring both to the liberation wars in Angola, Zimbabwe, and Namibia as well as the white military personnel of the former minority-ruled states.
15. Interview with DWNP official, October 11, 2013, Gaborone, no. 14.
16. See, e.g., "Botswana Disputes Account of 90 Elephant Poaching Deaths," *Africa Times*, September 6, 2018; "Botswana Rejects Claims of Elephant Poaching Surge," *Agence France-Presse*, September 20, 2018; K. de Greef, "Doubts Mount in Botswana over Charity's Claim of Elephant 'Poaching Frenzy,'" *New York Times*, September 28, 2018.
17. Interview with head of Anti-Poaching, March 31, 2014, Gaborone, no. 284.
18. See, e.g., J. Konopo, "Did Botswana Execute 'Poachers'?," *Mail & Guardian* (Johannesburg), November 23, 2023; T. Mongudhi, J. Konopo, and N. Ntibinyane, "Deadly Borders: 30 Namibians Killed through Botswana Shoot to Kill Policy," *The Namibian*, March 9, 2016; P. Tau, "Namibia Citizens Up in Arms over Botswana's 'Shoot to Kill' Approach," *CityPress News 24* (Johannesburg), November 12, 2020.

19. S. Kebonang, "Khama Lauds BDF for Anti-poaching Efforts," *Daily News* (Botswana), June 24, 2014.
20. The description of the specifics of the BDF's historical involvement in antipoaching relies on Dan Henk's 2007 monograph *The Botswana Defence Force in the Struggle for an African Environment*. While the BDF is primarily based in the north, the main law enforcement role in the west of the country, especially in the vast Central Kalahari Game Reserve (CKGR), is done by the Special Security Group, or SSG. The SSG is a paramilitary force that was initially constituted for riot control and other functions deemed inappropriate for unarmed police. Though not part of the BDF proper, the SSG has more in common with martial uses of force than the unarmed Botswana Police Service. Respondents in western Botswana typically do not distinguish between the SSG and regular BDF forces, referring to everyone engaged in antipoaching as "the army." Despite the BDF being primarily concentrated in the north, there is a BDF and DWNP antipoaching base at Lonetree on the Transkalahari Highway between Ghanzi Town and Kang. Fieldnotes 2014.
21. These units within the department are responsible for dealing with human-wildlife conflict and compensating Batswana for the loss of crops or property due to wild animals, or for injuries or deaths related to human-wildlife conflict.
22. Interview with DWNP CKGR liaison team, February 6, 2014, Ghanzi, no. 157.
23. Interview with DWNP regional wildlife officer, November 11, 2013, Maun, no. 50.
24. Interview with DWNP official, October 16, 2013, Gaborone, no. 16; interview with DWNP official, October 11, 2013, Gaborone, no. 13.
25. K. Keaketswe, "Botswana Intensifies Anti-poaching Efforts," *Daily News* (Botswana), January 28, 2016.
26. Interview with DWNP official, September 25, 2013, Gaborone, no. 6.
27. Interview with DWNP official, November 11, 2013, Maun, no. 52; interview with DWNP official, October 11, 2013, Gaborone, no. 13.
28. Interview with DWNP official, November 7, 2013, Maun, no. 46.
29. Interview with the DWNP Moremi Game Reserve liaison team, November 11, 2013, Maun, no. 51.
30. Interview with DWNP official, November 7, 2013, Maun, no. 45.
31. Interview with DWNP official, February 11, 2014, Ghanzi, no. 165.
32. Interview with head of Anti-Poaching, March 31, 2014, Gaborone, no. 284; fieldnotes May–July 2017.
33. Interview with DWNP official, October 11, 2013. Gaborone, no. 13.
34. Interview with resident, December 3, 2013, Mababe, no. 117.
35. Interview with DWNP official, September 25, 2013, Gaborone, no. 6.

36. Interview with head of Anti-Poaching, March 31, 2014, Gaborone, no. 284.
37. Interview with DWNP deputy director, October 14, 2013, Gaborone, no. 15.
38. Interview with conservation practitioner, October 24, 2013, Maun, no. 19.
39. Thompson, *Poaching Wars with Tom Hardy*.
40. See, e.g., "Did Botswana Execute 'Poachers'?" and "Namibia Citizens Up in Arms."
41. "BDF Commanders Justifies 'Shoot to Kill' against Poachers," *Sunday Standard* (Gaborone), June 11, 2015.
42. See the work by Botswana's local human rights NGO with regard to the death penalty. Ditshwanelo: The Botswana Centre for Human Rights, https://www.facebook.com/ditshwanelobotswana/.
43. Interview with human rights activist, January 24, 2014, Gaborone, no. 149.
44. Interview with human rights activist, January 24, 2014, Gaborone, no. 149. Significant legal challenges have been brought against the death penalty's constitutionality in the last several years. Many prominent lawyers actively and publicly oppose Botswana's application of capital punishment.
45. In fact, the extrajudicial killing of John Kalafatis, a suspect known to police, by security agents in Gaborone on May 13, 2009, resulted in national outrage and was the subject of vigorous debate (see Good 2009). As recently as my fieldwork in 2013–14, updates regarding the Kalafatis case would regularly make the pages of Gaborone's newspapers.
46. Interview with UN official, January 22, 2014, Gaborone, no. 147. See also Henk 2007.
47. Interview with director of the DWNP, March 28, 2014, Gaborone, no. 283; interview with conservation practitioner, September 26, 2013, Gaborone, no. 10; interview with photographic tourism operator, November 30, 2013, Maun, no. 111.
48. M. Mguni, "Masisi Hits Back on Elephant 'Poaching' Frenzy," *Mmegi* (Gaborone), September 10, 2018.
49. Interview with the DWNP Regional Wildlife Office, February 11, 2014, Ghanzi, no. 163.
50. Thompson, *Poaching Wars with Tom Hardy*. See also A. Leithead, "Why Elephants Are Seeking Refuge in Botswana," BBC, August 31, 2016.
51. "Convention and Protocol Relating to the Status of Refugees," UN High Commissioner for Refugees, http://www.unhcr.org/3b66c2aa10.html.
52. Interview with resident, December 5, 2013, Mababe, no. 127.
53. Interview with resident, December 5, 2013, Mababe, no. 127.
54. Interviews with community escort guides in Khwai, Sankuyo, Mababe, Boro, Ditshiping, and Maun, October–December 2013.
55. Interview with resident / community escort guide, December 2, 2013, Mababe, no. 112.

56. Interview with resident, November 22, 2013, Sankuyo, no. 81.
57. Interview with resident, November 22, 2013, Sankuyo, no. 81.
58. Interview with resident, February 26, 2014, Groot Laagte, no. 215.
59. Interview with DWNP regional wildlife officer, November 11, 2013, Maun, no. 50.
60. Interview with resident, February 23, 2014, Kacgae, no. 207.
61. Interview with conservation practitioner, February 8, 2014, Maun, no. 158.

Chapter 3: Democracy, the *Kgotla*, and Promises of Consent amid Conservation

1. A small part of this chapter is also included in LaRocco, A. A., and Mogende, E., "Fall from Grace or Back Down to Earth? Conservation and Political Conflict in Africa's 'Miracle' State," *Environment and Planning E: Nature and Space*, © 2022 by the authors, https://doi.org/10.1177/25148486221101553.
2. "Botswana to Ban Hunting over Wildlife Species Decline," BBC, November 29, 2012.
3. The ban was briefly mentioned during the president's State of the Nation address in November 2013 (two months before the ban's implementation) and was subsequently reported on state radio.
4. Interview with resident, February 22, 2014, Kacgae, no. 205.
5. Government of Botswana, *Vision 2016—a Long Term Vision for Botswana* (Gaborone: Government Printer, 1997), 47.
6. Government of Botswana, 39–40.
7. Government of Botswana, 11.
8. Ministry of Finance and Development Planning, *Mid-term Review of NDP 10: NDP 10 towards 2016* (Gaborone: Government Printer, 2013), 88.
9. "Freedom in the World 2021: Botswana," Freedom House, https://freedomhouse.org/country/botswana/freedom-world/2021.
10. K. Pelontle, "Public Has Say in Running of Country—Molale," *Daily News* (Botswana), June 17, 2015.
11. Government of Botswana, *Vision 2016*, 24.
12. Government of Botswana, 25.
13. Interview with village *kgosana*, November 25, 2013, Boro, no. 83.
14. Interview with conservation practitioner, September 23, 2013, Gaborone, no. 5.
15. Interview with DWNP official, September 25, 2013, Gaborone, no. 6.
16. Interview with DWNP official, November 7, 2013, Maun, no. 45.
17. Interview with DWNP official, November 7, 2013, Maun, no. 45.
18. Interview with San activist, March 4, 2014, New Xade, no. 231; interview with village kgosi, February 20, 2014, East Hanahai, no. 194; second group interview with residents, December 4, 2013, Mababe, no. 120; interview

with resident, March 11, 2014, Bere, no. 253; interview with MP, September 25, 2013, Gaborone, no. 8; interview with MP, January 30, 2014, Gaborone, no. 152; interview with MP, September 25, 2013, Gaborone, no. 7.
19. Interview with resident, March 5, 2014, New Xade, no. 237; interview with resident, February 21, 2014, Kacgae, no. 198; interview with resident, November 27, 2013, Xuoxao, no. 102.
20. Interview with resident, December 12, 2013, Khwai, no. 139.
21. Interview with conservation practitioner, October 24, 2013, Maun, no. 19.
22. Interview with San activist, February 4, 2014, Ghanzi, no. 155.
23. First group interview with residents, November 20, 2013, Sankuyo, no. 69.
24. See, e.g., from Gulbrandsen: "However, if anybody questions major policy directions which favour those who are already wealthy and privileged, they are, as I have observed on a few occasions, effectively silenced.... The wealthy—and hence dominant—members of the *kgotla* will argue forcefully, together with the government officials, that all the policies in question will benefit the nation. Even if some 'industrious' people gain particular benefits from them, that too will help poor people, albeit indirectly" (2012, 246).
25. Interview with village kgosi, February 23, 2014, Kacgae, no. 206.
26. Interview with resident, December 12, 2013, Khwai, no. 139.
27. Interview with resident, December 12, 2013, Khwai, no. 139; interview with resident, November 21, 2013, Sankuyo, no. 68.
28. Interview with resident, November 26, 2013, Ditshiping, no. 95.
29. Interview with resident, November 27, 2013, Xuoxao, no. 104.
30. Interview with resident, November 25, 2013, Boro, no. 87.
31. Interview with resident, February 28, 2014, Qabo, no. 222; interview with resident, February 19, 2014, West Hanahai, no. 179.
32. Interview with resident, November 25, 2013, Boro, no. 86.
33. Interview with resident, November 27, 2013, Xuoxao, no. 102. See also "It is not for the government to stop hunting without speaking with the people," interview with resident, November 21, 2013, Sankuyo, no. 71.
34. Interview with village kgosana, November 25, 2013, Boro, no. 82.
35. Interview with DWNP Moremi Game Reserve liaison team, November 11, 2013, Maun, no. 51.
36. Interview with Botswana Tourism Organisation official, January 28, 2014, Gaborone, no. 150.
37. The DWNP even attributes this to its recruitment problems, stating that those with the highest educational attainments in biology, for example, tend to be from urban areas and do not want to "go out into the bush." Interview with DWNP official, October 16, 2013, Gaborone, no. 16.
38. Batswana who lived or were educated in the Global North often recall with amusement how their Western peers at school or work were incredulous

when they said they had never been to a game reserve. Author's personal conversations during fieldwork.
39. Interview with resident, November 21, 2013, Sankuyo, no. 74.
40. Interview with resident, March 6, 2014, New Xade, no. 243.
41. Interview with San activist, March 4, 2014, New Xade, no. 231.
42. Interview with resident, December 3, 2013, Mababe, no. 114.
43. First group interview with residents, February 28, 2014, Qabo, no. 221.
44. First group interview with residents, February 28, 2014, Qabo, no. 221.
45. Interview with resident, March 13, 2014, Bere, no. 266.
46. Interview with DWNP deputy director, October 14, 2013, Gaborone, no. 15. See also T. Tebogo, "Controlling Human/Wildlife Conflict Remains Challenge," *Daily News* (Botswana), March 3, 2016.
47. Interview with resident, November 27, 2013, Xuoxao, no. 104.
48. Interview with resident, November 27, 2013, Xuoxao, no. 104.
49. Interview with MP, October 24, 2013, Maun, no. 20.
50. Interview with resident, December 12, 2013, Khwai, no. 139.
51. Interview with resident, November 25, 2013, Boro, no. 86.
52. C. Taylor, "Why Botswana's Election Could Be Decided by Elephants and Diamonds," BBC, October 22, 2019; P. Bax, "Elephants Can't Vote but They May Decide Botswana's Election," Bloomberg, May 16, 2019; R. Harvey, "Elephants Reduced to a Political Football as Botswana Brings Back Hunting," *The Conversation*, May 23, 2019.
53. L. De Waal, "Botswana Ignores Science and Reopens Hunting in Order to Gain Votes," *South African*, May 23, 2019.
54. Interview with resident, February 20, 2014, East Hanahai, no. 191. See also interview with residents, February 20, 2014, East Hanahai, no. 192.
55. While this analysis is based only on my own experience, it is possible to speculate that other Westerners interacting with these communities, most notably NGOs workers, may also be viewed as potential conduits to the Botswana state.

Chapter 4: Land and Ownership on the Conservation Estate

1. Fieldwork conversation with resident, March 4, 2014, Ghanzi District.
2. While seen as both ecologically important and potential economic boons, the delineation of WMAs severely limit the spectrum of possible livelihood options of those living inside them because, unlike other rural areas throughout the country, they are subject to control by the DWNP.
3. Interview with senior land officer, March 20, 2014, Ghanzi, no. 166.
4. Subterranean mineral resources remain state property throughout Botswana regardless of the land tenure regime.
5. Quoted in Zips-Mairitsch 2013, 262.

6. Interview with resident, December 12, 2013, Khwai, no. 139.
7. Interview with village *kgosi*, December 12, 2013, Khwai, no. 144.
8. Pan-San solidarities have not sprung up solely in response to contemporary politics but also have historical roots found in similarities in cosmological origin stories. Disparate groups across Botswana's north and west—the Bugakhwe, Ts'exa, Ju/'hoansi, Naro, and Hai//om—all have a similar origin story about the first man Khara/'una who comes from the Tsodilo Hills, an important spiritual location for many San groups, located in northwestern Botswana (Taylor 2000). Pan-San solidarity can be thought of not only as exclusively a reaction to the contemporary political situation but also as reflective of a connective history.
9. Parsons (2006) suggests that the late John Hardbattle, a key Naro San activist and organizer for the First People of the Kalahari, would not have wanted the movement for San recognition to become so narrowly focused on the CKGR alone, to the detriment of other issue areas. This is a sentiment that was echoed to me by one of his surviving family members. See interview with cattle farmer, March 1, 2014, Ghanzi, no. 227.
10. This is due in part to the acrimonious and antagonistic relationship that has developed between SI and the government of Botswana. See Solway 2009; Saugestad 2011.
11. Interview with resident, December 11, 2013, Khwai, no. 138.
12. Interview with resident, December 11, 2013, Khwai, no. 138.
13. Both communities are majority San, though the residents are from a different language group. The San of Khwai are Bugakhwe, and those from Mababe are Ts'exa.
14. Interview with resident, December 5, 2013, Mababe, no. 126.
15. Interview with resident, December 5, 2013, Mababe, no. 126.
16. Interview with resident, March 6, 2014, New Xade, no. 246.
17. Interview with DWNP CKGR liaison team, February 6, 2014, Ghanzi, no. 157.
18. Interview with cattle farmer and tourism operator, February 24, 2014, Ghanzi, no. 208.
19. Interview with DWNP official, November 15, 2013, Maun, no. 58.
20. Interview with cattle farmer and tourism operator, February 24, 2014, Ghanzi, no. 208.
21. Interview with cattle farmer and tourism operator, February 24, 2014, Ghanzi, no. 208.
22. Ministry of Environment, Wildlife and Tourism, "Hunting Ban in Botswana," news release, September 24, 2013, https://www.facebook.com/148228411926492/posts/press-release-hunting-ban-in-botswana-message-from-permanent-secretarythe-minist/500849569997706/.

23. See, e.g., the discussion of the ban in the 2014 State of the Nation address: "State of the Nation Address 2014," http://www.gov.bw/en/News/STATE-OF-THE-NATION-ADDRESS-BY-HIS-EXCELLENCY-LT-GEN-SERETSE-KHAMA-IAN-KHAMA/.
24. This is in contrast to subterranean mineral resources, which are invested with the state no matter what kind of land it sits under, often to the dismay of Ghanzi's private landowners. See interview with cattle farmer, March 1, 2014, Ghanzi, no. 227.
25. Interview with DWNP official, October 11, 2013, Gaborone, no. 13.
26. Interview with director of DWNP, March 28, 2014, Gaborone, no. 283.
27. Group interview with three white families from Ghanzi, March 16, 2014, Ghanzi, no. 268; interview with cattle farmer, February 17, 2014, Ghanzi, no. 173; interview with cattle farmer, March 10, 2014, Ghanzi, no. 249.
28. N. Ntibinyane, "Khama's Megaphone Diplomacy," Open Society Initiative for Southern Africa, October 4, 2013.
29. M. Mguni, "Mugabe Pokes Fun at Khama," *The Mmegi* (Gaborone), August 18, 2015; R. Gabathuse, "Khama's Diplomatic Tiff," *The Mmegi* (Gaborone), May 8, 2015; "Contrarian, Arrogant, and a Loner: Botswana's Khama Is Finally Thrust into the Spotlight; It Could Get Uncomfortable," *Mail & Guardian* (Johannesburg), August 23, 2015.
30. "Firebrand Malema Banned from Botswana," Yahoo News, September 12, 2014.
31. Group interview with three white families from Ghanzi, March 16, 2014, Ghanzi, no. 268.
32. Group interview with three white families from Ghanzi, March 16, 2014, Ghanzi, no. 268.
33. Interview with cattle farmer, February 17, 2014, Ghanzi, no. 173.
34. Interview with cattle farmer, February 14, 2014, Ghanzi, no. 170.
35. The Khama administration called for a rerun of the contested 2008 elections and declared that the 2013 polls were "not free and fair." "Botswana Faults Zimbabwe Election, Calls for Audit," Reuters, August 5, 2013.
36. Interview with hunting tourism operator, November 13, 2013, Maun, no. 54.
37. Interview with tourism operator, March 3, 2014, Ghanzi, no. 229.
38. First group interview with residents, February 28, 2014, Qabo, no. 221.
39. In early postcolonial development projects concerned with resettlement of so-called Remote Area Dwellers, the question of private property was inviolate. Land in western Botswana was not going to be given back to its original inhabitants, so government policy had to cultivate solutions to cope with a significant population of dispossessed citizens (Wily 1982). This situation, in part, motivated villagization policies commonplace in Botswana's western provinces.
40. Interview with San activist, January 23, 2014, Gaborone, no. 148.

41. Interview with MP, September 25, 2013, Gaborone, no. 8.
42. Interview with resident, March 13, 2014, Bere, no. 262.
43. A frequent term pejoratively used to describe non-African Batswana is "Motswana by papers," which implies a less "legitimate" kind of citizenship.
44. Interview with conservation practitioner, October 24, 2013, Maun, no. 19.
45. Interview with resident, March 13, 2014, Bere, no. 266.
46. The delineation of protected areas is not simply a colonial exercise. While all protected areas were gazetted prior to independence, WMAs were created in 1986, twenty years into Botswana's statehood. This decision more than doubled the size of the conservation estate.
47. Interview with San activist, January 23, 2014, Gaborone, no. 148.
48. Interview with resident, December 5, 2013, Mababe, no. 127.
49. Interviewees from both the DWNP and the community of private landowners agreed that there were limitations to the type of conservation restrictions that could be implemented on private land.
50. Interview with conservation practitioner, February 8, 2014, Maun, no. 158.
51. Interview with resident, March 5, 2014, New Xade, no. 239.
52. Interview with San activist, March 4, 2014, New Xade, no. 231.
53. Interview with resident, March 5, 2014, New Xade, no. 239.
54. Interview with DWNP CKGR liaison team, February 6, 2014, Ghanzi, no. 157. See also Poteete 2009a.
55. Interview with DWNP official, February 4, 2014, Ghanzi, no. 154.
56. Interview with Department of Forestry official, February 10, 2014, Ghanzi, no. 160.
57. Interview with resident, March 5, 2014, New Xade, no. 237.
58. Interview with resident, March 6, 2014, New Xade, no. 246.

Chapter 5: Infrastructure and the Contours of Settlement, Tourism, and Conservation

1. Portions of this chapter were published in Annette A. LaRocco, "Infrastructure, Wildlife Tourism, (Il)legible Populations: A Comparative Study of Two Districts in Contemporary Botswana," *Environment and Planning E: Nature and Space* 3, no. 4 (2020): 1074–95, © 2019 by the author, https://doi.org/10.1177/2514848619877083.
2. Mokoros are traditional dugout canoes used primarily by Bayei residents to navigate the delta. They have become a central feature of the tourism industry in the Okavango. See Mbaiwa and Darkoh 2009.
3. Interview with village *kgosana*, November 25, 2013, Boro. See also interview with resident, November 27, 2013, Xuoxao, no. 103.
4. The Ramsar Convention on Wetlands of International Importance Especially as Waterfowl Habitat enumerates ecologically significant wetland areas around the world. See https://www.ramsar.org/.

5. Interview with resident, March 4, 2014, New Xade, no. 233.
6. Fieldwork observations, January–March 2014, Ghanzi District.
7. Fieldwork observations, September–December 2013, Northwest District; fieldwork observations, January–March 2014, Ghanzi District.
8. Interview with resident and NGO employee, February 13, 2014, D'Kar, no. 169.
9. Interview with conservation practitioner, September 9, 2013, Gaborone, no. 2.
10. Interview with district development officer, February 5, 2014 Ghanzi, no. 156.
11. Fieldwork observations, March 2014, New Xade.
12. Interview with resident, March 6, 2014, New Xade, no. 242.
13. Interview with resident, March 6, 2014, New Xade, no. 243.
14. Interview with San activist, January 23, 2014, Gaborone, no. 148.
15. Interview with district development officer, February 5, 2014, Ghanzi, no. 156.
16. First group interview with residents, November 20, 2013, Sankuyo, no. 63.
17. Interview with village kgosi, November 19, 2013, Maun, no. 61.
18. Interview with resident, November 22, 2013, Sankuyo, no. 80.
19. Interview with resident, December 5, 2013, Mababe, no. 128.
20. *Makgoa* means either "white people" or "tourists," depending on the context. However, for all intents and purposes, the vast majority of tourists are white.
21. Interview with resident, November 26, 2013, Ditshiping, no. 95.
22. Both Xuoxao and Ditshiping are village members of the Okavango Kopano Mokoro Community Trust, which encompasses six delta villages that together had been allocated community rights to benefit from the resources in the Wildlife Management Area designated as NG32.
23. Botswana's Community-Based Natural Resource Management (CBNRM) policy empowers communities to create community-based organizations, often known as community trusts, to facilitate their participation in CBNRM.
24. Interview with resident, November 26, 2013, Ditshiping, no. 99.
25. Interview with resident, November 26, 2013, Ditshiping, no. 99.
26. Interview with resident, November 26, 2013, Ditshiping, no. 99.
27. Interview with DWNP official, November 11, 2013, Maun, no. 52; interview with Department of Forestry official, February 10, 2014, Ghanzi, no. 160.
28. Interview with MP, September 25, 2013, Gaborone, no. 8. The respondent's recitation of the distances between these villages is somewhat inaccurate. The distance between Mahalapye and Palapye is seventy-five kilometers. The distance between Palapye and Serowe is forty-five kilometers. However, the sentiment described remains apt.

29. However, many urban elites still have homesteads in these traditional villages.
30. Interview with resident, November 22, 2013, Sankuyo, no. 81.
31. Interview with resident, November 27, 2013, Xuoxao, no. 104.
32. Interview with resident, December 12, 2013, Khwai, no. 139. See also interview with resident, December 12, 2013, Khwai, no. 142.
33. Fieldwork observations September–December 2013, Northwest District.
34. Interview with resident, December 5, 2013, Mababe, no. 127.
35. Interview with photographic tourism operator, November 30, 2013, Maun, no. 111.
36. Interview with BTO official, November 8, 2013, Maun, no. 47.
37. Interview with BTO official, November 8, 2013, Maun, no. 47. This was echoed in Ditshiping, a village close to the core area of the delta.
38. Interview with resident, November 26, 2013, Ditshiping, no. 95.
39. Interview with resident, November 27, 2013, Xuoxao, no. 103.
40. Khwai Development Trust annual general meeting, December 10, 2013, Khwai.
41. From group interview with residents, November 27, 2013, Xuoxao, no. 106.

Chapter 6: Conservation Restrictions and the Construction of Criminalized Identities

1. Interview with village kgosi, February 18, 2014, West Hanahai, no. 174.
2. Where other authors or primary source material refer to this group as "Basarwa" or "RADs," I have left it as in the original.
3. Botswana categorically rejects any claims of indigeneity made by its citizens and the incumbent rights associated with indigeneity. A 2006 presidential press release stated, "Our contention as Botswana is that all black Africans are of African origin. It has to be appreciated that the situation in Africa is different from that of the Americas and Australia. Unlike in both North and Latin America and countries such as Australia and New Zealand, we did not emigrate from elsewhere in Africa, we have always belonged here" (quoted in Zips-Mairitsch 2013, 49; see also Ditshwanelo 2002).
4. The Harvard Kalahari Research Group, led by Richard B. Lee and Irven DeVore, began in the early 1960s and conducted anthropological research with the !Kung San in the Dobe area of northwestern Botswana.
5. Wilmsen's 1989 book *Land Filled with Flies: A Political Economy of the Kalahari* kicked off the Kalahari debate. Other well-known revisionists are James Denbow and Adam Kuper.
6. Interview with conservation practitioner, February 8, 2014, Maun, no. 158.
7. Interview with resident, March 4, 2014, New Xade, no. 232.
8. Interview with conservation practitioner, February 8, 2014, Maun, no. 158.

9. Interview with Department of Forestry official, February 10, 2014, Ghanzi, no. 160.
10. Interview with resident, November 27, 2013, Xuoxao, no. 101.
11. Interview with Department of Forestry official, February 10, 2014, Ghanzi, no. 160. Zips-Mairitsch (2013) says, "We should not forget, however, that these obligations only apply in the case of commercial use of resources. All citizens of Botswana enjoy the fundamental right of ensuring their subsistence" (265n32).
12. Interview with District Development officer, February 5, 2014, Ghanzi, no. 156.
13. Interview with resident, February 13, 2014, D'Kar, no. 169.
14. Fieldwork observations in Ghanzi District, January–March 2014.
15. Interview with residents, March 5, 2014, New Xade, no. 236.
16. Interview with village kgosi, February 18, 2014, West Hanahai Botswana, no. 174.
17. Interview with village kgosi, February 18, 2014, West Hanahai Botswana, no. 174.
18. Nustad (2015) also observes this in Isimangaliso (St. Lucia) Wetland Park in South Africa.
19. Interview with resident, March 13, 2014, Bere, no. 262.
20. Interview with resident, February 22, 2014, Kacgae, no. 201.
21. Interview with resident, February 20, 2014, East Hanahai, no. 191; interview with resident, December 3, 2013, Mababe, no. 117.
22. Interview with DWNP Community-Based Natural Resource Management officer, February 10, 2014, Ghanzi, no. 159.
23. Interview with conservation practitioner, February 8, 2014, Maun, no. 158.
24. Interview with resident, February 21, 2014, Kacgae, no. 195.
25. Interview with resident, February 19, 2014, West Hanahai, no. 179.
26. Interview with district development officer, February 5, 2014, Ghanzi, no. 156.
27. Interview with resident, February 18, 2014, West Hanahai, no. 178.
28. Interview with resident, February 19, 2014, West Hanahai, no. 186.
29. Fieldwork interviews with DWNP officials, February–March 2014, Ghanzi. See also Good 2002.
30. Interview with resident, February 19, 2014, West Hanahai, no. 179.
31. Interview with resident, March 13, 2014, Bere, no. 262.
32. Interview with resident, February 21, 2014, Kacgae, no. 195.
33. Interview with residents, February 21, 2014, Kacgae, no. 198.
34. Interview with regional wildlife officer, February 11, 2014, Ghanzi, no. 163.
35. Interview with residents, February 20, 2014, East Hanahai, no. 192. At the time of this research, one Botswana pula (BWP) was worth approximately $0.10. For context, 150 BWP is approximately $15. The maximum

month's wage in the government's Ipelegeng public works program at the time was 400 BWP ($40).
36. Interview with resident, February 19, 2014, West Hanahai, no. 186.
37. Some women have been savvy enough to acquire donor funding to bulk-buy eggshells, but they are the exception. I met one woman, relatively well educated and at ease using donor buzzwords in talking about her craft, who was able to secure funding from a South African organization to buy six kilograms of raw eggshells to make into beads. Conversations with resident, February 18–20, 2014, West Hanahai, no. 179.
38. Interview with resident, February 19, 2014, West Hanahai, no. 186.
39. Interview with resident, February 19, 2014, West Hanahai, no. 186.
40. Kiema 2010, 123.
41. Fieldwork observations, January–March 2014, Ghanzi District.
42. Interview with village *kgosana* (headman), March 11, 2014, Bere, no. 253. See also K. Pelontle, "Culture Has Commercial Value," *Daily News* (Gaborone), July 23, 2015.
43. One example among many is the Gaborone headquarters of the Botswana Tourism Organisation, which features San-inspired murals and art. Fieldwork observations. September 2013–March 2014. See also Zips-Mairitsch 2013.
44. "We Neither Hunt Naked nor with Bows and Arrows," *Sunday Standard* (Gaborone), December 8, 2014. An example from the private sector is the Grasslands Safari Lodge approximately eighty kilometers from Ghanzi Town. It was known for many years as the Grasslands Bushman Lodge and used stereotypical representations of San people in its logo and on other promotional material (like a large billboard on the Transkalahari Highway). The operation replaced the human figures in its logo with an oryx in 2022.
45. Interview with BTO official, February 10, 2014, Ghanzi, no. 161.
46. Interview with resident, February 21, 2014, Kacgae, no. 197.

Chapter 7: Promises of Modernity and Failures of Development on the Conservation Estate

1. Portions of this chapter were published in Annette A. LaRocco, "Botswana's Hunting Ban and the Transformation of Game-Meat Cultures, Economies and Ecologies," *Journal of Southern African Studies* 46, no. 4 (2020): 723–41, copyright © 2020 The Editorial Board of the Journal of Southern African Studies, reprinted by permission of Informa UK Limited, trading as Taylor &Francis Group, www.tandfonline.com, on behalf of The Editorial Board of the Journal of Southern African Studies.
2. "The Battle of Botswana's Big Men," *The Economist*, August 29, 2019.

3. S. O'Grady, "Botswana Overturns Ban on Hunting," *Washington Post*, May 23, 2019.
4. C. Torchia, "Botswana Hits Back at Critics on Anti-poaching Policy," Associated Press, September 9, 2018.
5. D. Carrington, "Wildlife Summit Votes Down Plan to Allow Sale of Huge Ivory Stockpile," *The Guardian*, August 22, 2019.
6. Interview with district development officer, February 5, 2014, Ghanzi, no. 156.
7. Lost in the commonplace subsistence/commercial hunting dichotomy are the nuanced views of hunting's sociocultural significance recounted by individuals living in the Botswana Kalahari ecosystem and described in this chapter and elsewhere. See, e.g., the description of San hunting practices in a memoir about Central Kalahari Game Reserve written by Kuela Kiema, a Kua San. He describes hunting as "a socio-economic and cultural activity that has been passed on from generation to generation ... for our economic and traditional welfare" (Kiema 2010, 145).
8. Interview with resident, February 19, 2014, West Hanahai, no. 184.
9. See, e.g., "Special Issue: Hunting in Contemporary Africa," *Journal of Contemporary African Studies* 34, no. 1 (2016).
10. See also "Special Issue: Farm Dwellers, the Forgotten People? Consequences of Conversions to Private Wildlife Production in South Africa," *Journal of Contemporary African Studies* 32, no. 2 (2014).
11. Government of Botswana, *Unified Hunting Regulations (Fauna Conservation Act)* (Government Printer: Gaborone, 1979).
12. This was a view still commonly expressed during my 2013–14 interviews with government officials in Gaborone as well as at district offices in Maun and Ghanzi Township.
13. Interview with local government official, February 10, 2014, Ghanzi, no. 160.
14. In interviews with government wildlife officials, hunting was frequently referred to as backwards and a relic of a time before Botswana became a middle-income country. See also *BTV News Special: London Conference on the Illegal Wildlife Trade*, BTV (Botswana), February 23, 2014.
15. Interview with director of DWNP, March 28, 2014, Gaborone, no. 283.
16. Interview with regional wildlife officer, February 11, 2014, Ghanzi, no. 163.
17. "Botswana to Ban Hunting over Wildlife Decline," BBC, November 29, 2012.
18. Government of Botswana, *Wildlife Conservation and National Parks Act*, Act No. 28 of 1992 (Gaborone: Government Printer, 1992).
19. Interview with DWNP official, September 25, 2013, Gaborone, no. 6.
20. Interview with DWNP deputy director, October 14, 2013, Gaborone, no. 15.

21. Interview with director of DWNP, March 28, 2014, Gaborone, no. 283.
22. Interview with regional wildlife officer, February 11, 2014, Ghanzi, no. 163.
23. Interview with resident, December 4, 2013, Mababe, no. 124.
24. Interview with cattle farmer and tourism operator, February 24, 2014, Ghanzi, no. 203.
25. Interview with local government official, February 10, 2014, Ghanzi, no. 160.
26. N. Onishi, "A Hunting Ban Saps a Village's Livelihood," *New York Times*, September 13, 2015.
27. Ministry of Environment, Natural Resources Conservation, and Tourism, "Press Conference on Lifting of Hunting Suspension," Facebook, May 23, 2019, https://www.facebook.com/BotswanaGovernment/videos/315050712720812/.
28. T. Marima, "In Botswana, Elephant Hunting Divides Opinion," Al Jazeera English, August 6, 2019; I. Selatlhwa, "Masisi Blasts the West over Hunting Ban," *The Monitor*, February 25, 2019; M. Masisi, "Hunting Elephants Will Help Them Survive," *Wall Street Journal*, June 19, 2019.
29. Ministry of Environment, Natural Resources Conservation, and Tourism, "Press Conference on Lifting of Hunting Suspension"; Botswana Government (@BWGovernment), "Lifting of Hunting Suspension and Creation of a Citizen Empowerment Model for Tourism in Botswana," Twitter, May 23, 2019, 11:37 a.m., https://twitter.com/BWGovernment/status/1131584923054350337.
30. Interview with resident, February 21, 2014, Kacgae, no. 196.
31. B. Keakabetse, "After Hunting Buzz, Reality Sinks In," *Mmegi* (Gaborone), September 27, 2019.
32. M. Dube, "Botswana Issues Elephant Hunting Licenses, First since 2014," Voice of America, September 23, 2019, https://www.voanews.com/.
33. Botswana Government, "Lifting of Hunting Suspension."
34. Keakabetse, "After Hunting Buzz, Reality Sinks In."
35. Keakabetse.
36. Keakabetse.
37. *BTV News Special: London Conference on the Illegal Wildlife Trade*.
38. *BTV News Special: London Conference on the Illegal Wildlife Trade*.
39. *BTV News Special: London Conference on the Illegal Wildlife Trade*.
40. Interview with village *kgosi*, February 18, 2014, West Hanahai, no. 174.
41. Interview with resident, December 10, 2013, Khwai, no. 133; interview with resident, December 4, 2013, Mababe, no. 124; interview with San activist, March 4, 2014, New Xade, no. 231.
42. Interview with resident, March 5, 2014, New Xade, no. 238.
43. From first group interview with residents, February 27, 2014, Groot Laagte, no. 213.

44. Interview with cattle farmer and tourism operator, February 24, 2014, Ghanzi, no. 203.
45. Fieldwork observations, January–March 2014, Ghanzi District.
46. *BTV News Special: London Conference on the Illegal Wildlife Trade.*
47. Botswana Government, "Lifting of Hunting Suspension"; author's personal correspondence.
48. Interview with San activist, January 23, 2014, Gaborone, no. 148.
49. Interview with community trust manager, November 28, 2013, Maun, no. 110.
50. From interview with residents, March 4, 2014, New Xade, no. 230. See also interview with resident, March 6, 2014, New Xade, no. 243.
51. This is not to suggest that non-San Batswana do not consume game meat. They do. In fact, game meat is a sought-after consumer item among tourists and many urban residents in Gaborone. However, the regular consumption of game meat for subsistence is regarded as at odds with an emphasis on agropastoralism.
52. Interview with district development officer, February 5, 2014, Ghanzi, no. 156.
53. Interview with resident, February 19, 2014, West Hanahai, no. 181.
54. My respondent provides a clear contrast with an anecdote provided by former president Khama in a nationally televized interview: "When I go to some kgotla meetings, I remember one I had in the Ghanzi District recently. One young person stood up and said, *gore* we don't want to be seen as people who live out here in the rural areas—only given certain programs for people who live remote type of lifestyle. We want to be in the mainstream of Botswana,' and that is our responsibility as a government to do." *BTV News Special: London Conference on the Illegal Wildlife Trade.*
55. Interview with resident, December 12, 2013, Khwai, no. 139.
56. Fieldwork observations, January–March 2014, Ghanzi District.
57. Interview with resident, December 5, 2013, Mababe, no. 126.
58. Interview with resident, February 28, 2014, Qabo, no. 222.
59. Interview with San activist, March 4, 2014, New Xade, no. 231.
60. Interview with resident, March 6, 2014, New Xade, no. 243. See another exchange with a resident in New Xade:

> "Interviewee: When I was a young man, before we were removed from Central [the CKGR], there were many animals. We didn't finish the animals because we know better. Our fathers and grandfathers taught us how to hunt the animals and not to finish them. But then the Bakwena and the Bangwaketse [two of the eight Tswana-speaking groups] came to the Central [CKGR] and made us their slaves and began to finish our animals.
>
> "Author: Why did the Bakwena and the Bangwaketse come from their lands to the CKGR?

"Interviewee: Why? Because they had finished all their animals! There were no animals left in their lands! The Tswana killed off their animals and then came to take ours. Now the government says the animals belong to the government and to the *lekgoa* [white people, meaning tourists]. But the only animals left are ours." Interview with resident, March 4, 2014, New Xade, no. 233.

61. One respondent suggested that those decision-makers from Gaborone were "as good as tourists" because they understood so little about life in the rural areas of Botswana. Interview with village *kgosana*, November 25, 2013, Boro, no. 82.
62. Interview with San activist, January 23, 2014, Gaborone, no. 148.
63. From first group interview with residents, February 18, 2014, West Hanahai, no. 178.
64. Interview with DWNP official, February 4, 2014, Ghanzi, no. 154.
65. AFP, "Farmers and Animals Struggle in Drought-Hit Botswana," Phys .org, August 30, 2019; M. Dube, "Botswana Drought Makes Wasteland of Harvests, Livestock," Voice of America, November 29, 2019.
66. "Pillars: Environment and Climate Change," Southern African Development Community, accessed October 13, 2023, https://www.sadc.int/pillars/environment-climate-change.
67. Interview with conservation practitioner, February 8, 2014, Maun, no. 158.
68. First group interview with residents, February 18, 2014, West Hanahai, no. 178.
69. Fieldwork interviews, March 2014, New Xade.
70. Interview with resident, March 4, 2014, New Xade, no. 232; interview with resident, March 5, 2014, New Xade, no. 238; see also Kiema 2010 for similar examples in his memoir.
71. Interview with resident, February 18, 2014, West Hanahai, no. 177.
72. Interview with resident, March 5, 2014, New Xade, no. 238.
73. Interview with resident, March 13, 2014, Bere, no. 264. See also "There is no meat. The government killed us," interview with resident, February 27, 2014, Groot Laagte, no. 217.
74. Interview with resident, February 19, 2014, West Hanahai, no. 179; interview with resident, February 18, 2014, West Hanahai, no. 177.
75. First group interview with residents, February 28, 2014, Qabo, no. 221.
76. Interview with village kgosana, February 20, 2014, East Hanahai, no. 194.
77. Interview with DWNP official, September 25, 2013, Gaborone, no. 6.
78. Interview with kgosana, February 26, 2014, Groot Laagte, no. 211.
79. Interview with regional wildlife officer, February 11, 2014, Ghanzi, no. 163.
80. Interview with DWNP official, October 16, 2013, Gaborone, no. 16.
81. Interview with social and community development officer, February 18, 2014, West Hanahai, no. 176.

82. Interview with DWNP official, November 7, 2013, Maun, no. 45.
83. Interview with UN official, January 22, 2014, Gaborone, no. 147.
84. To enter the EU market, meat must originate from an area that has been certified free of foot-and-mouth disease (FMD) for over a year. Exports are only permitted from areas where no cattle vaccines for FMD have been administered in the twelve months before export. Areas in the north where FMD is endemic are considered the "red zone." Surrounding the red zone is the "yellow zone," where cattle vaccination is required and then the "blue zone," which acts as a buffer. Areas of the country where export is permissible are part of the "green zone."
85. Second group interview with residents, November 27, 2013, Xuoxao, no. 106; interview with village kgosi, November 25, 2013, Boro, no. 82.
86. Interview with conservation biologist, October 25, 2013, Maun, no. 21.
87. Fieldwork interviews, March 2014, New Xade.
88. Interview with resident, December 4, 2013, Mababe, no. 122.
89. Interview with MP, September 25, 2013, Gaborone, no. 8.
90. Interview with village kgosi, November 19, 2013, Maun, no. 61.
91. E. Mmolai, "Lamentations of Ngami Pastoralists," *Daily News* (Gaborone), June 29, 2015.
92. Interview with MP, September 25, 2013, Gaborone, no. 8.
93. Interview with resident, November 27, 2013, Xuoxao, no. 102.
94. Interview with village kgosi, December 12, 2013, Khwai, no. 144.
95. Interview with conservation practitioner, November 5, 2013, Maun, no. 41.
96. Interview with MP, September 25, 2013, Gaborone, no. 8; interview with resident, November 21, 2013, Sankuyo, no. 71; Elephants like to eat cultivated grains like maize and sorghum when available. Interviewees believed that elephants remember where crop fields are and can sense when the harvest is ripe.
97. The use of chili peppers as deterrents have failed to live up to its promise. Interview with conservation practitioner, November 5, 2013, Maun, no. 41; K. Mpofu, "Ngamiland Jumbos Afraid of Chillies," *Mmegi* (Gaborone), March 12, 2010. Complaints that the chili pepper method is not working are often met with suggestions that people redouble their efforts. K. Pelontle, "Human-Wildlife Co-existence Possible," *Daily News* (Gaborone), October 16, 2014.
98. Interview with DWNP official, November 11, 2013, Maun, no. 50.
99. Interview with DWNP official, November 7, 2013, Maun, no. 45.
100. Interview with resident, October 31, 2013, Shakawe, no. 36.
101. Interview with resident, October 30, 2013, Shakawe, no. 32.
102. Interview with DWNP official, November 7, 2013, Maun, no. 45. Molepolole is closer to sixty kilometers from Gaborone, but I have left the quotation as original.

103. Interview with village kgosi, October 29, 2013, Shakawe, no. 24.
104. Backyard gardens are prominently featured in the state media (*Daily News* and Radio Botswana). A UN official working on the poverty-eradication portfolio in partnership with the Ministry of Finance and Development Planning recounted the ways in which the backyard gardening initiative was strongly promoted by government figures.
105. L. Morwaeng, "Backyard Garden Brings Hope to Kweneng Community," *Daily News* (Gaborone), March 17, 2015; K. Seatla, "Backyard Garden Uplifts Kedisitse," *Daily News* (Gaborone), August 30, 2015.
106. "Worst Drought in 34 Years to Hit Botswana—Meteorological Services," *Sunday Standard*, September 13, 2015; Botswana Press Agency (BOPA), "Khama Declares Drought," *Daily News* (Gaborone), June 28, 2015.
107. Interview with resident, February 22, 2014, Kacgae, no. 201. See also "Maun Residents Shoot Down Poverty Eradication Initiatives," *Sunday Standard*, April 2, 2015.
108. "Maun Residents Shoot Down Poverty Eradication Initiatives."
109. Interview with conservation practitioner, February 8, 2014, Maun, no. 158.
110. Interview with resident, December 9, 2013, Khwai, no. 130.
111. Interview with resident, February 20, 2014, East Hanahai, no. 191. See also interview with resident, December 4, 2013, Mababe, no. 122.
112. Interview with resident, March 12, 2014, Bere, no. 255.
113. Interview with San activist, March 4, 2014, New Xade, no. 231.

Conclusion

1. Interview with DWNP official, October 16, 2013, Gaborone, no. 16.
2. Interview with resident, November 25, 2013, Boro, no. 90. See also interview with resident, December 3, 2013, Mababe, no. 117; interview with resident, December 4, 2013, Mababe, no. 122.
3. Fieldnotes, June–July 2017, Gaborone.

References

Abrahamsen, R. 2005. "Blair's Africa: The Politics of Securitization and Fear." *Alternatives: Global, Local, Political* 30 (1): 55–80.
Abrams, P. 1988. "Notes on the Difficulty of Studying the State (1977)." *Journal of Historical Sociology* 1 (1): 58–89.
Acemoglu, D., Johnson, S., and Robinson, J. A. 2002. *An African Success Story: Botswana.* London: Centre for Economic Policy Research.
Adams, W. M. 2020. "Geographies of Conservation III: Nature's Spaces." *Progress in Human Geography* 44 (4): 789–801.
Adams, W. M., and Mulligan, M. 2003. *Decolonizing Nature: Strategies for Conservation in a Post-colonial Era.* London: Earthscan Publications.
Agamben, G. 2005. *State of Exception.* Chicago: University of Chicago Press.
Agbese, P. O., and Kieh, G. K. 2007. *Reconstituting the State of Africa.* New York: Palgrave Macmillan.
Alden, C., and Anseeuw, W. 2009. *Land, Liberation and Compromise in Southern Africa.* New York: Palgrave Macmillan.
Alden Wily, L. 2001. "Reconstructing the African Commons." *Africa Today* 48 (1): 76–99.
———. 2008. "Custom and Commonage in Africa: Rethinking the Orthodoxies." *Land Use Policy* 25 (1): 43–52.
Alexander, J. 2006. *The Unsettled Land: State-Making and the Politics of Land in Zimbabwe, 1893–2003.* Oxford, UK: James Currey.
Amanor, K., and Moyo, S. 2008. *Land and Sustainable Development in Africa.* London: Zed Books.
Anand, N. 2017. *Hydraulic City: Water and the Infrastructures of Citizenship in Mumbai.* Durham, NC: Duke University Press.
Anderson, B. 1982. *Imagined Communities: Reflections on the Origin and Spread of Nationalism.* London: Verso.
Anderson, D. 2002. *Eroding the Commons: The Politics of Ecology in Baringo, Kenya, 1890s–1963.* Oxford, UK: James Currey.

Apostolopoulou, E., Chatzimentor, A., Maestre-Andrés, S., Requena-i-Mora, M., Alejandra Pizarro, A., and Bormpoudakis, D. 2021. "Reviewing 15 Years of Research on Neoliberal Conservation: Towards a Decolonial, Interdisciplinary, Intersectional and Community-Engaged Research Agenda." *Geoforum*, no. 124, 236–56.

Armstrong, S., and Bennett, O. 2002. "Representing the Resettled: The Ethical Issues Raised by Research and Representation of the San." In Chatty and Colchester, *Conservation and Mobile Indigenous Peoples*, 188–201.

Atlhopheng, J., and Mulale, K. 2009. "Natural Resource-Based Tourism and Wildlife Policies in Botswana." In Saarinen, *Sustainable Tourism in Southern Africa*, 134–49.

Awiti, A. O. 2012. "Stewardship of National Parks and Reserves in the Era of Global Change." *Environmental Development* 1 (1): 102–6.

Badiey, N. 2013. "The Strategic Instrumentalization of Land Tenure in 'State-Building': The Case of Juba, South Sudan." *Africa* 83 (1): 57–77.

Barnard, A. 1980. "Basarwa Settlement Patterns in the Ghanzi Ranching Area." *Botswana Notes and Records*, no. 12, 137–49.

———. 2006. "Kalahari Revisionism, Vienna and the 'Indigenous Peoples' Debate." *Social Anthropology* 14 (1): 1–16.

Barnes, J. J. 1991. "Development of Botswana's Wildlife Resources as a Tourist Attraction." In Pfotenhauer, *Tourism in Botswana*, 346–69.

———. 2001. "Economic Returns and Allocations of Resources in the Wildlife Sector of Botswana." *South African Journal of Wildlife Research* 31 (3/4): 141–53.

Bates, R. H. 1981. *Markets and States in Tropical Africa: The Political Basis of Agricultural Policies*. Berkeley: University of California Press.

Bauer, G., and Taylor, S. D. 2005. *Politics in Southern Africa: State and Society in Transition*. Boulder, CO: Lynne Rienner.

Beinart, W. 2003. *The Rise of Conservation in South Africa: Settlers, Livestock, and the Environment 1770–1950*. Oxford: Oxford University Press.

Beinart, W., and Hughes, L. 2007. *Environment and Empire*. Oxford: Oxford University Press.

Bennett, B. S. 2002. "Some Historical Background on Minorities in Botswana." In Mazonde, *Minorities in the Millennium*, 5–16.

Berry, S. 1993. *No Condition Is Permanent: The Social Dynamics of Agrarian Change in Sub-Saharan Africa*. Madison: University of Wisconsin Press.

———. 2009. "Property, Authority and Citizenship: Land Claims, Politics and the Dynamics of Social Divisions in West Africa." *Development and Change* 40 (1): 23–45.

Biersteker, T. J., and Weber, C. 1996. *State Sovereignty as Social Construct*. Cambridge: Cambridge University Press.

Blaikie, P. 2006. "Is Small Really Beautiful? Community-Based Natural Resource Management in Malawi and Botswana." *World Development* 34 (11): 1942–57.

Bluwstein, J., and Lund, J. F. 2018. "Territoriality by Conservation in the Selous-Niassa Corridor in Tanzania." *World Development*, no. 101, 453–65.

Bocarejo, D., and Ojeda, D. 2016. "Violence and Conservation: Beyond Unintended Consequences and Unfortunate Coincidences." *Geoforum*, no. 69, 176–83.

Bodilenyane, K. 2012. "Botswana's Executive President: Implications for Democracy." *Journal of Public Administration and Governance* 2 (4): 188–201.

Bolaane, M. M. 2013. *Chiefs, Hunters and San in the Creation of the Moremi Game Reserve, Okavango Delta: Multiracial Interactions and Initiatives, 1956–1979*. Osaka: National Museum of Ethnology.

Boone, C. 2003. *Political Topographies of the African State: Territorial Authority and Institutional Choice*. Cambridge: Cambridge University Press.

———. 2007. "Property and Constitutional Order: Land Tenure Reform and the Future of the African State." *African Affairs* 106 (425): 557–86.

———. 2013. "Land Regimes and the Structure of Politics: Patterns of Land-Related Conflict." *Africa* 83 (1): 188–203.

———. 2014. *Property and Political Order in Africa: Land Rights and the Structure of Politics*. Cambridge Studies in Comparative Politics. Cambridge: Cambridge University Press.

Boone, C., and Lund, C. 2013. "Introduction: Land Politics in Africa—Constituting Authority over Territory, Property and Persons." *Africa* 83 (1): 1–13.

Borras, S. M., Hall, R., Scoones, I., White, B., and Wolford, W. 2011. "Towards a Better Understanding of Global Land Grabbing: An Editorial Introduction." *Journal of Peasant Studies* 38 (2): 209–16.

Botlhomilwe, M. Z., and Sebudubudu, D. 2011. "Limited Freedom and Intolerance in Botswana." *Journal of Contemporary African Studies* 29 (3): 331–48.

Bourdieu, P. 1977. *Outline of a Theory of Practice*. Translated by Richard Nice. Cambridge: Cambridge University Press.

———. 1991. *Language and Symbolic Power*. Cambridge, MA: Harvard University Press.

Brandt, F. 2016. "Power Battles on South African Trophy-Hunting Farms: Farm Workers, Resistance and Mobility in the Karoo." *Journal of Contemporary African Studies* 34 (1): 165–81.

Brockington, D. 2002. *Fortress Conservation: The Preservation of the Mkomazi Game Reserve, Tanzania*. Oxford, UK: James Currey.

———. 2005. "The Contingency of Community Conservation." In *Rural Resources and Local Livelihoods in Africa*, edited by Homewood, K., 100–120. New York: Palgrave Macmillan.

———. 2009. *Celebrity and the Environment: Fame, Wealth and Power in Conservation*. London: Zed Books.
Brockington, D., and Duffy, R. 2011. *Capitalism and Conservation*. Chichester, UK: Wiley-Blackwell.
Brockington, D., Duffy, R., and Igoe, J. 2008. *Nature Unbound: Conservation, Capitalism and the Future of Protected Areas*. London: Earthscan.
Brockington, D., and Scholfield, K. 2010. "The Work of Conservation Organisations in Sub-Saharan Africa." *Journal of Modern African Studies* 48 (1): 1–33.
Brown, C. 2020. "Botswana Votes 2019: Two-Party Competition and the Khama Factor." *Journal of Southern African Studies* 46 (4): 703–22.
Brownlie, S., and Botha, M. 2009. "Biodiversity Offsets: Adding to the Conservation Estate, or 'No Net Loss'?" *Impact Assessment and Project Appraisal* 27 (3): 227–31.
Bugday, A. 2016. "Environmental Problems and Surge in Civil-Military Cooperation: The Case of the Botswana Defence Force." *Armed Forces and Society* 42 (1): 192–210.
Büscher, B. 2016. "'Rhino Poaching Is Out of Control!' Violence, Race and the Politics of Hysteria in Online Conservation." *Environment and Planning A* 48 (5): 979–98.
Büscher, B., Dressler, W. H., and Fletcher, R. 2019. *Nature Inc: Environmental Conservation in the Neoliberal Age*. Tucson: University of Arizona Press.
Büscher, B., and Fletcher, R. 2015. "Accumulation by Conservation." *New Political Economy* 20 (2): 273–98.
———. 2018. "Under Pressure: Conceptualising Political Ecologies of Green Wars." *Conservation and Society* 16 (2): 105–13.
———. 2019. "Towards Convivial Conservation." *Conservation and Society* 17 (3): 283–96.
———. 2020. *The Conservation Revolution: Radical Ideas for Saving Nature beyond the Anthropocene*. London: Verso.
Büscher, B., Fletcher, R., Brockington, D., Sandbrook, C., Adams, W. M., Campbell, L., Corson, C., Dressler, W., Duffy, R., Gray, N., Holmes, G., Kelly, A., Lunstrum, E., Ramutsindela, M., and Shanker, K. 2017. "Half-Earth or Whole Earth? Radical Ideas for Conservation, and Their Implications." *Oryx*, no. 51, 407–10.
Büscher, B., and Ramutsindela, M. 2016. "Green Violence: Rhino Poaching and the War to Save Southern Africa's Peace Parks." *African Affairs* 115 (458): 1–22.
Butcher, J. 2007. *Ecotourism, NGOs and Development: A Critical Analysis*. London: Routledge.
Butt, B. 2012. "Commoditizing the Safari and Making Space for Conflict: Place, Identity and Parks in East Africa." *Political Geography* 31 (2): 104–13.

Buzan, B., Wæver, O., and de Wilde, J. 1998. *Security: A New Framework for Analysis*. Boulder, CO: Lynne Rienner.

Cafaro, P., Butler, T., Crist, E., Cryer, P., Dinerstein, E., Kopnina, H., and Noss, R. 2017. "If We Want a Whole Earth, Nature Needs Half: A Response to Büscher et Al." *Oryx* 51 (3): 400.

Campbell, A. 2004. "Establishment of Botswana's National Park and Game Reserve System." *Botswana Notes and Records*, no. 36, 55–66.

Carruthers, J. 1995. *The Kruger National Park: A Social and Political History*. Scottsville, South Africa: University of Natal Press.

———. 2012. "Environmental History in Africa." In *A Companion to Global Environmental History*, edited by McNeil, J. R., and Mauldin, E. S., 96–115. Chichester, UK: Blackwell.

Castree N. 2008. "Neoliberalising Nature: Processes, Effects, and Evaluations." *Environment and Planning A: Economy and Space* 40 (1): 153–73.

Cavanagh, C., and Benjaminsen, T. 2014. "Virtual Nature, Violent Accumulation: The 'Spectacular Failure' of Carbon Offsetting at a Ugandan National Park." *Geoforum*, no. 56, 55–65.

Chalfin, B. 2010. *Neoliberal Frontiers: An Ethnography of Sovereignty in West Africa*. Chicago: University of Chicago Press.

Chatty, D., and Colchester, M. 2002. *Conservation and Mobile Indigenous Peoples: Displacement, Forced Settlement, and Sustainable Development*. New York: Berghahn Books.

Chebanne, A. M. 2003. "The Dangers of Ethnic Groups Relocation: The Case of the CKGR Khoe and San Communities." *Botswana Notes and Record*, no. 35, 89–97.

Clapham, C. 1996. *Africa and the International System: The Politics of State Survival*. Cambridge: Cambridge University Press.

Clark, C. J., Poulsen, J. R., Malonga, R., and Elkan, P. W. 2009. "Logging Concessions Can Extend the Conservation Estate for Central African Tropical Forests." *Conservation Biology* 23 (5): 1281–93.

Cloete, E. 2008. "Africa's 'Charismatic Megafauna' and Berlin's 'Two Concepts of Liberty': Postcolony Routes to Utopia?" *Politikon* 35 (3): 257–76.

Cook, A., and Sarkin, J. 2010. "Is Botswana the Miracle of Africa? Democracy, the Rule of Law, and Human Rights versus Economic Development." *Current Law Journal* 19 (2): 453–89.

Corson, C. 2010. "Shifting Environmental Governance in a Neoliberal World: US AID for Conservation." *Antipode* 42 (3): 576–602.

Corson, C., Gruby, R., Witter, R., Hagerman, S., Suarez, D., Greenberg, S., Bourque, M., Grayh, N., and Campbell, L. M. 2014. "Everyone's Solution? Defining and Redefining Protected Areas at the Convention on Biological Diversity." *Conservation and Society* 12 (2): 190–202.

Damonte, G. N. 2016. "The 'Blind' State: Government Quest for Formalization and Conflict with Small-Scale Miners in the Peruvian Amazon." *Antipode* 48 (4): 956–76.

Danevad, A. 1995. "Responsiveness in Botswana Politics: Do Elections Matter?" *Journal of Modern African Studies* 33 (3): 381–402.

Das, V., and Poole, D. 2004. *Anthropology in the Margins of the State*. Santa Fe, NM: School of America Research Press.

Datta, K., and Murray, A. 1989. "The Rights of Minorities and Subject Peoples in Botswana: A Historical Evaluation." In Molutsi and Holm, *Democracy in Botswana*, 58–73.

Death, C. 2016a. "Green States in Africa: Beyond the Usual Suspects." *Environmental Politics* 25 (1): 116–35.

———. 2016b. *The Green State in Africa*. New Haven, CT: Yale University Press.

De Bont, R. 2017. "A World Laboratory: Framing the Albert National Park." *Environmental History* 22 (3): 404–32.

de Jager, N., and du Toit, P. 2012. Introduction to *Friend or Foe? Dominant Party Systems in Southern Africa: Insights from the Developing World*, edited by de Jager, N., and du Toit, P. Tokyo: United Nations University Press.

de Jager, N., and Sebudubudu, D. 2017. "Towards Understanding Botswana and South Africa's Ambivalence to Liberal Democracy." *Journal of Contemporary African Studies* 35 (1): 15–33.

de Jager, N., and Taylor, I. 2015. "Democratic Contestation in Botswana." In *Democratic Contestation on the Margins: Regimes in Small African Countries*, edited by Metelits, C., and Matti, S., 25–48. Lanham, MD: Lexington Books.

DeMotts, R., Haller, T., Hoon, P., and Saum, R. 2009. "Dynamics of Common Pool Resource Management in the Okavango Delta, Botswana." *Development Southern Africa* 26 (4): 569–83.

DeMotts, R., and Hoon, P. 2012. "Whose Elephants? Conserving, Compensating, and Competing in Northern Botswana." *Society and Natural Resources* 25 (9): 1–15.

Devine, J. 2014. "Counterinsurgency Ecotourism in Guatemala's Maya Biosphere Reserve." *Environment and Planning D* 32 (6): 984–1001.

Devine, J., and Baca, J. 2020. "The Political Forest in the Era of Green Neoliberalism." *Antipode* 52 (4): 911–27.

Dietz, R. W., and Czech, B. 2005. "Conservation Deficits for the Continental United States: An Ecosystem Gap Analysis." *Conservation Biology* 19 (5): 1478–87.

Dominguez, L., and Luoma, C. 2020. "Decolonising Conservation Policy: How Colonial Land and Conservation Ideologies Persist and Perpetuate Indigenous Injustices at the Expense of the Environment." *Land* 9 (65): 1–22.

Dongol, Y., and Neumann, R. 2021. "Statemaking through Conservation: The Case of Post-conflict Nepal." *Political Geography*, no. 85, 1–13.
Doty, R. 1996. *Imperial Encounters. The Politics of Representation in North-South Relations*. Minneapolis: University of Minnesota Press.
Dowie, M. 2009. *Conservation Refugees: The Hundred-Year Conflict between Global Conservation and Native Peoples*. Cambridge, MA: MIT Press.
Duffy, R. 2002. *A Trip Too Far: Ecotourism, Politics, and Exploitation*. London: Earthscan.
———. 2010. *Nature Crime: How We're Getting Conservation Wrong*. New Haven, CT: Yale University Press.
———. 2014. "Waging a War to Save Biodiversity: The Rise of Militarized Conservation." *International Affairs* 90 (4): 819–34.
———. 2016. "War, by Conservation." *Geoforum*, no. 69, 238–48.
Duffy, R., Massé, F., Smidt, E., Marijnen, E., Büscher, B., Verweijen, J., Ramutsindela, M., et al. 2019. "Why We Must Question the Militarisation of Conservation." *Biological Conservation*, no. 232, 66–73.
Duffy, R., St. John, F., Büscher, B., and Brockington, D. 2015. "The Militarisation of Anti-Poaching: Undermining Long Term Goals?" *Environmental Conservation* 42 (4): 345–48.
Dunlap, A., and Fairhead, J. 2014. "The Militarisation and Marketisation of Nature: An Alternative Lens to 'Climate-Conflict.'" *Geopolitics* 19 (4): 937–61.
Dunn, K. C. 2001. "Madlib #32: The (Blank) African State; Rethinking the Sovereign State in International Relations Theory." In *Africa's Challenge to International Relations Theory*, edited by Dunn, K. C., and Shaw, T. M., 46–63. Basingstoke, UK: Palgrave Macmillan.
———. 2009. "Contested State Spaces: African National Parks and the State." *European Journal of International Relations* 15 (3): 423–46.
Dutta, A. 2020. "Forest Becomes Frontline: Conservation and Counterinsurgency in a Space of Violent Conflict in Assam, Northeast India." *Political Geography* 77 (102117): 1–10.
Dwyer, M., Ingalls, M., and Baird, I. 2016. "The Security Exception: Development and Militarization in Laos's Protected Areas." *Geoforum*, no. 69, 207–17.
Dzingirai, V. 2003. "The New Scramble for the African Countryside." *Development and Change* 34 (2): 243–63.
Ellis, S. 1994. "Of Elephants and Men: Politics and Nature Conservation in South Africa." *Journal of Southern African Studies* 20 (1): 53–69.
Engel, U., and Nugent, P. 2010. *Respacing Africa*. Boston: Brill.
Eriksen, S. S. 2011. "Regimes, Constituencies and the Politics of State Formation: Zimbabwe and Botswana Compared." *International Political Science Review* 33 (3): 261–78.

Fairhead, J., Leach, M., and Scoones, I. 2012 "Green Grabbing: A New Appropriation of Nature?" *Journal of Peasant Studies*, no. 39, 237–61.

Fawcus, P., and Tilbury, A. 2000. *Botswana: The Road to Independence*. Gaborone: Pula Press and Botswana Society.

Ferguson, J. 2005. "Seeing like an Oil Company: Space, Security, and Global Capital in Neoliberal Africa." *American Anthropologist* 107 (3): 377–82.

Ferketic, J. S., Latimer, A. M., and Silander, J. A. 2010. "Conservation Justice in Metropolitan Cape Town: A Study at the Macassar Dunes Conservation Area." *Biological Conservation* 143 (5): 1168–74.

Fletcher, R. 2010. "Neoliberal Environmentality: Towards a Poststructuralist Political Ecology of the Conservation Debate." *Conservation and Society* 8 (3): 171–81.

Floyd, R. 2010. *Security and the Environment: Securitisation Theory and US Environmental Security Policy*. Cambridge: Cambridge University Press.

Fox, G. R. 2018. "The 2017 Shooting of Kuki Gallmann and the Politics of Conservation in Northern Kenya." *African Studies Review*, no. 61, 210–36.

Fuller, R. A., McDonald-Madden, E., Wilson, K. A., Carwardine, J., Grantham, H. S., Watson, J. E., Klein, C. J., Green, D. C., and Possingham, H. P. 2010. "Replacing Underperforming Protected Areas Achieves Better Conservation Outcomes." *Nature* 466 (7304): 365–67.

Gabay, C., and Death, C., eds. 2014. *Critical Perspectives on African Politics*. Oxford: Routledge.

Gadd, M. E. 2005. "Conservation Outside of Parks: Attitudes of Local People in Laikipia, Kenya." *Environmental Conservation* 32 (1): 50–63.

Gardner, B. 2017. "Elite Discourses of Conservation in Tanzania." *Social Semiotics* 27 (3): 348–58.

Garland, E. 2008. "The Elephant in the Room: Confronting the Colonial Character of Wildlife Conservation in Africa." *African Studies Review* 51 (3): 51–74.

Gibson, C. C. 1999. *Politicians and Poachers: The Political Economy of Wildlife Policy in Africa*. Cambridge: Cambridge University Press.

Gillett, S. 1970. "Notes on the Settlement in the Ghanzi District." *Botswana Notes and Records*, no. 4, 52–55.

Gissibl, B., Hohler, S., and Kupper, P., eds. 2012. *Civilizing Nature: National Parks in Global Historical Perspective*. Oxford: Berghahn Books.

Gladney, D. C. 1998. *Making Majorities: Constituting the Nation in Japan, Korea, China, Malaysia, Fiji, Turkey, and the United States*. Stanford, CA: Stanford University Press.

Gohain, S. 2019. "Selective Access: or, How States Make Remoteness." *Social Anthropology* 27 (2): 204–20.

Gombay, N. 2014. "'Poaching'—What's in a Name? Debates about Law, Property, and Protection in the Context of Settler Colonialism." *Geoforum*, no. 55, 1–12.

Good, K. 1992. "Interpreting the Exceptionality of Botswana." *Journal of Modern African Studies* 30 (1): 69–95.

———. 1993. "At the Ends of the Ladder: Radical Inequalities in Botswana." *Journal of Modern African Studies* 3 (2): 203–30.

———. 1996. "Authoritarian Liberalism: A Defining Characteristic of Botswana." *Journal of Contemporary African Studies* 14 (1): 29–51.

———. 1999. "Enduring Elite Democracy in Botswana." *Democratization* 6 (1): 50–66.

———. 2002. *The Liberal Model and Africa: Elites against Democracy*. New York: Palgrave.

———. 2008. *Diamonds, Dispossession and Democracy in Botswana*. Oxford: James Currey.

———. 2009. "The Presidency of General Ian Khama: The Militarization of the Botswana 'Miracle.'" *African Affairs* 109 (435): 315–24.

Good, K., and Taylor, I. 2007. "Mounting Repression in Botswana." *Commonwealth Journal of International Affairs* 96 (390): 275–87.

———. 2008. "Botswana: A Minimalist Democracy." *Democratization* 15 (4): 750–65.

Gressier, C. 2011. "Safaris into Subjectivity: White Locals, Black Tourists, and the Politics of Belonging in the Okavango Delta, Botswana." *Identities: Global Studies in Culture and Power* 18 (4): 352–76.

———. 2014. "Experiential Autochthony in the Okavango Delta, Botswana." *Anthropological Forum: A Journal of Social Anthropology and Comparative Sociology* 24 (1): 1–20.

———. 2015. *At Home in the Okavango: White Batswana Narratives of Emplacement and Belonging*. New York: Berghahn Books.

Griffiths, I. L. 1995. *The African Inheritance*. London: Routledge.

Grove, R. 1995. *Green Imperialism: Colonial Expansion, Tropical Island Edens and the Origins of Environmentalism, 1600–1800*. Cambridge: Cambridge University Press.

Grovogui, S. N. 2001. "Sovereignty in Africa: Quasi-statehood and Other Myths in International Relations Theory." In *Africa's Challenge to International Relations Theory*, edited by Dunn, K. C., and Shaw, T. M., 29–45. Basingstoke, UK: Palgrave Macmillan.

Gulbrandsen, Ø. 1995. "'The King Is King by the Grace of the People': Control and Exercise of Power in Subject-Ruler Relations." *Comparative Studies in Society and History* 37 (3): 415–44.

———. 1996. "Living Their Lives in Courts: Counter-hegemonic Force of the Tswana *Kgotla* in the Bechuanaland Protectorate." In *Inside and Outside the Law*, edited by Harris, O., 125–56. London: Routledge.

———. 2012. *The State and the Social: State Formation in Botswana and Its Precolonial and Colonial Genealogies*. Oxford: Berghahn.

Gupta, A. 2015. "An Anthropology of Electricity from the Global South." *Cultural Anthropology*, no. 30, 555–68.

Gupta, A., and Ferguson, J. 1992. "Beyond 'Culture': Space, Identity, and the Politics of Difference." *Cultural Anthropology* 7 (1): 6–23.

Hagmann, T., and Péclard, D. 2011. *Negotiating Statehood: Dynamics of Power and Domination in Africa*. Chichester, UK: Wiley-Blackwell.

Hall, R. 2011. "Land-Grabbing in Southern Africa: The Many Faces of the Investor Rush." *Review of African Political Economy* 38 (12): 193–214.

Hambira, W. L., Saarinen, J., and Moses, O. 2020. "Climate Change Policy in a World of Uncertainty: Changing Environment, Knowledge, and Tourism in Botswana." *African Geographical Review* 39 (3): 252–66.

Hansen, L. 2012. "Reconstructing Desecuritisation: The Normative-Political in the Copenhagen School and Directions for How to Apply It." *Review of International Studies* 38 (3): 525–46.

Hansen, T. B., and Stepputat, F. 2001. Introduction to *States of Imagination: Ethnographic Explorations of the Postcolonial State*, edited by Hansen, T. B., and Stepputat, F., 1–38. Durham, NC: Duke University Press.

Harvey, D. 2006. *The Limits to Capital*. New York: Verso.

Harvey, P., and Knox, H. 2015. *Roads: An Anthropology of Infrastructure and Expertise*. Ithaca, NY: Cornell University Press.

Helle-Valle, J. 2002. "Seen from Below: Concepts of Politics and the State in a Village in Botswana." *Africa* 72 (2): 179–202.

Hendlin, Y. H. 2014. "From Terra Nullius to Terra Communis: Reconsidering Wild Land in an Era of Conservation and Indigenous Rights." *Environmental Philosophy* 11 (2): 141–74.

Henk, D. 2007. *The Botswana Defence Force in the Struggle for an African Environment*. New York: Palgrave Macmillan.

Herbst, J. I. 2000. *States and Power in Africa: Comparative Lessons in Authority and Control*. Princeton, NJ: Princeton University Press.

Hermans, J. 1977. "Official Policy towards the Bushmen of Botswana: A Review, Part I." *Botswana Notes and Records*, no. 9, 55–67.

Hillbom, E. 2008. "Diamonds or Development? A Structural Assessment of Botswana's Forty Years of Success." *Journal of Modern African Studies* 46 (2): 191–214.

———. 2011. "Botswana: A Development-Oriented Gate-Keeping State." *African Affairs* 111 (442): 67–89.

———. 2012. "Botswana: A Development-Oriented Gate-Keeping State; A Reply to Ian Taylor." *African Affairs* 111 (444): 477–82.

Hitchcock, R. K. 1991. "Tourism and Sustainable Development among Remote Area Populations in Botswana." In Pfotenhauer, *Tourism in Botswana*, 161–72.

———. 1996. "Subsistence Hunting and Special Game Licenses in Botswana." *Botswana Notes and Records*, no. 28, 55–64.

———. 1999. "A Chronology of Major Events Relating to the Central Kalahari Game Reserve." *Botswana Notes and Records*, no. 31, 105–17.

———. 2001. "'Hunting Is Our Heritage': The Struggle for Hunting and Gathering Rights among the San of Southern Africa." In Anderson and Ikeya, *Parks, Property, and Power*, 139–56.

———. 2002. "'We Are the First People': Land, Natural Resources and Identity in the Central Kalahari, Botswana." *Journal of Southern African Studies* 28 (4): 797–824.

———. 2006. "'We Are the Owners of the Land': The San Struggle for the Kalahari and Its Resources" In *Updating the San: Image and Reality of an African People in the 21st Century*, edited by Hitchcock, R. K., Ikeya, K., Biesele, M., and Lee, R. B., 229–56. Osaka: National Museum of Ethnology.

Hitchcock, R. K., and Holm, J. D. 1993. "Bureaucratic Domination of Hunter-Gatherer Societies: A Study of the San in Botswana." *Development and Change* 24 (2): 305–38.

Hitchcock, R. K., Ikeya, K., Biesele, M., and Lee, R. B. 2006. Introduction to *Updating the San: Image and Reality of an African People in the 21st Century*, edited by Hitchcock, R. K., Ikeya, K., Biesele, M., and Lee, R. B., 1–42. Osaka: National Museum of Ethnology.

Hitchcock, R. K., Johnson, M., and Haney, C. E. 2004. "Indigenous Women in Botswana: Changing Gender Roles in the Face of Dispossession and Modernization." In Hitchcock and Vinding, *Indigenous Peoples' Rights in Southern Africa*, 166–82.

Hitchcock, R. K., Sapignoli, M., and Babchuk, W. A. 2011. "What about Our Rights? Settlements, Subsistence and Livelihood Security among Central Kalahari San and Bakgalagadi." *International Journal of Human Rights* 15 (1): 62–88.

Hitchcock, R. K., and Vinding, D. 2001. "A Chronology of Major Events Relating to the Central Kalahari Game Reserve II: An Update." *Botswana Notes and Record*, no. 33, 61–72.

———, eds. 2004. *Indigenous Peoples' Rights in Southern Africa*. Copenhagen: International Work Group for Indigenous Affairs.

Hodgetts, T., Burnham, D, Dickman, A., Macdonald, E., and Macdonald, D. 2019. "Conservation Geopolitics." *Conservation Biology* 33 (2): 250–59.

Holmes, G. 2011. "Conservation's Friends in High Places: Neoliberalism, Networks, and the Transnational Conservation Elite." *Global Environmental Politics* 11 (4): 1–21.

Holmes, G., and Cavanagh, C. 2016. "A Review of the Social Impacts of Neoliberal Conservation: Formations, Inequalities, Contestations." *Geoforum*, no. 75, 199–209.

Homewood, K., and Sullivan, S. 2004. "Natural Resources: Use, Access, Tenure and Management." In *Eastern and Southern Africa: Development*

Challenges in a Volatile Region, edited by Potts, D., and Bowyer-Bower, T. A. S., 118–66. New York: Pearson Education.

Hoon, P. and Maclean, L. M. 2014. "Introduction: The Politics of Local Communities and the State in Africa." *African Studies Quarterly* 15 (1): 1–11.

Hübschle, A. 2017. "The Social Economy of Rhino Poaching: Of Economic Freedom Fighters, Professional Hunters and Marginalized Local People." *Current Sociology* 65 (3): 427–47.

Hughes, D. M. 2010. *Whiteness in Zimbabwe: Race, Landscape, and the Problem of Belonging*. New York: Palgrave Macmillan.

Hulme, D., and Murphree, M. 1999. "Communities, Wildlife and the 'New Conservation' in Africa." *Journal of International Development* 11 (2): 277–85.

Hwedi, O. 2001. "The State and Development in Southern Africa: A Comparative Analysis of Botswana and Mauritius with Angola, Malawi and Zambia." *African Studies Quarterly* 5 (1): 19–31.

Igoe, J. 2010. "The Spectacle of Nature in the Global Economy of Appearances: Anthropological Engagements with the Spectacular Mediations of Transnational Conservation." *Critique of Anthropology*, no. 30, 375–97.

———. 2017. *The Nature of Spectacle: On Images, Money, and Conserving Capitalism*. Tucson: University of Arizona Press.

Igoe, J., Neves, K., and Brockington, D. 2010. "A Spectacular Eco-tour around the Historic Bloc: Theorising the Convergence of Biodiversity Conservation and Capitalist Expansion." *Antipode*, no. 42, 486–512.

Iliffe, J. 1987. *The African Poor: A History*. Cambridge: Cambridge University Press.

Jackson, R. H. 1990. *Quasi-states: Sovereignty, International Relations, and the Third World*. Cambridge: Cambridge University Press.

Jackson, R., and Rosberg, C. J. 1982. "Why Africa's Weak States Persist: The Empirical and the Juridical in Statehood." *World Politics* 35 (1): 1–24.

Jerven, M. 2010. "Accounting for the African Growth Miracle: The Official Evidence—Botswana, 1965–1995." *Journal of Southern African Studies* 36 (1): 73–94.

Keeley, J., and Scoones, I. 2003. *Understanding Environmental Policy Processes: Cases from Africa*. London: Earthscan.

Kelly, A. B. 2011. "Conservation Practice as Primitive Accumulation." *Journal of Peasant Studies* 38 (4): 683–701.

Kelly, A. B., and Gupta, A. C. 2016. "Protected Areas: Offering Security to Whom, When and Where?" *Environmental Conservation* 43 (2): 172–80.

Kelly, A. B., and Ybarra, M. 2016. "Green Security in Protected Areas." *Geoforum*, no. 69, 161–75.

Kepe, T. 2009. "Shaped by Race: Why 'Race' Still Matters in the Challenges Facing Biodiversity Conservation in Africa." *Local Environment: The International Journal of Justice and Sustainability*, 14 (9): 871–78.

Kgomotso, P. K. 2011. "Global Environmental Agreements and Local Livelihoods: How the Internationalisation of Environmental Resources Shapes Access to and Control over Wetland Resources in the Okavango Delta, Botswana." DPhil diss., University of Sussex.

Kiema, K. 2010. *Tears for My Land: A Social History of the Kua of the Central Kalahari Game Reserve, Tc'amnqoo.* Gaborone: Mmegi.

Kliskey, A. D. 1998. "Linking the Wilderness Perception Mapping Concept to the Recreation Opportunity Spectrum." *Environmental Management* 22 (1): 79–88.

Koot, S. 2019. "The Limits of Economic Benefits: Adding Social Affordances to the Analysis of Trophy Hunting of the Khwe and Ju'/hoansi in Namibian Community-Based Natural Resource Management." *Society and Natural Resources* 32 (4): 417–33.

Koot, S., Büscher, B., and Thakholi, L. 2022. "The New Green Apartheid? Race, Capital and Logics of Enclosure in South Africa's Wildlife Economy." *Environment and Planning E: Nature and Space.* https://doi.org/10.1177/25148486221110438.

Kuper, A. 1970. *Kalahari Village Politics: An African Democracy.* Cambridge: Cambridge University Press.

———. 2003. "Return of the Native." *Current Anthropology* 44 (3): 389–95.

LaRocco, A. A. 2016. "The Comprehensive Hunting Ban: Strengthening the State through Participatory Conservation in Contemporary Botswana." In *The Politics of Nature and Science in Southern Africa*, edited by Ramutsindela, M., Miescher, G., and Boehi, M., 179–207. Basel: Basler Afrika Bibliographien.

———. 2019. "The Biodiversity for Life (B4L) Flagship Initiative: The EU, Africa, and Biodiversity Conservation" in *EU Development Policies: Between Norms and Geopolitics*, edited by Thiel, M., Maier, S., and Beringer, S. L., 55–77. New York: Palgrave Macmillan.

———. 2020a. "Botswana's Hunting Ban and the Transformation of Game-Meat Cultures, Economies and Ecologies." *Journal of Southern African Studies* 46 (4): 723–41.

———. 2020b. "Infrastructure, Wildlife Tourism, (Il)legible Populations: A Comparative Study of Two Districts in Contemporary Botswana." *Environment and Planning E: Nature and Space* 3 (4): 1074–95.

LaRocco, A. A., and Mogende, E. 2022. "Fall from Grace or Back Down to Earth? Conservation and Political Conflict in Africa's 'Miracle' State." *Environment and Planning E: Nature and Space.* https://doi.org/10.1177/25148486221101553.

Leach, M., and Mearns, R. 1996. *The Lie of the Land: Challenging Received Wisdoms on the African Environment.* Oxford, James Currey.

Leftwich, A. 2000. *States of Development: On the Primacy of Politics in Development.* Cambridge, UK: Polity.

Leith, J. C. 2005. *Why Botswana Prospered*. Montreal: McGill-Queen's University Press.

Lekorwe, M. H. 1989. "The Kgotla and the Freedom Square: One-Way or Two-Way Communication?" In Molutsi and Holm, *Democracy in Botswana*, 216–30.

Livingston, J. 2019. *Self-Devouring Growth: A Planetary Parable as Told from Southern Africa*. Durham, NC: Duke University Press.

Lukes, S. 1974. *Power: A Radical View*. London: Macmillan.

Lund, C. 2008. *Local Politics and the Dynamics of Property in Africa*. Cambridge: Cambridge University Press.

———. 2013. "The Past and Space: On Arguments in African Land Control." *Africa* 83 (1): 14–35.

Lunstrum, E. 2014. "Green Militarization: Anti-poaching Efforts and the Spatial Contours of Kruger National Park." *Annals of the Association of American Geographers* 104 (4): 816–32.

———. 2017. "Feed Them to the Lions: Conservation Violence Goes Online." *Geoforum*, no. 79, 134–43.

Lunstrum, E., and Ybarra, M. 2018. "Deploying Difference: Security Threat Narratives and State Displacement from Protected Areas." *Conservation and Society* 16 (2): 114–24.

Mabele, M. B. 2017. "Beyond Forceful Measures: Tanzania's 'War on Poaching' Needs Diversified Strategies More than Militarized Tactics." *Review of African Political Economy* 44 (153): 487–98.

MacKenzie, J. M. 1988. *The Empire of Nature: Hunting, Conservation, and British Imperialism*. Manchester: Manchester University Press.

Maclean, L. M. 2010. *Informal Institutions and Citizenship in Rural Africa: Risk and Reciprocity in Ghana and Côte d'Ivoire*. Cambridge: Cambridge University Press.

Madzwamuse, M. 2010. "Adaptive or Anachronistic? Maintaining Indigenous Natural Resource Governance Systems in Northern Botswana." In Nelson, *Community Rights, Conservation and Contested Land*, 241–68.

Mafela, Lily. 2009. "Changing Livelihoods, Language Use and Language Shifts amongst Basarwa of Botswana." *International Journal of Multilingualism* 6 (3): 229–45.

Magole, L. I. 2009. "Common Pool Resource Management among San Communities in Ngamiland, Botswana." *Development Southern Africa* 26 (4): 597–610.

Magome, H., and Murombedzi, J. C. 2003. "Sharing South African National Parks: Community Land and Conservation in a Democratic South Africa." In Adams, and Mulligan, *Decolonizing Nature*, 108–34.

Makgala, C. J. 2019. "The Manifesto Experiment and Internal Electioneering in the Botswana Democratic Party." *Journal of African Elections* 18 (2): 134–57.

Malope, P., and Batisani, N. 2008. "Land Reforms That Exclude the Poor: The Case of Botswana." *Development Southern Africa* 25 (4): 383–97.

Mamdani, M. 1996. *Citizen and Subject: Contemporary Africa and the Legacy of Late Colonialism.* Princeton, NJ: Princeton University Press.

Mann, M. 1984. "The Autonomous Power of the State: Its Origins, Mechanisms and Results." *European Journal of Sociology*, no. 25, 185–213.

Marijnen, E. 2018. "Public Authority and Conservation in Areas of Armed Conflict: Virunga National Park as a 'State within a State' in Eastern Congo." *Development and Change* 49 (3): 790–814.

Marijnen, E., De Vries, L., and Duffy, R. 2021. "Conservation in Violent Environments: Introduction to a Special Issue on the Political Ecology of Conservation amidst Violent Conflict." *Political Geography* 87 (102253): e1–e3. https://doi.org/10.1016/j.polgeo.2020.102253.

Marijnen, E., and Schouten, P. 2019. "Electrifying the Green Peace? Electrification, Conservation and Conflict in Eastern Congo." *Conflict, Security and Development*, no. 1, 15–34.

Marijnen, E., and Verweijen, J. 2016. "Selling Green Militarization: The Discursive (Re)production of Militarized Conservation in the Virunga National Park, Democratic Republic of the Congo." *Geoforum*, no. 75, 274–85.

Martin, G. 2012. *Game Changer: Animal Rights and the Fate of Africa's Wildlife.* Berkeley: University of California Press.

Mascia, M. B., Pailler, S., Krithivasan, R., Roshchanka, V., Burns, D., Mlotha, M. J., Roeber Murray, D., and Peng, N. 2014. "Protected Area Downgrading, Downsizing, and Degazettement (PADDD) in Africa, Asia, and Latin America and the Caribbean, 1900–2010." *Biological Conservation*, no. 169, 355–61.

Massé, F. 2018. "Topographies of Security and Multiple Spatialities of (Conservation) Power: Verticality, Surveillance, and Space-Time Compression in the Bush." *Political Geography*, no. 67, 56–64.

———. 2019. "Anti-poaching's Politics of (In)visibility: Representing Nature and Conservation amidst a Poaching Crisis." *Geoforum*, no. 98, 1–14.

Massé, F., and Lunstrum, E. 2016. "Accumulation by Securitization: Commercial Poaching, Neoliberal Conservation, and the Creation of New Wildlife Frontiers." *Geoforum*, no. 69, 227–37.

Matunga, H. 1995. *Maori Recreation and the Conservation Estate.* Information Paper No. 6. Canterbury, New Zealand: Centre for Maori Studies and Research, Lincoln University.

Maundeni, Z. 2002. "State Culture and Development in Botswana and Zimbabwe." *Journal of Modern African Studies* 40 (1): 105–32.

———. 2004. "Mutual Criticism and State/Society Interaction in Botswana." *Journal of Modern Africa Studies* 42 (4): 619–36.

———. 2005. *40 Years of Democracy in Botswana, 1965–2005*. Gaborone: Mmegi House.

Mazonde, I. 2002a. "The San in Botswana and the Issue of Subjectivities: National Disintegration or Cultural Diversity?" In Mazonde, *Minorities of the Millennium*, 57–71.

———, ed. 2002b. *Minorities of the Millennium: Perspectives from Botswana*. Gaborone: Lentswe la Lesedi.

———. 2004. "Equality and Ethnicity: How Equal Are San in Botswana?" In Hitchcock and Vinding, *Indigenous Peoples' Rights in Southern Africa*, 134–51.

Mbabazi, P., and Taylor, I. 2005. *The Potentiality of "Developmental States" in Africa: Botswana and Uganda Compared*. Dakar: Council for the Development of Social Science Research in Africa.

Mbaiwa, J. E. 2005. "Enclave Tourism and Its Socio-economic Impacts in the Okavango Delta, Botswana." *Tourism Management* 26 (2): 157–72.

———. 2017. "Poverty or Riches: Who Benefits from the Booming Tourism Industry in Botswana?" *Journal of Contemporary African Studies* 35 (1): 93–112.

———. 2018. "Effects of the Safari Hunting Tourism Ban on Rural Livelihoods and Wildlife Conservation in Northern Botswana." *South African Geographical Journal* 100 (1): 41–61.

Mbaiwa, J. E., and Darkoh, M. 2009. "Socio-economic Impacts of Tourism in the Okavango Delta, Botswana." In Saarinen, *Sustainable Tourism in Southern Africa*, 210–30.

Mbaiwa, J. E., and Hambira, W. L. 2020. "Enclaves and Shadow State Tourism in the Okavango Delta, Botswana." *South African Geographical Journal* 102 (1): 1–21.

———. 2023. "Can the Subaltern Speak? Contradictions in Trophy Hunting and Wildlife Conservation Trajectory in Botswana." *Journal of Sustainable Tourism* 31 (5): 1107–25.

Mbaiwa, J. E., Stronza, A., and Kreuter, U. 2011. "From Collaboration to Conservation: Insights from the Okavango Delta, Botswana." *Society and Natural Resources* 24 (4): 400–411.

Mbaria, J., and Ogada, M. 2016. *The Big Conservation Lie*. Auburn, WA: Lens & Pens.

McGahey, D. J. 2008. "Maintaining Opportunism and Mobility in Drylands: The Impact of Veterinary Cordon Fences in Botswana." DPhil diss., University of Oxford.

Meskell, L. 2011. *The Nature of Heritage: The New South Africa*. Chichester, UK: Wiley-Blackwell.

Migdal, J. S. 1988. *Strong Societies and Weak States: State-Society Relations and State Capabilities in the Third World*. Princeton, NJ: Princeton University Press.

Mogalakwe, M. 2003. "Botswana: An African Miracle or a Case of Mistaken Identity?" *Pula: Botswana Journal of African Studies* 17 (1): 85–94.

———. 2006. "From Pre-colony to Post-colony: Continuities and Discontinuities in Political Power Relations and Governance in Botswana." *Journal of African Elections* 5 (2): 5–20.

Mogalakwe, M., and Nyamnjoh, F. 2017. "Botswana at 50: Democratic Deficit, Elite Corruption and Poverty in the Midst of Plenty." *Journal of Contemporary African Studies* 35 (1): 1–14.

Mogende, E., and Ramutsindela, M. 2020. "Political Leadership and Non-state Actors in the Greening of Botswana." *Review of African Political Economy* 47 (165): 399–415.

Mogomotsi, G., and Madigele, P. 2017. "Live by the Gun, Die by the Gun: Botswana's Shoot-to-Kill Policy as an Anti-poaching strategy." *SA Crime Quarterly*, no. 60, 51–59.

Mogwe, A. 1992. *Who Was (T)here First? An Assessment of the Human Rights Situation of Basarwa in Selected Communities in the Gantsi District, Botswana*. Occasional Paper No. 10. Gaborone: Botswana Christian Council.

Molomo, M. G. 2000. "Understanding Government and Opposition Parties in Botswana." *Commonwealth and Comparative Politics* 38 (1): 65–92.

———. 2001. "Civil-Military Relations in Botswana's Developmental State." *African Studies Quarterly* 5 (2): 37–59.

———. 2008. "Sustainable Development, Ecotourism, National Minorities and Land in Botswana." In *Land and Sustainable Development in Africa*, edited by Amanor, K., and Moyo, S., 157–83. London: Zed Books.

Molosi-France, K. 2018. "A Relational View of San Poverty in Botswana: A Case Study of Khwee and Sehunong." *South African Review of Sociology* 49 (3–4): 1–15.

Molutsi, P., and Holm, J. 1989. *Democracy in Botswana*. Gaborone: Macmillan.

Mompati, T., and Prinsen, G. 2000. "Ethnicity and Participatory Development Methods in Botswana: Some Participants Are to Be Seen and Not Heard." *Development in Practice* 10 (5): 625–37.

Mosley, J., and Watson, E. 2016. "Frontier Transformations: Development Visions, Spaces and Processes in Northern Kenya and Southern Ethiopia." *Journal of East African Studies* 10 (3): 452–75.

Moyo, S., O'Keefe, P., and Sill, M. 1993. *The Southern African Environment: Profiles of the SADC Countries*. London: Earthscan.

Murdock, E. 2021. "Conserving Dispossession? A Genealogical Account of the Colonial Roots of Western Conservation." *Ethics, Policy and Environment* 24 (3): 235–49.

Murombedzi, J. C. 2003. "Devolving the Expropriation of Nature: The 'Devolution' of Wildlife Management in Southern Africa." In Adams and Mulligan, *Decolonizing Nature*, 135–71.

———. 2010. "Agrarian Social Change and Post-colonial Natural Resource Management Interventions in Southern Africa's 'Communal Tenure' Regimes." In Nelson, *Community Rights, Conservation and Contested Land*, 241–68.

Must, E., and Hovorka, A. 2019. "Co-opting Cattle Spaces: Women, Cattle, and Empowerment in Northwestern Botswana." *Environment and Planning E: Nature and Space* 2 (4): 922–43.

Mwangi, F., Zhang, Q., and Wang, H. 2022. "Development Challenges and Management Strategies on the Kenyan National Park System: A Case of Nairobi National Park." *International Journal of Geoheritage and Parks* 10 (1): 16–26.

Nelson, F. 2010. *Community Rights, Conservation and Contested Land*. London: Earthscan.

Neumann, R. P. 1998. *Imposing Wilderness: Struggles over Livelihood and Nature Preservation in Africa*. Berkeley: University of California Press.

———. 2000. "Primitive Ideas: Protected Area Buffer Zones and the Politics of Land in Africa." In *Producing Nature and Poverty in Africa*, edited by Broch-Due, V., and Schroeder, R., 220–42. Uppsala: Nordiska Afrikainstitutet.

———. 2001. "Disciplining Peasants in Tanzania: From Coercion to Self-Surveillance in Wildlife Conservation." In Peluso and Watts, *Violent Environments*, 305–27.

———. 2004a. "Moral and Discursive Geographies in the War for Biodiversity in Africa." *Political Geography* 23 (7): 813–37.

———. 2004b. "Nature-State-Territory: Toward a Critical Theorization of Conservation Enclosures." In *Liberation Ecologies: Second Edition*, edited by Peet, R., and Watts, M., 195–217. London: Routledge.

———. 2005. "Model, Panacea, or Exception? Contextualizing CAMPFIRE and Related Programs in Africa." In *Communities and Conservation: Histories and Politics of Community-Based Natural Resource Management*, edited by Brosius, P., Tsing, A., and Zerner, C., 177–93. London: Altamira Press.

Ngo'ong'ola, C. 1997. "Land Rights for Marginalized Ethnic Groups in Botswana, with Special Reference to the Basarwa." *Journal of African Law*, no. 411, 1–26.

Norton, D. A. 2000. "Conservation Biology and Private Land: Shifting the Focus." *Conservation Biology* 14 (5): 1221–23.

Norton-Griffiths, M., and Southey, C. 1995. "The Opportunity Costs of Biodiversity Conservation in Kenya." *Ecological Economics* 12 (2): 125–39.

Noss, R., Dobson, A. P., Baldwin, R., Beier, P., Davis, C. R., Dellasala, D. A., Francis, J., Locke, H., Nowak, K., Lopez, R., Reining, C., Trombulak, S. C., and Tabor, G. 2012. "Bolder Thinking for Conservation." *Conservation Biology*, no. 26, 1–4.

Nteta, D., Hermans, J., and Jezkova, P. 1997. *Poverty and Plenty: The Botswana Experience*. Gaborone: Botswana Society.

Nthomang, K. 2004. "Relentless Colonialism: The Case of the Remote Area Development Programme (RADP) and the Basarwa in Botswana." *Journal of Modern African Studies* 42 (3): 415–35.

Ntsebeza, L., and Hall, R. 2007. *The Land Question in South Africa: The Challenge of Transformation and Redistribution*. Johannesburg: HSRC Press.

Nugent P. 2018. "Africa's Re-enchantment with Big Infrastructure: White Elephants Dancing in Virtuous Circles?" In *Extractive Industries and Changing State Dynamics in Africa*, edited by Schubert J., Engel, U., and Macamo, E., 22–40. New York: Routledge.

Nustad, K. G. 2015. *Creating Africas: Struggles over Nature, Conservation and Land*. London: Hurst.

Nyamnjoh, F. B. 2002. "Local Attitudes towards Citizenship and Foreigners in Botswana: An Appraisal of Recent Press Stories." *Journal of Southern African Studies* 28 (4): 755–75.

———. 2004. "Reconciling 'the Rhetoric of Rights' with Competing Notions of Personhood and Agency in Botswana." In *Rights and the Politics of Recognition in Africa*, edited by Englund, H., and Nyamnjoh, F. B., 33–63. London: Zed Books.

———. 2007. "'Ever-Diminishing Circles': The Paradoxes of Belonging in Botswana." In *Indigenous Experience Today*, edited by Cadena, M., and Starn, 305–32. Oxford: Berg.

Nyati-Ramahobo, L. 2002a. "From a Phone Call to the High Court: Wayeyi Visibility and the Kamanakao Association's Campaign for Linguistic and Cultural Rights in Botswana." *Journal of Southern African Studies* 28 (4): 685–709.

———. 2002b. "Ethnic Identity and Nationhood in Botswana." In Mazonde, *Minorities in the Millennium*, 17–28.

———. 2009. *Minority Tribes in Botswana: The Politics of Recognition*. London: Minority Rights Group International.

Odell, M. 1985. "Local Government: Traditional and Modern Roles of the Village Kgotla." In Picard, *Evolution of Modern Botswana*, 61–83.

Ojeda. D. 2012. "Green Pretexts: Ecotourism, Neoliberal Conservation and Land Grabbing in Tayrona National Natural Park, Colombia." *Journal of Peasant Studies* 39 (2): 357–75.

Okello, M. M., Kenana, L., and Kieti, D. 2012. "Factors Influencing Domestic Tourism for Urban and Semiurban Populations around Nairobi National Park, Kenya." *Tourism Analysis* 17 (1): 79–89.

Oldekop, J. A., Holmes, G., Harris, W. E., and Evans, K. L. 2016. "A Global Assessment of the Social and Conservation Outcomes of Protected Areas." *Conservation Biology*, no. 30, 133–41.

Ong, A. 2000. "Graduated Sovereignty in South-East Asia." *Theory, Culture and Society* 17 (4): 55–75.

Painter, J. 2006. "Prosaic Geographies of Stateness." *Political Geography* 25 (7): 752–74.

Palfrey, R., Oldekop, J., and Holmes, G. 2021 "Conservation and Social Outcomes of Private Protected Areas." *Conservation Biology* 35 (4): 1098–110.

Parry, D. C., and Campbell, B. M. 1990. "Wildlife Management Areas of Botswana." *Botswana Notes and Records*, no. 22, 65–77.

Parson, J. 1984. *Botswana: Liberal Democracy and the Labor Reserve in Southern Africa*. Boulder, CO: Westview.

Parsons, N. 2006. "Unravelling History and Cultural Heritage in Botswana." *Journal of Southern African Studies*, 32 (4): 667–81.

Parsons, N., Henderson, W., and Tlou, T. 1995. *Seretse Khama: 1921–1980*. Gaborone: Macmillan.

Peluso, N. L., and Lund, C. 2011. "New Frontiers in Land Control: Introduction." *Journal of Peasant Studies* 38 (4): 667–81.

Peluso, N. L., and Vandergeest, P. 2011. "Political Ecologies of War and Forests: Counterinsurgencies and the Making of National Natures." *Annals of the Association of American Geographers* 101 (3): 587–608.

Peluso, N. L., and Watts, M. 2001. *Violent Environments*. Ithaca, NY: Cornell University Press.

Pennaz, A. K., Ahmadou, M., Moritz, M., and Scholte, P. 2018. "Not Seeing the Cattle for the Elephants: The Implications of Discursive Linkages between Boko Haram and Wildlife Poaching in Waza National Park, Cameroon." *Conservation and Society* 16 (2): 125–35.

Peters, P. E. 1994. *Dividing the Commons: Politics, Policy, and Culture in Botswana*. Charlottesville: University of Virginia Press.

———. 2004. "Inequality and Social Conflict over Land in Africa." *Journal of Agrarian Change* 4 (3): 269–314.

Pfotenhauer, L., ed. 1991. *Tourism in Botswana*. Gaborone: Botswana Society.

Picard, L. A. 1985. *The Evolution of Modern Botswana*. London: Rex Collings.

———. 1987. *The Politics of Development in Botswana: A Model for Success?* Boulder, CO: Lynne Rienner.

Pillay. S. 2018. "Thinking the State from Africa: Political Theory, Eurocentrism and Concrete Politics." *Politikon* 45 (1): 32–47.

Poteete, A. R. 2009a. "Defining Political Community and Rights to Natural Resources in Botswana." *Development and Change* 40 (2): 281–305.

———. 2009b. "Is Development Path Dependent or Political? A Reinterpretation of Mineral-Dependent Development in Botswana." *Journal of Development Studies* 45 (4): 544–71.

———. 2012. "Electoral Competition, Factionalism, and Persistent Party Dominance in Botswana." *Journal of Modern African Studies* 50 (1): 75–102.

―――. 2015. "Election Note: Botswana's 2014 Parliamentary Elections." *Electoral Studies*, no. 40, 444–47.
Poteete, A. R., and Ribot, J. C. 2011. "Repertoires of Domination: Decentralization as Process in Botswana and Senegal." *World Development* 39 (3): 439–49.
Rabinowitz, B. 2018. *Coups, Rivals and the Modern State: Why Rural Coalitions Matter in Sub-Saharan Africa*. Cambridge: Cambridge University Press.
Radcliffe, S. A. 2001. "Imagining the State as a Space: Territoriality and the Formation of the State in Ecuador." In *States of Imagination: Ethnographic Explorations of the Postcolonial State*, edited by Hansen, T. B., and Stepputat, F., 123–45. Durham, NC: Duke University Press.
Ramutsindela, M. 2007. *Transfrontier Conservation in Africa: At the Confluence of Capital, Politics, and Nature*. Wallingford, UK: CABI.
―――. 2015. "Extractive Philanthropy: Securing Labour and Land Claim Settlement in Private Nature Reserves." *Third World Quarterly* 36 (12): 2259–72.
―――. 2016. "Wildlife Crime and State Security in South(ern) Africa: An Overview of Developments." *Politikon* 43 (2): 159–71.
―――. 2017. "Greening Africa's Borderlands: The Symbiotic Politics of Land and Borders in Peace Parks." *Political Geography*, no. 56, 106–13.
Ramutsindela, M., and Büscher, B. 2019. "Environmental Governance and the (Re-)Making of the African State." *Oxford Research Encyclopedia of Politics*. https://oxfordre.com/politics/view/10.1093/acrefore/9780190228637.001.0001/acrefore-9780190228637-e-903.
Ramutsindela, M., and Sinthumule, I. 2017. "Property and Difference in Nature Conservation." *Geographical Review* 107 (3): 415–32.
Ranger, T. 1999. *Voices from the Rocks: Nature, Culture and History in the Matopos Hills of Zimbabwe*. Oxford: James Currey.
Regan, T. 1985. "The Case for Animals Rights." In Singer, *In Defence of Animals*, 13–26.
Ribot, J. C., and Peluso, N. L. 2003. "A Theory of Access." *Rural Sociology* 68 (2): 153–81.
Rihoy, L., and Maguranyanga, B. 2010. "The Politics of Community-Based Natural Resource Management in Botswana." In Nelson, *Community Rights, Conservation and Contested Land*, 55–78.
Risse, T. 2011. *Governance without a State? Policies and Politics in Areas of Limited Statehood*. New York: Columbia University Press.
Roberts, S. 1985. "The Tswana Polity and 'Tswana Law and Custom' Reconsidered." *Journal of Southern African Studies* 12 (1): 75–87.
Robins, S. 2003. "Whose Modernity? Indigenous Modernities and Land Claims after Apartheid." *Development and Change* 34 (2): 265–86.
Robinson, J. A., and Parsons, Q. N. 2006. "State Formation and Governance in Botswana." *Journal of African Economies* 15 (1): 100–140.

Roodt, V. 1993. *The Shell Field Guide to the Common Trees of the Okavango Delta and Moremi Game Reserve.* Gaborone: Shell.

Ross, K. 1987. *Okavango: Jewel of the Kalahari.* New York: Macmillan.

Saarinen, J., ed. 2009. *Sustainable Tourism in Southern Africa: Local Communities and Natural Resources in Transition.* Bristol, UK: Channel View Publications.

Samatar, A. I. 1999. *An African Miracle: State and Class Leadership and Colonial Legacy in Botswana Development.* Portsmouth, NH: Heinemann.

Samatar, A. I., and Samatar, A. I. 2002. *The African State: Reconsiderations.* Portsmouth, NH: Heinemann.

Sapignoli, M. 2012. "Local Power through Globalised Indigenous Identities: The San, the State, and the International Community." PhD diss., University of Essex.

———. 2018. *Hunting Justice: Displacement, Law, and Activism in the Kalahari.* Cambridge: Cambridge University Press.

Saugestad, S. 2001. *The Inconvenient Indigenous: Remote Area Development in Botswana, Donor Assistance and the First People of the Kalahari.* Uppsala: Nordic Africa Institute.

———. 2011. "Impact of International Mechanisms on Indigenous Rights in Botswana." *International Journal of Human Rights* 15 (1): 37–61.

Saxer, M., and Andersson, R. 2019. "The Return of Remoteness: Insecurity, Isolation and Connectivity in the New World Disorder." *Social Anthropology* 27 (2): 140–55.

Schapera, I. (1970) 2021. *Tribal Innovators: Tswana Chiefs and Social Change 1795–1940.* Reprint, London: Routledge.

———. 1984. *A Handbook of Tswana Law and Custom.* London: Oxford University Press.

Schroeder, R. A. 2018. "Moving Targets: The 'Canned' Hunting of Captive-Bred Lions in South Africa." *African Studies Review* 61 (1): 8–32.

Scott, J. 1998. *Seeing Like a State: How Certain Schemes to Improve the Human Condition Have Failed.* New Haven, CT: Yale University Press.

———. 2009. *The Art of Not Being Governed: An Anarchist History of Upland Southeast Asia.* New Haven, CT: Yale University Press.

Seabo, B., and Nyenhuis, R. 2021. "Botswana's 2019 General Elections: A Referendum on General Ian Khama." *African Studies Review* 64 (4): 854–83.

Sebudubudu, D., and Botlhomilwe, M. Z. 2012. "Interrogating the Dominant Party System in Botswana." In *Friend or Foe? Dominant Party Systems in Southern Africa: Insights from the Developing World,* edited by de Jager, N. and du Toit, P., 115–31. Tokyo: United Nations University Press.

Selby, H. 1991. "Hunting as a Component of Tourism in Botswana." In Pfotenhauer, *Tourism in Botswana,* 370–78.

Selolwane, O. D. 2007. "Statecraft in Botswana: Renegotiating Development, Legitimacy, and Authority." In Agbese, and Kieh, *Reconstituting the State of Africa*, 33–73.

Shinn, J. E. 2018. "Toward Anticipatory Adaptation: Transforming Social-Ecological Vulnerabilities in the Okavango Delta, Botswana." *Geographical Journal*, no. 184, 179–91.

Shinn, J. E., and Hall-Reinhard, A. 2019. "Emphasizing Livelihoods in the Study of Social-Ecological Systems: Insights from Fishing Practices in the Okavango Delta, Botswana." *South African Geographical Journal* 101 (1): 121–39.

Sikor, T., and Lund, C. 2009. "Access and Property: A Question of Power and Authority." *Development and Change* 40 (1): 1–22.

Singer, P. 1985. *In Defence of Animals*. Oxford: Basil Blackwell.

Sinthumule, I. 2017. "Resistance against Conservation at the South Africa Section of Greater Mapungubwe (Trans)frontier." *Africa Spectrum* 52 (2): 53–77.

Snijders, D. 2012. "Wild Property and Its Boundaries: On Wildlife Policy and Rural Consequences in South Africa." *Journal of Peasant Studies* 39 (2): 503–20.

Solway, J. 2002. "Navigating the 'Neutral' State: 'Minority' Rights in Botswana." *Journal of Southern African Studies* 28 (4): 711–29.

———. 2004. "Reaching the Limits of Universal Citizenship: 'Minority' Struggles in Botswana." In *Ethnicity and Democracy in Africa*, edited by Berman, B., Eyoh, D., and Kymlicka, W., 129–48. Oxford: James Currey.

———. 2009. "Human Rights and NGO 'Wrongs': Conflict Diamonds, Culture Wars and the 'Bushman Question.'" *Africa* 79 (3): 321–45.

Solway, J., and Nyati-Ramahobo, L. 2004. "Democracy in the Process: Building a Coalition to Achieve Political, Cultural and Linguistics Rights in Botswana." *Canadian Journal of African Studies* 38 (3): 603–21.

Spinage, C. A. 1991. *History and Evolution of the Fauna Conservation Laws of Botswana*. Gaborone: Botswana Society.

Stedman, S. J. 1993. *Botswana: The Political Economy of Democratic Development*. Boulder, CO: Lynne Rienner.

Strang, D. 1996. "Contested Sovereignty: The Social Construction of Colonial Imperialism." In *State Sovereignty as Social Construct*, edited by Biersteker, T. J., and Weber, C., 22–49. Cambridge: Cambridge University Press.

Swanepoel, J. 2013. "Custodians of the Cape Peninsula: A Historical and Contemporary Ethnography of Urban Conservation in Cape Town." Master's thesis, Stellenbosch University.

Swatuk, L. A. 2005. "From Project to Context: Community-Based Natural Resource Conservation in Botswana." *Global Environmental Politics* 5 (3): 95–124.

Sylvain, R. 2014. "Essentialism and the Indigenous Politics of Recognition in Southern Africa." *American Anthropologist* 116 (2): 251–64.

Taiepa, T., Lyver, P., Horsley, P., Davis, J., Bragg, M., and Moller, H. 1997. "Co-management of New Zealand's Conservation Estate by Maori and Pakeha: A Review." *Environmental Conservation* 24 (3): 236–50.

Taylor, I. 2003. "As Good as It Gets? Botswana's Democratic Development." *Journal of Contemporary African Studies* 21 (2): 215–31.

———. 2006. "The Limits of the 'African Miracle': Academic Freedom in Botswana and the Deportation of Kenneth Good." *Journal of Contemporary African Studies* 24 (1): 101–22.

———. 2012. "Botswana as a 'Development-Oriented Gate-Keeping state': A Response." *African Affairs* 111 (444): 466–76.

Taylor, I., and Mokhawa, G. 2003. "Not Forever: Botswana, Conflict Diamonds and the Bushmen." *African Affairs* 102 (407): 261–83.

Taylor, M. 2000. "Life, Land and Power: Contesting Development in Northern Botswana." PhD diss., University of Edinburgh.

———. 2001. "Narratives of Identity and Assertions of Legitimacy: Basarwa in Northern Botswana" In Anderson and Ikeya, *Parks, Property, and Power*, 157–82.

———. 2002. "The Shaping of San Livelihood Strategies: Government Policy and Popular Values." *Development and Change* 33 (3): 467–88.

———. 2004. "The Past and Future of San Land Rights in Botswana." In Hitchcock and Vinding, *Indigenous Peoples' Rights in Southern Africa*, 152–65.

Tlou, T. 1985. *A History of Ngamiland, 1750 to 1906: The Formation of an African State*. Gaborone: Macmillan Botswana.

Toulmin, C., and Quan, J. 2000. *Evolving Land Rights, Policy, and Tenure in Africa*. London: IIED.

Trogisch, L. and Fletcher, R. 2022. "Fortress Tourism: Exploring Dynamics of Tourism, Security and Peace around the Virunga Transboundary Conservation Area." *Journal of Sustainable Tourism* 30 (2–3): 352–71.

Tsie, B. 1996. "The Political Context of Botswana's Development Performance." *Journal of Southern African Studies* 22 (4): 599–616.

Turner, R. L. 2009. "Politics Where the Wild Things Are: Nature Tourism, Property Rights, Traditional Leadership, and the State in Rural Botswana and South Africa." PhD diss., University of California, Berkeley.

Twyman, C. 1998. "Rethinking Community Resource Management: Managing Resources or Managing People in Western Botswana?" *Third World Quarterly* 19 (4): 745–70.

———. 2000. "Livelihood Opportunity and Diversity in Kalahari Wildlife Management Areas, Botswana: Rethinking Community Resource Management." *Journal of Southern African Studies* 26 (4): 783–806.

Uribe, S. 2018. "Illegible Infrastructures: Road Building and the Making of State-Spaces in the Colombian Amazon." *Environment and Planning D: Society and Space* 37 (5): 886–904.

Vandergeest, P., and Peluso, N. L. 1995. "Territorialization and State Power in Thailand." *Theory and Society* 24 (3): 385–426.

———. 2015. "Political Forests." In *The International Handbook of Political Ecology*, edited by R L Bryant, 162–75. Northampton, UK: Edward Elgar.

Vaughan, O. 2003. *Chiefs, Power, and Social Change: Chiefship and Modern Politics in Botswana, 1880s–1990s*. Trenton, NJ: Africa World Press.

Verhoeven, H. 2014. "Gardens of Eden or Hearts of Darkness? The Genealogy of Discourses on Environmental Insecurity and Climate Wars in Africa." *Geopolitics* 19 (4): 784–805.

von Richter, W., and Butynski, T. 1973. "Hunting in Botswana." *Botswana Notes and Records*, no. 5, 191–208.

Wæver, O. 1995. "Securitization and Desecuritization" In *On Security*, edited by Lipschutz, R., 46–86. New York: Columbia University Press.

Watson, J. E. M., Venter, O., Lee, J., Jones, K. R., Possingham, H. P., and Allan, J. R. 2018. "Protect the Last of the Wild." *Nature*, no. 563, 27–30.

Weber, C. 1998. "Performative States." *Millennium: Journal of International Studies* 27 (1): 77–95.

Weldemichel, T. G. 2020. "Othering Pastoralists, State Violence and the Remaking of Boundaries in Tanzania's Militarised Wildlife Conservation Sector." *Antipode* 52 (5): 1496–518.

Werbner, R. 2002. "Cosmopolitan Ethnicity, Entrepreneurship and the Nation: Minority Elites in Botswana." *Journal of Southern African Studies* 28 (4): 731–53.

———. 2004. *Reasonable Radicals and Citizenship in Botswana: The Public Anthropology of Kalanga Elites*. Bloomington: Indiana University Press.

Williams, M. C. 2003. "Words, Images, Enemies: Securitization and International Politics." *International Studies Quarterly* 47 (4): 511–31.

Wilmsen, E. N. 1989. *Land Filled with Flies: A Political Economy of the Kalahari*. Chicago: University of Chicago Press.

———. 2002. "Mutable Identities: Moving beyond Ethnicity in Botswana." *Journal of Southern African Studies* 28 (4): 825–41.

Wilson, E. O. 2016. *Half-Earth: Our Planet's Fight for Life*. London: Liveright.

Wily, E. 1982. "A Strategy of Self-Determination for the Kalahari San (the Botswana Government's Programme of Action in the Ghanzi Farms)." *Development and Change* 13 (2): 291–308.

Wiseman, J. A. 1998. "The Slow Evolution of the Party System in Botswana." *Journal of Asian and African Studies* 33 (3): 241–64.

Witter, R. 2021. "Why Militarized Conservation May Be Counter-productive: Illegal Wildlife Hunting as Defiance." *Journal of Political Ecology* 28 (1): 176–92.

Witter, R., and Satterfield, T. 2019. "Rhino Poaching and the 'Slow Violence' of Conservation-Related Resettlement in Mozambique's Limpopo National Park." *Geoforum*, no. 101, 275–84.

Wright, V. C. 2016. "Turbulent Times: Fighting History Today in Tanzania's Trophy Hunting Spaces." *Journal of Contemporary African Studies* 34 (1): 40–60.

Wuerthner, G., Crist, E., and Butler, T., eds. 2015. *Protecting the Wild Parks and Wilderness: The Foundation for Conservation*. Washington, DC: Island Press.

Wylie, D. 1990. *A Little God: The Twilight of Patriarchy in a Southern African Chiefdom*. London: Wesleyan University Press.

Ybarra, M. 2017. *Green Wars: Conservation and Decolonization in the Maya Forest*. Oakland: University of California Press.

Youatt, R. 2020. *Interspecies Politics: Nature, Borders, States*. Ann Arbor: University of Michigan Press.

Zips-Mairitsch, M. 2013. *Lost Lands? (Land) Rights of the San in Botswana and the Legal Concept of Indigeneity in Africa*. Berlin: Lit Verlag.

Government and Gray Literature

Ditshwanelo. 2002. *Supplementary Report for the Committee on the Elimination of Racial Discrimination*. Gaborone: Ditshwanelo.

Government of Botswana. 1968. *Tribal Land Act*. Act No. 54 of 1968. Government Printer: Gaborone.

———. 1979. *Unified Hunting Regulations (Fauna Conservation Act)*. Government Printer: Gaborone.

———. 1986. *Wildlife Conservation Policy*. Government Paper No. 1 of 1986. Government Printer: Gaborone.

———. 1992. *Wildlife Conservation and National Parks Act*. Act No. 28 of 1992. Government Printer: Gaborone.

———. 1994. *Ostrich Management Plan Policy*. Government Paper No. 1 of 1994. Government Printer: Gaborone.

———. 1997. *Vision 2016—a Long Term Vision for Botswana*. Presidential Task Group on a Long Term Vision for Botswana. Government Printer: Gaborone.

Ministry of Environment, Wildlife and Tourism. 2013. *Press Release: Hunting Ban in Botswana*. Gaborone: Government Printer.

Ministry of Finance and Development Planning. 2013. *Mid-term Review of NDP 10: NDP 10 towards 2016*. Gaborone: Government Printer.

Report of the Presidential Commission. 2000. *Inquiry into Sections 77, 78 and 79 of the Constitution, November 2000 (Balopi Commission)*. Gaborone: Government Printer.

Roy Sesana, Keiwa Setlhobogwa and Others v. The Attorney General. MISCA No. 52 of 2002 (High Court). Botswana.

UNEP-WCMC, IUCN, and NGS. 2018. Protected Planet Report 2018. Cambridge, Gland, and Washington, DC: UNEP–World Conservation Centre, IUCN, and National Geographic Society.

Video Sources

BTV News Special: London Conference on the Illegal Wildlife Trade. BTV (Botswana). February 23, 2014. Author in possession of recorded copy.

Linfield, M., Berlowitz, V., and Fothergill, A., dirs. Elephant. Los Angeles: Disney+, 2020.

Thompson, E., dir. Poaching Wars with Tom Hardy. Aired August 29, 2013, on ITV, Burning Bright Productions.

Index

Page numbers in *italics* refer to figures and tables.

Africa: and African bush elephant, 4, 85; and African states, 51–52, 63–66, 131–32, 157–58, 318; agriculture in, 33, 34, 56, 57; and antipoaching policy, 98–99; apartheid in, 64, 65, 86, 302; Cape Town in, 37; capital investment in, 200; and Central Africa, 68; colonial rule in, 13; and consensus, 118; and the conservation estate, 5–7, 9–10, 11, 17, 22, 27, 28, 30, 35–37, 61; countries in, 6, 17, 27, 96; demographics of, 316; and development plans, 195; and eastern Africa, 6, 76; European settlement in, 157–58; first inhabitants of, 233; and French colonial empire, 34; and "green grabbing" of land, 17–18; and hunter-gatherers, 231; and Khoesan languages, 231; land ownership in, 17; land tenure regimes in, 170–71; minority rule in, 63–64; Mozambique in, 78, 224; and nature tourism, 196; political parties in, 54; and postcolonial states, 32, 37, 63, 76, 170; private military firms in, 82–83; protected areas in, 13, 22, 67–68, 76, 77, 78; and race, 17, 162; and raw materials, 60; and rural areas, 4, 9–10, 30–37; and rural experiences, 11, 30, 31, 34, 35, 36, 37; Rwanda in, 65; and the Serengeti, 209; Somalia in, 52; and South Africa, 173, 177, 302; and southern Africa, 5, 6, 62, 63–64, 65, 78, 86, 87, 102, 158, 162, 170, 171, 172, 173, 231, 233, 254, 264, 265, 293; state building in, 22, 23, 27, 30–32, 34, 37, 46–47, 173, 313; sub-Saharan region of, 13, 17; terrorist groups in, 77; and urban experiences, 11, 35; urbanization of, 31; and violence, 76; voting blocs in, 31; and wilderness, 61, 191–92; Zambia in, 85, 98. *See also* Botswana; Gabon; Kenya; Namibia; South Africa; states; Tanzania; Zimbabwe

African State: Reconsiderations (Samatar and Samatar), 52

Agamben, Giorgio, 79, 98, 99, 133

Aichi, Japan, 19, 20

America, 118

Anaya, James, 160

Art of Not Being Governed, The (Scott), 195

authority: and coercion, 46, 47, 73–74, 75, 129; and colonial land control, 30; and conflict over wildlife, 62; and conservation estates, 46, 73, 87, 88, 91, 103–4, 105, 129, 130, 133–34, 140–41, 283, 306, 308; and consultation, 130; and control of resources, 3, 29; and control of territory, 3, 29, 83; and democracy, 117–18, 120–21; and environment, 29, 83, 283; and expertise, 136–37; and the *kgotla*, 126–31; and land, 29, 103–4, 125, 184; and landowners, 184; and legitimacy, 105–6; and limitation on mobility, 30; and local authority, 134; and permits, 168; political, 3, 7, 14, 65–66, 119, 126–31, 274; and rural experiences, 30, 32; and San people, 234–35; and securitization, 79–86, 89, 103–4, 115; and spatial control, 103–4;

authority (*cont.*)
  and the state, 25, 29, 75, 80–81, 106–7, 108, 116, 120; and state authority, 3, 4, 27, 29, 30, 47–49, 56, 73–75, 79–80, 86, 89, 94–95, 98, 99, 102, 107, 111, 119, 120, 127–28, 168, 176, 189–90, 192, 242, 243, 255; and state building, 23, 29–30, 46, 127, 148; structuring of, 69, 74, 93, 308; and subjectivities, 9, 66, 308; and territory, 188; and traditional authorities (*dikgosi*), 156; and Tswana authority, 65, 66, 118, 126; and urban experiences, 32; and use of force, 83

backyard gardens, 296, 299–301
Balopi Commission, 65
Bamangwato *morafe* (kingdom), 216
Batswana: and Bakgalagadi people, 159, 164; and Basarwa (San), 231, 275, 276, 277, 281, 282; and Central Kalahari Game Reserve (CKGR), 277, 283; and citizenship, 75, 115, 116, 133–34, 135, 206, 240, 256, 278, 305–6; and conservation, 74, 75, 100, 101, 133, 148; on the conservation estate, 96, 100–101, 103, 118–19, 139–40, 216, 240–41; and conservation policies, 136–37; culture of, 167; definition of, 8; and elders' knowledge, 282–83; and elites, 172; European-descended, 66–67, 69; and food gathering, 205, 229, 242; and foraging, 103, 184; and game meat, 262, 265, 281, 289; and hunter-gatherers, 243–44, 256, 274, 281; and hunting lottery, 271–72; and Indian-descended people, 66–67; and inequality, 206; and infrastructure, 207; and Kalanga people, 66–67, 166; and the kgotla, 115, 121–22; and land rights, 152, 166, 186–87; and limitation on mobility, 103–4, 194; and livelihoods, 101, 103, 133, 183–84; and marginalization, 166, 210; and Naro San, 279–80; and national stability, 117; and natural resources, 257; non-Tswana, 63, 66–67, 69, 121–22, 130–31, 166–67; and resource use, 137; rights of, 133, 138, 164, 166, 186; and rural areas, 11, 135–37; and San people, 66, 67, 68, 92, 114, 122, 137, 151, 154, 159–62, 164, 165–68; and securitization, 92,

100–101, 103; and social services, 207; and state building, 309; and Tswana group, 63, 64, 65–69, 118, 164; and unity, 117; white, 63, 68, 173, 174, 181–82; as wilderness guides, 191
beadwork, 248–49, 250, 252, 253, 254, 255, 256, 258, 280
Botswana: 10th National Development Plan of, 119–20; and Afrikaners, 68, 181, 254, 286; and agrarian production, 56, 135, 203, 263, 296–300; and assimilation, 63, 67, 122, 138, 146, 234, 236, 246, 259, 263, 264, 281, 282, 288, 289, 290, 311; and Bakgalagadi, 231; and Basarwa (San), 165, 204, 229, 231, 234, 244, 255, 256, 257, 258, 273; and basic services, 159, 160–61, 202–3, 207; and Basubiya, 68; and Batawana (a Tswana subgroup), 68–69, 156, 174; and Bayei, 68, 129, 231, 237; and Bechuanaland Protectorate, 63, 154, 155, 157–58, 167, 263, 265; and Bere, 45, 139, 181, 182, 245, 251, 301; and Boro village, 133, 142, 197, 294, 306; and "buffalo fences," 293–94, 295; and cattle farming, 201, 262–63, 264, 276, 279–80, 285–87, 290, 292, 294, 301; cattle posts (*moraka*) in, 134, 135, 154, 156; and census records, 64, 200–201, 232; Central District in, 216; and Central Kalahari, 18, 67–68, 125; and Central Kalahari Game Reserve (CKGR), 217, 218, 222, 223; Chobe District in, 68, 140; Chobe River in, 38; and citizenship, 237, 305; citizens of, 8, 10, 63, 69, 75, 100, 121, 125–27, 129, 138, 140–41, 156, 161, 162, 164, 173, 177–78, 190, 194, 221, 230–31; citizen-state relations in, 4, 10, 42–43, 46–49, 75, 100, 126–31, 172, 192–93; and civil rights, 119; climate of, 208, 299; and coercion, 132, 148; and colonialism, 172, 173; colonial rule in, 56, 64, 210; and commercialization, 303; and Community-Based Natural Resource Management (CBNRM) program, 266, 305; and consensus, 118, 138, 141–42; conservation areas in, 4, 5–6, 18, 27, 36, 37–39, 51, 61–62, 67–68, 69, 100–104, 145, 172, 196, 316;

Index

Constitution of, 65; and consultation, 12, 27, 124, 126–31, 138, 141–42, 165, 167, 204; and coronavirus pandemic, 58; and crime, 103, 104, 106; culture of, 63, 118, 121, 135, 161, 174, 230, 245, 248, 256, 257, 258, 259, 260, 262, 264, 275, 276, 279, 280, 281, 284; death penalty in, 96–97; and democracy, 12, 42, 48, 52, 53, 54–56, 74, 86, 115–21, 122, 129, 138–39, 141; and Department of Wildlife and National Parks (DWNP), 291; deportation of critics of, 162; and development, 52, 58, 160, 161, 162, 191, 193, 197, 199, 201, 206, 207, 215, 217–19, 221, 222, 234, 235, 240, 247, 256, 262, 263, 264, 265, 270, 271, 273, 274–75, 277, 279–80, 285, 288, 290–92, 294, 300, 305–6; as a developmental state, 263, 277, 301–2; diamond industry of, 58, 60, 162, 162, 188, 199, 202, 263, 305; Ditshiping in, 45, 211–14, 212, 215, 219, 293; eastern area of, 154, 157, 302; and economic crisis, 277; and economic growth, 207, 284; and economy, 51–58, 64, 69, 101, 135, 162, 197, 199, 200, 201, 221, 222, 233, 234, 236, 246–48, 256, 262, 263, 270, 273, 274, 279, 280, 281, 302; ecosystems of, 198, 246–47, 300–301; education in, 89, 112, 121, 142, 186, 202, 253; elephants of, 37, 56, 61–62, 85, 101–2, 104, 123–24, 134, 139–40, 262, 269–72, 278, 296, 314; elite class of, 55, 56, 180–81, 182, 199–200, 262; environmental histories of, 37, 56; and equality, 12, 53, 65, 139, 181, 206; and ethnicity, 53, 63–65, 68, 69, 118–19, 127, 133, 156, 166, 173, 183, 201, 207, 231–33, 237, 244, 266, 275–76, 312; and ethnolinguistic minorities, 53, 63, 64, 65, 67–69, 118–19, 122, 126, 165, 229–35, 275–76; and European settlers, 158, 172–73, 200; and evictions, 198, 231, 239; fieldwork in, 1–3, 38–46, 47, 73, 84, 96, 104, 114–15, 124–26, 136, 142, 147, 151, 152, 159, 164–66, 177, 179–80, 205, 213, 215, 222, 239, 240, 267, 285, 299, 305, 306; and Francistown, 158, 216–17; Gaborone in, 1, 41, 45, 92, 97, 130, 132, 137, 157, 158, 204, 206, 210, 216–17, 283, 288, 297, 298, 305, 306, 314; and gap between policy and practice, 12, 27, 165, 267, 300; and gathering and hunting, 234, 235, 236, 256–57, 263, 267, 290, 300, 303; and Ghanzi District, 39, 41, 44, 45, 67–68, 100, 106, 110, 126–27, 139, 151, 159, 170, 173–74, 177, 180, 182, 187–88, 200, 201–3, 206, 207, 220, 237, 239, 240, 245, 249, 252–53, 266, 267, 268, 282, 286, 288, 299; and Ghanzi Town, 202, 242, 253, 258; government of, 41–44, 47–48, 52–54, 56, 59, 64, 66, 67, 83, 89–95, 96, 98, 99–100, 105, 111, 117–33, 139, 141, 144, 146–48, 159–61, 162, 164, 165, 170, 175, 181, 200–207, 209–10, 213–15, 216, 229, 232, 234–35, 250, 251–54, 262, 263, 266, 277, 280, 284, 295, 299; and government seed program, 296; and Greater Mapungubwe area, 171; and Groot Laagte village, 106, 276; and Hambukushu, 68, 231; and health clinics, 202; and Herero, 68; and House of Chiefs, 65; and hunting and gathering, 242–43, 257, 267; ideology of, 63, 121; illiteracy rate in, 53; independence of, 43, 52–53, 54, 55, 56, 63, 64, 117, 118, 154, 162, 167, 171, 172, 263, 284; and indigeneity, 232, 233, 284; and indigenous people, 65, 67, 95, 101, 108, 138, 160–61, 184, 189, 251; and inequality of economic and social relations, 53–54, 55, 67, 232, 304, 313; and infrastructure, 48, 49, 58, 159, 192–97, 201–24, 305; and international community, 131, 134–35, 145, 147–48, 161–62; and international relations, 87–88, 96, 98, 177; and ivory trade, 143, 261; and the Kalahari debate, 232–34; and the Kalahari region, 38, 114, 191, 198, 199, 218, 237, 263, 285–86, 299; Kaudwane in, 160; Kgalagadi District in, 100, 267; and the *kgotla*, 232, 274, 299, 312; and Khwai community trust, 129; and Khwai village, 103–4, 125, 136, 141, 165, 166, 167, 208, 211, 218, 219, 280, 293, 300; and land and resources, 3, 74, 103, 128, 131, 152; land tenure regimes in, 36, 48, 153, 167, 173–74, 180, 190, 198;

Batswana (cont.)
languages of, 62, 63, 68, 121, 229, 231, 253; and limitation on mobility, 202, 203, 205, 210; and livelihoods, 161, 183–84, 205, 234, 236–37, 247, 257, 274, 275, 280, 291, 300, 304, 309, 311; Mababe in, 136, 138, 183, 184, 208, 210, 239, 268, 282, 293; and maintenance of conservation estate, 56, 89–90, 92, 94; maps of, 40, 41; Maun in, 69, 90, 110, 123, 174, 199, 208, 210, 211, 212, 219, 242, 271, 291, 293, 297; meaning of, 63; media in, 97, 98, 114, 117, 126–27, 137–38, 145, 162, 272, 273, 274, 299; military of, 97, 105, 107, 112, 147, 184, 306; and minerals, 160, 174, 188, 200; and Ministry of Environment, Natural Resources Conservation and Tourism (MENT), 56; and Ministry of Environment, Wildlife and Tourism (MEWT), 1; and minority rule, 102, 108; and modernization, 53, 220–21, 273, 285, 289, 292; and Molepolole village, 314; as monoethnic polity, 64; and Motswana, 8, 63, 101, 121, 131, 173, 182, 234, 272; multicultural reality of, 64, 65, 66–67; National Archives of, 313; and national unity, 63–65, 117; and natural resources, 58–59, 66, 103, 117, 122–23, 132, 139, 144–45, 160, 188, 200, 201, 230, 234, 240–42, 244–46, 254–56, 264, 267, 268, 270, 289, 292, 295, 302; New Xade in, 136, 151, 160, 165, 168, 187, 188, 200, 201, 202, 204, 205, 206, 237, 274, 279, 283; and non-Tswana people, 127, 154, 165, 183, 198, 231–32, 253; north and west of, 156, 157, 164, 173, 193, 194, 198, 207, 220–22, 235, 265, 295–96, 301, 315; Northwest District of, 39, 41, 44, 45, 67, 68–69, 133, 140, 156, 158, 166, 173–74, 183, 198, 199, 207–20, 221, 237, 239, 293, 294, 300; Okavango Delta in, 38, 68, 101, 143, 174, 180, 191, 198, 199, 200, 202, 208, 209, 210, 211–13, 215, 218, 219, 220, 222, 223, 242, 281, 293, 294, 301; and Okavango region, 198, 222, 224, 237, 294, 300; and Ovambo people, 68; parliament of, 54–55; police of, 97, 99, 105; and policing of human behavior, 93; political parties in, 66; and postcolonialism, 10, 42–43, 47, 52–53, 56, 64, 65, 66, 68, 117, 118, 119, 121–22, 126, 127, 133, 172, 201, 234, 263, 265; poverty in, 53, 200, 205, 234, 246, 249, 252, 255–56, 265, 267–68, 270, 272, 277, 290, 291, 292, 294–96, 299, 301; power in, 54–55, 65–66, 67, 74, 93, 124, 127–31, 136, 144, 146, 148; precolonial era of, 153–54; presidents of, 42, 64, 98, 124–26, 130, 133, 142–43, 145, 159, 167, 177, 179, 210, 216, 261, 266–67, 268, 269, 274, 277, 289; private landowners in, 44, 158, 170–82, 186; protected areas in, 17, 39, 67–68, 93–94, 103, 108, 125, 135, 151–52, 156–61, 164, 180, 183–86, 198, 203, 207, 231, 239, 286, 302; and race, 181–82, 190; and relationship between state and citizens, 42–43, 48, 63, 74–75, 100, 121, 132–34, 135, 164–70, 184, 193–94, 206, 208, 215, 221, 236–37, 278–79, 309; and relocation of residents, 4, 151, 159–61, 164–67, 168, 170, 186, 201, 202, 203, 204, 219, 220, 221, 222–23, 294, 310; and removal of people, 125, 158–62, 164–65, 180, 184, 200, 207, 217–18, 223; and repressive practices, 66, 162; Republic of, 8; and resettlement communities, 201–6, 240, 249, 268, 279–80, 282, 300; and resettlement of residents, 180, 201, 203, 240, 279–80; and resources, 239, 247, 263–64, 284; and resource-use policies, 137, 203, 206, 262, 282; and resource-use restrictions, 1, 92, 130, 134, 164, 201, 262, 268; and resource-use rights, 161, 186, 242; and roads, 207, 210–11, 216, 217, 219, 221; and rule of law, 98, 99–100, 121; and rural areas, 37, 48, 49, 60, 69, 104, 131–32, 134, 135, 137, 142, 143, 208, 216–17, 223–24, 237–39, 241, 292, 302, 309; rural development in, 230, 294–96, 302–4, 311; and rural subjects, 10, 11, 49, 69; and rural-urban divide, 192, 216; Sankuyo in, 45, 103, 105, 109, 125–26, 129, 136, 207, 208, 210, 217, 293, 294–95; San people in, 66, 67, 68, 92,

114, 122, 137, 151, 154, 159, 160, 161, 162, 164–67, 168, 180, 183, 184–87, 190, 201, 202, 204, 206, 207, 231–35, 237, 239, 242, 243, 248–49, 252, 253, 255, 256–60, 262, 263, 265, 266, 270, 274, 275, 276, 278, 279, 280–82, 284, 286–88, 289, 303; and securitization, 47–48, 82–91, 92, 104–7, 115, 140–41, 276; and sedentarization, 194, 203, 207, 222; and Serowe village, 157; and Setswana, 45, 63, 214–15, 229, 231, 232, 253, 280; and settlement, 157–58, 201, 203, 206, 219, 220, 222, 224; and shoot-to-kill policy, 95–100, 112; and social order or organization, 164, 213–15; and social programs, 266, 267, 270, 292; and social services, 201, 202, 204–7, 213, 218; and social trespass, 92; southern area of, 164; and sovereignty, 87, 111, 112, 145; state building in, 8–12, 27, 47, 63, 64, 69, 74, 121, 126, 127, 138, 148, 173, 192, 221, 222, 234, 277, 278, 283, 284, 307; and subjectivities, 46, 65–66, 251; success of, 51–53, 55–56, 266; and surveillance, 108, 110, 309; and Tawana land, 155, 156; and Transkalahari Highway, 202; and transmission of disease, 292–93; tribes of, 65; and Tsodilo Hills historical site, 68; and Tswana chieftaincies (*merafe*), 153–54; and Tswanadom, 63, 64, 121–22, 281; Tswana ethnic chauvinism in, 53; and Tswana institutions, 127, 146, 232; and Tswana "mainstream," 230–31, 234, 262, 263, 284, 290; and Tswana majoritarianism, 64, 257, 259; and Tswana-speaking groups, 63, 65, 66–67, 118, 121, 126, 134, 154, 156, 157, 164, 174, 183, 186, 232, 234, 276, 283, 284; and Tswana villages, 217; University of, 1; and urban areas, 139, 145, 158, 202, 216–17; urbanization of, 37; and use of force, 83, 84, 85, 107, 115, 147, 148, 167; and violence, 66, 89, 102, 103, 252, 297; and wealth creation, 60, 285, 292; and welfare programs, 253, 266, 277, 289, 291; western region of, 193; and West Hanahai, 279–80, 285; white citizens of, 63, 68, 173–74, 176, 177–78, 254; and white settlers, 151; women in, 66, 122, 125, 229, 238, 248, 250–55; and world's natural heritage, 47, 68, 220; and Xuoxao, 213, 218, 219, 220, 294. See also Batswana; conservation estate; data collection; poaching

Botswana Defence Force (BDF), 73, 83, 85, 87, 88–90, 91, 94, 96, 98, 99, 103, 106. *See also* conservation; conservation estate; poaching

Botswana Democratic Party (BDP), 54, 142–43, 144, 178, 216, 261

Bourdieu, Pierre, 107, 108

British South Africa Company, 158

carbon offset or sequestration, 19–20, 317

Central Kalahari Game Reserve (CKGR), 18, 67–68, 125, 151, 152, 153, 157, 159–69, 162, 185, 198. See also Botswana; wildlife

Chobe National Park, 18, 68, 143, 159, 164, 167, 183–84, 198, 223, 239

Citizen and Subject: Contemporary Africa and the Legacy of Late Colonialism (Mamdani), 32

community-built bridges, 213–15, 214, 218

conservation: and "Accumulation by Conservation," 60; and African state formation, 27, 28, 37, 51; and animal rights, 62; and armed rangers, 82; in Australia, 14; and authority, 9, 14, 30, 74–75; and biodiversity conservation, 2, 3–7, 9, 13–14, 17, 19, 21, 27, 29, 43, 46, 47, 59–60, 61, 76, 80–83, 91, 152, 156, 230, 237, 246, 291, 307, 317, 318; and Botswana Defence Force (BDF), 123; Botswana's focus on, 37, 56, 88; and Botswana's securitized conservation estate, 83, 87–95, 130; and capital extraction, 224; and Central Kalahari Game Reserve (CKGR), 294; and charismatic species, 74, 85, 88, 134; and coercion, 76, 79, 81, 82–83, 89, 91, 95, 105–7; and collection permits, 244–46, 250–51; and colonialism, 156–57; and commercialization, 236, 246–47; and commitment to green values, 5; and communities, 215–16; and Community-Based Natural Resource Management (CBNRM) program, 59, 186;

conservation (cont.)
and community escort guides, 104–5, 106; and conservation biology, 14, 15, 22; and conservation policies, 4, 6–7, 10, 11, 13, 15, 18, 19–20, 22, 27, 28, 37, 48, 74, 82, 83, 87, 89, 92, 95–100, 111, 115, 123, 124, 128, 131, 140, 143–46, 148, 157, 164, 190, 225, 235–36, 246–47, 249, 250, 259, 261, 273, 283, 284–85, 288, 289, 290, 300, 302, 305–7; and conservation science, 36; and control of resources and territory, 307; and Department of Wildlife and National Parks (DWNP), 87, 89–92, 100, 112, 139, 140, 179; and development, 230, 259, 262, 274, 308; and dispossession, 101, 158; and "eco-communities," 36–37; and ecology, 19–22, 28, 36–37, 74, 88, 92, 93; enforcement of, 47, 48, 73–74, 81, 87–95, 96, 103, 104–7, 110, 112, 124, 240, 251–52; in Europe, 27; and experts, 134, 136–37, 244; and fortress conservation, 76; and game farms, 170, 254–55; and game reserves, 164, 198, 317; and global heritage, 198; of globally important species, 4, 20, 81, 101–2, 123–24, 134; global movement for, 13, 19, 20, 145, 313; and Global North, 13–14; and government, 2, 10–11, 13–14, 131–34; and hunting, 278; impacts of, 318; and inequality, 57; and international institutions, 3, 12–13, 19; international movement for, 61, 134; and the Kalahari region, 300; land devoted to, 18, 19, 203; and land tenure regimes, 190; and law, 241–43, 245, 247, 250–51, 252; and limitation on residency, 251; and livelihoods, 284; and local knowledge, 137, 283–85; and London, 123–24, 160; and Makgadikgadi Pans National Park, 159, 164; and marine and coastal areas, 19; militarization of, 78–81, 83, 105; and movements of capital and ideas, 7, 81–82; neoliberalization of, 14, 18, 57–58, 60, 81; and New York City, 123–24; in New Zealand, 14; and nongovernmental organizations (NGOs), 3, 20, 44, 78, 82, 83, 98, 134, 160; in North America, 27; and Nxai Pan National Park, 159, 164; and ostrich eggshells, 230, 247–52, 254–55; and parks, 19, 27, 103, 135, 164, 167, 169–70, 171, 203, 207, 240, 266, 317; and participation in programs, 185–86, 188; and payment-for-ecosystem models, 318; and policing of human behavior, 9, 82, 240–41, 308; political economy of, 62; politics of, 27–28, 79, 82, 103; and postcolonial states, 156, 307; potential for, 316; and power, 14, 111–12; and private corporations, 3; and private land ownership, 176–77; and private military firms, 82–83; and race, 179; and "Remote Area Dwellers" (RADs), 231–32; resistance to, 12, 48, 136–37; and resources, 14, 21, 123, 147, 188, 230, 242, 251–52, 262; and restrictions, 181, 205, 236, 244, 251–52, 270, 292, 295; and rurality, 28, 36, 37, 132; and rural-urban divide, 7–8, 49; and securitization, 75, 77–78, 79, 83, 95–100, 103, 104–5, 108–11, 115, 132, 141; and spatial control, 28, 46; and spatial organization, 164; and spectacle, 57; and the state, 6–9, 28–30, 100, 102–4, 110–11, 136–37; and state building, 8–9, 27–30, 37, 46, 111, 152–53, 190, 317, 318; and statehood, 13; and subjectivities, 46, 57, 100–103, 230; and tourism, 61–62; and urban spaces, 28, 37; and veldt products, 246; and village conservation trusts, 104; and violence, 75, 76, 78, 81; and wilderness spaces, 61, 225; and wildlife, 34, 59, 75, 134–35, 139–41; and world's protected areas, 220. *See also* Africa; conservation estate; tourism; wildlife

Conservation Biology (Dietz and Czech), 15

conservation estate: and African countries, 17, 18, 27, 28, 30, 37–38; and agrarian production, 22, 33–35, 302; and air travel, 211; and Asia, 6; and authority, 319; and biodiversity conservation, 4, 9, 13–14, 15, 19, 21, 27, 36, 80–81, 110, 156; and Botswana Defence Force (BDF), 129; and Botswana's ecosystems, 38, 39, 68; and Botswana's history, 63, 68, 108, 143, 153–54, 156–58; and Botswana's securitized conservation estate, 47–48, 74–75, 82, 85, 100–101, 107–11, 127–28; and boundaries, 239–41; and the Caribbean, 6; and cash economy, 303; and cattle, 277, 289, 292, 294, 295, 296, 300, 302; and Central Kalahari Game Reserve (CKGR), 286; and citizenship, 9–10, 11, 15–16, 41, 48, 49, 100, 121, 122, 123, 127–28, 134–35, 140–41, 148, 152–53, 174, 186, 217, 292, 309–11; and citizen-state relations, 310–11, 316, 318; in the climate crisis, 317; coercion on, 75, 89, 129; and commercialization, 247–49, 255–56, 259; and communal identity, 275; and community, 124, 125–16, 129, 144; and Community-Based Natural Resource Management (CBNRM) program, 39, 144–45, 186, 187–89, 268, 271, 291–92; concept of, 4, 7, 8–9, 12–17, 15, 103; and Crown land, 154; dehumanization of people on, 100–101, 108; and Department of Wildlife and National Parks (DWNP), 56, 89, 90–92, 139, 140; and dependency on government, 290–92, 300–301, 302, 311; and development, 229, 234, 247, 253, 309; and discourse, practice, and technology, 24, 95–100; and ecology, 13, 17, 21–22, 35–36, 38, 172, 286, 301, 304, 316; and economic commodification, 316; and economy, 16, 59, 248–49; and ethnicity, 8, 67, 281; and ethnolinguistic claims, 138; and ethnolinguistic minorities, 229; and expansionism, 13, 20, 21–22, 50, 158; and experts, 132, 138; farming on, 296–97; and fishing, 242; and food insecurity, 272, 296–97; and game meat, 271, 272, 287–88; and gathering, 237–47, 250; and Ghanzi's estate, 178; and the Global North, 61, 81, 135, 136; and Global South, 316; and hunter-gatherers, 237–39, 303; and hunting ban, 114–15, 132, 136, 273, 276; infrastructure in, 38–39, 48–49, 192–94, 201–2, 209, 210–11, 217, 220–23, 225, 306, 313; and international institutions or systems, 19–20, 46–47, 131, 309; in the Kalahari region, 207; and lack of transportation, 253; and landowners, 180, 187; and land politics, 29–37, 48, 187; and land tenure, 38, 39, 48, 182–83; and Latin America, 6; and limits on residency, 38; and livelihoods, 36, 38, 47, 92, 137, 229, 256, 259, 268–69, 270, 276, 286, 298–99, 304; and local levels, 225; and marginalization, 144, 147–48, 242, 253, 259, 271, 286, 306; militarization of, 99, 105–6, 127, 129, 147; and Nairobi National Park, 37; and national rural development, 38, 286; and natural resources, 92, 128, 248; and natural sciences, 14, 36; and negotiation, 311; Ngamiland in, 143; in non-Tswana areas, 67, 127, 259; and non-Tswana Batswana, 63, 69, 127, 146; in northern conservation areas, 104, 143, 223, 269; and ostrich eggshells, 247–52, 249, 254–55, 258, 313; and parks, 5, 15, 35, 56, 152, 157, 159, 201; and payment-for-ecosystem models, 18, 20; and people of Botswana, 8–9, 47–48, 67–69, 100–101, 105–6, 108–10, 124, 127–33, 136–37, 139, 157, 225, 242, 246, 254–56, 259, 289, 297–99, 303; and percentage of African land, 5–6, 37, 67–68, 152, 157; and poacher as foreigner, 107, 108, 109; and politics, 5, 9, 13, 14, 15, 21–22, 116, 318; and power, 12, 13, 107–8; and privately owned land, 171–72, 175–77, 182, 312; and private wildlife ranches, 18, 175–77; and protected areas, 14, 18–22, 103, 157; and protection of animals, 209, 283; and race, 153, 175, 182; and relationship between state and citizen, 15, 46–47, 49, 59, 86, 102–7, 111, 112–13, 115–16, 131–34, 136, 137–39, 142, 167–70, 184, 192, 204, 209–11, 224, 245–46, 248, 252–53, 255, 291, 307, 309; and relocation of residents, 206, 217; and removal of people, 68, 158–61, 167, 170, 201; and resistance, 115, 116, 137, 148; and resources, 12, 47, 89, 110, 111, 229, 239, 240, 244–46, 248–49, 255–56, 271, 274–75, 277, 295–96, 301; restrictions on, 49, 239, 240–41, 247, 290, 301; and roads, 207–8, 253, 306; and rural communities, 89, 137, 253, 272, 315; and rural differentiation, 307–8;

conservation estate (*cont.*)
and rural politics, 18, 30–31, 32, 75, 139; rural resistance to, 9, 11, 12, 46; and rural spaces, 9–10, 16, 30–37, 43, 46, 75, 231; and rural-urban divide, 49, 137; and safari hunting, 266; and San people, 257; and securitization, 39, 47–48, 81, 82–86, 95, 96–103, 108–10, 112, 116, 145–46, 148, 184, 308, 310, 312; and service provision, 225; and shoot-to-kill victims, 97; size of, 94; and social order or organization, 48, 172; and social sciences, 15; as sociopolitical category, 38–39, 46, 116, 138, 224, 239, 308, 315, 316; and spatial organization, 165, 166, 172, 220; and the state, 308, 319; and state building, 5, 7, 9, 11–12, 15, 16, 21, 22, 28, 46–47, 49, 62, 69, 93, 138, 152, 153, 192–93, 237, 259, 303, 306, 307, 309, 310, 316; state use of, 124–25; and subjectivities, 10, 43, 46, 49, 62, 131, 190, 192, 217, 230, 242–43, 302, 309–10; and territory, 319; and *therisanyo* (consultation), 142, 144, 145–46, 148, 210; and transfrontier conservation areas, 18, 87, 171; and Tuli Block, 157; types of, 14, 15, 18, 34–35, 38–39, 171; and urban areas, 30, 315–16; and use of force, 95; and value of cultural practices, 303; and veldt products, 237, 238, 240, 241, 244; and village development committees, 44; and violence, 310; and voting, 138; and welfare programs, 236; and Western gaze, 48; western region of, 222, 271, 276; and wilderness spaces, 34–35, 67, 135–36; and Wildlife Management Areas (WMAs), 35, 38, 39, 157; and wildlife products, 236, 271. See also Central Kalahari Game Reserve (CKGR); hunting; land; wildlife
Convention on Biological Diversity (CBD), 19, 20
Convention on International Trade in Endangered Species of Wild Fauna and Flora (CITES), 261
Copenhagen School, 75, 79, 80, 86, 98

data collection, 38–46, 67, 123
Death, Carl, 7, 8, 22, 24, 26–27, 152, 207.

See also *Green State in Africa, The* (Death)
democracy: and 2019 national election, 42, 142–44; and accountability, 115, 117, 138, 147; and authority, 117–18, 119, 120, 124, 147; and Botswana's securitized conservation estate, 129, 142, 145–47; and citizenship, 137–42, 310; and community levels, 117, 120, 124, 144–45; and consensus, 120, 142, 145, 146; and consent of the people, 118, 119, 146–47; and conservation, 309; and the conservation estate, 308; decentralized, 117; and democratic norms, 74, 116, 120, 121, 129, 142; and democratic rights, 53, 54, 119, 121, 142; and *dikgotla*, 48, 66, 115, 117–28, 120, 122, 124; and electoral democracy in Botswana, 53, 54–55, 86, 115–16, 118, 119, 120, 121, 142–48; and "freedom squares," 120; and indigenous democratic traditions, 126; participation in, 12, 48, 115, 116, 119, 120, 122, 129, 145–47, 309; and presidential power, 54–55; and race, 173; and resistance, 146; scholarship about, 52, 54; and state building, 115, 116; and *therisanyo* (consultation), 118–20, 122–30, 138, 141–42; and Umbrella for Democratic Change (UDC), 143, 144; and voting, 115, 116, 138, 139, 141, 142, 145, 312

Elephants (film), 61–62
environment: access to, 271; and activist groups, 20–21; and African state building, 7, 22; and biodiversity conservation, 6, 20, 50, 73, 76; and Botswana's ecosystems, 38, 39; and cattle production, 263, 286; and climate change, 21, 50, 286, 314, 315, 317–18; and community levels, 117; and conservation policies, 3, 5, 6–7, 79, 318; and Department of Wildlife and National Parks (DWNP), 123, 313, 315; and development, 222; and ecosystems, 203; and education, 90, 91, 105; and food gathering, 236, 237–39, 240, 242–45; and forests, 20, 79; and fossil fuels, 5; and global heritage, 13, 20, 39; and governance, 26–27, 79;

Index   389

and Half-Earth coalition, 6, 20–21; histories of, 5, 37; human relations with, 3, 13, 56–57, 203, 273; and hunting or gathering, 203, 232, 273; and the *kgotla*, 122–23; management of, 14, 19–20, 76, 117; and Ministry of Environment, Natural Resources Conservation and Tourism (MENT), 56, 267; and national security, 312; and ostrich eggshells, 236, 251; and payment-for-ecosystem models, 317; and people-free areas, 221; policies about, 42, 43, 76, 79, 141, 261, 301; and political authority, 3; political nature of, 2–3, 26, 29, 42; protection of, 104–5, 106; and roads, 208; and San people, 232–33, 289; and securitization, 89, 93, 107–8; and social sciences, 20–21; and social welfare, 301; and solar farms, 318; and the state, 307; stewardship of, 282, 283–84; and thatching grass, 237, 238; and world's protected areas, 12–13, 19–22, 27, 68. *See also* Convention on Biological Diversity (CBD)
European Union, 292–93

Freedom House, 120

Gabon, 6, 17, 85
Global North, 61, 77, 135, 136, 139, 199, 274
Global South: and coerciveness of conservation, 76; and colonial land control, 6; and government, 16; and "green grabbing" of land, 18; poor people in, 21; postcolonies of, 3, 5; and securitization, 77, 81; and state building, 26; and world's protected areas, 6, 12–13, 19, 21, 30, 37–38, 316, 317
Good, Kenneth, 55
"green grabbing," 17–18
Green State in Africa, The (Death), 8, 26

Hardy, Tom, 73
Harvard Kalahari Research Group, 232
hunting: and animal rights, 266; and animals and plants, 236, 258, 282; ban on, 1, 4, 42, 74, 82, 110–11, 114–15, 123, 124, 125–29, 132, 143, 144, 153, 172, 175–77, 179, 180, 182, 225, 258, 261, 263, 265, 266–70, 272, 273, 275, 276–79, 281, 285, 288–90, 295, 312; and citizen hunting licenses, 271–73, 280; clandestine, 110, 111, 276; commercial safari, 44, 178–79, 261, 262, 264, 265, 266, 268, 269, 276, 285; and Community-Based Natural Resource Management (CBNRM) program, 266; and Controlled Hunting Areas (CHAs), 157, 179, 269; and Department of Wildlife and National Parks (DWNP), 106, 111; and ecology, 278; as an economic strategy, 267; and elephants, 262, 278; ending of, 215, 268; and environment, 264; and establishment of parks, 159; and game meat, 263–64, 275–81, 285, 290; and game ranches, 170, 175–76, 179, 180–81, 276; and game reserves, 156–57, 266; and hunter-gatherers, 160, 238, 267; and identity, 270, 275–76; and illegal activities, 84, 107; and livelihoods, 115, 267, 270, 271, 276, 278, 280, 290; and media reports, 114–15; and natural resources, 230, 270, 271; noncommercial, 264, 265, 271, 272, 273, 277–78, 280–81, 288, 289, 290; and nonendangered animals, 278; and people's traditions, 256, 270, 271, 272, 274–76; and policy changes, 143–44, 267–70, 271; and private landowners, 179; and quotas, 107, 266, 267, 268–70, 276, 295; and rights, 265–68, 277–78, 288; San reliance on, 275–76; and Special Game Licences, 159, 261, 262, 264, 265–68, 270, 271–72, 274–75, 277, 281, 288, 289, 300; and the state, 132, 179, 266–67, 288; and state building, 236; subsistence, 265, 266, 270, 273, 276, 281, 286, 300; trophy, 258, 261, 264, 272; and Tswana-speaking groups, 265; and wild meat, 205, 269, 270, 271, 272. *See also* poaching

identity: and Botswana's polity, 161, 264; and centralized villages, 164; and citizenship, 256, 262; communal, 275; and the conservation estate, 18, 46, 243–44, 251, 259–60, 262, 308; and conservation programs, 235; and criminalized identities, 49, 230, 251–52; and development, 259;

identity (*cont.*)
and ethnicity, 8, 18, 229, 237, 259, 283, 284; formation of, 4, 5, 69, 270; and game meat, 275–76, 279; and gathering and hunting, 243–47, 250–52, 279, 281; and identity-based claims, 237, 252, 259–60, 282; individual, 275; and livelihoods, 18, 46, 234–36, 281; and modes of resistance, 312–13; national, 27, 63, 306; non-Tswana, 236, 241, 281; poachers', 110, 112–13; political, 29, 62, 290; and political claims, 187; and political subjectivities, 10; politics, 127, 183; and race, 18, 181; and San people, 165, 233–35, 256–60; and the state, 25, 52; and state building, 23, 259; and subjectivities, 49; and Tswana-speaking groups, 259, 284; and undifferentiated rights, 10–11; and Western ideals, 235

Kenya, 6, 17, 96, 171
kgosi (chief), 41–42, 44, 118, 126–27, 128, 154, 156–57, 165, 197, 229, 294–95
kgotla, 48, 66, 115, 117–31, 138, 142, 146, 147, 148, 202, 204, 205. *See also* authority; Botswana; democracy
Khama, Ian, 42, 124–25, 126, 167, 177, 261, 262, 273, 274
Khama, Seretse, 64, 88, 96, 118, 142, 143, 159, 167, 216
Khama, Tshekedi, 95
Khama Rhino Sanctuary, 157
Kiema, Kuela, 187, 256, 274

land: access to, 6, 110, 152, 168, 173, 292; and the African state, 27–30, 33–34, 35, 128, 152–53, 157–58, 170–72; agricultural, 30, 158; alienation from, 17, 153, 158, 312; and armed forces, 103; and authority, 29; boards, 156, 174; and Botswana's history, 159; capital of, 60; and cattle farms, 176, 179, 200, 222; and cattle posts (*moraka*), 154, 156; characteristics of, 174; claims, 222; and class, 174; and commercial freehold farms, 202; communal/tribal, 18, 35, 36, 38, 153, 156, 171, 174; and community-mapping, 185; competition for, 22, 29; and conservation, 29, 128, 153, 164, 165, 171–72; and conservation policies, 33–34, 128; control over, 6, 9, 14, 28, 29, 46, 58, 308, 310; Crown, 154, 155, 156, 157; dispossession, 167, 172, 201; disputes over, 1, 29; and evictions, 1, 125, 158, 159, 162, 194, 223, 231; and expansionism, 220; farm, 154, 158, 203; and game farms, 175, 176–82, 254, 258, 268, 276, 278; and game reserves, 162, 164, 167, 183–84, 189; and Ghanzi Farm Block, 68, 158; and Ghanzi Land Board, 154; and Ghanzi wildlife ranch, 18; and a global commons, 20; governance of, 7, 27–30, 33–34, 152, 183, 187, 190; and hunting and gathering, 183–84; and inequality, 170; and infrastructure, 217; and landowners, 189–90; and land-use patterns, 205; and limitation on mobility, 192; and livelihoods, 156, 161, 183–84; and Lobatse, 158; and Mababe village, 167, 183–84; and marginalization, 172, 190; militarization of, 103–4, 184; and nongovernmental organizations (NGOs), 161, 162; non-use of, 18, 29, 34–35; and ownership, 48, 66, 151–54, 158, 164, 167, 168, 170–72, 173, 175–77, 182–90, 192, 207; and political space, 17–20, 29–30, 33; politics, 166–67; politics of, 34–37, 62, 171–72, 192; and postcolonialism, 3, 6–7, 159; and power, 171–72; private freehold, 18, 35, 36, 44, 45, 48, 67, 68, 151, 153, 154, 156–58, 161, 167, 170, 171–74, 176, 178, 180, 183, 184, 187, 278; and private property, 55, 153, 170–77, 179, 180, 184, 189, 190, 225; as property, 28, 29, 33, 170; and race, 170, 171, 172–74, 177, 180; and resettlement villages, 161; and resources, 3–4, 29, 58–59, 104, 110, 152, 153, 158, 161; restrictions on, 34; and rights, 74, 152, 158, 160, 161, 164, 166, 167, 168, 171, 172, 185–87; rural, 30–33, 158, 308, 310; and rural communities, 171; setting aside of, 5–8, 17, 19, 37–38; and settlements, 36, 152, 158; and spatial control, 48; and spatial organization, 168–69, 201; state, 18, 35, 36, 38, 112, 153, 156–57, 170, 171, 174, 179, 186, 187; and the state, 167–70, 174, 178,

Index

184; and state building, 3, 28–30, 34, 152–53, 172; and Tati Concession, 158; and Tawana Land Board, 174; tenure, 28, 29, 35, 36, 38, 39, 153, 154, 167, 168, 170, 172–74, 178–79, 182–84, 312; and territory, 28, 29, 31, 46, 48, 69, 95, 151, 152, 153, 154, 158, 168, 170, 172, 183, 185, 186, 187, 189–90, 192, 193, 194, 196, 206, 207, 239, 309; and tourism, 57, 222; trespassing on, 109, 184; and Tribal Grazing Land Policy, 286; and Tribal Land Act, 156; and tribal reserves, 154, 155, 156; and tribal territory, 187; and Tswana areas, 157; and Tswana chieftaincies (*merafe*), 153–54, 156; Tswana organization of, 154, 156; and Tuli Block wildlife ranch, 18, 30, 158; "unoccupied," 30, 183; use of, 18, 19, 29, 33, 36, 40, 154, 164, 183, 201, 235; and white people, 17, 158, 181–82; and wilderness spaces, 49, 73, 156, 208, 209, 217, 218–20, 221, 223, 224; and wildlife, 42–43, 156–57, 203; and Zimbabwe's Fast Track Land Reform, 177, 178. *See also* Central Kalahari Game Reserve (CKGR); conservation estate; *Sesana and Others v. the Attorney General*; wildlife

Lion King, The (film), 61
Lord's Resistance Army, 77

Mamdani, Mahmood, 8, 32, 35
Markle, Meghan, 62
Masisi, Mokgweetsi, 42, 96, 98, 142–43, 144, 145, 261, 262, 269, 271, 288, 290
Merafhe, Mompati, 235–36
Mmusi, Peter, 118
Mogae, Festus, 274
Mokolodi Game Reserve, 157
Moremi Game Reserve, 18, 68, 135, 158–59, 164, 165, 167, 198, 211, 223
Mugabe, Robert, 177, 178

Namibia, 17, 54, 96, 98, 158, 173
Nature Needs Half, 20

Pilane, Sidney, 162, 164
poaching: and antipoaching decisions, 130, 134, 140; and antipoaching patrols, 24, 73, 90, 94–95, 105; and antipoaching sign, *109*; and antipoaching strategies, 1, 4, 74, 75, 98, 112–13, 312; and armed antipoaching operations, 81, 82–83, 88, 99, 261; and Botswana Defence Force (BDF), 73, 83, 88–90, 91, 94, 98; and Botswana's antipoaching policy, 82, 84, 89–90, 91, 95–100, 112–13; and crime, 82, 94, 97, 99, 100; and cross-border raids, 86; definition of, 82; and dehumanization, 112; and Department of Wildlife and National Parks (DWNP), 84, 85, 86, 87, 94, 98, 110; and elephants, 101; and human rights, 96, 98; and hunting ban, 111; and ivory wars, 76; and military, 47, 73–74, 84–86, 88–90, 93, 95, 97–99, 101, 107; as a national security issue, 83–85, 96, 98, 99–100; and poachers, 75, 78, 84, 85, 87, 92, 93, 96, 97, 99, 107–12, 240–41, 244, 251, 276, 281, 310; and Poaching Wars, 73–74; and resources, 189; and securitization, 74, 75, 77, 84–100, 101, 107, 108–9, 110, 112; and shoot-to-kill policy, 87–88, 95–100, 112; and subjectivities, 107; and terrorism, 78, 82; and use of force, 134; and violence, 82, 108, 112

Poaching Wars (documentary), 73–74, 82
Political Topographies of the African State: Territorial Authority and Institutional Choice (Boone), 32
politics: and African politics, 7, 12, 17, 18, 27–28, 30–37, 48, 54, 62, 100–103, 118, 142–46, 177; and agency, 130; and authoritarianism, 54; and biodiversity conservation, 9, 19, 80–81; in Botswana, 63–64, 74, 148; and centralized villages, 164; and conservation, 317; and conservation estates, 9, 15–22, 142–48; and consultation, 144, 148; and corporations, 6; and debate, 80, 81; electoral, 88, 142–45; environmental, 316; and environmental goals, 19–22, 78, 81; ethnic, 65, 165–66; and ethnicity, 233; and the *kgotla*, 129–30, 143; of land, 7, 17–22, 27–28, 33–36, 166–67, 173, 183; and language, 63; and minority ethnic groups, 65, 66–67; and natural resources, 6, 145; nature of, 2, 3, 4, 32, 69, 318;

politics (*cont.*)
and nongovernmental organizations (NGOs), 6; and Okavango MP, 216; and policy changes, 144–45; and political authority, 3, 14; and political ecology, 6, 7, 17, 307, 318; and political economy, 3, 7, 53, 232–33; and the political forest, 16–17, 36; and political parties, 54, 142–44; and political rights, 119; and power of the executive, 54–55; and precolonial political traditions, 118; of protected areas, 5–8, 17, 35–36; and race, 48, 162, 172–73, 182; and rights to resources, 74, 186; rural, 30–37; and social sciences, 16; and spatial organization, 192; and the state, 23, 25, 192; and state building, 307; and subjectivities, 100, 103; and Tswana chieftaincies (*merafe*), 154; and wildlife, 102–3, 139. See also Botswana Democratic Party (BDP); democracy

Property and Political Order: Land Rights and the Structure of Politics in Africa (Boone), 32

protected area downgrading, downsizing, and degazettement (PADDD), 21–22, 151–52

Remote Area Dwellers Programme, 67, 201

Rhodes, Cecil, 158

Seeing Like a State (Scott), 24, 200
self-reliance, 214–15
Selous Game Reserve, 198
Sesana and Others v. the Attorney General, 151, 159, 160, 162, 164, 166
slavery, 154
South Africa, 6, 17, 27, 36–37, 54, 64, 65, 78, 98, 155, 158, 171. See also Africa
Southeast Asia, 15, 17, 195–96, 317
State and the Social, The (Gulbrandsen), 65–66
states: African, 6–11, 13–14, 17, 23, 25, 26–33, 82–83, 121, 131–32, 152, 153–54, 162, 195, 224, 306; armed agents of, 129; and authority, 75, 84, 88–89, 109–10, 124, 130–33, 146, 148, 159, 194; borders of, 93, 112; and citizenship, 2, 3, 4, 5, 8, 10, 11, 25, 29, 31, 75, 100, 127, 133, 139, 148, 164, 167, 182, 235–36, 247; and citizens' mobility, 195; and coercion, 82–83, 100; and colonialism, 17, 30, 32, 39, 153, 154; and communities, 190; and consensus, 131; and consent of the people, 130, 134, 146, 148, 306, 312; and conservation estates, 4, 5–6, 7, 10–11, 25, 27, 38–39, 51, 116, 130–34, 152–53; and conservation's benefits, 305; and consultation, 116, 128, 130–34, 145–48; and contested land, 29; and control of natural resources, 3–4, 14, 28, 29, 58–60, 152; and cultural specificity, 312; and debate, 98, 124; and democracy, 2, 31; and development, 195, 230; developmental, 52, 58, 59; environmental, or "green," 7, 8, 26–27, 152; and equality of citizens, 11, 12, 133, 165; and ethnically heterogeneous territory, 63; and ethnicity, 52, 63; of exception, 79–80, 94, 98, 99, 104, 133; formation of, 65, 112; and freedom of movement, 128; functions of, 7; and Global North, 274; and identities, 230; and indigenous rights, 65; and inequality, 66; and infrastructure, 192–97, 201–2, 224; and institutional securitization, 86; institutions of, 13, 66, 127; and land, 4, 5–7, 27–30, 31, 131, 152–53, 189, 193, 205; and legibility versus illegibility, 195–97; and limitation on mobility, 201; and livelihoods, 230; and local elites, 33; and local levels, 126, 127–30, 132–33; and marginalization, 195; and military governments, 129; military personnel of, 39, 47; and modernization, 201; and movements of capital, 194; nation-, 230, 263, 270; and national resources, 174; and nation building, 5; and natural resources, 7, 48, 82, 103, 130, 230; nature of, 26; Nordic, 27; and participation, 27, 181; and political economy, 7; politics of, 15–16, 25, 26–27; and postcolonialism, 6, 7, 8, 25, 26, 28, 30–32, 36, 153; post-Soviet, 5; and power, 128, 130, 147, 194, 195, 309; power of, 26, 31–33, 35, 75, 82–83, 98, 107, 118, 128, 225; and practical securitization, 86;

and private landowners, 180; and private property rights, 48, 225; and public education, 24; and public works initiatives, 254; and refugees, 102; relationship between citizen and, 8, 9–11, 32, 35–36, 41, 46–47, 49, 86, 102–4, 107–13, 115, 122, 128–34, 140–41, 147–48, 154, 162, 193–95, 310; and relocation of people, 153, 201; and resettlement communities, 224; resistance to, 49, 115, 141, 142, 153, 186, 188, 190, 194, 196, 210, 213, 221, 225, 237, 251, 259, 308, 311–12; and resources, 110, 112, 128, 152, 188–89, 236; and the rural experience, 30, 31–34, 49, 137; and rural-urban divide, 9, 31, 32, 33; and securitization, 79–82, 86, 109–13, 148; services of, 221; and settlement on land, 29; social construction of, 22–26; and social order or organization, 4, 22, 25, 29, 32, 35, 194; and sovereignty, 15–16, 22–23, 24, 83, 111, 112, 152; and spatial control, 194, 221; spectrum of, 52; and state building, 2, 3, 4, 5, 7, 8, 9–12, 15–17, 22–24, 25–32, 36, 46–49, 69, 76, 100, 116, 121–22, 133, 135, 164, 179, 196, 233, 270, 311; and statehood, 2, 6, 11, 22–23, 27, 31, 52, 86, 117; and subject formation, 112; and subjectivities, 15, 75, 121, 128; and surveillance, 11, 84, 87, 94, 95, 106, 111, 189, 241; and territory, 4, 7, 16, 24, 25, 84, 94, 152, 164–66, 170, 186; and Tswana merafe, 153–54, 186; and undifferentiated rights, 10–11; and the unitary state, 10, 63, 301, 302; and use of force, 81, 83, 84, 95–96, 104–5; and violence of conservation, 78, 96; Weberian ideas of, 23–24, 25; white-ruled, 64; and wilderness spaces, 194, 195–96, 236. See also conservation estate; democracy; *Green State in Africa, The* (Death)
States of Imagination (Hansen and Stepputat), 25–26

Tanzania, 6, 17, 27, 37, 68, 78, 85, 96, 198, 209
tourism: and access to parks, 169–70; and accommodations for tourists, 202, 205, 210, 219, 256; and Batswana, 135, 218; and Botswana Tourism Organisation (BTO), 219; business of, 145, 162, 171, 190, 193, 199–200, 219, 220, 263, 317; and celebrity conservationists, 61, 62; and commercial safaris, 44, 60, 61, 82, 134, 135, 139, 191, 197, 198, 199, 209; and communities, 125, 200; and concern about wildlife, 84–85; and the conservation estate, 198; and conservation policies, 305–6; and development, 197–98, 200; eco-, 221; economic benefits of, 10–11, 36, 57–58, 60, 135, 140, 172, 198–99; and employment, 205; and European-descended Batswana, 69; and fears of relocation, 219; and infrastructure, 201–2, 208, 218–20, 224, 225; and international tourists, 60–61, 134–35, 136, 199, 306; and militarism, 78, 82; and Ministry of Environment, Natural Resources Conservation and Tourism (MENT), 56; and natural resources, 251; and Okavango Delta region, 220; operators, 41, 44, 218–19, 222, 306; and peoplelessness, 310; photographic, 44, 60, 174; political economy of, 196; and pristine landscapes, 219; public-private partnerships in, 58; and race, 173, 182; and role of spectacle, 61–62; and safari tourists, 272; and San people, 162, 257, 258; and securitization, 82, 104; studies, 14; and tourists' preferences, 49, 61, 135, 193, 194, 196, 197, 199, 200, 209, 219–20, 222, 224; and white people, 172, 173, 182; wilderness, 61, 135, 191, 192, 193, 196–98, 224; wildlife, 20, 34, 47, 56–57, 58, 60, 69, 101, 134–35, 140, 196, 197, 200, 209, 223, 257
tribalism, 64, 65

Umbrella for Democratic Change (UDC), 143, 144
Unified Hunting Regulations, 265
United Kingdom, 2, 73, 118, 154, 157
United Nations, 12, 13, 39, 68, 77, 160–61, 198

veterinary fences, 292, 294, 304
Vision 2016—a Long Term Vision for Botswana (Government of Botswana), 117, 118, 119–21, 142, 146, 215

wildlife: access to, 265, 266; and animals and plants, 58, 159; and armed antipoaching operations, 83, 96; and armed civilian officers, 42; and Ban Ki-moon's statement, 77; Botswana's, 37, 48, 56–62, 82, 83, 100–103, 112, 139–41, 174–77, 291; and buffalo, 292, 293; and cattle, 287, 292, 293, 294; and Central Kalahari Game Reserve (CKGR), 200, 201, 203, 205, 206; and charismatic species, 4, 10, 37, 47, 48, 61–62, 77, 81, 100–102, 112, 123, 134, 140, 271–72; and citizen-state relations, 309; and community guides, 42; and conflict with humans, 1, 59, 90, 91, 106, 123–24, 139, 145, 269, 297–98, 314; and conservation, 308; and crime, 77–78, 82, 85, 102, 106; and Department of Wildlife and National Parks (DWNP), 56, 83, 89, 106, 111, 157, 168, 176, 185, 186, 187, 245, 253, 258, 268, 289, 305; eating of, 106, 272, 283; and elephants, 4, 37, 56, 81, 101–2, 104, 123–24, 134, 139–40, 269–72, 297, 298, 300, 314; encroachment of, 314; and extinction, 88, 137, 283; and fences, 269, 297; and forests, 16; and freehold land, 174–77; and game, 208, 209, 273; and game farms, 180–81, 225; and game ranches as buffer zones, 269; and Global North, 77, 139; and hippopotamus, 212, 212; human relationships with, 1, 13, 38, 42–43, 46, 56–57, 59, 62, 75, 82, 102–3, 104, 106, 110, 132, 139, 140–41, 152, 160, 282; and human rights, 102; and hunting ban, 278; and illegal activities, 84, 108, 273; and infrastructure, 201–2, 224; and land zones, 67, 156–57; locations of, 18, 157; management of, 90, 94, 103, 104, 137, 140, 157, 197, 262, 269, 270, 291, 317; and migration, 76, 269; and Ministry of Environment, Wildlife and Tourism (MEWT), 175; needs of, 139, 140, 142; and ostriches, 250, 254; ownership of, 174–75; and poaching, 75, 82, 85, 86, 105, 107, 140; populations of, 37, 38, 59, 102; and private wildlife ranches, 14, 18; and problem animal control, 90, 91, 106, 140; products from, 4, 107; protection of, 100–102, 103, 111, 112, 116, 136–37, 140, 299, 301, 303; proximity of, 10, 11, 48, 75, 101, 102, 103, 104, 132, 136, 137, 139, 140, 147, 283, 284, 295, 296–97, 306, 309, 310, 314–15; reserves, 201; and resources, 174, 241; and rhinoceros, 81, 157, 175; and rights, 186; and roads, 209; and small animals, 268; spaces of, 316; and state building, 10, 34; and subjectivity, 101, 102, 139; and terrorism, 77; tourism, 20, 34, 47, 57, 60, 69, 209; and trophy dealer's licenses, 252–55; and Tswana people, 200; and Tuli Block, 175; use of, 304; and use of chili pepper, 297, 298; and use of force, 81; and Wildlife Conservation and National Parks Act, 250, 267; and Wildlife Conservation Policy, 157; and Wildlife Management Areas (WMAs), 35, 38, 39, 103, 152, 179, 200, 203, 266; and wild meat, 271; and World Wildlife Day, 77; and World Wildlife Fund, 78. *See also* conservation; hunting; poaching

Wilmsen, Edwin, 232

Zimbabwe, 17, 96, 98, 158, 173, 177, 178